RESEARCH HANDBOOK ON WORK–LIFE BALANCE

Research Handbook on Work–Life Balance

Emerging Issues and Methodological Challenges

Edited by

Sonia Bertolini

Department of Cultures, Politics and Society, University of Turin, Italy

Barbara Poggio

Department of Sociology and Social Research, University of Trento, Italy

EE Edward Elgar
PUBLISHING

Cheltenham, UK • Northampton, MA, USA

© Sonia Bertolini and Barbara Poggio 2022

All rights reserved. No part of this publication may be reproduced, stored in a retrieval system or transmitted in any form or by any means, electronic, mechanical or photocopying, recording, or otherwise without the prior permission of the publisher.

Published by
Edward Elgar Publishing Limited
The Lypiatts
15 Lansdown Road
Cheltenham
Glos GL50 2JA
UK

Edward Elgar Publishing, Inc.
William Pratt House
9 Dewey Court
Northampton
Massachusetts 01060
USA

Paperback edition 2023

A catalogue record for this book
is available from the British Library

Library of Congress Control Number: 2021949005

This book is available electronically in the **Elgar**online
Sociology, Social Policy and Education subject collection
http://dx.doi.org/10.4337/9781788976053

ISBN 978 1 78897 604 6 (Hardback)
ISBN 978 1 78897 605 3 (eBook)
ISBN 978 1 0353 2364 7 (Paperback)

Printed and bound by CPI Group (UK) Ltd, Croydon, CR0 4YY

Contents

Contributors

Myrto Anastassiadou is a researcher and PhD student at the Department of Business and Public Administration of the University of Cyprus. She holds an MSc in Sociology (Research) from the London School of Economics in England and a BA in Sociology and Human Resource Management from Rutgers University–New Brunswick. Her research interests are within the area of work–life balance and specifically the examination of the experiences of invisible minorities in the workplace and how they are managing their identities.

Anne E. Barrett is Professor of Sociology and Director of the Pepper Institute on Aging and Public Policy at Florida State University in Tallahassee, Florida. Her research examines two themes: social relationships' effects on health in middle and later life and the social structural patterning and health consequences of subjective aging. Her recent publications include examinations of ageist responses to the COVID-19 pandemic and aging body reminders' effects on age identity in later life.

Sonia Bertolini is an associate professor at the University of Turin's Department of Cultures, Politics and Society, where she teaches Sociology of Work. Her research interests concern youth labour market entry, female labour market participation, labour market flexibilization and transition to adult life, the sociology of professions and the study of artistic professions. She has been involved in international projects and has been the coordinator of the Italian team in the European project Social Exclusion of Youth in Europe: Cumulative Disadvantage, Coping Strategies, Effective Policies and Transfer (EXCEPT), Horizon 2020. She is a member of the Management Committee of the COST (European Cooperation in Science and Technology) Action YOUNG-IN. Among her recent publications are: Bataille, P., Bertolini, S., Casula, C., and Perrenoud, M. (2020), "From atypical to paradigmatic? The relevance of the study of artistic work for the sociology of work", *Sociologia del lavoro*, 157; and Unt, M., Gebel, M., Bertolini, S., Deliyanni-Kouimtzis, V., and Hofaecker, D. (eds), 2021, *Social Exclusion of Youth in Europe*, Bristol University Press.

Rossella Bozzon is Assistant Professor in Sociology at the Department of Social and Political Sciences of the University of Milan. She is a member of the European Research Council Project SHARE – Seizing the Hybrid Areas of Work by Re-Presenting Self-Employment (2017–2022). Her research interests include family and labour market transformations, non-standard employment relations, gender inequalities and quantitative methods.

Simone Braun, holder of an MA in Sociology, is a researcher at the Institut für Mittelstandsforschung Bonn. From 2014 to 2020 she was a researcher and lecturer at the Faculty of Educational Sciences (Institute for Social Work and Social Policy) at the University of Duisburg-Essen. Formerly she was a researcher in survey methodology of the German Family Panel pairfam (Panel Analysis of Intimate Relationships and Family Dynamics) at LMU Munich. She specializes in the fields of quantitative research methods and family sociology.

Anna Carreri is Assistant Professor of Sociology of Work and Sociology of Organizations at the Department of Human Sciences of University of Verona, Italy, and affiliated with the Research Centre SEIN – Identity, Diversity & Inequality Research, University of Hasselt, Belgium. Her research is conducted mainly through qualitative methods from an intersectional and critical perspective. Her main research interests are work–life issues and the quality of working life in relation to changes in the labour market and organizational models. Currently, she is involved in research concerning gender inequalities in academic careers.

Julia Cook is Lecturer in Sociology at the University of Newcastle, Australia, where she codirects the Newcastle Youth Studies Network. Her research interests include the sociology of youth, time and housing, and her most recent research addresses young adults' pathways into home ownership and their navigation of debt and financial assistance. She is a chief investigator on the Australian Research Council-funded Life Patterns project, a 30-year longitudinal study following school leavers into middle age, with colleagues from the University of Melbourne.

Marjan De Coster is a PhD student at the Research Center SEIN – Identity, Diversity & Inequality Research of Hasselt University and at the Department of Work and Organization of KU Leuven. Previous projects she participated in mainly focused on work–life balance policy, gender (in)equality and flexible work. Her doctoral research draws on the work of Judith Butler to study vulnerable lives and resistance under neoliberal governance through a performative lens.

Annalisa Dordoni is a research fellow at the Department of Sociology and Social Research of the University of Milano-Bicocca. Her main research interests lie in gender studies and contemporary social changes within the areas of labour and everyday life. She is working on a research project on the transformations of gender identities, with particular reference to changes in masculinity and the role of new media, using qualitative research methods, online and offline ethnography, interviews and focus groups.

Rachel Douglas is a member of the faculty of the Department of Education and Human Services at Florida State College at Jacksonville in Florida. She studies gender, leisure, aging and urban sociology, examining how individuals and communities reflect, reinforce and challenge social inequalities. Her latest research on women's solo travel experiences has been published in *Sociological Forum* and the *Journal of Women & Aging*.

Ulla Forseth is Professor in Sociology at the Department of Sociology and Political Studies at the Norwegian University of Science and Technology, Trondheim. She teaches courses in Sociological Theory, Gender, Work and Organization, the Norwegian Model of Work and Welfare and Research Design. Her research fields are wide and include gender, work, organization, welfare, power, risk, health and safety, regulation and industrial relations. She is also interested in techniques of fieldwork and the application of narratology and memory work.

Jeanne Ganault is a PhD student in Sociology at the Center for Research in Economics and Statistics and the Observatoire sociologique du changement (Science Po). Her research focuses on workers' time autonomy and time use depending on gender and class. Her research interests include the gender division of labour, intersectionality in time use and time constraints, work–life conflict, life-course analysis and quantitative and qualitative methodological considerations.

Caroline Gatrell is Professor of Organization Studies at the University of Liverpool Management School. Her research centres on work, family and health, which she explores from a socio-cultural perspective. She is a Fellow of the Academy of Social Sciences and of the British Academy of Management. In 2020 she was awarded the British Academy of Management Research Medal. She is presently General Editor of the *Journal of Management Studies* and Chair of the Research Committee, Chartered Association of Business Schools.

Kathleen Gerson is Collegiate Professor of Sociology at New York University, where she studies the sources, shapes and implications of the revolutions in gender, work and private life in the US and globally. The author of six books, including *The Unfinished Revolution: Coming of Age in a New Era of Gender, Work, and Family* and, most recently, *The Science and Art of Interviewing*, she is writing a book about Americans' strategies for reconciling work and caregiving in the new economy.

Emily Hallgren is a sociologist and doctoral candidate who studies the intersections of gender, work and health. Her work has been featured in prestigious journals, including the *American Journal of Public Health* and *Journal of Health and Social Behavior*. She strongly believes in applying sociology beyond the classroom to affect policy and cultural change. She has worked with organizations including the Scholars Strategy Network and New America's Better Life Lab on projects to translate research to the public and policymakers.

Suvi Heikkinen is a postdoctoral researcher and programme leader at Jyväskylä University School of Business and Economics. Her research interests include ethics in working life, particularly social sustainability and equality, and management and leadership in different contexts. Her work has been published in journals like *Gender, Work and Organization*, the *Journal of Business Ethics* and the *International Journal of Human Resource Management*.

Dirk Hofäcker, Dr. rer. soc., is Professor of Quantitative Methods of Social Research at the Faculty of Educational Sciences (Institute for Social Work and Social Policy) at the University of Duisburg-Essen. Formerly he was Research Fellow and Project Leader at the Mannheim Centre for European Social Research (MZES). He specializes in the fields of quantitative research methods and international welfare state comparison.

Marjut Jyrkinen is Professor in Working Life Equality and Gender Studies at the University of Helsinki, and director of a research consortium on sustainable working life, funded by the Strategic Research Council at the Academy of Finland. Her research interests relate to gender, power and intersectionalities in management and organizations and society. Her research has been published in, for example, *Gender, Work and Organization*, the *Journal of Business Ethics* and *Work, Employment & Society*.

Emilia Kangas is a project manager in Seinäjoki University of Applied Sciences. Her main research interests are in gender in management and leadership, work–family relationships and women's leadership development. She studied fatherhood in leadership and management at the University of Jyväskylä. She is currently working with the topics of hybrid work–life and women's opportunities for new work in rural areas. Her research has been published both nationally and internationally on topics related to gender and leadership.

Mauro Migliavacca is Associate Professor of Economic Sociology at the University of Genoa, where he teaches Economic Sociology, Social Inequalities and Welfare Systems. His current research is focused on comparative analysis of social policies, social inequality and social vulnerability, with particular focus on the dynamics affecting the transformations of the labour market, the family and the working conditions of young people.

Annalisa Murgia is Associate Professor of Sociology at the Department of Social and Political Sciences, University of Milan, and Visiting Senior Research Fellow at the Centre for Employment Relations, Innovation and Change of the University of Leeds. She is the PI of the European Research Council project SHARE – Seizing the Hybrid Areas of Work by Re-Presenting Self-Employment. Her research interests focus on precariousness, emerging forms of organizing and gender differences in organizations.

Rosy Musumeci is Assistant Professor of the Sociology of Cultural and Communication Processes at the University of Turin. Her main research interests are work–life balance in the transition to parenthood, working careers and job insecurity, and gender imbalances in academic institutions. Another topic is the role of expert and scientific knowledge in the construction of adequate parenting, children's well-being and care. Among her recent publications is (editor, with A. Santero) *Fathers, Childcare and Work: Cultures, Practices and Policies* (Emerald 2018).

Manuela Naldini is Full Professor of Sociology of the Family at the University of Turin's Department of Cultures, Politics and Society, and a fellow at the Collegio Carlo Alberto. She has coordinated several national and international research projects on topics related to family changes, comparative studies of welfare states, gender studies, work–family reconciliation issues, the transition to parenthood, migrant families and more recently gendering academia.

Jessica Noblitt is a doctoral candidate in Sociology at Florida State University in Tallahassee, Florida. Her research focuses on sexual minority status, age and gender as social factors that influence physical and mental health. Her recent projects include analyses of sexual minority status' effects on health behaviours over the life course and the effect of same-sex partner loss on psychological well-being.

Ariane Pailhé, holder of a PhD in Economics, is Senior Researcher at the French Institute for Demographic Studies (INED) in Paris. Her multidisciplinary research focuses on the dynamics of individual life courses from a gender perspective. She is interested in work–family inter-relationships, the division of housework and childcare, employment uncertainty and fertility, family behaviour of migrants and their descendants, and public policy evaluation. She has extensive experience in general population surveys as a survey user and survey designer at the national and international levels.

Barbara Poggio is Vice Rector for Equality and Diversity of the University of Trento and Coordinator of the Center for Interdisciplinary Gender Studies of the same university. She is a full professor at the Department of Sociology and Social Research, where she teaches Sociology of Work and Sociology of Organizations. She has carried out several studies and research about the social construction of gender, with a special focus on cultural and symbolic dimensions. She coordinated several international projects on gender, work and organizations, and in particular on gender and science, gender and entrepreneurship, work–life balance and fatherhood. Her current research interests mainly deal with gender and scientific careers, organizational gender policies and work precariousness.

Epp Reiska graduated in Sociology with an MA and works as a research assistant at the Institute of International Social Studies at Tallinn University. Her main tasks include providing administrative support for the institute's research projects and managing the journal *Studies of Transition States and Societies*, published by the institute.

Barbara J. Risman is Editor of *Gender & Society*, the most highly cited American journal about gender. She has served as both President of the Board of Directors and Executive Director of the Council on Contemporary Families. She has also served as President of the Southern Sociological Society and Vice-President of the American Sociological Association. Dr. Risman believes fervently that sociologists have a responsibility to do good research and publicize and share it beyond the classroom to the public with policymakers.

Kristine Warhuus Smeby is Associate Professor in Sociology at Queen Maud University of Early Childhood Education (DMMH). She manages and teaches courses in Leadership, Cooperation and Educational Development. Her research fields include gender, organization, strategic leadership, democratic professionalism, parental participation, the transition from early childhood education and care (ECEC) to school, process quality in ECEC institutions and qualitative methods.

Eleni Stavrou is a professor at the University of Cyprus. She was Director of Programs and Operations of the Center for Family Enterprise at George Washington University. She has published widely, including articles in various academic journals, like the *British Journal of Management*, *Human Resource Management*, the *Journal of Organizational Behavior*, the *Journal of Business Ethics*, *Entrepreneurship Theory and Practice*, the *International Journal of Human Resource Management* and the *Journal of International Business Studies*. Her research interests include work–life issues, strategic and comparative human resource management, and intergenerational transitions in family firms. She is also involved in helping businesses with various human resource management issues, especially intergenerational transitions in family firms.

Kadri Täht is Professor of Sociology at Tallinn University. Her research interests include labour market transitions and interactions between work and family. She is currently the principal investigator of the research project "Reducing the Gender Wage Gap (REGE)" (2019–2021) funded by Estonian Research Council and forms part of Estonian country team in Horizon2020 project "Social Exclusion of Youth in Europe: Cumulative disadvantage, coping strategies, effective policies and transfer" (2020–2023).

Marge Unt is Professor of Comparative Sociology and the Head of the Institute of International Social Studies at Tallinn University. Her research interests are in the life-course in comparative perspective, namely the youth transitions in adulthood, inequalities in early career and in late career and the moderating role of social institutions. She was the Principal Investigator (PI) of the H2020 project Social Exclusion of Youth in Europe: Cumulative Disadvantage, Coping Strategies, Effective Policies and Transfer (EXCEPT-project.eu). Currently she is Co-PI of the Gender Wage Gap in Estonia project funded by the European Regional Fund, and leads the Estonian team in the Horizon2020 projects Platform Labour in Urban Spaces: Fairness, Welfare, Development (PLUS) and Closing Gaps in Social Citizenship: New Tools to Foster Social Resilience in Europe (EUROSHIP).

Dan Woodman is TR Ashworth Professor of Sociology and Deputy Associate Dean Research

Impact and Engagement in the Faculty of Arts at the University of Melbourne, Australia. He is President of the Council for the Humanities, Arts and Social Sciences and Immediate Past President of the Australian Sociological Association. He is a chief investigator on the Australian Research Council-funded Life Patterns study.

Patrizia Zanoni is a full professor at the Faculty of Business Economics of Hasselt University, where she leads the research center SEIN – Identity, Diversity & Inequality Research, and Chair in Organization Studies at the Utrecht School of Governance of Utrecht University. Drawing on critical traditions, her research investigates the relation between diversity – involving gender, ethnicity, disability and age – and organizing processes, dynamics of control and resistance, work-related identities and unequal valuation. She is Co-Editor-in-Chief of *Organization*.

1. Introduction to the *Research Handbook on Work–Life Balance*

Sonia Bertolini and Barbara Poggio

Two years ago, when we received the proposal to engage in an editorial project for a handbook on work–life balance research, we were hesitant to accept, aware of the increasingly contested and problematic nature of the very construct of 'work–life balance'. However, we eventually decided to accept the invitation, with the idea of collating not so much an exhaustive compendium of the research works focused on the relationship between work and other dimensions of the biographical experience of individuals, but rather a text offering both theoretical reflections and empirical research examples illustrating the multiple strategies through which the different articulations that characterize this intersection can be analyzed. Our aim was to devise a text not only able to account for the richness of lenses and perspectives, together with their translation and actualization into specific research practices and methodological choices, but that would also shed light on its potentialities yet to be thoroughly explored.

We believe the final result matches these objectives to some extent and that the volume offers a rather broad and articulated selection of reflections and contributions focused on how research is carried out and could be carried out when it comes to the relationship between working life and other life areas; also in light of the controversies the work–life balance construct carries and especially the changes that have characterized these areas over the last few years, with the gradual dissolution of the boundaries between the different domains, and also as a result of the processes of digitalization. In this regard, it should be remembered how, just as we were composing the volume, we found ourselves confronted with the consequences of the Covid-19 pandemic and its overbearing impact on everyone's lives. The recent months' events have deeply affected both our way of working and our way of managing personal and family relationships and commitments, producing situations where the boundaries between the different dimensions suddenly appeared blurred, thus generating the need to redefine our analytical and interpretative frameworks.

Observing what was happening around us further consolidated our awareness that the theme addressed in this volume called for approaches other than those constrained within thematic or methodological boundaries, and to some extent it also pushed us to rethink the structure we had originally designed, which was based on a distinction between contributions according to the level of articulation (macro, meso and micro). Many of the texts in this volume prove in fact problematic when attempting to delimit or label it within a single category or boundary. In particular, on a methodological level, the book features numerous mixed-methods contributions, aiming to answer the same research question through different lenses, as well as contributions characterized by methodological pluralism, aimed at answering different research questions by combining data provided by different methods. This trend highlights how what the literature describes as work–life balance has become an increasingly complex terrain for the combination of a plurality of different factors. Among these, for example, are the rise in number of dual-earner couples and the ongoing redefinition of family roles; the higher life expectancy; the weakening of the welfare systems, now unable to respond to the intensified complexity of social life; the differentiation and individualization of life and work experiences; the surge in jobs and work contracts with flexible hours generating intermittent work periods; and the consequences of the growing digitalization of labor, including the redefinition of workplaces, an acceleration of which we have witnessed during the pandemic with the various forms of home working. In this scenario, the adoption of multi-focus methodologies allows us to highlight how the ways and times in which we reconcile family and work are being redefined, and to better grasp the underlying processes. Further enriching the picture is also the emergence of new research techniques and methodologies, made possible in particular by the development of digital technologies, which offer the possibility of pursuing new research avenues to investigate traditional as well as new research questions, representing an addition to more established tools and approaches.

The first part of the volume aims to outline the theoretical and methodological framework of the book. The chapter written by Anna Carreri, Annalisa Dordoni and Barbara Poggio introduces the scientific debate on work–life balance, starting from a short reconstruction of the history of the concept, from the emphasis on the conflict between the separate spheres to the more recent urges to abandon it, because of its many limitations and biases. Moreover, the authors here outline the main thematic axes around which the debate on work–life balance has developed, such as gender and generation, but also those that should be better considered, by adopting an intersectional approach in the analysis of the relationship between work and other spheres of life. Finally, the ongoing changes, implications and challenges posed by the Covid-19 pandemic are considered, in order to identify the possible trajectories and perspectives opening up for future research agendas.

Chapter 3, by Sonia Bertolini and Rosy Musumeci, reflects on the methodological implications of work–life balance conceptual constructs and theoretical approaches previously described. The authors here identify some of the main recurrences, criticalities and potentialities in the research approaches studying work–life balance. Empirical methods and research designs are closely intertwined with analytical goals: the methodological choices depend on the research questions and conceptual constructs, and vice versa. The chapter illustrates the main research designs and empirical methods used in work–life balance, and the main innovations arising from studies and reflections presented in the chapters of this edited volume and from the wider literature on work–life balance, as well as the consequences and challenges that the Covid-19 pandemic may present in terms of doing research on work–life balance and the approach to fieldwork.

The second part includes three contributions which reflect on the opportunity to adopt multilevel research approaches and perspectives, along gender and temporal axes.

The first, written by Emily Hallgren and Barbara J. Risman, stresses the importance of adopting a multilevel analytical approach to research on work–life balance, within a gender structure theory. They argue that research on work–life balance should be contextualized at different levels of analysis: individual, interactional and macro-level. Even where a single study focuses on a single level of analysis, it is important to take into consideration the overall gender structure within which work–life balance needs, assets and practices are framed. Moreover, they suggest that both the material and cultural aspects of this structure should be considered and analyzed, showing how they are closely intertwined. In the last part of the chapter, the authors offer a set of recommendations regarding research on work–life balance based on the chapter's main assumptions, and present a couple of examples. One of them is a multilevel model of lagged generational change, useful to explain the slow progress toward equality in the gender division of work and comparative research. Based on interviews with working mothers from four cities in four different countries, it is aimed at studying the relationship between cultural ideology and state policies in influencing working mothers' work–life balance experiences and perceptions.

A second relevant perspective from which the relationship between professional and private life can be considered is that of life-course research. In their contribution, Jeanne Ganault and Ariane Pailhé highlight how work–life balance research and literature has been predominantly cross-sectional, and suggest the opportunity to adopt a life-course standpoint instead, which would be able to offer a dynamic conceptualization of work–life reconciliation issues and capture the changes occurring over time. The chapter presents a review of the recent works on reconciling work life and private life, focusing on the objective and subjective measures of the work–life conflict throughout our life course. Four different measuring methods are identified: by exploring employment and family trajectories over the life course, by studying paid and unpaid work time throughout the life course, by identifying work–life strategies linked to life-course events, and finally by analyzing perceptions of work–life conflict through the life course.

The opportunity to adopt an unusual perspective based on a temporal perspective in the study of work–life balance is recommended and explored by Anne E. Barrett, Rachel Douglas and Jessica Noblitt in a chapter that focuses on work–life balance in the second half of life. While research on the reconciliation between work life and private life usually tends to mainly consider the experience of relatively young, employed adults caring for small children, this contribution aims to expand the research scope by considering work–life balance in middle and later life and making aging more explicit. In particular, the authors identify three main themes: the long-term effects of work–life balance in early adulthood; the issue of care work for spouses or partners, older family members and grandchildren; and leisure in later life. This widening of the temporal horizon could bring several benefits to both the research and the design of public policies.

Comparative research based on quantitative methods is at the heart of Part III. In Chapter 7, Dirk Hofäcker and Simone Braun combine different levels of explanation about the persistence of inequality in the division of unpaid work, considering both the micro and macro level. While the first perspective highlights the role of individual (economic) resources in making the division of work among spouses economically rational, the other stresses the relevance of traditional gender norms within society. The authors provide an example of how advanced methods of multilevel regression models can be used to empirically explore such relationships, in a comparative way. Results show that, apparently, societies largely rejecting a traditional male-breadwinner model provide both a supportive normative framework as well as institutionalized support for a more equal division of labor between the sexes, as reflected in the reconciliation-oriented policies of Scandinavian countries.

The chapter by Rossella Bozzon and Annalisa Murgia uses a quantitative methodology to study how the heterogeneous category of self-employed workers experience work–family conflict. Basing their work on the European Working Conditions Survey (sixth edition), the authors develop an empirical exercise starting from a descriptive basis and then referring to a series of multilevel models, aimed at analyzing how subjective work-to-family conflict and family-to-work conflict vary across different types of self-employment, dependent employment and informal work. Their analysis shows that, despite the high level of autonomy and control over their working conditions, the self-employed with employees and the solo self-employed workers share such overwhelming work demands that they end up experiencing a higher perception of work–family conflict. Moreover, they demonstrate that job-related resources and demands play different roles in mediating subjective work–family conflict, according to the type of self-employment.

The fourth part includes contributions adopting qualitative approaches based on longitudinal, discursive and narrative perspectives. Manuela Naldini's chapter illustrates the theoretical and methodological challenges of longitudinal qualitative study, focusing on the transition to parenthood and the work–family balance of dual-earner couples in Italy. The work is based on interviews with mothers and fathers about their desires, values, choices and practices before and after their transition into parenthood. The background for the analysis is the life-course perspective and, in particular, one of the key principles in the analysis of transitions, that of 'linked lives'. The analysis, based on a longitudinal perspective, reveals a number of signs of change, and thus of variability in parents' behavior. Among mothers, some redefined their priorities in favor of the family, finding a balance by applying for part-time work or reducing their job commitments, while others decided, despite the uncertainties and difficulties, to stay in the labor market, not simply out of need but also following strong personal motivations and a sense of identity rooted in their professional or non-domestic lives. As for fatherhood, the study revealed areas of continuity but also a break with the past, as well as a significant variability in motivations and behavior, and a group of fathers who are coming to grips with men's 'dual presence' in the workplace and the domestic sphere.

In their chapter, Suvi Heikkinen, Marjut Jyrkinen and Emilia Kangas show how discourse analysis can be used in order to study work–family issues, with a specific focus on the fathers' experience. The adoption of methodological approaches based on language and discourse offers the opportunity to better understand how people interpret their experiences and the emotions and feelings associated with them. In particular, they present two empirical examples where a discursive analytical perspective is used to study work–family issues from a male perspective in the Finnish context. The first is aimed at revealing how media discourses portray fatherhood in the context of work life, while the second is aimed at studying the discursive ways in which working fathers make sense of emotions in their daily experience of work and family life. Discourse analysis emerges as a useful approach to analyze the complex intersections between work and family, shedding light on meanings that often remain unexplored. Moreover, it allows for a temporal and space-specific framework, as well as a multi-layered investigation of work–life balance.

The chapter by Kristine Warhuus Smeby and Ulla Forseth explores work–life balance by using a narrative approach. Their research aims to study the experiences of some of the first fathers who took the ten-week paternity leave introduced in Norway, and its impact on the promotion of work–life balance within the couples. The authors analyze narratives elicited during in-depth interviews with working fathers who experienced the full length of the father's quota in one continuous period, when the mothers were back at work. Their contribution is focused on the interplay of three logics: state-regulated welfare schemes, work organizations and individual agency. It allows them to bring forth underlying frames and patterns regarding fathers' practical and emotional involvement and how they re-construct their identities as caretakers, developing new practices of masculinity. At the same time, it reveals balance, tension and conflict between responsibilities at home and at work.

The fifth part includes chapters that combine different sources of data and different methodologies. Kathleen Gerson and Mauro Migliavacca focus on how current economic and social changes have affected the ways people organize work, care and gender relationships, with special attention to the US case. By adopting a mixed-methods approach that uses both quantitative and qualitative data to highlight critical issues in the understanding of the connections between gender, work and care in the new economy, this chapter offers some tools for analyzing the transformation of the work–family relationship in a variety of national and local settings. In the first section, the authors use demographic and related data sources to compare the trends and major axes that characterize changes in work–family relations in the US and Europe. The results of qualitative research based on 120 in-depth interviews with American adults living and working in the heart of the new economy are presented. They also discuss the strengths and limitations of the mixed-methods approach.

A similar approach is used by Kadri Täht, Marge Unt and Epp Reiska, who consider the effect of child-care facilities on labor market participation among young adults in Estonia, where access to affordable and good-quality public care is considered high. Quantitative data from the Estonian Time Use Survey (2009) allow for the study of the detailed time use of household members, including participation in paid work and time spent on care. These data are complemented with interviews selected from an Estonian study to illustrate how the use of formal and informal child-care may affect young parents' labor market participation. The authors use the life stories of two young mothers with low education to illuminate their coping strategies and challenges in combining working and parenting. The results showed that having access to early care facilities reduces the chances of being unemployed or inactive, especially for women.

The opportunity of using a combination of quantitative and qualitative methodologies and multilevel analysis is argued in the next chapter, where Eleni Stavrou and Myrto Anastassiadou discuss research on flexible-work arrangements and diversity. The chapter proposes a multilevel comparative framework, articulated on three levels: the individual, the meso/organizational and the macro/supra-organizational. It is maintained that, in this way, it would be possible to gain a more holistic and in-depth understanding of these issues, particularly suited to the study of diverse demographic groups and invisible minorities. Moreover, the authors suggest that proximal and distal outcomes should be incorporated in the examination of flexible-work arrangements. Finally, the use of non-parametric methods is recommended in work–life balance research and, in particular, in research on flexible-work arrangements and diversity.

The last part of the volume is dedicated to a number of research contributions where the authors adopted innovative research methods that benefit from the use of digital and visual technologies. This is a particularly interesting and promising field, probably destined for further development, especially in the light of recent occurrences (during the pandemic, much research has been carried out using these methods, because of the particular limitations for the time being).

The first contribution in this section, by Julia Cook and Dan Woodman, is based on the use of a combination of digital and interview-based methods with Australian young adults in heterosexual partnerships. The study aims to show how the rise of dual-income households, together with that of nonstandard hours in paid employment, has resulted in an increasing need to schedule and manage lives, and thus a contextual feeling of precarity. The participants were asked to write posts on a mobile phone app every day for a week and then discuss the posts in an interview. The analysis was focused on scheduling and organization of time, considering work–life interferences and leisure time, and it allows them to highlight the gendered dimension of organizing and managing shared time. In the last section of the chapter, the authors offer some useful insights into the challenges and potential of digital qualitative data collection.

A second example of research based on digital resources is offered by Caroline Gatrell's chapter, which introduces the use of netnography (or internet research) to study work–life balance. The author discusses the benefits and disadvantages of using this method in a non-participative form: distant netnography; that is, observing interactions within internet spaces through open-access websites, without personally joining these communities. In particular, she used this method to qualitatively study work–life balance among pregnant and breastfeeding employees. As with the majority of methodologies that use the internet, netnography poses some ethical problems: researchers can observe participants without them being aware of it, and have access to a large quantity of data. At the same time, the author has continued to gather data from websites and discussion groups which are publicly accessible, and within which users usually choose an internet 'identifier' which anonymizes them. In this way, this 'distant' form of netnography preserved women's anonymity in a manner in which other media methods might not have done.

Finally, Marjan De Coster and Patrizia Zanoni introduce readers to the use of visual methodologies, adopting a performative onto-epistemological stance. Two empirical cases are considered: in the first, they used visual elicitation during interviews with project workers; in the second, visual material uploaded online by a group of media influencers, subsequently used to elicit narratives about their experiences. Through the analysis of the collected material, the authors show how visuals offer an anti-narrative space in interview settings, where a more 'entangled subjectivity' can be performed beyond their narrative inscription in the work–life dichotomy. Moreover, they show how the conflict experienced by the participants is not between pre-defined roles in work and personal life, but it reflects the struggle of constituting an ethical self through multiple relations of accountability across work and private life.

PART I

THEORETICAL AND METHODOLOGICAL FRAMEWORK

2. Work–life balance and beyond: premises and challenges

Anna Carreri, Annalisa Dordoni, and Barbara Poggio[1]

INTRODUCTION

Writing an introductory chapter on work–life balance within a publication aimed at exploring the perspectives and strategies to tackle this subject proves to be a demanding challenge, both because the literature on this subject is extremely vast and it would not be possible, nor is it our intention, to give an exhaustive account of it, and because the construct itself of work–life balance has long been the object of criticism and deconstruction, due to the many problems and ambivalences it embodies.

When reflecting on which argumentative strategy we should use to approach this task, we decided to start from the very genesis of the concept, to highlight its weaknesses and underlying biases. These include the risk of describing work as a distinct domain from other spheres of life – in the first instance, the family – thus falling within a framework that is tied to a model and ideology of production, specifically located in time and space, as in the Fordist one. This chapter will recall some of the main articulations that took shape, starting from the original idea of work–life balance, in particular those of 'conflict' or 'enhancement/enrichment' and 'work–life boundary' or 'family-friendliness', laying out their premises and limitations.

The main thematic axes around which the reflection on work–life balance has developed will also be identified: starting from gender, other dimensions such as generation and class will then be considered, so as to adopt an intersectional approach in the analysis of the relationship between work and other spheres of life.

Finally, some possible further development trajectories of the debate will be outlined in the concluding section, taking the most relevant ongoing changes into account, including the Coronavirus pandemic, during which this text was written.

1. THE 'WORK–LIFE BALANCE' CONSTRUCT: PREMISES AND LIMITATIONS

Scholars who attempted to chronicle the history of the 'work–life balance' concept and, more generally, of the larger work–life field in academic research, pinpointed its beginning in some publications from the late 1970s, although the work–family interface had begun to arouse scientific interest prior to that (Rapoport and Rapoport, 1965, 1969). The year 1977 saw two influential publications clearly raise the issue of the inter-relations between work and family, thus allowing a deeper understanding of non-work activities to be encompassed in employment research: the book *Work and Family in the United States: A Critical Review and Agenda for Research and Policy* by Rosabeth Moss Kanter (1977), and the article 'The Work-Family Role System' by Joseph H. Pleck (1977). Both these publications, grounded in two different disciplines – sociology the former and psychology the latter – emphasize the interdependence between the organization of paid work and family labor, and point to the fact that the way in which people reconcile work activities and care responsibilities is not a private experience but the result of complex interdependencies between economic and socio-cultural contingencies. Moreover, they criticize the concept of 'separate spheres' due to its tendency to reify the division of social experience into public/male and private/female worlds, and to overlook the interactions between them (see also Pleck, 1976).

In particular, sociologist Kanter attacked the prevailing assumption that workplaces and jobs must be designed to separate work from family demands, and the belief that workers should sacrifice family/personal responsibilities in order to be successful on the job (Kossek and Groggins, 2014). Owing to its relationship with feminist studies, which from the 1960s onwards began to challenge Parsonian concepts of dividing labor along gendered lines, Kanter's book brought the issue of 'work–family' to the forefront of organizations and research as a pressing concern for the quality of women's working life. The question of 'balance' therefore arises as a 'problem' that concerns women, mothers in particular, when their participation in the labor market in Western countries not only grows enormously, but is also positively hoped for and becomes the subject of corporate and governmental policies (Naldini and Saraceno, 2011).

The scholarship has only recently broadened its scope to include – albeit still to a much lesser extent – men and other types of families, such as same-sex, and other realms of 'life' other than caring for children and domestic work, such as leisure and community activities (Gatrell et al., 2013; Özbilgin et al., 2011). However, the concept of an 'ideal worker' model through which workers are indoctrinated to be good employees is still embodied by a male individual to this day, thus reflecting the traditional gendered division of labor (see Blair-Loy, 2003; Gatrell et al., 2017). Moreover, in the neoliberal economy, paid employment continues to eclipse family, leisure and community in the developed as well as in the developing world (see Gambles et al., 2006; Shockley et al., 2018). This also happens in ways that are relatively new compared to those highlighted by the first work–life balance scholars. For example, it has been shown how new technologies and new management practices that push towards greater flexibility bring with them new expectations about employees' greater autonomy for the integration of care work and paid work, as well as constant availability in light of intensification and precarization of the work (see Moore et al., 2018; Pérez-Zapata et al. 2016).

Interestingly, the idea of separate spheres, a legacy of the Fordist conceptualization of work, has also had a long-lasting impact on the distribution of themes within the scientific community. In fact, it created a break between studies that are focused on work and how work demands are affected by family responsibilities and those more focused on family and how family demands are affected by work commitments, thus limiting the ability of scholars to integrate different perspectives and explore the multiple interconnections of the phenomenon (Gatrell et al., 2013; Wharton, 2006). In the larger scope of work–life academic literature, which is grounded in distinct and poorly integrated disciplines – mainly sociology, social policy research, management studies, psychology and demography – the work–life balance concept itself is contested and lacks an established definition (Gatrell et al., 2013; Gregory and Milner, 2009; Lewis et al., 2007).

The scientific debate is marked by controversy with regard to the use of the term 'work–family' or 'work–life'. The term 'work–family' has been criticized for conjuring up images of an ideal-type of male-breadwinner family and not acknowledging different aspects of life other than childcare. The term 'work–life' was adopted in the 1990s in response to those criticisms, and deemed as more inclusive. However, it presents limitations: for example, it loses analytic sharpness because it can potentially include any aspect of life and it may suggest an artificial separation between work and life, as if work were not part of life (Bloom, 2016; Fleetwood, 2007; Gambles et al., 2006; Glucksmann, 2005; Lewis et al., 2007).

Yet, the umbrella term 'balance' itself is not static despite its popularity, even at the international policy level, and the way it is conceptualized is shaped in response to different pressures and concerns, and based on various assumptions within the work–life balance field. It was initially understood by researchers as signifying low levels of role conflict between the domains of life and a good functioning at both work and home, which are viewed as in equilibrium with each other with a 'roughly equal' distribution of individual time and energy (Wayne et al., 2016). Traditionally, researchers thought of a 'win–lose' relationship between work and family, and assumed that individuals have limited resources in terms of time and energy to allocate to their life roles as a zero-sum game. Therefore, most research in the field of work–life balance has been conducted (and is still being conducted) on the construct of 'work–family conflict' (Barnett and Gareis, 2006; Bianchi and Milkie, 2010; Kossek and Groggins, 2014), which emanates out of role theory (Kossek et al., 2011; Powell et al., 2019). In their seminal work, Greenhaus and Beutell (1985) defined the work–family conflict as a form of inter-role conflict where the role pressures from the work and family domains are mutually incompatible and viewed as competing actors for an individual's time, energy and behavior, on and off the job. Studies that used this construct defined a role as involving behavioral expectations associated with a position in a social structure and led us to progress in understanding the types, directions and sources of conflict to help organizations and governments to better design appropriate interventions to support work–life balance (Kossek and Groggins, 2014). Therefore, if on one hand the construct of separate spheres has been strongly questioned in work–life literature, which has emphasized how 'work' and 'family' realms are not to be conceived separately, on the other hand the close interdependence between them was primarily understood in an oppositional and conflictual way. In this sense, family and work have been conceptualized as areas that pose incompatible demands. Within this dominant frame, the effects of navigating multiple roles are viewed on the one hand in psychological terms, such as increased stress, anxiety or even a depressive syndrome with negative consequences on the stability of couple relationships and the quality of parents–children relationships; and on the other hand in organizational terms, such as a decrease in job satisfaction, an increase in absenteeism and, more generally, effects of burnout.

In contrast to the concept of 'conflict', a new stream of work–life research has emerged on 'work–family enhancement' (see Ruderman et al., 2002) or 'work–family enrichment' (see Greenhaus and Powell, 2006). This line of research has argued that work and family can also enrich and complement each other and that taking on multiple roles can be beneficial to both men and women as long as the roles are of good quality and the individual highly identifies with them (see Chapter 10 by Heikkinen et al. in this book). In particular, these studies have illustrated how the effects of having multiple roles can show as rewards and skills from one domain (such as income or learning how to manage people) that can help one perform better in the other, as well as psycho-physical well-being and the quality of social relationships. Indeed, the main assumption of this perspective lies in conceiving an individual's energy and time as potentially expandable resources rather than as resources of a fixed and limited quantity (Barnett and Hyde, 2001).

Another recent strand of research has started looking at the processes of balancing relationships between work and family. Increasing attention has been given to the concept of the 'work–family boundary' (Ashforth et al., 2000; Clark, 2000; Nippert-Eng, 1996), which scholars employ to refer to how individuals create (or do not create) clear boundaries between the different domains of their daily lives. Examples are segmentation, integration or more mixed processes (Kossek, 2016); that is, how, why and leading to which consequences individuals keep work and personal roles segmented, integrated or mixed. This line of research has allowed for the study of the 'fit' between effective boundary practices and those desired by individuals (Ammons, 2013), and the directionality of individuals' boundary practices to understand whether subjects tend to integrate or separate their family sphere from their work sphere (for example, by taking or not taking their children into the office) or vice versa, integrating or separating work from family (for example, by taking or not taking work home) (Ashforth et al., 2000; Kossek et al. 2012).

Although the concept of the work–family boundary allows us to shed some light on the processes of balancing relationships between work and home, and not only look at the outcomes of 'conflict' in negative terms or of 'enhancement/enrichment' (sometimes also 'harmonization') in positive ones, the boundary construct, like the other key concepts, positions work–life balance as a matter of individual choice and responsibility with regard to establishing priorities and organizing schedules (Lewis and Beauregard, 2018). This weakness is partly reflected in another key concept of the work–life research field: the label 'family-friendly' for workplace practices and policies. This label rhetorically implies an employee-centered focus and the idea that these policies and practices are 'favors' granted to employees for their personal work–life balance and well-being. However, critics argue that the label might mask the fact that these policies and practices, such as cost-savings and constant availability, in fact serve the interests of employers (Fleetwood, 2007; Gatrell and Cooper, 2008; Harvey, 2005; S. Lewis et al., 2007, 2017). This is framed within the general shift in responsibility for well-being from state to individual promoted by neoliberal political rationality and governance, in which state-provided goods and provisions (for example, state-funded childcare centers) are largely replaced with various market-based services to be chosen by subjects (for example, organizational voucher schemes through which parents are offered some financial support for their choice of privately-operated day-care) (Fleetwood, 2007; Gambles et al., 2006; Lewis and Beauregard, 2018). Moreover, the so-called family-friendly policies often belie a traditional view of the division of care work and paid work based on gender and outdated assumptions about ideal workers (see Dumas and Sanchez-Burks, 2015; Lewis et al., 2007). The scholarship has showed that those who use these practices – most likely women – often experience professional isolation and fewer networking opportunities, as well as a lesser reputation among colleagues and superiors for being less committed to the organization, and lower career advancement prospects (Beauregard, 2011; Leslie et al., 2012).

The key concepts of conflict, enhancement/enrichment, work–family boundary and family-friendly have enabled us to make great strides in the flourishing work–life research field but all may overlook the diverse, embedded, mixed and messy ways in which individuals manage family, work and community life, not all of which involve balance or the condition of being 'out-of-balance' (Gambles et al., 2006; Hobson, 2014; Rajan-Rankin, 2016). Furthermore, work–life research has been criticized for its problematic assumptions about individualism and individual choice, gender and power neutrality, the concept of balance as something that should and could be reached, and more generally the binary thinking (see, for example, Bloom, 2016; Fleetwood, 2007; Lewis et al., 2007; Ollier-Malaterre, 2010; Özbilgin et al., 2011; Ransome, 2007).

More recently, as we will see in the next paragraph, work–life balance research is taking steps forward to overcome these limitations by embracing critical and transdisciplinary interpretative keys that are able to take into account multiple and interrelated levels (see Chapter 4 by Hallgren and Risman in this book). The scientific debate in the work–life field, and the adoption of a broad spectrum of methods (see Chapter 3 by Bertolini and Musumeci in this book), is proving to be fruitful, as the following chapters will show. Where the research will take us in terms of theory-building and production of specific researchable questions is hard to tell. Besides, work–life balance has already proven to be a dynamic construct whose meaning changes to reflect shifting contexts and times (Fleetwood, 2007; Gambles et al., 2006; Hobson, 2014; S. Lewis et al., 2007, 2017). Therefore, we expect other key concepts to be elaborated in response to current and future concerns to better understand the interdependencies between work and the rest of life and to design more effective social and corporate policies.

Some management scholars have hypothesized that work–life balance, despite being a concept that helped to raise awareness about the issue and unveil an interrelated system of distribution of care work and paid work along gender lines, now constitutes a barrier preventing both scholarship and practice from thinking more widely about the diversity of experiences to the point of proposing to abandon it (Lewis and Beauregard, 2018; Lewis et al., 2007; S. Lewis et al., 2017). On the other hand, the proliferation of key concepts under a single umbrella term poses the risk of making the construct of work–life balance more ambiguous, nebulous and boundless, namely a grand concept of inconsistent usage, in which our gains in extensional coverage tend to be matched by losses in connotative precision.

We believe that, even in the face of the disruptive changes brought about by the Covid-19 pandemic, as we will see in more detail at the end of the chapter, new questions will not be long in being asked by scholarship, tackling the very concept of work–life balance as well as posing new challenges on a methodological level (see Chapter 3 in this book). We shall find out in the future whether these developments will lead to the abandonment of the balance construct, which among its merits has the potential to put into dialogue different disciplines, as shown by the growing number of networks and calls for papers in journals and conferences, or to the formation of a sort of meta-concept and truly transdisciplinary construct.

2.   WORK–LIFE BALANCE AXES AND PERSPECTIVES

This section will provide theoretical coordinates to approach the literature on work–life balance, undoubtedly vast and multifaceted. First of all, we deem it useful to grasp the 'impulse' of work–life balance.

As Connell wrote,

> the idea of "work/life balance" is a conservative expression of a radical impulse […] for justice, specifically gender equality, and for the fuller life made possible for everyone by just human relations […] expressed as a demand for "balance" because of the impossibility of realizing equality within an institutional system that subordinates home to economy. (2005, 378)

Since the beginning, the research field exploring the interconnections between work and life has been closely linked to women's rights and gender issues. While the number of women employed in the labor market has increased significantly in recent decades, an equally rapid and impactful social change in gender roles, and in particular in social expectations regarding care and domestic work, did not occur (Perrons et al., 2007).

Therefore, the first axis to be considered when studying work–life balance is that of gender. Work–life balance issues were initially conceived and implemented in the framework of the criticism of sexual division of labor (Rubin, 1975) and the institutionalization of politics for gender equality and women's rights in both spheres, starting with the first conceptualization of gender as a social and historical construction which places women on a subordinate level with respect to men (Scott, 1986). In fact, it is now consolidated evidence in the literature that gender has a very close relationship with power with respect to the relationships between men and women, inside and outside of the labor market, and that gender outlines the boundaries of the possibility of social action, defining norms, codes of behavior, social roles, circumscribing dynamics and structures that determine status and prestige (Bourdieu, 1990; Connell, 1987).

Today, women are present in working environments that were previously typically male, or hold top positions in organizations, but the structure that orders and regulates our societies, even though in different ways, still does it on the basis of gender (Schnurr et al., 2020). Empirical and theoretical studies have used different lenses to investigate gender issues in the field of work–life balance; for example, a 'cultural' and 'institutional' frame, often in order to observe these issues from a comparative point of view, using a 'gender regimes perspective' (Bose, 2015; Pascall and Lewis, 2020; Sümer, 2016; Tomlinson, 2007) or an 'organizational cultures perspective' (Benschop and Verloo, 2011; Gherardi, 1996; Gherardi and Poggio, 2001; P. Lewis et al., 2017). These perspectives allow us to underline that institutions, organizations and their cultures are not neutral, but gendered (Acker, 1990, 1992; Williams et al., 2012).

A work–life imbalance is more profound where it is still culturally taken for granted that domestic and care work are female prerogatives, and where the institutional infrastructure does not take into account gender equality as a key issue. Even in recent years, comparative research has given empirical evidence with regard to differences between countries, recognizing some where gender stereotypes are still deeply present and equality policies are just starting to be implemented (Salazar Benítez, 2016; Saraceno, 2018), and others whose labor markets and economies are also affected by job insecurity and stagnation or crisis, although featuring a more gender-equal cultural background and stronger gender-equality policies (Grönlund et al., 2017; Teigen and Skjeie, 2017).

However, because work–life balance historically arose as a female issue, starting from the assumption – taken for granted for years – that women and particularly mothers are the only ones who need it (Connell, 2005; Risman and Davis, 2013), reconciliation rights and resulting policies were almost exclusively designed for women and are still affected by this initial bias (Saraceno and Keck, 2011). This bias is also present in the work–life balance research field – conditioning also the methodological and sampling choices, as underlined in Chapter 3. In this way, work–life balance arrangements are also designed and used as gendered: the traditional cultural norms and gendered representations are reproduced. Childcare can be represented as the most taken-for-granted reason for requesting and using these arrangements, and 'private' lives of women can be conceptualized as 'only family' life, solely characterized by care duties, not hobbies, passions nor interests (Mescher et al., 2010).

Nevertheless, societies have gone through important transformations. In the last decades, there have been relevant changes in gender practices and relationships, as well as in models of parenthood and ways of starting families. The reconceptualization of family models is a current goal to achieve in the field of work–life balance: several studies have dealt with themes such as work–life balance of both men and women (Emslie and Hunt, 2009); the work–life balance of men, in particular fathers (Crespi and Ruspini, 2015, 2016); and the process of de-institutionalization of the male-breadwinner family model (Cannito, 2018). Although the change has not yet fully occurred, work–life balance policies have changed over time, from being conceptualized and constructed with the aim of bringing women into the labor market to being designed and implemented today for the well-being of both males and females.

A second fundamental axis in the field of work–life balance research is the axis of class. Social class is important with respect to conciliation: especially in historical periods affected by economic crisis and austerity, different classes or economic groups can experience very different everyday lives, despite being placed inside the same geographical context and institutional framework (Chatrakul Na Ayudhya et al., 2019; Lewis et al., 2017; Warren, 2014, 2020). The problems of reconciliation can be investigated within the working class, focusing on blue- or white-collar or service workers with low wages; or within the privileged class, studying managing directors, business owners and high-income professionals. The studies have been unevenly distributed; most have focused on work–life balance, reconciliation and gender inequalities in high-skilled occupations and qualified professions – in a sample-selection approach that ends up including only some social groups and not others, from a class point of view as well as from a gender perspective, as argued in the next chapter.

Scholars have observed work–life balance issues in management and women's access to managerial positions, focusing, for example, on the difficulty women may encounter when reconciling work and private or family life in the course of their career. These are often linked to organizational aspects, such as the glass-ceiling process, informal norms and cultural representations related to decision-making positions and leadership, or coping strategies in the work–life balance of women and men, to conform to or bypass organizational norms (Guillaume and Pochic, 2009). There has also been analysis on the discourses of work–life balance in the academic sector, that can be self-represented by female academics as a personal management task, an unachievable ideal, as detrimental to their careers or unmentionable at work. These discourses respond to the gendered attitudes about paid work and unpaid care that women configure when attempting to create a work–life balance, showing how gendered organizational cultures, when internalized, can be the very premises for them to fail to manage this balance (Toffoletti and Starr, 2016).

There are also studies on the work–life balance and the well-being of the working class, albeit some scholars have underlined their scarcity (Warren, 2015, 2016). Numerous studies have recently started to analyse work–life balance with regard to flexibility of working times, shift work and Sunday or holiday work (Jacobs and Padavic, 2015; Lefrançois et al., 2017; Ravenswood and Harris, 2016; Van Eck et al., 2020). These work schedules are primarily experienced by the working class and above all in the service sector, where non-standard working hours are now the norm (Boulin, 2013).

According to the literature on low-skilled and low-paid workers, non-standard working times have negative consequences on well-being and everyday life, leading to conditions of stress, powerlessness and even alienation (Dordoni, 2017), more deeply for women and especially for mothers, who are compelled to face flexible schedules together with the economic strain of paying for public or private childcare (Dordoni, 2018). Moreover, in the last few years, both unemployment and part-time employment – especially the involuntary kind – has increased in several countries because of the economic crisis, accompanied by an increase in poverty risk (Horemans et al., 2016). Involuntary part-time work is associated more with women than with men (Denia and Guillú, 2019; Pech et al., 2020) and in-work poverty has been investigated taking into account work–life balance and childcare policies (Lohmann and Marx, 2018; Saraceno et al., 2020).

Another relevant axis in the study of work–life balance is the axis of generation, which can be articulated in research and reflections focused on aging and youth. In the last few years, the aging process of the population, together with the postponement of the retirement age implemented by many countries, raised new issues and problems – highlighted in Chapter 3 from the methodological point of view – such as the higher need for care and assistance for the elderly who no longer work, in terms of both paid (Ravenswood and Harris, 2016) and unpaid work (Bouget et al., 2017) on one hand, and the demand for reconciliation policies for the aged who are still working on the other (Anderson, 2019; Baltes and Young, 2007; Phillips and Siu, 2012). The generational approach allows us to analyse work–life balance issues from a different point of view and to detect how they change and translate into daily life in different age groups.

Regarding youth work, the most relevant point to be outlined is that contemporary economic structures have changed over time and are now extremely marked by flexibilization processes. This has led to the spread of temporary contracts, which inevitably affect young people's everyday life and life planning through creating difficulty when addressing autonomy, and thus their transition into adulthood, economic vulnerability and precariousness of life. Young people's work–life balance is today conditioned by their flexible and precarious working conditions, associated with uncertainty, insecurity and diminished control at work, which may contribute to work–life imbalance (Bohle, 2016).

Work flexibility intended as non-standard work, characterized by temporary contracts, shift work and flexible schedules, leads to a lack of guarantees and labor protection, such as parental leave, and is negatively interfering with work–life balance (Dizaho et al., 2017). The rise in precarious employment is most markedly affecting service sector workers, whose precarious or temporary work is associated with adverse outcomes, including low control over working hours, work–life conflict and stress. Empirical evidence shows that temporary workers perceive themselves as less in control of their working hours than permanent workers (McNamara et al., 2011), and that job insecurity and precariousness also affect professionals as knowledge workers, with a negative impact on their work–life balance, especially for women (Carreri, 2020).

Flexibility is an ambivalent concept because it can refer to flexible work arrangements mutually agreed by workers and employers with the aim of improving work–life balance, but also to a condition of instability that is intrinsic in a form of flexibility that was not chosen by workers, such as in the case of a temporary job with a flexible schedule. As written on the European Institute for Gender Equality (EIGE) website: 'Flexible working arrangements, such as opportunities to transition between part-time and full-time work, flexibility in working hours and remote work, typically give employees a greater ability to control how much, when and where they can work.'[2] By this definition, flexibility is conceived as a set of working arrangements implemented with the aim to 'give employees a greater ability to control' their work, in terms of pace of work, working times and working space. Nevertheless, as previously argued, flexibilization processes have led to the growth of temporary and precarious jobs.

The key issue concerns the workers' autonomy and the employer's control. The effect of the implementation of flexibility arrangements depends on the degree of workers' autonomy in the workplace, on their possibility of having a voice in decisional and organizational processes. In the EIGE's definition, working times are decided 'bottom up' by the company in dialogue with workers, and this translates the flexibility into positive work–life balance organizational practices (Chung and Van der Lippe, 2020; Smithson and Stokoe, 2005). On the contrary, flexibility that is not associated with workers' autonomy, as we have seen with temporary jobs and involuntary part-time, shift and Sunday work, translates into precariousness of life, sometimes into vulnerability and in-work poverty, and often into work–life balance difficulties.

Gender, class and generation are today the most regarded axes in work–life balance literature; not the only ones, however. In the last few years, scholars have started to take into consideration and incorporate other dimensions in the debate, such as race, nationality and ethnicity, taking into account the multiple identity group memberships of each individual, and critically reviewing the existing work–life balance literature, through the lenses of diversity (Mulinari and Selberg, 2013; Özbilgin et al., 2011).

More and more aspects, factors and categories are now being taken into account – as observed in the next chapter – in order to achieve a more complex and inclusive vision of work–life balance (Dennissen et al., 2020; Hutchinson, 2018; Sang and Powell, 2013). With the aim of overcoming a heteronormative vision of the family, work–life balance issues concerning LGBTQ+ workers have recently been investigated (Sawyer et al., 2017; Stavrou and Solea, 2021). Other research has considered family strategies for balancing caregiving and work in families with disabled children (Lewis et al., 2000) or the application of new technologies and remote work for workers with disabilities or workers who have family members with disabilities (Igeltjørn and Habib, 2020). Lastly, recent research has investigated work–life balance with an intersectional approach, framing the experiences of migrant workers, considering, for example, their legal and employment restrictions (Au et al., 2020) or their experiences as self-employed parents (Munkejord, 2017).

Many of these contributions examine the influence of the interweaving of these dimensions on work–life issues by adopting an intersectional perspective, with the aim of broadening the field to new aspects and factors. Individuals can recognize themselves in multiple identities according to their qualities and characteristics, and the combination and intersection of these qualities produces substantively distinct life experiences.

Moreover, cumulative negative outcomes stem from having several stigmatized identities: those who belong to multiple marginalized identity groups risk being made socially invisible because they do not represent a prototype for their overarching group. This occurs when the wider culture's ideology holds a certain set of qualities as the standard; that is, male, white and heterosexual in certain parts of the world (Purdie-Vaughns and Eibach, 2008).

An intersectional point of view allows us to make the invisible visible as well as reinforcing work–life balance issues in organizations and enhancing inclusivity. Today, it is crucial to promote work–life balance, well-being at work and job satisfaction while recognizing multiple identities and intersected identity groups who suffer from greater stigmatization (Ryan and Briggs, 2020). Observing and understanding the different work–life experiences of individuals can guide institutions and organizations in developing more inclusive and equitable policies, as well as giving the researchers a valuable opportunity to extend work–life balance research (Beauregard et al., 2020).

3.   NEW PERSPECTIVES FOR STUDYING THE INTERSECTION BETWEEN WORK AND OTHER LIFE DOMAINS

Having outlined the genesis and development of the work–life balance construct, shed light on some of its main ambivalences and defined the main axes along which the debate has developed over time, in this last section we attempt to identify emerging issues and future prospects, with a focus on present-day ongoing changes, including the implications of the Covid-19 pandemic, which emerged at an advanced stage of the writing process of this book but could not possibly be disregarded. In fact, it may very well be that this unexpected event, which so heavily impacted our lives, could represent the starting point for a reflection on the possible developments of the debate. The pandemic, as always happens with catastrophes and emergencies of this scale, has acted as a sort of magnifying glass for the analysis of the structures and processes that characterize our experience of daily life, which would not always be easily recognizable otherwise. The Covid-19 emergency has brought to light widespread contradictions and social imbalances by taking them to the extreme, in particular in terms of the intertwining of work and private life. As soon as many found themselves confined within their domestic walls, it became evident how an analytic construct based on the existence of two distinct domains, work on the one hand and private life on the other, had become intrinsically problematic and insufficient on the heuristic level.

During the months of the pandemic, much instant-research was carried out, in which various aspects related to the relationship between work and other domains of personal life were considered, exploring topics such as remote work, the consequences of the closure of schools and home-schooling, the division of care tasks and the consequences of the crisis on female employment. Much of the research featured interpretative readings that criticized classical approaches to work–life balance and were aimed at soliciting new perspectives and new paradigms, not only on the theoretical and interpretive level, but also on the methodological one (see Chapter 3 in this book).

The several authors who over the last few years have criticized the separation – somehow implicit in the work–life balance construct – between work and 'non-work', have seen their theories thoroughly confirmed in the face of the pandemic experience. Reality undoubtedly appears more complex and indefinite than what the construct of work–life balance allows us to guess, the intertwining between its domains much more nuanced, differentiated and located in relation to different dimensions, from socio-economic to temporal and spatial ones. The development of new technologies plays a key role in this picture, especially with digital devices intensifying the processes of work flexibilization. Various studies (Nam, 2014; Sungdoo and Hollensbe, 2018) have already highlighted how the spread of increasingly sophisticated technologies has made it possible to overcome the previously existing limits between the workplace and the home, on both a physical and temporal level: with connected devices, work can now be carried out in different times and locations. Boundaries therefore become increasingly permeable and flexible (Weaver McCloskey, 2016), with consequences affecting workers' quality of life and room for reconciliation. The pandemic has acted as an extremely powerful accelerator of this process. The number of people engaged in virtual work has increased exponentially (Berg et al., 2020). If the working-from-home solution has often been listed among the means capable of favoring work–life reconciliation (Allen et al., 2015b), it should nevertheless be noted that the conditions that characterized it in this particular situation were actually rather different from those that could in fact make remote work a resource to foster the balance between work and personal life. In this case, people worked continuously from home for the whole week, often without a clear definition of working hours, simply by moving the activities that they would previously carry out in the office to their home.

Being unable to resort to external support due to schools and day-care facilities being closed, parents also found themselves compelled to provide assistance to non-self-sufficient family members and support for their children's home-schooling. Moreover, everyone being at home at all times greatly increased the housework load. This made the gender asymmetries in the division of roles within families more explicit: the greater demand in family work commitment has in fact burdened the female component more significantly (Craig and Churchill, 2021), creating a sort of gender backlash. However, it should be remembered that – especially in cases where women were key workers – fathers' involvement and commitment has greatly increased (Qian and Fuller, 2020).

Working remotely, perhaps being unable to isolate in a quiet room and having nobody who would take care of toddlers and young children, has inevitably worsened the condition of fatigue and stress, as well as accentuating the conflict between work demands, potentially coming at any time and invading personal times and spaces, and those related to family responsibilities, which could represent factors of interruption and distraction during working hours.

The situation appeared particularly problematic for families with a disadvantaged background, belonging to minority groups, who were immigrants, or with members with disabilities, or in the cases of single parents. The latter condition is also much more common among women: a survey conducted in the US has shown that only 20 percent of single parents have managed to organize themselves in order to work from home (Alon et al., 2020).

At the same time, the pandemic has allowed us to observe the very differences that exist between different types of work, precisely with regard to the use of technologies. Not all families had access to the devices required to work remotely or for their children's home-schooling. The shift to remote work has not occurred across all job positions. For example, there is a significant number of workers, so-called 'key workers' (the majority of whom are women), who continued to work outside their homes, in health care, social work and essential retail jobs (Robertson and Gebeloff, 2020). They did so at a high risk of contracting the virus at work and then carrying it home to their families.

The critical issues related to the pandemic are not limited to the lockdown period, but also extend to the consequences that this crisis will have in the medium and long term. The scenario we are looking at is that of an amplification of the imbalance, to the detriment of the female component. Unlike what happened with previous economic recessions, which had mainly affected the so-called 'cyclical' sectors (among them construction, manufacturing and transport), characterized by a prevalence of a male workforce, the current crisis has mainly penalized those sectors defined as 'anticyclical', and in particular those activities in which the risk of infection was higher due to closer interpersonal contact, such as care services, but also catering, tourism and retail, in which women represent the majority of the workforce (Alon et al., 2020).

In countries where work and labor suffer from a lower degree of protection, the increase in female unemployment (to a greater extent than male) had already been observed during the first instances of the emergency, especially for those working in key sectors and in conditions of greater precariousness. In the US, statistics showed that, as early as March 2020, 59 percent of unemployment benefits applications had been filed by women (Bureau of Labor Statistics, 2020). Furthermore, it was observed that the reduction in women's working hours risked generating a 'downward spiral' that could lead to labor force exit (Stone, 2007) or negative consequences in terms of career and salary (Rhubart, 2020).

Another group of female workers who are being deeply affected by the pandemic are those who work part-time or are self-employed, business owners and those who before the crisis already had an irregular income, often exactly in order to manage their care commitments with greater flexibility, which the uncertain circumstances precipitated by the pandemic have made even more vulnerable (OECD, 2020).

What are the main implications of the ongoing changes with respect to the future research agenda? What are the trajectories and perspectives opening for those who intend to study the intersection between work and the other areas of personal life?

In the first instance, looking at the issue on the basis of a dichotomous categorization between work and life (as if work were not a part of life), or between 'work' and 'non-work', now proves to be insufficient. In fact – today more than ever – the articulation of the relationship between work and other life domains is much more complex than what a dichotomous representation could ever convey. It is therefore necessary to adopt a more explicitly multidimensional approach able to do justice to the complexity of the phenomenon (Hall et al., 2013; Powell et al., 2019).

Secondly, despite the significant changes that have occurred over time, gender remains a crucial factor in the differentiation of expectations, practices and opportunities. It is therefore necessary to continue to take gender implications into account when studying work–life balance structures and practices, not only considering the changes that have occurred over time and the progressive reduction of the gap, but also paying close attention to the factors that can 'turn the clock back in time', as seen in the face of the pandemic crisis. However, the focus on gender must be integrated and enriched by the inclusion of other dimensions and diversity components that can influence the work–life interrelation, such as socio-economic class, ethnicity, sexual orientation and religion, and by adopting a perspective capable of analysing the influence produced by the intersection of these dimensions (Ammons and Edgell, 2007; Özbilgin et al., 2011; Sawyer et al., 2017).

Thirdly, it is today crucial to bear in mind that the work–family interface as a subject of analysis is located in a specific socio-cultural context, conditioned by national welfare policies and regimes, as well as companies and organizations' specific strategies and practices, and the different family models that connote different territories, which today tend to intertwine and contaminate each other as a result of the processes of globalization (Allen et al., 2015a). In this respect, it would be useful to extend scholarly attention to realities that are scarcely considered today.

In the fourth instance, we should dedicate greater consideration to the changes that have characterized the very ways in which we work, with particular respect to the differentiation of work forms and methods. The traditional work–life balance concept appears to be strongly tied to the Fordist model, whereas our contemporary reality is certainly much more varied. The processes of growing precariousness, fragmentation and individualization of work deeply affect its intertwining with other life domains and cannot possibly be disregarded. Moreover, we deem it necessary to reflect on how research to date has mainly focused on certain categories of workers (in particular in managerial and professional careers, as highlighted by Casper et al., 2007), and forgotten others that, especially in light of recent events, would deserve more attention (think, for example, of essential workers, but also the self-employed).

Finally, it is essential to develop analytical frameworks that add the recent technological changes to the equation, with the awareness that the development of technologies significantly affects the intertwining of the work experience and other life domains, helping to define and shape them, as well as generating previously unseen balances and intersections. On this front, it also appears necessary to adopt critical lenses that also allow us to highlight the possible risks of these processes, which range from the creation of new forms of digital divide to the possibility of generating phenomena of alienation and loss of those protections and opportunities that are tied to the interaction with other life dimensions.

NOTES

1. This chapter is a collaborative effort; nevertheless, if for academic reasons individual authorship has to be attributed, Anna Carreri wrote Section 1, Annalisa Dordoni Section 2 and Barbara Poggio the Introduction and Section 3.
2. See https://eige.europa.eu/gender-equality-index/thematic-focus/work-life-balance/flexible -working-arrangements (last accessed on 14 December 2020).

REFERENCES

Acker, J. (1990), 'Hierarchies, jobs, bodies: A theory of gendered organizations', *Gender & Society*, **4**(2), 139–158.

Acker, J. (1992), 'From sex roles to gendered institutions', *Contemporary Sociology*, **21**(5), 565–569.

Allen, T. D., K. A. French, S. Dumani and K. M. Shockley (2015a), 'Meta-analysis of work–family conflict mean differences: Does national context matter?', *Journal of Vocational Behavior*, **90**, 90–100.

Allen, T. D., T. D. Golden and K. M. Shockley (2015b), 'How effective is telecommuting? Assessing the status of our scientific findings', *Psychological Science in the Public Interest*, **16**(2), 40–68.

Alon, T. M., M. Doepke, J. Olmstead-Rumsey and M. Tertilt (2020), 'The impact of COVID-19 on gender equality' (CRC TR 224 Discussion Paper Series), University of Bonn and University of Mannheim, accessed 19 January 2021 at www.crctr224.de/en/research-output/discussion-papers/discussion-paper -archive/2020/the-impact-of-covid-19-on-gender-equality-titan-alon-matthias-doepke-jane-olmstead -rumsey-michele-tertilt.

Ammons, S. K. (2013), 'Work-family boundary strategies: Stability and alignment between preferred and enacted boundaries', *Journal of Vocational Behavior*, **82**(1), 49–58.

Ammons, S. K., and P. Edgell (2007), 'Religious influences on work–family trade-offs', *Journal of Family Issues*, **28**(6), 794–826.

Anderson, R. (2019), 'Work-life balance over the course of working life', in Mikkel Barslund (eds), *Policies for an Ageing Workforce: Work-Life Balance, Working Conditions and Equal Opportunities*, Brussels: CEPS – Centre for European Policy Studies, pp. 1–5, accessed 19 January 2021 at www .ceps.eu/ceps-publications/policies-for-an-ageing-workforce/.

Ashforth, B. E., G. E. Kreiner and M. Fugate (2000), 'All in a day's work: Boundaries and micro role transitions', *Academy of Management Review*, **25**(3), 472–491.

Au, W. C., U. Chatrakul Na Ayudhya, Y. S. Tan and P. K. Ahmed (2020), 'The work-life experiences of an invisible workforce: The case of live-in women migrant domestic workers in Malaysia', *Equality, Diversity and Inclusion: An International Journal*, **39**(5), 567–583.

Baltes, B. B., and L. M. Young (2007), 'Aging and work/family issues', in G. Adams and K. Shultz (eds), *Aging and Work in the 21st Century*, Mahway, NJ: Lawrence Erlbaum Associates, pp. 251–275.

Barnett, R. C., and K. C. Gareis (2006), 'Role theory perspectives on work and family', in M. Pitt-Catsouphes, E. E. Kossek and S. Sweet (eds), *The Work and Family Handbook: Multi-Disciplinary Perspectives and Approaches*, Mahwah, NJ: Lawrence Erlbaum Associates, pp. 209–221.

Barnett, R. C., and J. S. Hyde (2001), 'Women, man, work, and family: An expansionist theory', *American Psychologist*, **56**(10), 781–796.

Beauregard, T. A. (2011), 'Corporate work-life balance initiatives: Use and effectiveness', in S. Kaiser, M. Ringlstetter, D. R. Eikhof and M. Pina e Cunha (eds), *Creating Balance? International Perspectives on the Work-Life Integration of Professionals*, Berlin: Springer, pp. 193–208.

Beauregard, T. A., M. Adamson, A. Kunter, L. Miles and I. Roper (2020), 'Diversity in the work–life interface: Introduction to the special issue', *Equality, Diversity and Inclusion: An International Journal*, **39**(5), 465–478.

Benschop, Y., and M. Verloo (2011), 'Gender change, organizational change, and gender equality strategies', in E. Jeanes, D. Knights and P. Yancey Martin (eds), *Handbook of Gender, Work and Organization*, Hoboken, NJ: Wiley-Blackwell, pp. 277–290.

Berg, J., S. Bonnet and C. Soares (2020), 'Working from home: Estimating the worldwide potential', VoxEU, accessed 19 January 2021 at https://voxeu.org/article/working-home-estimating-worldwide-potential.

Bianchi, S. M., and M. A. Milkie (2010), 'Work and family research in the first decade of the 21st century', *Journal of Marriage and Family*, **72**(3), 705–725.

Blair-Loy, M. (2003), *Competing Devotions: Career and Family among Women Financial Executives*, Cambridge, MA: Harvard University Press.

Bloom, P. (2016), 'Work as the contemporary limit of life: Capitalism, the death drive, and the lethal fantasy of "work–life balance"', *Organization*, **23**(4), 588–606.

Bohle, P. (2016), 'Work-life conflict in 'flexible work': Precariousness, variable hours and related forms of work organization', in I. Iskra-Golec, J. Barnes-Farrell and P. Bohle (eds), *Social and Family Issues in Shift Work and Non-Standard Working Hours*, New York, NY: Springer, pp. 91–105.

Bose, C. E. (2015), 'Patterns of global gender inequalities and regional gender regimes', *Gender & Society*, **29**(6), 767–791.

Bouget, D., C. Saraceno and S. Spasova (2017), 'Towards new work-life balance policies for those caring for dependent relatives?', in B. Vanhercke, S. Sabato and D. Bouget (eds), *Social Policy in the European Union: State of Play 2017*, Brussels: European Trade Union Institute, accessed 19 January 2021 at www.etui.org/publications/books/social-policy-in-the-european-union-state-of-play-2017, pp. 155–179.

Boulin, J. Y. (2013), 'Working on Sunday: Regulations, impacts and perceptions of the time use practices', in D. Henckel, B. Könecke, R. Zedda and S. Stabilini (eds), *Space–Time Design of the Public City*, Dordrecht: Springer, pp. 21–35.

Bourdieu, P. (1990), 'La domination masculine', *Actes de la recherche en sciences sociales*, **84**(1), 2–31.

Bureau of Labor Statistics (2020), *The Employment Situation: March 2020*, accessed 5 May 2020 at www.bls.gov/news.release/archives/empsit_04032020.pdf.

Cannito, M (2018), 'Fathers and parental leave: The role of the work environment and the gendered family friendliness in the private sector', *Polis*, **32**(2), 217–244.

Carreri, A. (2020), 'Control on the 'boundary-work' in work-life articulation for flexible knowledge workers: Insights into gender asymmetries', *Social Sciences*, **9**(6), 107.

Casper, W. J., L. T. Eby, C. Bordeaux, A. Lockwood and D. Lambert (2007), 'A review of research methods in IO/OB work-family research', *Journal of Applied Psychology*, **92**(1), 28–43.

Chatrakul Na Ayudhya, U., R. Prouska and T. A. Beauregard (2019), 'The impact of global economic crisis and austerity on quality of working life and work-life balance: A capabilities perspective', *European Management Review*, **16**(4), 847–862.

Chung, H., and T. Van der Lippe (2020), 'Flexible working, work–life balance, and gender equality: Introduction', *Social Indicators Research*, **151**, 365–381.

Clark, S. C. (2000), 'Work/family border theory: A new theory of work/family balance', *Human Relations*, **53**(6): 747–770.

Connell, R. (1987), *Gender and Power: Society, the Person and Sexual Politics*, Stanford, CA: Stanford University Press.

Connell, R. W. (2005), 'Work/life balance, gender equity and social change', *Australian Journal of Social Issues*, **40**(3), 369–383.

Craig, L., and B. Churchill (2021), 'Dual-earner parent couples' work and care during COVID-19', *Gender, Work & Organization*, **28**(S1), 66–69.

Crespi, I., and E. Ruspini (2015), 'Transition to fatherhood: New perspectives in the global context of changing men's identities', *International Review of Sociology*, **25**(3), 353–358.

Crespi, I., and E. Ruspini (eds) (2016), *Balancing Work and Family in a Changing Society: The Fathers' Perspective*, Basingstoke: Palgrave Macmillan.

Denia, A., and M. D. Guillú (2019), 'The gender gap in involuntary part-time employment: The case of Spain', *International Journal of Business and Social Science*, **10**(12), 169–182.

Dennissen, M., Y. Benschop and M. Van den Brink (2020), 'Rethinking diversity management: An intersectional analysis of diversity networks', *Organization Studies*, **41**(2), 219–240.

Dizaho, E. K., R. Salleh and A. Abdullah (2017), 'Achieving work life balance through flexible work schedules and arrangements', *Global Business & Management Research*, **9**, 455–465.

Dordoni, A. (2017), 'Times and rhythms of the retail shift work: Two European case studies – Immediate gratification and deregulation of shop opening hours', *Sociologia del lavoro*, **146**, 156–171.

Dordoni, A. (2018), 'Gender and time inequalities: Retail work and the deregulation of shop opening hours', *Sociologia Italiana – AIS Journal of Sociology*, **12**, 161–172.

Dumas, T. L., and J. Sanchez-Burks (2015), 'The professional, the personal, and the ideal worker: Pressures and objectives shaping the boundary between life domains', *Academy of Management Annals*, **9**(1), 803–843.

Emslie, C., and K. Hunt (2009), '"Live to work" or "work to live"? A qualitative study of gender and work–life balance among men and women in mid-life', *Gender, Work and Organization*, **16**(1), 151–172.

Fleetwood, S. (2007), 'Why work–life balance now?' *International Journal of Human Resource Management*, **18**(3), 387–400.

Gambles, R., S. Lewis and R. Rapoport (2006), *The Myth of Work Life Balance: The Challenge of Our Time for Men, Women and Societies*, Chichester: John Wiley & Sons.

Gatrell, C., C. L. Cooper and E. E. Kossek (2017), 'Maternal bodies as taboo at work: New perspectives on the marginalizing of senior women in organizations', *Academy of Management Perspectives*, **31**(3), 239–252.

Gatrell, C. J., S. B. Burnett, C. L. Cooper and P. Sparrow (2013), 'Work–life balance and parenthood: A comparative review of definitions, equity and enrichment', *International Journal of Management Reviews*, **15**(3), 300–316.

Gatrell, C. J., and C. L. Cooper (2008), 'Work-life balance: Working for whom?' *European Journal of International Management*, **2**(1), 71–86.

Gherardi, S. (1996), 'Gendered organizational cultures: Narratives of women travellers in a male world – Gender', *Work & Organization*, **3**(4), 187–201.

Gherardi, S., and B. Poggio (2001), 'Creating and recreating gender order in organizations', *Journal of World Business*, **36**(3), 245–259.

Glucksmann, M. (2005), 'Shifting boundaries and interconnections: Extending the "total social organisation of labour"', *Sociological Review*, **53**(Suppl. 2), 19–36.

Greenhaus, J., and N. Beutell (1985), 'Sources of conflict between work and family roles', *Academy of Management Review*, **10**(1): 76–88.

Greenhaus, J., and G. Powell (2006), 'When work and family are allies: A theory of work-family enrichment', *Academy of Management Review*, **31**(1), 72–92.

Gregory, A., and S. Milner (2009), 'Editorial: Work–life balance – A matter of choice?', *Gender, Work & Organization*, **16**(1), 1–13.

Grönlund, A., K. Halldén and C. Magnusson (2017), 'A Scandinavian success story? Women's labour market outcomes in Denmark, Finland, Norway and Sweden', *Acta Sociologica*, **60**(2), 97–119.

Guillaume, C., and S. Pochic (2009), 'What would you sacrifice? Access to top management and the work–life balance', *Gender, Work & Organization*, **16**(1), 14–36.

Hall, D. T., E. E. Kossek, J. P. Briscoe, S. Pichler and M. D. Lee (2013), 'Nonwork orientations relative to career: A multidimensional measure', *Journal of Vocational Behavior*, **83**(3), 539–550.

Harvey, D. (2005), *A Brief History of Neoliberalism*, Oxford: Oxford University Press.

Hobson, B. (ed.) (2014), *Worklife Balance: The Agency and Capabilities Gap*, Oxford: Oxford University Press.

Horemans, J., I. Marx and B. Nolan (2016), 'Hanging in, but only just: Part-time employment and in-work poverty throughout the crisis', *IZA Journal of European Labor Studies*, **5**(1), 5.

Hutchinson, D. (2018), 'Work-life balance in the workplace', in C. de Aquino and R. Robertson (eds), *Diversity and Inclusion in the Global Workplace*, Cham: Palgrave Macmillan, pp. 185–200.

Igeltjørn, A., and L. Habib (2020), 'Homebased telework as a tool for inclusion? A literature review of telework, disabilities and work-life balance', in M. Antona and C. Stephanidis (eds), *Universal Access in Human-Computer Interaction: Applications and Practice*, Cham: Springer, pp. 420–436.

Jacobs, A. W., and I. Padavic (2015), 'Hours, scheduling and flexibility for women in the US low-wage labour force', *Gender, Work & Organization*, **22**(1), 67–86.

Kanter, R. M. (1977), *Work and Family in the United States: A Critical Review and Agenda for Research and Policy*, New York, NY: Russell Sage Foundation.

Kossek, E. E. (2016), 'Managing work-life boundaries in the digital age', *Organizational Dynamics*, **45**(3), 258–270.

Kossek, E. E., B. B. Baltes and A. Mathews (2011), 'Innovative ideas on how work–family research can have more impact', *Industrial and Organizational Psychology*, **4**(3), 426–432.

Kossek, E., and A. Groggins (2014), 'Work life balance' in D. Guest and D. Needle (eds), *Wiley Encyclopedia of Management, Volume 5: Human Resource Management*, Chichester: Wiley, pp. 1–4.

Kossek, E. E., M. N. Ruderman, P. W. Braddy, and K. M. Hannum (2012), 'Work–nonwork boundary management profiles: A person-centered approach', *Journal of Vocational Behavior*, **81**(1): 112–28.

Lefrançois, M., K. Messing and J. Saint-Charles (2017), 'Time control, job execution and information access: Work/family strategies in the context of low-wage work and 24/7 schedules', *Community, Work & Family*, **20**(5), 600–622.

Leslie, L. M., C. F. Manchester, T. Y. Park and S. A. Mehng (2012), 'Flexible work practices: A source of career premiums or penalties?', *Academy of Management Journal*, **55**(6), 1407–1428.

Lewis, P., Y. Benschop and R. Simpson (2017), 'Postfeminism, gender and organization', *Gender, Work and Organization*, **24**(3), 213–225.

Lewis, S., D. Anderson, C. Lyonette, N. Payne and S. Wood (2017), 'Public sector austerity cuts in the UK and the changing discourse of work–life balance', *Work, Employment and Society*, **31**(4), 586–604.

Lewis, S., and T. A. Beauregard (2018), 'The meanings of work–life balance: A cultural perspective', in K. M. Shockley, W. Shen and R. C. Johnson (eds), *The Cambridge Handbook of the Global Work–Family Interface*, Cambridge: Cambridge University Press, pp. 720–732.

Lewis, S., R. Gambles and R. Rapoport (2007), 'The constraints of a 'work–life balance' approach: An international perspective', *International Journal of Human Resource Management*, **18**(3), 360–373.

Lewis, S., C. Kagan and P. Heaton (2000), 'Managing work-family diversity for parents of disabled children: Beyond policy to practice and partnership', *Personnel Review*, **29**(3), 417–430.

Lohmann, H., and I. Marx (eds) (2018), *Handbook on In-Work Poverty*, Cheltenham, UK and Northampton, MA, USA: Edward Elgar Publishing.

McNamara, M., P. Bohle and M. Quinlan (2011), 'Precarious employment, working hours, work-life conflict and health in hotel work', *Applied Ergonomics*, **42**(2), 225–232.

Mescher, S., Y. Benschop, and H. Doorewaard (2010), 'Representations of work-life balance support', *Human Relations*, **63**(1), 21–39.

Moore, S., S. Tailby, B. Antunes and K. Newsome (2018), '"Fits and fancies": The Taylor Review, the construction of preference and labour market segmentation', *Industrial Relations Journal*, **49**(5–6), 403–419.

Mulinari, P., and R. Selberg (2013), 'Intersectional directions in working life research: A proposal', *Nordic Journal of Working Life Studies*, **3**(3), 81–98.

Munkejord, M. C. (2017), 'His or her work–life balance? Experiences of self-employed immigrant parents', *Work, Employment and Society*, **31**(4), 624–639.

Naldini, M., and C. Saraceno (2011), *Conciliare famiglia e lavoro. Vecchi e nuovi patti tra i sessi e le generazioni*, Bologna: Il Mulino.

Nam, T. (2014), 'Technology use and work-life balance', *Applied Research in Quality of Life*, **9**(4), 1017–1040.

Nippert-Eng, C. (1996), *Home and Work: Negotiating Boundaries through Everyday Life*, Chicago, IL: University of Chicago Press.

OECD (2020), *Distributional Risks Associated with Non-Standard Work: Stylised Facts and Policy Considerations*, Paris: OECD, accessed 18 January 2021 at https://read.oecd-ilibrary.org/view/?ref

=134_134518-2bfush541w&title=Distributional-risks-associated-with-nonstandard-work-Stylised -facts-and-policy-considerations.

Ollier-Malaterre, A. (2010), 'Contributions of work–life and resilience initiatives to the individual/ organization relationship', *Human Relations*, **63**(1), 41–62.

Özbilgin, M. F., T. A. Beauregard, A. Tatli and M. P. Bell (2011), 'Work–life, diversity and intersection-ality: A critical review and research agenda', *International Journal of Management Reviews*, **13**(2), 177–198.

Pascall, G., and J. Lewis (2020), 'Emerging gender regimes and policies for gender equality in a wider Europe', *Journal of Social Policy*, **33**(3), 373–394.

Pech, C., E. Klainot-Hess and D. Norris (2020), 'Part-time by gender, not choice: The gender gap in involuntary part-time work', *Sociological Perspectives*, **64**(2), accessed 18 January 2021 at https://doi .org/10.1177/0731121420937746.

Pérez-Zapata, O., A. Serrano Pascual, G. Álvarez-Hernández and C. Castaño Collado (2016), 'Knowledge work intensification and self-management: The autonomy paradox', *Work Organisation, Labour & Globalisation*, **10**(2), 27–49.

Perrons, D., L. McDowell, C. Fagan, K. Ray and K. Ward (2007), 'Gender, social class and work-life balance in the new economy', in R. Crompton, S. Lewis and C. Lyonette (eds), *Women, Men, Work and Family in Europe*, London: Palgrave Macmillan, pp. 133–151.

Phillips, D. R., and O. L. Siu (2012), 'Global aging and aging workers', in J. W. Hedge and W. C. Borman (eds), *The Oxford Handbook of Work and Aging*, Oxford: Oxford University Press, pp. 11–32.

Pleck, E. (1976), 'Two worlds in one: Work and family', *Journal of Social History*, **10**(2), 178–195.

Pleck, J. H. (1977), 'The work-family role system', *Social Problems*, **24**(4), 417–427.

Powell, G. N., J. H. Greenhaus, T. D. Allen and R. E. Johnson (2019), 'Advancing and expanding work-life theory from multiple perspectives', *Academy of Management Review*, **44**(1), 54–71.

Purdie-Vaughns, V., and R. P. Eibach (2008), 'Intersectional invisibility: The distinctive advantages and disadvantages of multiple subordinate-group identities', *Sex Roles*, **59**(5–6), 377–391.

Qian, Y., and S. Fuller (2020), 'COVID-19 and the gender employment gap among parents of young children', *Canadian Public Policy*, **46**(2), 89–101.

Rajan-Rankin, S. (2016), 'Paternalism and the paradox of work–life balance: Discourse and practice', *Community, Work & Family*, **19**(2), 227–241.

Ransome, P. (2007), 'Conceptualizing boundaries between "life" and "work"', *International Journal of Human Resource Management*, **18**(3), 374–387.

Rapoport, R., and R. N. Rapoport (1965), 'Work and family in contemporary society', *American Sociological Review*, **30**(3), 381–394.

Rapoport, R., and R. N. Rapoport (1969), 'The dual-career family. A variant pattern and social change', *Human Relations*, **22**(1), 3–30.

Ravenswood, K., and C. Harris (2016), 'Doing gender, paying low: Gender, class and work–life balance in aged care', *Gender, Work & Organization*, **23**(6), 614–628.

Rhubart, D. (2020), 'Gender disparities in caretaking during the COVID-19 pandemic', *Population Health Research Brief Series*, accessed 18 January 2021 at https://lernercenter.syr.edu/2020/06/04/ ds-18/.

Risman, B., and G. Davis (2013), 'From sex roles to gender structure', *Current Sociology*, **61**(5/6), 733–755.

Robertson, C., and R. Gebeloff (2020), 'How millions of women became the most essential workers in America', *New York Times*, April 18.

Rubin, G. (1975), 'The traffic in women: Notes on the "political economy" of sex', in R. R. Reiter (ed.), *Toward an Anthropology of Women*, New York, NY: Monthly Review Press, pp. 157–210.

Ruderman, M. N., P. J. Ohlott, K. Panzer and S. N. King (2002), 'Benefits of multiple roles for manage-rial women', *Academy of Management Journal*, **45**(2), 369–386.

Ryan, A. M., and C. Q. Briggs (2020), 'Improving work-life policy and practice with an intersectionality lens', *Equality, Diversity and Inclusion*, **39**(5), 533–547.

Salazar Benítez, O. (2016), 'The fragility of gender equality policies in Spain', *Social Sciences*, **5**(2), 1–17.

Sang, K., and A. Powell (2013), 'Equality, diversity, inclusion and work–life balance in construction', in A. Dainty and M. Loosemore (eds), *Human Resource Management in Construction: Critical Perspectives*, New York, NY: Routledge, pp. 187–220.

Saraceno, C. (2018), 'Beyond the stereotype: The obstacle course of motherhood in Italy', in P. Morris and P. Willson (eds), *La Mamma*, New York, NY: Palgrave Macmillan, pp. 215–235.

Saraceno, C., D. Benassi and E. Morlicchio (2020), *Poverty in Italy: Features and Drivers in a European Perspective*, Bristol: Policy Press.

Saraceno, C., and W. Keck (2011), 'Towards an integrated approach for the analysis of gender equity in policies supporting paid work and care responsibilities', *Demographic Research*, **25**(11), 371–406.

Sawyer, K. B., C. Thoroughgood and J. Ladge (2017), 'Invisible families, invisible conflicts: Examining the added layer of work-family conflict with LGB families', *Journal of Vocational Behavior*, **103**(A), 23–39.

Schnurr, S., O. Zayts, A. Schroeder and C. Le Coyte-Hopkins (2020), '"It's not acceptable for the husband to stay at home": Taking a discourse analytical approach to capture the gendering of work', *Gender, Work & Organization*, **27**(3), 414–434.

Scott, J. W. (1986), 'Gender: A useful category of historical analysis', *American Historical Review*, **91**(5), 1053–1075.

Shockley, K. M., W. Shen and R. C. Johnson (eds) (2018), *The Cambridge Handbook of the Global Work–Family Interface*, Cambridge: Cambridge University Press.

Smithson, J., and E. H. Stokoe (2005), 'Discourses of work–life balance: negotiating "genderblind" terms in organizations', *Gender, Work and Organization*, **12**(2), 147–168.

Stavrou, E., and E. Solea (2021), 'In the eye of the beholder: Employee sexual orientation, perceived supervisory support for life beyond work and job satisfaction', *Human Resource Management Journal*, **31**(1), 225–241.

Stone, P. (2007), *Opting out? Why Women Really Quit Careers and Head Home*, Berkeley, CA: University of California Press.

Sümer, S. (2016), *European Gender Regimes and Policies: Comparative Perspectives*, London: Routledge.

Sungdoo, K., and E. Hollensbe (2018), 'When work comes home: Technology-related pressure and home support', *Human Resource Development International*, **21**(2), 91–106.

Teigen, M., and H. Skjeie (2017), 'The Nordic gender equality model', in O. Knutsen (ed.), *The Nordic Models in Political Science: Challenged, But Still Viable?* Bergen: Fagbokforlaget, pp. 125–147.

Toffoletti, K., and K Starr (2016), 'Women academics and work–life balance: Gendered discourses of work and care', *Gender, Work & Organization*, **23**(5), 489–504.

Tomlinson, J. (2007), 'Employment regulation, welfare and gender regimes: A comparative analysis of women's working-time patterns and work–life balance in the UK and the US', *International Journal of Human Resource Management*, **18**(3), 401–415.

Van Eck, D., L. Dobusch and M. Van den Brink (2020), 'The organizational inclusion turn and its exclusion of low-wage labor', *Organization*, **28**(2), accessed 18 January 2021 at https://doi.org/10.1177/1350508420966743.

Warren, T. (2014), 'Economic crisis, work–life balance and class', *Social Policy Review*, **26**, 11–28.

Warren, T. (2015), 'Work–life balance/imbalance: The dominance of the middle class and the neglect of the working class', *British Journal of Sociology*, **66**(4), 691–717.

Warren, T. (2016), 'Work-life balance and class: In search of working class work-lives', in D. Anderson, S. Lewis, C. Lyonette, N. Payne and S. Wood (eds), *Work-Life Balance in Times of Recession, Austerity and Beyond*, Abingdon: Routledge, pp. 112–130.

Warren, T. (2020), 'Work-life balance, time and money: Identifying the work-life balance priorities of working class workers', *Bulletin of Comparative Labour Relations*, accessed 18 January 2021 at http://eprints.nottingham.ac.uk/id/eprint/40675.

Wayne, J. H., M. M. Butts, W. J. Casper and T. D. Allen (2016), 'In search of balance: An empirical integration of multiple meanings of work-family balance', *Personnel Psychology*, **70**(1), 167–210.

Weaver McCloskey, D. (2016), 'Finding work-life balance in a digital age: An exploratory study of boundary flexibility and permeability', *Information Resources Management Journal*, **29**(3), 53–70.

Wharton, A. S. (2006), 'Understanding diversity of work in the 21st century and its impact on the work-family area of study', reprinted in M. Pitt-Catsouphes, E. E. Kossek and S. Sweet (eds)

(2015), *The Work and Family Handbook: Multi-Disciplinary Perspectives and Approaches*, Hove: Psychology Press, pp. 17–39.

Williams, C. L., C. Muller and K. Kilanski (2012), 'Gendered organizations in the new economy', *Gender & Society*, **26**(4), 549–573.

3.   Doing research on work–life balance
Sonia Bertolini and Rosy Musumeci[1]

1.   INTRODUCTION

Having seen (in Chapter 2) chronological reconstruction of the genesis and subsequent development of the work–life balance (WLB) conceptual construct (and research), its premises and its limits, in this chapter we aim to describe and discuss the main peculiarities of undertaking research on WLB. This has presented some trends and shifts over time, and more recently it has been challenged – as we will try to show at the end of this chapter – by the global COVID-19 pandemic.

Methodological reviews which explore designs, data sources and analytic techniques addressing work–life and work–family balance are rare (among these: Casper et al. 2007, Chang et al. 2010, Greenhaus and Parasuraman 1999). In this chapter, we do not aspire to review all the existent studies, which – as also observed in the previous chapter – would be a huge feat; rather, we will try to identify some of the main recurrences, criticalities and potentialities in approaches to research on WLB, relying on the chapters included in this edited volume as well as on the wider literature, with particular regard to the most recent developments (over the last 10 to 15 years or so).

More precisely, we reflect on the methodological implications of WLB conceptual constructs and theoretical approaches described in Chapter 1. Empirical methods and research designs are indeed closely intertwined with analytical goals. Methodological choices depend on the research questions and conceptual constructs, and vice versa.

In the paragraphs that follow, we firstly illustrate the main research designs and empirical methods used in WLB research and the samples involved; we then present the main innovations arising from studies and reflections presented in the chapters of this edited volume and from wider literature on WLB; finally, we reflect on the consequences and challenges that the COVID-19 pandemic may present in terms of doing research on WLB and approaches to fieldwork. The contexts and literature we consider are mainly from Europe and, in minor measure, the United States.

2.   RESEARCH DESIGNS, METHODOLOGICAL CHOICES AND SAMPLES

In this section, we describe and discuss how social scientists investigate the area of WLB, in relation to empirical methods, the main research questions addressed and the samples involved. Empirical methods and analytical goals are closely intertwined. Methodological choices depend on the theoretical approaches adopted and conceptual constructs (illustrated in Chapter 1), and vice versa, even if – as Powell et al. (2019) have recently observed – work–life theory has not always kept up with the explosion in research.

Some clarification is needed when talking about *how* WLB scholars conduct and design research on WLB, the empirical methods adopted and the samples involved. As stated by Ollier-Malaterre et al. (2013), national contexts shape the production of knowledge (what is produced and how) by scholars who are themselves embedded in a given culture and socio-institutional system, and whose samples are embedded in national contexts too. In particular, the authors note that the way scholars design research and interpret findings may be influenced by their own cultural frames of reference and work–life experience. Here, we do not aspire to account for the country specificities involved when engaging in work–life and/or work–family research (the greater part of which is located in Europe and the United States), but we reflect on general trends.

According to Lewis et al. (2007), the huge recent growth in attention to WLB might give the impression that this is a new area of interest. However, as was shown in Chapter 1, dilemmas relating to the management of paid work alongside other life domains, especially family, have been the object of research for several – at least five – decades (see, for example, Rapoport and Rapoport 1965, Powell et al. 2019). Here, we look mainly at developments that have occurred in more recent decades.

Many studies use quantitative and qualitative methods. Quantitative methods involve objective measurements and statistical analysis of data collected through polls, questionnaires and surveys, or by manipulating pre-existing statistical data using computational techniques; qualitative methods aim to understand how people interpret their experiences, and the kinds of meanings they attribute to these, often by analysing interviews or focus groups conducted with individuals and groups.

According to Heikkinen et al. (Chapter 10 in this volume), research employing quantitative methodologies significantly outweighs qualitative approaches (Beigi and Shirmohammadi 2017, Casper et al. 2007). The levels of analysis are different, but they all contribute to answering the question of whether WLB is freely determined by individuals or whether it is constrained by a wide range of factors operating at a micro (individual), meso (organizational) or macro level. In this last case, the focus of analysis is on exploration of the impact of national institutional contexts, rules, regulations and formal policies on men's and women's ability to effect a choice in shaping their careers and their day-to-day commitments (Gregory and Milner 2009), as well as the cultural logics that influence people's imagined options and choices throughout their life cycle (Hallgren and Risman, Chapter 4 in this volume).

As stated by Stavrou and Anastassiadou (Chapter 14 in this volume), research on WLB has predominantly been approached from a micro, individual employee perspective; therefore, a micro-individualistic focus which analyses individual decision-making is the most explored level among the three. Nevertheless, as the authors have outlined, recently research on WLB has expanded to meso and even macro levels of analysis (Ilies et al. 2007, Kopelman et al. 2006, McCarthy et al. 2013, O'Neill et al. 2009).

Adoption of a qualitative approach can be based on a plurality of tools, more often than not on (different types of) discursive interviews (for an in-depth one, see, for example, Gerson and Damaske 2020) but also thematic analysis of media contents. Contributions based on ethnographic techniques are almost non-existent; among these is the study by Bichard et al. (2014) exploring the values held by individuals in their performance of everyday or 'quotidian' rituals in family life, focusing on mobile workers who may be away from home and family for extended and/or regular periods of time. As observed by the authors, during the course of the research a key hurdle emerged, revolving around gaining access to families for the purposes of conducting traditional ethnographic studies, since, for many mobile workers who are separated from their family on a regular basis, the idea of having an ethnographic researcher present during what becomes very limited family time has proved difficult to negotiate. Therefore, the researchers have had to develop design interventions that enable ethnographic data to be obtained effectively when both the researcher and the researched are away from the field site, namely the family home. Another ethnographic study of WLB is that by Bourne and Forman (2014), which – drawing on Weber's ideal types of social action – questions whether, for women business owners, the flexibility of their occupation is truly an advantage to balancing work and other aspects of life. Some autoethnographic studies have also been carried out. Among these is, for example, the contribution of Cohen et al. (2009), which was based on data generated in autoethnographic conversations between the three authors; in their article, they critique the prevailing metaphor of WLB and offer – they affirm – a conceptualization of the relationship between work and non-work aspects of life that is more dynamic and less reductionist, and in which emotions, as well as issues of autonomy, control and identity, are integral features.

Innovative methods seem to be a rarity and an exception; for example, visual and digital methods included in so-called netnography – that is, ethnography applied to the internet (for an example of application of this method to WLB, see, for example, Gatrell's Chapter 16 in this volume, exploring WLB among pregnant and breastfeeding employees). Furthermore, mixed methods – which combine qualitative and quantitative data – are not frequent, although they are increasing.

If we look at the samples used in studies, much of the existent work–life research has been conducted on restricted populations with little diversity (Powell et al. 2019). Following Casper et al. (2007), most of what researchers know about (work–life) issues is based on the experiences of heterosexual, Caucasian, managerial and professional employees whose lives involve traditional family arrangements. Moreover, little consideration has been given to care-receivers as compared to caregivers (Moss and Deven 2015).

In particular, the focus on work–*family* conflict (Kahn et al. 1964, Lewis and Cooper 1999) (before) and (after) balance – shown in Chapter 1 – has had consequences in terms of socio-demographic characteristics (when these are reported[2]), starting from the age variable – with much research focusing on WLB for employed youngsters or young adults caring for small children – and being approached from a short-term (or medium-term) perspective (Ganault and Pailhé, Chapter 5 in this volume).

Following the shift from the conceptual construct of work–family to that of work–life (Gatrell et al. 2013, Lewis et al. 2007; see Chapter 1 for more information on this), studies have considered life in a broader and more inclusive sense, rather than seeing 'family' as exclusively parents caring for children, including, as examples, new forms of family, child-lessness, friendship and leisure, and so on. But despite this turn, studies which conceptualize their research designs as work–life are relatively small compared to those which use the narrower 'work–family' term. Considering publications referring to the period from 1987 to 2006, only 9 per cent of quantitative studies and 26 per cent of qualitative studies specifically examined work–life issues (Chang et al. 2010).

In Chapter 6 in this volume, Barrett et al. observe that very few studies analyse WLB in middle and later life, leaving – they say – many questions unanswered about WLB in these phases of the life course and during retirement. They show the benefits for theory that expanding the temporal scope of WLB research could have: clarifying the concept of unpaid work and facilitating research into its shifting interface with paid work across the life course, and drawing attention to leisure as a central but underexamined component of life and also to individuals' changing investment in it as they age. In terms of empirical research, the authors make the case for more WLB research that takes into account the long-term consequences of WLB in early adulthood, and shifting meanings of care work as individuals age, through various care-provider, and perhaps care-recipient, roles. Among the few studies which analyse WLB in middle and later life is, for example, that of Emslie and Hunt (2009), based on semi-structured interviews with men and women in Scotland aged between 50 and 52, which aimed to compare participants' experiences of WLB.

Moreover, as noted by Smeby and Forseth (Chapter 11 in this volume), research on work–family and work–life balance has mainly used surveys or interviews and has focused on working mothers with children and/or middle-class, dual-career parents (Gatrell et al. 2013, Seierstad and Kirton 2015), and these sampling choices have led to inequity within the research, marginalizing other groups such as working fathers and/or parents with low social capital (Gatrell et al. 2013).

In particular, regarding the gender and marital status variable, as a consequence of the prevailing theoretical perspectives in WLB study discussed in the previous chapter, much of the qualitative and quantitative social studies continues to focus on women/mothers (white, middle-class, married and with professional careers,[3] as outlined by Heikkinen et al. in this volume) – contributing to reproducing the idea that care is a female issue. However, recently a more male-gendered perspective on work and family-life balance (Holter 2007) has spread, and research on fatherhood and men-only samples has increased, facilitating a better grasp of persistence and changes in cultural and social models, ideals and fatherhood practices. Much of this has been from a one-country or one-context perspective, and few cases have adopted a comparative perspective such as that of Halrynjo (2009), who presented an analysis of men's experience of WLB and the strategies they develop, drawing on a sample of structured interviews with 102 men from six countries (Austria, Bulgaria, Germany, Israel, Norway and Spain), working in either technical and financial organizations or social and health-related organizations.

As with wider WLB studies (Lewis et al. 2007), research on this topic reflects social, economic and workplace developments and concerns, shifting in response to new trends. Although the traditional family model with a male breadwinner is less widespread today than in the past, due to the growth of women's participation in the labour market, it continues to be the predominant 'ideal' model, so to speak (Blossfeld et al. 2005, Holter 2007), and even more egalitarian couples seem to resist a more equitable ideal involving fathers and mothers doing exactly the same things in the same way (Saraceno 2018), especially in certain countries. Moreover, in a workplace environment, the norm continues to be full-time, continuously employed (male) workers (Moss and Deven 2015). Work organizations' claims on male workers' presence and commitment are intensified by the demands of a globalized marketplace (Kvande 2009). Gender differences persist, for example, with regard to men's uptake of parental leave, which, although rising, is still low (OECD 2016) and shorter in duration, compared to women's uptake (Castro-García and Pazos-Moran 2016, Magaraggia 2015). State and work organizations can be enabling or disenabling forces for paternal childrearing and parental leave-taking. This can also emerge when using a qualitative approach grounded on a micro-individual level. This is the case with Smeby and Forseth's narrative analysis (in this volume) of the impact of earmarked parental leave for fathers' WLB in work organizations. They explored child-caring and individual agency in a sample of fathers in Norway; these fathers were 'pioneers' in a tra-ditionally feminine arena, since, for the first time, the Norwegian state was providing men with the opportunity to take 10 weeks' earmarked paternal leave. The authors' narrative approach has highlighted how individual experiences, at the micro level, relate to structures and cultures on the meso and macro levels. Despite the state-implemented policy of fathers' quotas at the macro level, work organizations at the meso level may influence fathers' individual experience of managing to balance work obligations and family responsibilities during their paternal leave period. Other qualitative approaches used in this volume can help to better investigate – in a non-traditional way – the different layers and meanings from macro, meso and micro per-spectives; and the intersections between work and family as a complex bundle of, and standing in relation to, societal policies, work–life conditions, organizational norms and fatherhood. This is the case with the chapter by Heikkinen et al. The authors combine discursive analysis of how media (business magazines and the most widely read daily newspaper) discourses on fatherhood have developed during the last two and a half decades in Finland, with a study of the emotions and feelings talk of employees who are fathers, with respect to WLB.

Together with the persistence of gender differences, research has shown that there are some visible changes among younger generations in terms of gender roles, attitudes and behaviours that are more egalitarian than those of their parents' generation (Cichy et al. 2007). One of the main indicators of these changes is the way that men perceive and practise fatherhood (particularly with regard to small children), which, in turn, reflects changes in men's ideals and practices of maleness. Caring practices (Doucet 2006, Featherstone 2009, Miller 2010, Ranson 2015) and 'intimate' emotional bonds (Dermott 2008) have been increasingly acknowledged at social and cultural levels as crucial components of 'good fatherhood', with the father's presence being seen as important for children's well-being and proper socialization. More and more contemporary fathers express the need to be – and actually are – more involved in child-care than their forefathers were (Bosoni 2011, Musumeci and Santero 2018, Sabbadini and Cappadozzi 2011). In many cases, studies are based on samples of fathers in a single country or on case studies in limited geographical areas; and cross-country research on these new fathers, especially involving non-Western countries, is still limited (Crespi and Ruspini 2016, Pattnaik 2013), with the exception of Europe and North America (Eydal and Rostgaard 2015, Hobson 2002, Hobson and Fahlén 2009). Moreover, much research on fathers looks to focus narrowly on just one aspect of the relationship between care, employment and gender, such as fathers and leave, which runs the risk of not seeing and understanding under-representation of men in all forms of caring (Moss and Deven 2015).

To sum up, WLB research was initially concentrated on samples of mothers. Studies then also began to involve fathers, and recent research has included parental couples (in particular, on WLB in the transition to parenthood, see Grunow and Evertsson (2016, 2019) for a com-parative perspective; and Naldini's Chapter 9 in this volume).

One of the social categories studied less extensively is that of single adult workers without dependent children. Quoting the title of a qualitative study by Casper et al. (2016), their family lives, personal demands and how they manage work and non-work are 'hidden'. According to the authors' study (based on both a literature review and interviews), singles without dependent children have a variety of family, relationship and personal demands, which often compete with work, leading to inter-role conflict. Moreover, most interview participants indicated that their role as a family member was highly valued and of greater importance than their work role. Taken together, the findings refute the view of many work–family researchers that singles without dependent children 'have no family', and they argue for their inclusion in studies of the work–family interface.

In terms of the occupational groups and social classes included in WLB research samples, studies interviewing or focusing on lower-wage workers and poor households are in a minority (Tracey 2015). Among these, see, for example, Täht et al.'s Chapter 13 in this volume on work–family reconciliation among disadvantaged households in Estonia. Only 7.5 per cent of publications used samples from manual occupational groups exclusively or lower-skilled service/clerical workers (Chang et al. 2010). Among these, for example, is the study by Warren et al. (2009) on low-waged women's (and men's) choices in England in relation to their caring and employed lives. This was a mixed-methods study combining a quantitative analysis of the British Household Panel Survey and interviews with a sample of 35 male–female couples, in order to investigate their childcare strategies. The results showed that men's long working hours create a strain on family life as well as on women's ability to access better paid employment. Rather than greater provision of formal childcare, the authors identified a strong demand for a reduction in working hours and for parental leave policies in order to give both men and women a better balance between work and family, particularly for low-waged couples.

An occupational group that has become of increasing interest in recent decades in terms of WLB research on labour market transformations is that of people working in flexible and temporary forms of employment.

A peculiarity of WLB research and of the explanations for it (as pointed out by Nieuwenhuis and Kossek 2017) is that of it being work-focused rather than family-focused. Family diversity is increasing, with dual-earner families becoming more common, as well as singles and single-parent families. Each of these family forms has its own unique work–family needs and way of using the time available. National policies, organizations and managers clearly play a crucial role in shaping trends in WLB, but family trends may also affect WLB independently of what happens in the workplace, and (as the authors note) these deserve to be given significant attention in future work on WLB.

According to Warren (2017), moreover, the academic debate around WLB is too heavily time-dominant and time-based. The centrality of time within conceptualization of WLB has led to a focus on the needs and work lives of the middle classes and to neglect of the priorities and concerns of working-class workers; it has also determined the ways in which balance/imbalance is measured and how it shapes policy discourse and development. The author – while recognizing that having enough time is at the core of a balanced work life – underlines that it is not the only ingredient, and nor is it one that dominates the narratives of the working classes, for whom financial hardship is a serious threat to work–life balancing.

3.   NEW RESEARCH QUESTIONS AND INNOVATIVE METHODS IN THE WORK–LIFE FIELD

As stated earlier, empirical methods depend on the research questions, and new research questions aimed at exploring emerging social issues and problems can necessitate new research methods and empirical approaches or innovation of existing ones.

Research on WLB comes from a rich interdisciplinary tradition (Shockley and Shen 2016), and the list of disciplines that engage in such study is highly varied, including sociology, economics, psychology, family studies, political science, demography and women's studies.

Despite this, research on WLB has only recently started to adopt a multidisciplinary approach (Pitt-Catsouphes et al. 2006) and embrace several theoretical perspectives and methodologies. Nowadays (and more so than in the past), studies utilize a combination of different and multiple perspectives, research designs, methods (for example, so-called mixed methods), types of indicators and tools. Behind what we might define the 'multidisciplinary and multi-method trend' – or 'methodological pluralism' (to use the expression coined by Stavrou and Anastassiadou in this volume) – in WLB research lie challenges and concerns linked to the increasing complexity of the phenomenology of work–life intertwining. Moreover, behind it there is a greater awareness that extensive and comprehensive understanding (and generation of such phenomenology) requires an approach just as complex and complete, holistic (although not idiosyncratic) and able to take into account and manage the variety of cultural, structural and institutional factors operating at different levels: micro (individual), meso (organizational) and macro (values, policy and legislation). As stated in Gerson and Migliavacca's Chapter 12 in this volume (with particular reference to work–family studies), 'A main characteristic of work and family studies is the linked nature of their topics and the complexity this produces in their research foci.'

The lens of cross-country comparison has also increased recently. According to Annor's (2016) review of cross-national studies of work–family conflict (focusing on the influences of cultural, institutional and economic factors), although combining work and family responsibilities has become an increasingly challenging task for employees in virtually every nation, a large part of the studies on work–family conflict have focused predominantly on Western and developed nations. According to Powell et al. (2019), little attention has been paid to experiences of the work–life interface across several regions of the world, such as the Middle East, Africa and South Asia, with very little representation in work–life research (Allen et al. 2015). Thus, it is important to keep in mind that the generalizability of work–life research across the globe remains uncertain. Recent cross-national research on WLB is narrow in scope, with most studies mainly focusing on identifying differences in prevalence of the phenomenon across national contexts. Ollier-Malaterre and Foucreault's (2016) review of comparative research on individuals' work–life experiences shows that more of this research has focused on cultural factors impacting on experiences at country level (for example, individualism/collectivism and gender egalitarianism) than on institutional factors (for example, public policy and provisions, and family structures) or economic ones (for example, stage of development and unemployment rates); moreover, it shows that it is only work–life conflict that has been truly investigated empirically (and not work–life enrichment, WLB or boundary management).

With the shift from work–family to work–life balance (described in Chapter 1), work–life research has expanded in scope and coverage over time, considering life in a broader and more inclusive sense (including, as examples, friendship and leisure), rather than regarding family as exclusively revolving around childcare. This has occurred, in part, as a result of the increased diversity of workplaces, families and lifestyles (for example, the increase in singlehood and childlessness), and partly as a consequence of methodological innovations and growth of communities of researchers focused on the work–life nexus (Bianchi and Milkie 2010). Therefore, new research questions, other social categories (in addition to those traditionally considered by researchers) and 'new' topics have emerged as areas of study. Some of these are related to the following: gender, sexual orientation, new family forms (for example, same-sex families), generations, WLB in middle and later life, singlehood, childlessness, ethnicity, migration, multicultural and intercultural issues, diversity and intersectionality, maternal employment and child outcomes, family policies in organizations, (dis)ability (LaWanda and Shinew 2014, Lindemann 2017), changes in labour markets and in modes of working (Las Heras et al. 2017) (for example, in relation to greater labour market deregulation and the related diffusion of atypical employment contracts, and also in relation to technology and the changes it generates in people's integration of work and family life today), and the 2008–2009 financial and economic crisis (Ammons and Kelly 2015, Lewis et al. 2017). However, these kinds of research remain marginal. Much remains to be done, and as noted by Wharton (2012), more research is needed to address the work–life challenges of the 21st century.

Below, we reflect on some of these recent WLB research developments, focusing on research and methods proposed or described in the chapters of this volume as well as in the wider literature.

3.1   Quantitative Studies

With this type of study in particular, one of the problems is availability of data and the type of data available for studying WLB, which can condition the research question and choice of samples.

In fact, another element missing from research concerning WLB is the fact that samples are often mainly composed of dependent workers with typical contracts, working full-time and in permanent positions. This implies that there is a lack of studies regarding reconciliation issues among atypical workers. A contract can be atypical in terms of its temporal dimension, because it is fixed-term; or it may be atypical in terms of the number of daily working hours, a part-time contract that includes flexible time as collaborations, or self-employment. In both these cases, there are problems of reconciliation issues which are different from those of dependent workers. In the first case, because workers cannot bank on renewal of their contract, planning such a reconciliation issue could be very hard. These workers are often in countries with a segmented labour market and do not have access to the same social protection (that is, maternity provisions) that typical workers do. In the second case, because public services such as early childhood services have standard opening hours (as in Fordist society; that is, 9 to 5), these contracts include flexible working.

Workers in professions that include shifts in their work (for example, nurses) face the same problems. It is often the case that women take on more unpaid work,[4] with atypical work contracts. In the case of temporary jobs, for example, in the European Union (27 countries) in 2019, on average this was more evident for female young adults: among 25- to 34-year-olds, the percentage of temporary employees (out of the total number of employees) was 2.7 percentage points higher than that for men in the same age group (21.2 vs 18.5 per cent; among 15- to 64-year-olds, the gender gap was only +1 p.p.). In Latvia, the gender gap was +11.5 p.p., compared to countries where the share of women among temporary employees is lower, for example, as in Germany (-0.4 p.p.) (source: authors' calculation based on Eurostat database).

Among the few studies on atypical/flexible work arrangements, the study by Russell et al. (2009) examines the impact of three main types of flexible work arrangements on employees' perception of work–life stress and their ability to carry out their caring responsibilities, based on an analysis of the first national survey of employees in Ireland. Their basic hypothesis is that flexible work arrangements (flexitime or flexible working hours, part-time work and working from home) will reduce work–life conflict because they give employees greater choice. The authors observe that uptake of flexibility is gendered and that women are considerably more likely than men to work part-time or to experience other forms of flexibility that reduce their earnings, and men are more likely than women to work from home. In line with this approach, Stavrou and Anastassiadou present (in this volume) a review of studies and combined methodologies (methodological pluralism) for studying flexible work arrangements and employee diversity across different contexts, combining micro, meso and macro levels.

An often-neglected occupational group in work–family research, in terms of the effect on dependent workers, is that of self-employed workers, while greater attention has been devoted to employees and less to the autonomous (among the quantitative and qualitative interview studies focusing on self-employed workers, see Annink et al. 2016, and Hilbrecht and Lero 2014).

Today, it is particularly important to focus on this category because of the recent growth in self-employed workers (especially those without employees) and diffusion of hybrid job positions that challenge the boundaries between dependent and independent employment. In this volume, an interesting piece of quantitative research on self-employment is that in Chapter 8 by Bozzon and Murgia. In their study, the authors use the European Working Conditions Survey (6th edition; Eurofound 2017) to develop an empirical exercise aimed at analysing how subjective work-to-family conflict and family-to-work conflict vary across different types of self-employment, dependent employment and informal work. Their results show that

> Despite having the highest availability of autonomy and control over their job conditions, the self-employed with employees and the genuine SSE [solo self-employed workers] share such overwhelming job demands (job pressures, responsibilities and commitment over their business) that they end up increasing the perception of work–family conflict. Only dependent SSE, with job-related demands closer to those of employees, perceive a lower conflict, reaching levels of subjective work-to-family conflict similar to those of employees.

Looking at an innovative contribution regarding sample composition, the work by Las Heras et al. (2017) is interesting because of their focus on managers in different areas of the world (Africa, the Middle East, Asia, Europe and North America). The methodology is mainly quantitative, through surveys of firms, but other contributions are based on qualitative methods, using interviews with managers. The authors also focus on the impact of technology on WLB, introducing a theme very central today: information technology carried the promise of autonomy and control over when and where to perform work (Mazmanian et al. 2013) by allowing asynchronous communications (Barber and Santuzzi 2015) and by enabling people to work from various times and in various locations, thus offering flexibility and control over work (Valcour and Hunter 2005). This ease of access to communicate in an asynchronous way has led to a blurring of work and non-work boundaries. They stress that on the one hand this could facilitate a work–family balance by increasing employees' control over their work periods and enabling them to balance work and family pressures creatively (Murray and Rostis 2007). But on the other hand, it can lead to overloading of the boundary between time for work and time for a private life.

Finally, we would like to underline two quantitative studies which particularly illustrate the fact that less attention has been paid to this population; that is, women employed in low-wage jobs in the United Kingdom, and middle-aged employees in Norway. Warren et al. (2009), in fact, analyse the ways in which the gendered nature of employment shapes the choices of low-waged women in England in relation to their caring and employed lives, using data from the British Household Panel Survey. Low-waged women represent a sizeable proportion of the female workforce, and their employment is characterized by low hourly wages and a high preponderance of part-time work. Familiar WLB measures, such as flexitime or job-sharing, are not available to them. Since their partners are often also in low-wage employment or not employed, these women also have limited access to private childcare.

The work of Gautun and Hagen (2010) studied how common it is for middle-aged employees to experience a balance between work and caring for their parents, and to what extent this affects their behaviour in working life. They analysed data from a representative survey conducted in Norway in 2007. One finding was that seven out of 10 respondents (with one or both parents still living) were both employed and caring for elderly parents. Fifty-seven per cent had experienced difficult situations in coping with both. The most preferable arrangement was flexible working hours, and it was found that employees prefer the possibility of reducing or staggering working hours, or the option of working from home if necessary.

3.2   Qualitative: Longitudinal, Narrative and Visual Studies

According to Ganault and Pailhé in this volume, most of the literature on reconciling professional and private life has been cross-sectional. WLB is generally studied at a specific point in people's lives, and studies also mainly focus on single events; for instance, the effect of parenthood or marriage on work and family trade-offs. Moreover, fewer have investigated work–life conflict through a life-course approach (Moen and Sweet 2004).

An innovative method that seems to address this issue and fill this gap (and which has recently been used in WLB research) is that of qualitative longitudinal studies. Qualitative longitudinal analysis facilitates observation of variations in expectations and behaviour in different phases of the life course. The advantage of this methodological approach is acknowledgement of the fact that individuals are dynamic and interactive, having preferences that can vary over time with regard to structural, institutional and economic constraints, but also in relation to different phases of the course of life and to the interaction between life partners (Bertolini and Musumeci 2018). This approach calls into question economic and sociological theories of the labour market which assume that individuals' preferences are stable, as in the following: human capital theory (Becker 1964), which assumes, for example, that educational levels structure individual preferences in an almost deterministic way; Hakim's preferences theory (2000), according to which women's preferences for differing combinations of family work and paid employment are the primary determinant of employment decisions; or sociological theories emphasizing the effect of one's education in terms of emancipation (Reyneri 2011).

All these prospects do not explain variations in preferences over individuals' life course, but they presume a static actor in time who, having obtained a degree, does not change anymore.

Instead, these preferences are not immutable, and they also tend to be redefined in relation to the institutional context, cultural reference models and socioeconomic constraints.

When we study WLB, it is very important to take into account this perspective as it is, in fact, a typical topic; that is, where men and women redefine their preferences to take into account different periods and transitions in their lives. The decisions to be made are more interconnected and more complex, and people's roles are less predetermined, with couples seeing the necessity of reconciling family needs with those of both partners in the relationship.

Studies using this approach are innovative, but they need specific methodological tools such as interview narratives or qualitative longitudinal studies. Finally, variations in preferences are influenced by the interaction between people – in particular, friends and family members – but the transition to being in a couple is also affected by interaction with partners. Studies that interview both partners in a couple can partly reconstruct such interactions in terms of influence and conflict.

Some studies, through narrative interviews, show that preferences for allocation of time to paid and unpaid work can vary over the life course. Young women tend to invest more when they first enter the labour market (Bertolini 2006).

Other studies have explored this theme. For example, McRae's work (2003) provides an empirical examination of women's work histories following the birth of their first child, their attitude to their role, and the relationship between attitudes and work history; and in the light of these analyses, the aptness of Hakim's Preference Theory (Hakim 2000) as an explanation for the position of women in the British labour market is considered. The analysis of longitudinal data fails to support the Preference Theory's central argument that women in Britain and North America (countries where women live 'in the new scenario') have genuine, unconstrained choice in terms of how they wish to live their lives. Instead, it is argued that a complete explanation of women's labour market choices after childbirth (and the outcomes of these choices) depends as much on understanding the constraints that differentially affect women as it does on understanding their personal preferences.

Cano-Lòpez (2014) also tested Hakim's theory by analysing variance among women's opinions, attitudes, and preferences towards work and family throughout their lives, and affirms that '[T]here aren't three types of women but in fact all women are simultaneously ambivalent towards work and the family. Preferences aren't static; they are adjusted according to two factors: one is micro (maternity, death of a family member etc.) and the other macro (economic recession, reduction in salaries etc.).' Cano-Lòpez also argues that '[A]nalysis of the 23 biographies of women has shown a multitude of nuances that operate precisely against the affirmations of Hakim.'

In line with this approach, the work coordinated by Grunow and Evertsson (2016, 2019) is interesting (Bertolini and Musumeci 2018, Naldini 2016) because they observe how expectations and preferences in different spheres vary in couples during the transition to parenthood. In particular, in nine European countries, dual-earner couples had been interviewed separately (both males and females) before and after the birth of their first baby, using the same trace of interview. This allowed comparison of how the individuals had changed before and after the baby's birth, and also changes within the couple; for example, comparing the father and the mother. In particular, this methodology facilitated exploration of different ways in which dual-earner couples in contemporary welfare states plan for, realize and justify how they share work and childcare during the transition to parenthood. The results are comparative and underlined couples' beliefs and negotiations in the wider context of national institutional structures.

One important result relates to the shift in preferences before and after birth of a baby, and how meso-level friends and family, and macro levels (for example, the institutional context), shape the preferences of similar couples in different countries.

In this volume, the chapter by Naldini uses this type of approach. In-depth interviews with mothers and fathers before and after arrival of their first child enabled us to make effective use of an approach based on continuous comparison of men and women over time, in an effort to interpret similarities and differences between the two genders in terms of desires, values, choices, relationships, feelings, practices and experiences.

The life-course perspective and, in particular, one of the key principles in the analysis of transitions (that of 'linked lives') (Elder 1995, Elder et al. 2003) proved useful in longitudinal analysis of the interviews. This was especially useful in couples' narratives, where it was possible to see that the WLB strategies adopted in daily life are enacted at the level of the couple and the family. In other words, the notion of 'linked lives' sheds light on the interconnections between the father's and the mother's work and childcare careers, and the two partners' different trajectories, and seeing how they relate to the biographies of their own parents (that is, the latter's role as grandparents).

Using the same life-course approach, Emslie and Hunt (2009) conducted semi-structured interviews with men and women in mid-life (aged 50 to 52 years) in order to compare their experiences of WLB. Their qualitative, small-scale research was based on a small, representative subsample of a larger longitudinal database, and they used an approach that sought to integrate gender more fully into such interpretations, in particular Sue Campbell Clark's 'work–family border' theory, which aims to explain how people 'manage and negotiate the work and family spheres and the borders between them in order to attain balance' (Clark 2000, p. 750). Their results revealed how work–life strains were experienced by interviewees over the life course in a gendered way, with women using images of 'juggling' to describe their coping strategies, and middle-class women in particular expressing their sense of sacrifice. The male interviewees, on the other hand, were found to accept work–life conflict as natural. Women discussed their current problems of juggling a variety of roles (despite having no young children at home), while men confined their discussion of such conflicts to the past, when their children were young. However, diversity among men (some of whom 'worked to live', while others 'lived to work') and women (some of whom constructed themselves in relation to their families, while others positioned themselves as 'independent women') was apparent, as were some commonalities between men and women (with both men and women constructing themselves as 'pragmatic workers'). Emslie and Hunt's article, like that of Warren et al. (2009), also highlights the impact of social class position on work–life choices. The manual workers in their sample tended to display pragmatic attitudes towards paid employment and had a stronger sense than middle-class women of boundaries between work and home life. Thus, work–life boundaries are not only gendered but are also mediated by people's socioeconomic position, and in addition, as Emslie and Hunt show, they may shift over the life course as gender identities are reconfigured.

In our volume, we want to underline the presence of a chapter which studies pregnancy using an innovative methodology – netnography – in a non-participative form: distant netnography; that is, observing interactions within internet space through open-access sites, but not personally joining these communities. Accordingly, distant ethnography is a qualitative method for exploring WLB among pregnant and breastfeeding employees. This particular methodology has some ethical problems, as with the majority of methodologies that use the internet, given that researchers can observe participants without them being aware of this, and at the same time, researchers can access a large quantity of data.

3.3 Mixed Methods

Up to the mid-1980s, qualitative and quantitative approaches were strongly polarized (Freshwater 2007). They were seen as deriving from different theoretical underpinnings with very different methods and quite separate orientations: one approach directed towards objectivity and the other towards subjectivity (Letherby et al. 2013).

The outcome of this was that people argued fiercely for the superior capacities of one camp or the other, and combinations were almost never to be seen. Ten years later, Tashakkori and Teddlie (2003) asserted that '[M]ixed method is the combination of qualitative and quantitative approaches in the methodology of a study […] [M]ixed-methods research has evolved to the point where it is a separate methodological orientation with its own worldview, vocabulary and techniques' (p. x). In fact, social life and lived realities are multidimensional, and our understandings will be impoverished and may be inadequate if we view these phenomena only along a single dimension (Mason 2011). This idea is particularly important when we study WLB (a complex field) between work and family life and leisure time, and it is constructed in the interaction with institutions and with family members, especially with partners.

According to Small (2011), it is possible to mix different types of data in two ways using the confirmation or the complementary approach. In the first case, the researcher collects different kinds of data to measure the same phenomenon. In this case, the finality is to ensure that the findings do not depend primarily on a particular kind of data collection. The promise of confirmatory designs is clearest when alternative types of data produce conflicting results. The second case (the complementary model; Small 2011) implies using different types of data that generate different kinds of knowledge, in order to investigate the same research question. Quantitative data describe the behaviour of people, and qualitative data intercept people's expectations, norms and values, allowing researchers to reconstruct the strategies and mechanisms behind behaviours.

The study by Guillaume and Pochic (2019), combining quantitative and qualitative data (60 interviews with career managers, top managers and high-potential talent, both men and women), was conducted in a major French utility company and focused on the subject of diversity; specifically, on the issue of women's access to top management positions. The richness of the data used allowed the authors to firstly identify the difficulties that women may encounter in the course of their occupational career, linked to organizational aspects, including 'glass ceiling' processes, and social and cultural representations attached to leadership. The other perspective of this research focused on the different strategies that women and men build to either conform to organizational norms or bypass them. Guillaume and Pochic showed that policies are inadequate for tackling both highly formal recruitment and promotion procedures (based on educational attainment through competition) and informal processes that favour 'unencumbered' workers, or those with the kinds of relational resources that make it possible for their spouse to follow them.

Organizational practices are based on an underlying set of traditional gender values regarding households' division of labour, which assumes that managers are male. Women apply different strategies to address this situation, according to the authors. Some single women, and women in dual-career households, decide to pursue a typical male career pattern. They do not relinquish their careers because they earn enough to employ domestic carers, and they live in a country where public childcare provision is also relatively plentiful. Others choose an alternative career model, resisting forced mobility at the risk of an implicit 'withdrawal from the competition for power', or constructing joint mobility strategies with their spouse (Guillaume and Pochic 2009). Drew and Murtagh (2005) examined experience of, and attitudes towards, WLB among female and male senior managers in a major Irish organization, using both quantitative and qualitative data. All female managers and a sample of male managers were surveyed using a combination of interviews and focus groups. WLB emerged as a major issue impeding the career progression of female managers.

In this book, most chapters use a mixed-methods approach. In particular, Täht et al. analyse the effect of childcare facilities on labour market participation among young adults in Estonia. This country constitutes an interesting case, with a high rate of labour market participation among women, including women with (young) children. Despite high labour market attachment among men and women, the employment careers of women are marked by rather long career breaks for childcare purposes (one and a half to three years per child). Respectively, the main burden and challenge of returning to the labour market after a (long) career break falls disproportionally on women. Quantitative data from the Estonian Time Use Survey (2009) facilitate detailed study of allocation of time among household members, including participation in paid work and time spent on care. The survey provides data on both use of externally sourced childcare (for example, public childcare and grandparents) and internally sourced support (for example, grandparents living in the household). These data are complemented by selected interviews featuring two synopses from Estonia, to illustrate how use of formal and informal childcare may affect young parents' labour market participation.

In Chapter 17 in this volume, De Coster and Zanoni use visual methodologies as a way to capture complex 'work lives'. In this case, the authors show how different kinds of data can emerge using different methodologies studying the same research questions. Visual methods, as a research approach, offer an anti-narrative space, where more 'entangled subjectivity' can be performed in interview settings. In other words, the authors argue that '[T]he use of visuals creates affordances for participants to "queer the frame of legibility" [thereby] allowing them to emerge beyond their narrative inscription in the binary.'

Visuals allow participants to constitute themselves before their narrative inscription in the binary framework. The authors show that the trade-off between visual and narrative performances additionally reveals how the 'conflict experienced' by participants is not a consequence of a symbolic struggle against gendered norms about the division of work and private life.

4.   THE CHALLENGE OF THE COVID-19 PANDEMIC: FUTURE DIRECTIONS, EMERGENCY-DRIVEN, TO ADVANCE EMPIRICAL RESEARCH

At the time of writing this chapter, the world had been battling with the COVID-19 pandemic for nearly a year, ever since the virus was first recorded in China in late 2019.

The restrictive measures put in place by governments in an attempt to control the infection – social distancing, school closures and lockdowns – have created turmoil in families' lives in many countries.

Will this global pandemic have consequences for research on WLB, and if the answer is yes, how? In what way does it challenge WLB research?

Here, we reflect on two directions: firstly, whether (and how) the COVID-19 pandemic has changed the type of research questions being asked about WLB; and secondly, whether (and how) it has stimulated development and use of innovative research methods, compared to the past.

The COVID-19 pandemic seems to be generating a very intense debate around work–life conciliation policies and personal experiences in the public debate and in scientific research. In particular, one of the main themes explored by researchers (especially sociologists and psychologists) during the COVID-19 pandemic has been the characteristics, experiences and consequences of working from home on one hand, and of distance learning for children, given the closure of educational institutions in order to contain the pandemic, on the other. The two things are strictly intertwined, since parents have been experiencing working from home while their children have been experiencing distance learning, which, in turn, affects the ability of many of them to work. In 'normal' times and circumstances, working from home can have many advantages – for example, from an economic point of view (with lower travel expenses being incurred) and/or in terms of well-being, as well as in reconciling WLB.[5] However, when this is forced, prolonged over time and accompanied by the closure of schools and childcare services, it can be difficult to combine work, study and family life in one space, and creating a new routine that works for the whole family can be a very difficult task. In this frame, researchers are questioning issues such as the consequences of new everyday routines at an individual level (for present and future individual well-being and work productivity) and at a macro level, in terms of social inequalities.

During lockdowns, a large proportion of the workforce worldwide has been instructed to work remotely (if job functions make this possible) by companies across different business sectors. Organizations that were previously familiar with teleworking, as well as organizations that have not hitherto experimented with working from home, have been sending their employees home, creating conditions for the most extensive mass-teleworking experiment in history (International Labour Organization 2020).

In terms of distance learning, according to the United Nations (2020), the COVID-19 pandemic has created the largest disruption of education systems in history, affecting nearly 1.6 billion learners in more than 190 countries, and the closure of schools and other learning spaces has impacted on 94 per cent of the world's student population.

Some of the leading questions are specifically located at the micro level: how are these new work, childcare and school learning arrangements subjectively perceived, experienced in everyday practices and managed (and coped with) by family members? What kind of consequences are they having for gender roles within couples with respect to the distribution of care and domestic tasks (innovative practices or re-traditionalizing practices)? What impact will this mode of work have on men's and women's working careers?[6]

Socio-sanitary conditions determined by the COVID-19 pandemic and the restrictive measures put in place to control contagions challenge the 'traditional' way of conducting fieldwork on WLB, especially qualitative social research conducted face to face *with* people: interviews, focus groups, participant observation and ethnographies, and so on. Social distancing forces researchers to readjust and use innovative research methods to avoid in-person interactions until the emergency is over. For example, discursive interviews are mostly conducted remotely via Skype or other telecommunications applications providing a video-chat facility and enabling voice calls to be made via computers, tablets, smartphones and other mobile devices over the internet. Obviously, social research has been conducted online for many years, and it is not a novelty, but it is now spreading widely because of COVID-19, and, above all, online social research is being done in a different context and situation to that of the past as a consequence of the necessity (not through choice) to manage fieldwork that was initially intended to be carried out using face-to-face methods.

Qualitative social research undertaken via online interview settings therefore involves empirical material being collected in a different manner to the face-to-face methods formerly used. An online interview has pros and cons, some (not all) of which are linked to the fact that interviewer–interviewee interactions are computer-mediated. In this kind of interview setting, the interviewee and interviewer do not share the same *physical* space, but rather a *virtual* place.

Online interviews could make interview appointments easier (if people are in good health) and less time-consuming (obviating the need for participants to leave home, for example, and simply requiring them to turn on a PC or smartphone to 'start' the process); moreover, people are more confined and may be feeling bored or restless and therefore may welcome the opportunity to be part of a research project (Cannito and Scavarda 2020). On the other hand, it is also true that in a situation where normal routines are disrupted, people may feel uncertain and worried.

Moreover, it could be more difficult for the interviewee (but also for the interviewer), when having to work from home and deal with school closures, to find a suitable moment to have the interview conversation without interference from other members of the family (children playing or doing distance learning, and/or a partner also trying to work from home). At the same time, these 'disturbances' could be of interest to a social researcher studying WLB, although the issue then arises of how he or she could obtain and manage this supplementary empirical material for study motifs from an ethical point of view; for example, an interviewee may need to give authorization/informed consent for this kind of use, but at the same time this kind of request could discourage the potential interviewee from participating in the study. In general, it is very important to consider privacy issues in these contexts, and researchers must also take into account that people may be living in environments where they are subjected to harassment, violence or surveillance by other family members.

Another aspect related to remote interviews concerns non-verbal communication. This is an important source of information for social researchers, which could be missing or lacking in a non-face-to-face interview, especially if a camera is not used. Other problems may arise due to internet malfunctions, which could make it hard to conduct an interview and could lead to a poor-quality conversation.

Some studies on balancing work and family life during the COVID-19 pandemic have also used (or are using) visual methods; in this case, researchers provide research participants with questions or prompts and ask them to use a camera (often on their smartphone) to take photos or make videos about their everyday practices and interactions, which they then share with the researchers. This is, for example, the case with Carreri and Dordoni's (2020) study of the WLB experiences of academics. The empirical material consists of narrative interviews conducted online with researchers in social sciences and humanities disciplines in the early stages of their academic career (fellows and temporary researchers), and pictures representing people working from home during the pandemic.

Another example of research using innovative methods to investigate WLB, exploring the challenges that people face and their experience of the COVID-19 crisis, is that of Plotnikof et al. (2020). They use a collage of stories, snapshots, vignettes, photos and other reflections relating to everyday life, in order to catch a glimpse of 'corona life' and its micropolitics of multiple, often contradictory, claims on practices, as many academics live, work and care at home. The study recounts concerns, dreams, anger, hope, numbness and passion emerging among academics from across the world in response to the crisis, and the authors explore constitutive relations of resistance, care and solidarity in these dis/organizing times of contested spaces, identities and agencies, as those involved live, work and care at home during lockdowns.

One possible research path could be aimed at exploring the impact of the COVID-19 pandemic on WLB policies and services in particular, to disentangle whether (and how) the present crisis can be a boost to their expansion, enhancement and innovation, in order to adapt them to the challenges of securing a WLB, or, rather, to ascertain whether it will lead (or has led) to a move away from traditional arrangements. According to an online survey conducted in Italy during the pandemic, of 3,000 people aged between 18 and 85,[7] two-thirds expressed a negative opinion of institutions or preferred not to answer. Only a third of families felt supported by institutions during this critical phase, with families being overloaded in terms of accountability for the large number of activities, which has, in turn, necessitated some form of delegation in an attempt to find solutions to the problem of managing complexity.

With regard to research methods in the future and in general in situations like the current COVID-19 pandemic, where distancing and lockdowns are needed temporally (and/or enforced), the following ways of doing fieldwork could be potentiated (Lupton 2020): individual or familial diaries/journaling, epistolary interviews, re-enactment videos (asking participants to make their own re-enactment videos using their phone or providing them with a wearable video camera and then sharing videos online with the researchers), documentary photography, autoethnography[8] (defined by Ellis et al. (2011, p. 1) as 'an approach to research and writing that seeks to describe and systematically analyse (*graphy*) personal experience (*auto*) in order to understand cultural experience (*ethno*)'), online discussion platforms and netnography (which facilitates analysis of the conversations of online textual communities) (Kozinets 2010). In this respect, important issues arise regarding the role of the research participant. In fact, many of these methods require the active involvement of the 'object' of study, whose role is also crucial in determining the quality of the empirical material collected. It therefore becomes extremely important to know how to motivate people to participate fully, as well as being aware that they are able to technically manage such methods.

NOTES

1. This chapter is a collaborative effort. Nevertheless, if for academic reasons individual authorship has to be attributed, Rosy Musumeci wrote Sections 1, 2 and 4, and Sonia Bertolini Subsections 3.1, 3.2 and 3.3.
2. According to Chang et al. (2010), in fact, much relevant information regarding samples (for example, marital status, child characteristics, race, hours worked, education and occupation) is omitted from descriptions of work–family research.
3. Some qualitative studies focus on women working in male-dominated professions. As an example, see Watts's (2009) microanalysis and mesoanalysis of WLB strategies employed by women in a male-dominated profession (that is, engineering) in the UK's 'long hours' culture.
4. In the United States, women aged 15–64 spent 241 minutes per day on unpaid work; that is, +66% in comparison to men (who devoted 145 minutes to it). In Organisation for Economic Co-operation and Development (OECD) countries, on average, women spent even more time on unpaid work,

compared to men: 262.4 minutes per day, which is nearly double that of men (135.8 minutes) (authors' calculation, based on the OECD database).

5.   Although, regarding this last point, in Italy's case research carried out by the Valore D Association on a sample of 1,300 workers (more than 93 per cent of whom were 'smart' working) has shown that one in three women and one in five men admit they struggle to reconcile work and family life.

6.   In the Italian context, for example, many surveys have been implemented regarding a specific workplace – the university – in order to analyse transformations, experiences and the consequences of working from home and of distance learning.

7.   The 'Famiglia al tempo del Covid-19' research project has been conducted by a group of psycho-social researchers from the University Centre for Family Studies and Research at the Catholic University in Milan, directed by Camillo Regalia, together with the Human Highway company.

8.   Among recent contributions using autoethnography to analyse experiences of living and working from home (and reconciling these) during the COVID-19 pandemic (with particular regard to the academic context and work), see Guy and Arthur (2020), Pruulmann-Vengerfeldt (2020) and Utoft (2020).

REFERENCES

Ahn, N., and P. Mira (2001), 'A note on the changing relationship between fertility and female employ-ment rates in developed countries', *Journal of Population Economics*, **4**, 667–682.

Allen, T.D., K.A. French, S. Dumani, and K.M. Shockley (2015), 'Meta-analysis of work-family conflict mean differences: does national context matter?' *Journal of Vocational Behavior*, **90**, 90–100.

Ammons, S.K., and E.L. Kelly (eds) (2015), *Work and Family in the New Economy* (Research in the Sociology of Work, Volume 26), Bingley: Emerald Group.

Annink, A., L. den Dulk, and J.E. Amorós (2016), 'Different strokes for different folks? The impact of heterogeneity in work characteristics and country contexts on work–life balance among the self-employed', *International Journal of Entrepreneurial Behaviour & Research*, **22** (6), 880–902.

Annor, F. (2016), 'Work-family conflict: a synthesis of the research from cross-national perspective', *Journal of Social Sciences*, **12**, 1–13.

Barber, L.K., and A.M. Santuzzi (2015), 'Workplace telepressure and employee recovery', *Journal of Occupational Health Psychology*, **20** (2). DOI: 10.1037/a0038278.

Becker, G.S. (1964), *Human Capital: A Theoretical and Empirical Analysis, with Special Reference to Education*. University of Illinois at Urbana-Champaign's Academy for Entrepreneurial Leadership Historical Research Reference in Entrepreneurship. Available at SSRN: https://ssrn.com/abstract=1496221.

Beigi, M., and M. Shirmohammadi (2017), 'Qualitative research on work-family in the management field: a review', *Applied Psychology*, **66** (3), 382–433.

Bertolini, S. (2006), 'La conciliazione per le lavoratrici atipiche', *Economia e lavoro*, **XL** (1), 57–71.

Bertolini, S., and R. Musumeci (2018), 'Variations in work preferences in the transition to parenthood? Evidences from a qualitative longitudinal research on Italian couples', in 'La famiglia contesa. Le ridefinizioni della famiglia negli odierni conflitti della sfera pubblica', *AG About Gender – Rivista internazionale di studi di genere*, **14** (7), 95–123.

Bianchi, S.M., and M.A. Milkie (2010), 'Work and family research in the first decade of the 21st century', *Journal of Marriage and Family*, **72**, 705–725.

Bichard, J-A., P. Yurman, D. Kirk and D. Chatting (2014), 'Quotidian Ritual and Work–life Balance: An Ethnography of Not Being There', paper presented at the EPIC Conference, New York, September. www.epicpeople.org/quotidian-ritual-and-work–life-balance-an-ethnography-of-not-being-there/.

Blossfeld, H.-P., E. Klijzing, M. Mills and K. Kurz (eds) (2005), *Globalization, Uncertainty and Youth in Society*, London: Routledge.

Bosoni, M.L. (2011), 'Uomini, paternità e lavoro: la questione della conciliazione dal punto di vista maschile', *Sociologia e politiche sociali*, **14** (3), 63–86.

Bourne, K.A., and P.J. Forman (2014), 'Living in a culture of overwork: an ethnographic study of flexi-bility', *Journal of Management Inquiry*, **23** (1), 68–79.

Cannito, M., and A. Scavarda (2020), 'Childcare and remote work during the COVID-19 pandemic: ideal worker model, parenthood and gender inequalities in Italy', *Italian Sociological Review*, **10** (3S), 801–820.

Cano-Lòpez, T. (2014), 'Decisions on employment and the family: some considerations about the theory of preference', presentation at the 7th ESFR Congress, Families in the Context of Economic Crisis: Recent Trends in Multidisciplinary Perspective, Madrid, 3–6 September.

Carreri, A., and A. Dordoni (2020), 'Academic and research work from home during the COVID-19 pandemic in Italy: a gender perspective', *Italian Sociological Review*, **10** (3S), 821–845.

Casper, W., L. Eby, C. Bordeaux, A. Lockwood and D. Lambert (2007), 'A review of research methods in IO/OB work-family research', *Journal of Applied Psychology*, **92** (1), 28–43.

Casper, W.J., Marquardt, D.J., Roberto, K.J., and Buss, C. (2016), 'The hidden family lives of single adults without dependent children', in T.D. Allen and L.E. Eby (eds), *Oxford Handbook of Work and Family*, New York, NY: Oxford University Press, pp. 182–195.

Castro-García, C., and M. Pazos-Moran (2016), 'Parental leave policy and gender equality in Europe', *Feminist Economics*, **22** (3), 51–73.

Chang, A., P. McDonald and P. Burton (2010), 'Methodological choices in work–life balance research 1987 to 2006: a critical review', *International Journal of Human Resource Management*, **21** (13), 2381–2413.

Cichy, K.E., E.S. Lefkowitz and K.L. Fingerman (2007), 'Generational differences in gender attitudes between parents and grown offspring', *Sex Roles*, **57** (11), 825–836.

Clark, S.C. (2000), 'Work/family border theory: a new theory of work/family balance', *Human Relations*, **53** (6), 747–70.

Cohen, L., J. Duberley and G. Musson (2009), 'Work–life balance? An autoethnographic exploration of everyday home-work dynamics', **18** (3), 229–241.

Crespi, I., and E. Ruspini (2016), *Balancing Work and Family in a Changing Society: The Fathers' Perspective*, London: Palgrave.

Dermott, E. (2008), *Intimate Fatherhood: A Sociological Analysis*, London: Routledge.

Doucet, A. (2006), *Do Men Mother? Fathering, Care & Domestic Responsibility*, Toronto: University of Toronto Press.

Drew, E., and E.M. Murtaugh (2005), 'Work–life balance: senior management champions or laggards?', *Women in Management Review*, **20** (4), 262–278.

Elder, G.H., Jr (1995), 'The life-course paradigm: social change and individual development', in P. Moen, G.H. Elder Jr and K. Luscher (eds), *Examining Lives in Context: Perspectives on the Ecology of Human Development*, Washington, DC: American Psychological Association, pp. 101–139.

Elder, G.H., Jr, M.K. Johnson and R. Crosnoe (2003), 'The emergence and development of life course theory', in: J.T. Mortimer and M.J. Shanahan (eds), *Handbook of the Life Course*. Handbooks of Sociology and Social Research. Boston, MA: Springer.

Ellis, C., T.E. Adams and A.P. Bochner (2011), 'Autoethnography: an overview', *Forum Qualitative Sozialforschung/Forum: Qualitative Social Research*, **12** (1), Art. 10. www.qualitative-research.net/index.php/fqs/article/view/1589/3095.

Emslie, C., and K. Hunt (2009), '"Live to work" or "work to live": a qualitative study of gender and work–life balance among men and women in mid-life', in A. Gregory and S. Milner (eds), 'Special Issue on Work–Life Balance', *Gender, Work and Organization*, **16** (1), 151–172. https://onlinelibrary.wiley.com/doi/full/10.1111/j.1468-0432.2008.00434.x.

Eurofound (2017), *Income Inequalities and Employment Patterns in Europe Before and After the Great Recession*, Luxembourg: Publications Office of the European Union.

Eydal, G.B., and T. Rostgaard (eds) (2015), *Fatherhood in the Nordic Welfare States: Comparing Care Policies and Practice*, Bristol: Policy Press.

Featherstone, B. (2009), *Contemporary Fathering: Theory, Policy and Practice*, Bristol: Policy Press.

Freshwater, D. (2007), 'Reading mixed methods research: contexts for criticism', *Journal of Mixed Methods Research*, **1** (2), 134–146.

Gatrell, C.J., S.B. Burnett, C.L. Cooper and P. Sparrow (2013), 'Work–life balance and parenthood: a comparative review of definitions, equity and enrichment', *International Journal of Management Reviews*, **15**, 300–316.

Gautun, H., and K. Hagen (2010), 'How do middle-aged employees combine work with caring for elderly parents?', *Community, Work & Family*, **13** (4), 393–409.

Gerson, K., and Damaske, S. (2020), *The Science and Art of Interviewing*, Oxford: Oxford University Press.

Greenhaus, J.H., and S. Parasuraman (1999), 'Research on work, family, and gender: current status and future directions,' in G.N. Powell (ed.), *Handbook of Gender & Work*, London: SAGE, pp. 391–412.

Gregory, A., and S. Milner (2009), 'Editorial: work–life balance – a matter of choice?', *Gender, Work and Organization*, **16** (1), pp. 1–13.

Grunow, D., and M. Evertsson (eds) (2016), *Couples' Transitions to Parenthood: Analysing Gender and Work in Europe*, Cheltenham, UK and Northampton, MA, USA: Edward Elgar Publishing.

Grunow, D., and M. Evertsson (eds) (2019), *New Parents in Europe: Work-Care Practices, Gender Norms and Family Policies*, Cheltenham, UK and Northampton, MA, USA: Edward Elgar Publishing.

Guillaume, C., and S. Pochic (2019), 'What would you sacrifice? Access to top management and the work–life balance', in A. Gregory and S. Milner (eds), 'Special Issue on Work–Life Balance', *Gender, Work and Organization*, **16** (1), 14–36.

Guy, B., and B. Arthur (2020), 'Academic motherhood during COVID-19: navigating our dual roles as educators and mothers', *Gender, Work and Organization*, **27** (5), 887–899.

Hakim, C. (2000), *Work-Lifestyle Choices in the 21st Century*, Oxford: Oxford University Press.

Halrynjo, S. (2009), 'Men's work–life conflict: career, care and self-realization – patterns of privileges and dilemmas', in A. Gregory and S. Milner (eds), 'Special Issue on Work–Life Balance', *Gender, Work and Organization*, **16** (1), pp. 98–125.

Hilbrecht, M., and D.S. Lero (2014), 'Self-employment and family life: constructing work–life balance when you're "always on"', *Community, Work & Family*, **17** (1), 20–42.

Hobson, B. (ed.) (2002), *Making Men into Fathers: Men, Masculinities and the Social Politics of Fatherhood*, Cambridge: Cambridge University Press.

Hobson, B., and S. Fahlén (2009), 'Competing scenarios for European fathers: applying Sen's Capabilities and Agency Framework to work-family balance', *Annals of the American Academy of Political and Social Science*, **624** (1), 214–233.

Holter, O.G. (2007), 'Men's work and family reconciliation in Europe', *Men and Masculinities*, **9** (4), 425–456.

Ilies, R., K.M. Schwind and D. Heller (2007), 'Employee well-being: a multilevel model linking work and nonwork domains', *European Journal of Work and Organizational Psychology*, **16** (3), 326–341.

International Labour Organization (2020), *Teleworking During the COVID-19 Pandemic and Beyond: A Practical Guide*, Geneva: International Labour Organization.

Kahn, R.L., D.M. Wolfe, R.P. Quinn, J.D. Snoek and R.A. Rosenthal (1964), *Organizational Stress: Studies in Role Conflict and Ambiguity*, New York, NY: Wiley.

Kopelman, R., D. Prottas, C. Thompson and E. Jahn (2006), 'A multilevel examination of work–life practices: is more always better?', *Journal of Managerial Issues*, **18** (2), 232–253.

Kozinets, R.V. (2010), *Netnography: Doing Ethnographic Research Online*, Thousand Oaks, CA: SAGE.

Kvande, E. (2009), 'Work–life balance for fathers in globalized knowledge work: some insights from the Norwegian context', in A. Gregory and S. Milner (eds), 'Special Issue on Work–Life Balance', *Gender, Work and Organization*, **16** (1), pp. 58–72.

Las Heras, M., N. Chinchilla and M. Grau (eds) (2017), *The Work-Family Balance in Light of Globalization and Technology*, Newcastle upon Tyne: Cambridge Scholars Publishing.

LaWanda, H.C., and K.J. Shinew (2014), 'Leisure, work, and disability coping: "I mean, you always need that 'in' group"', *Leisure Sciences: An Interdisciplinary Journal*, **36**, 420–438.

Letherby, G., J. Scott and M. Williams (2013), 'Theorised subjectivity', in *Objectivity and Subjectivity in Social Research*, London: SAGE, pp. 79–102.

Lewis, S., Anderson, D., Lyonette, C., Payne, N., and Wood, S. (eds) (2017), *Work–Life Balance in Times of Recession, Austerity and Beyond*, Abingdon: Routledge.

Lewis, S., and C.L. Cooper (1999), 'The work-family research agenda in changing contexts', *Journal of Occupational Health Psychology*, **4** (4), 382–93.

Lewis, S., G. Richenda and R. Rapoport (2007), 'The constraints of a "work–life balance" approach: an international perspective', *International Journal of Human Resource Management*, **18** (3), 360–373.

Lindemann, K. (2017) 'Working on it: family narrative on masculinities, disability, and work–life balance', in A.F. Herrmann (ed.), *Organizational Autoethnographies: Power and Identity in Our Working Lives*, New York, NY: Routledge, pp. 59–70.

Lupton, D. (2020), 'Doing fieldwork in a pandemic', North West Social Science Doctoral Training Partnership/Economic and Social Reseearch Council. https://nwssdtpacuk.files.wordpress.com/2020/04/doing-fieldwork-in-a-pandemic2-google-docs.pdf.

Magaraggia, S. (2015), *Essere giovani e diventare genitori. Esperienze a confronto*, Rome: Carocci.

Mason, J. (2011), 'Mixing methods in a qualitatively driven way', *Qualitative Research*, **6** (1), 9–25.

Mazmanian, M., W.J. Orlikowski and J. Yates (2013), 'The autonomy paradox: the implications of mobile email devices for knowledge professionals', *Organization Science*, **24** (5), 1337–1357.

McCarthy, A., J.N. Cleveland, S. Hunter, C. Darcy and G. Grady (2013), 'Employee work–life balance outcomes in Ireland: a multilevel investigation of supervisory support and perceived organizational support', *International Journal of Human Resource Management*, **24** (6), 1257–1276.

McRae S. (2003) 'Constraints and choices in mothers' employment careers: a consideration of Hakim's preference theory', *British Journal of Sociology*, **54**(3), 317–38.

Miller, T. (2010), *Making Sense of Fatherhood: Gender, Caring and Work*, Cambridge: Cambridge University Press.

Moen, P., and S. Sweet (2004), 'From "work-family" to "flexible careers": a life-course reframing', *Community, Work & Family*, **7** (2), 209–26.

Moss, P., and F. Deven (2015), 'Leave policies in challenging times: reviewing the decade 2004–2014', *Community, Work & Family*, **18** (2), 137–144.

Murray, W.C., and A. Rostis (2007), 'Who's running the machine? A theoretical exploration of work stress and burnout of technologically tethered workers', *Journal of Individual Employment Rights*, OI: 10.2190/IE.12.3.F, Corpus ID: 144762886.

Musumeci, R., and A. Santero (eds) (2018), *Fathers, Childcare and Work: Cultures, Practices and Policies*, Bingley: Emerald Group.

Naldini, M. (ed.) (2016), *La Transizione alla genitorialità. Da Coppie Moderne a Famiglie Tradizionali* (*The Transition to Parenthood: From Modern Couples to Traditional Families*), Bologna: Il Mulino.

Nieuwenhuis, R., and E.E. Kossek (2017), 'Book review: *Work–Life Balance in Times of Recession, Austerity and Beyond*, edited by Suzan Lewis, Deirdre Anderson, Clare Lyonette, Nicola Payne and Stephen Wood, Abingdon, Routledge, 2017', *Community, Work & Family*, **21** (1), 106–109. 10.1080/13668803.2017.1388002.

O'Neill, J.W., M.M. Harrison, J. Cleveland, D. Almeida, R. Stawski and A.C. Crouter (2009), 'Work-family climate, organizational commitment, and turnover: multilevel contagion effects of leaders', *Journal of Vocational Behavior*, **74** (1), 18–29.

OECD (2016), *Parental Leave: Where Are the Fathers?* Organisation for Economic Co-operation and Development policy brief. www.oecd.org/policy-briefs/parental-leave-where-are-the-fathers.pdf.

Ollier-Malaterre, A., and A. Foucreault (2016), 'Cross-national work–life research: a review at the individual level', in T.D. Allen and L.E. Eby (eds), *Oxford Handbook of Work and Family*, New York, NY: Oxford University Press, pp. 315–332.

Ollier-Malaterre, A., M. Valcour, L. Den Dulk and E.E. Kossek (2013), 'Theorizing national context to develop comparative work–life research: a review and research agenda', *European Management Journal*, **31** (5), 433–447.

Pattnaik, J. (ed.) (2013), *Father Involvement in Young Children's Lives: A Global Analysis*, New York, NY: Springer.

Pitt-Catsouphes, M., E.E. Kossek and S. Sweet (2006), *The Work and Family Handbook: Multidisciplinary Perspectives, Methods and Approaches*, Mahwah, NJ: Lawrence Erlbaum.

Plotnikof, M., P. Bramming, L. Branicki, L.H. Christiansen, K. Henley, N. Kivinen, J.P. Resende de Lima, M. Kostera, E. Mandalaki, S. O'Shea, B. Özkazanç-Pan, A. Pullen, J. Stewart, S. Ybema and N. van Amsterdam (2020), 'Catching a glimpse: corona-life and its micropolitics in academia', *Gender Work Organization*, **27**, 804–826.

Powell, G.N., J.H. Greenhaus, T.D. Allen and R.E. Johnson (2019), 'Introduction to special topic forum: advancing and expanding work–life theory from multiple perspectives', *Academy of Management Review*, **44**, (1), 54–71.

Pruulmann-Vengerfeldt, P. (2020), 'The ways of knowing the pandemic with the help of prompted autoethnography', *Qualitative Inquiry*. https://doi.org/10.1177/1077800420960133.

Ranson, G. (2015), *Fathering, Masculinity and the Embodiment of Care*, London: Palgrave.

Rapoport, R., and R.N. Rapoport (1965), 'Work and family in contemporary society', *American Sociological Review*, **30** (3), 381–394.

Reyneri, E. (2011), *Sociologia del mercato del lavoro*, Bologna: Il Mulino.

Russell, H., P.J. O'Connell and F. McGinnity (2009), 'The impact of flexible working arrangements on work–life conflict and work pressure in Ireland', in A. Gregory and S. Milner (eds), 'Special Issue on Work–Life Balance', *Gender, Work and Organization*, **16** (1), 73–97.

Sabbadini, L.L., and T. Cappadozzi (2011), 'Essere padri: tempi di cura e organizzazione di vita', presentation at the workshop Men, Fathers and Work from Different Perspectives, Milan, 2 February 2011.

Saraceno, C. (2018), 'Foreword', in R. Musumeci and A. Santero (eds), *Fathers, Childcare and Work: Cultures, Practices and Policies*, Bingley: Emerald Group, pp. xvii–xviii.

Seierstad, C., and G. Kirton (2015), 'Having it all? Women in high commitment careers and work–life balance in Norway', *Gender, Work and Organization*, **22** (4), 390–404.

Shockley, K.M., and W. Shen (2016), 'Couple dynamics: division of labor', in T.D. Allen and L.E. Eby (eds), *Oxford Handbook of Work and Family*, New York, NY: Oxford University Press, pp. 125–139.

Small, M.L. (2011), 'How to conduct a mixed methods study: recent trends in a rapidly growing literature', *Annual Review of Sociology*, **37**, 57–86.

Tashakkori, A., and C. Teddlie (2003), *Handbook of Mixed Methods in Social & Behavioral Research*, Thousand Oaks, CA: SAGE.

Tracey, W. (2015), 'Work–life balance/imbalance: the dominance of the middle class and the neglect of the working class', *British Journal of Sociology*, **66** (4), 691–717.

United Nations (2020), *Policy Brief: Education During COVID-19 and Beyond*. www.un.org/development/desa/dspd/wp-content/uploads/sites/22/2020/08/sg_policy_brief_covid-19_and_education_august_2020.pdf.

Utoft, E.H. (2020), '"All the single ladies" as the ideal academic during times of COVID-19?', *Gender, Work and Organization*, **27** (5), 778–787.

Valcour, P.M., and L.W. Hunter (2005), 'Technology, organizations, and work–life integration', in E.E. Kossek and S.J. Lambert (eds), *Work and Life Integration: Organizational, Cultural, and Individual Perspectives*, Mahwah, NJ: Lawrence Erlbaum, pp. 61–84.

Warren, T. (2017), 'Work–life balance, time and money: identifying the work–life balance priorities of working class workers', *Bulletin of Comparative Labour Relations*, **97**.

Warren, T., E. Fox and G. Pascal (2009), 'Innovative social policies: implications for work–life balance among low-waged women in England', in A. Gregory and S. Milner (eds), 'Special Issue on Work–Life Balance', *Gender, Work and Organization*, **16** (1), pp. 126–150.

Watts J. (2009), 'Allowed into a man's world' meanings of work–life balance: perspectives of women civil engineers as 'minority' workers in construction', in A. Gregory and S. Milner (eds), 'Special Issue on Work–Life Balance', *Gender, Work and Organization*, **16** (1), pp. 37–57.

Wharton, A.S. (2012), 'Work and family in the 21st century: four research domains', *Sociology Compass*, **6** (3), 219–235.

PART II

MULTILEVEL PERSPECTIVES ALONG GENDER AND TEMPORAL AXES

4. Research on work–life balance: a gender structure analysis

Emily Hallgren and Barbara J. Risman

In this chapter, we argue that fundamentally work–life balance needs to be framed with gender theory. Industrial societies were organized so that the world of paid labor was designed for men and family work was delegated to women. We have a work–life balance problem because women now work for pay in the labor force but continue to assume a greater share of family work. Gender equality cannot exist in a society where men do not take on an equal share of family work. In order to address this fundamental issue, we use gender structure theory to argue for a multilevel analytical approach to research on work–life balance (Risman 2018a, 2018b). Most work–life balance scholarship concentrates on one level of analysis: either exploring individual gender ideologies and expectations for work–family arrangements, or the implications of household or workplace interactions, or the structure or culture of work organizations and nation-states. These different strands of inquiry have greatly advanced our understanding of how gender structures the relationship between work and home life, and the resulting work–life conflict or balance that workers experience. We argue that researchers of work–life balance should contextualize their findings with evidence at each level of analysis, even as any given study focuses on one level of analysis. Finally, research on work–life balance must attend to both the material and cultural aspects of the gender structure (Risman 2018a, 2018b). To create a society where men and women experience work–life balance, we must create a gender-egalitarian one.

We begin with an overview of the gender structure framework (Risman 2018a, 2018b). We then review existing literature on work–life balance organized by the level of analysis outlined within the framework. Next, we leverage gender structure theory to discuss how scholars can improve research on work–life balance through contextualization of their topic with research at other levels of analysis. We conclude with an overview of two research projects that push us forward toward internationally comparative work/family research which integrates research at each level of the gender structure to help move us toward the possibility of seeing a more equitable society.

GENDER STRUCTURE THEORY

We suggest that it is useful for work–life balance to be conceptualized within a gender structure framework (Risman 2018a, 2018b). Gender structure theory integrates previous gender theories into a multi-dimensional argument of gender as a social structure. Grounded in a conceptualization of structure as a dialectical process where causality is recursive (Giddens 1984), conceptualizing gender as a structure brings together research traditions on individual personal orientations, interpersonal interactions, and macro-level patterns. Gender structure theory posits a reflexive relationship between structure and individual action, such that individual action is always responding to existing structures in ways that either reinforce or challenge existing conditions. By theorizing gender as a structure, we can understand the way gender shapes ongoing practices at the individual, interactional, and macro level, and how, through these practices, gender as a structure is sustained, reproduced, and/or challenged.

The individual, interactional, and macro dimensions of the gender structure are interrelated, mutually constitutive, and reflexive. Furthermore, at each dimension, material and cultural processes shape gendered practices within that dimension of analysis and influence the way gender is done at other dimensions. Material processes involve physical bodies, laws, or geographical locations. Cultural processes are ideological or socially constructed ideas and ideologies that orientate people's perspectives and worldviews. Figure 4.1 illustrates the interconnections between the three dimensions of the gender structure, as well as the material and cultural processes operating within and between each dimension.

The individual level of the gender structure emphasizes the processes involved in the development of gendered selves and gendered ways of cognitively interpreting the social world. Bodies matter, and biological materiality surely plays a significant role in the historical construction of child rearing in industrial societies as women's work. Cultural processes play quite an important role in the development of gendered personalities and differential commitment to work and family roles.

Material and cultural processes also take place at the interactional dimension of the gender structure, and the patterns of expectations for both women and men in families and in workplaces. In West and Zimmerman's classic (1987) article on 'doing gender', they explain the way we hold each other accountable to behave in ways consistent with expectations for women or men. We also note the effect of culture in the way gender stereotypes frame how we interpret the behavior of others so that we more readily see men as more competent and agentic than women, and women as more nurturing than men (Ridgeway 2011, Ridgeway and Correll 2004). These cognitive biases influence men's and women's differential roles in and outside of families. In addition to these cultural processes, material experiences also play a role in gendering interactions. For example, the numerical representation of men and women in an office totally changes the dynamics (Bruni, Gherardi, and Poggio 2004). Research has found that as women's proportion of managers and corporate board members increase, so does gender equity for employees located below them in organizational hierarchies (Cohen and Huffman 2007; Cook and Glass 2014, 2015; Huffman, Cohen, and Pearlman 2010; Skaggs, Stainback, and Duncan 2012; Stainback, Kleiner, and Skaggs 2016). Stainback, Kleiner, and Skaggs (2016) find that female managers are likely to change the work/family policies for those who work for them. Hence, the number of women at the top of an organization can influence the work–life balance of the men and women who work for them.

The macro dimension of the gender structure includes both the rules and regulations that construct possibilities in institutions and the cultural logics that justify them. National policies create laws that shape and can reshape societal patterns of gender inequality. Gendered cultural logics influence people's imagined options and choices throughout their life-cycle. For women, balancing work and family often means justifying their decision to work by explaining that it is 'for the family' in order to meet the normative ideal that women are self-sacrificial and family-centered (Damaske 2011b). Men also face challenges in balancing work and family, but since cultural ideals of masculinity require breadwinning, men's life choices tend to be shaped by the expectation that they should 'have it all' – a wife, children, career, and a home.

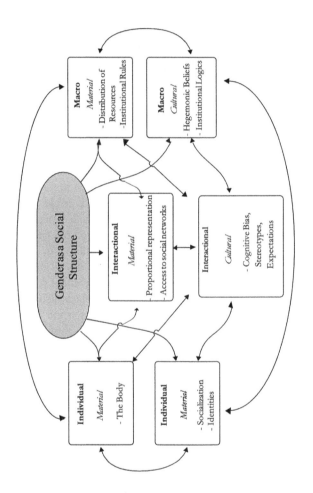

Source: Risman, B. J. (2017), 'Are millennials cracking the gender structure?', *Social Currents*, 4(3), p. 211.

Figure 4.1   *Gender as a social structure*

Yet, in order to attract a wife and buy the home, many men feel pressures to prioritize their career above all else (Townsend 2002). In some societies, such as the United States, men without stable jobs are not seen as viable husbands and so are less likely to marry (David and Wasserman 2013, Sawhill and Venator 2015, Wood 1995).

Gender structure theory provides a conceptual framework for understanding the way gender is reproduced through cultural and material processes taking place at individual, interactional, and macro dimensions. Gender structure theory emphasizes how change is like a game of dominoes: one move instigating others. For example, macro-level programs such as educational initiatives by federal governments encouraging young women to learn science and math can help develop individual-level preferences among young women to pursue jobs in STEM (science, technology, engineering, and mathematics) fields. Yet, the potential for change inspired by such macro and individual processes could ultimately be stunted by inter-actional processes – as women who study or work in STEM fields often face discrimination by colleagues and then alienation from their jobs, increasing the chance that they will 'opt out' of work, reinforcing women's responsibility for family labor. By thinking about gender as a multi-dimensional framework, we can start to make sense of dynamic patterns of change, both toward more equality as well as the pushback against it.

1.   WORK/LIFE BALANCE ANALYZED BY GENDER STRUCTURE

By applying gender structure to the study of work–life balance, we can examine how gender operates at the individual, interactional, and macro levels of social organization to shape the experience of work–life balance for workers and families. Our approach underscores the fact that gender fundamentally structures work–life balance, because both work and family are inherently gendered (Acker 1990, Ferree 2010). For example, Acker (1990) reveals how the apparently neutral concept of a 'job' is inherently gendered: it is based on the abstract ideal male worker, who has a wife to take care of all of his domestic concerns. For centuries, the family has been fundamentally structured by gender division and the oppression of women (Hartsock 1987), and the household remains a primary site where gender is produced and prac-ticed (Ferree 2010). However, new and diverse family forms are challenging the traditional gendered organization of families (Blackstone and Greenleaf 2015, Green 2015, Smock and Manning 2015). By applying gender structure theory to the field of work–life balance we can examine how and where traditional notions of gender are reinforced or challenged at each level of analysis, and how these processes shape the possibilities for work–life balance.

Below we organize our review by each level of analysis. We begin with an overview of research on work–life balance at the individual level, focusing on gendered selves and expec-tations for work–family arrangements, as well as changes in personal gender ideologies over time. At the interactional level, we review findings on how social interaction in the household and the workplace shapes work–life balance arrangements. Regarding interactional research in the household, we discuss literature on couples' strategies for work–life balance, as well as changing gender division in contributions to household labor. In terms of workplace inter-action, we review literature on how bias, including the 'motherhood penalty' and flexibility bias, disadvantages mothers and all workers who seek arrangements that improve work–life balance. At the macro level, we explore literature on how organizational structure and culture, as well as state-level policies and cultural ideologies, shape the realities and possibilities for work–life balance.

2.   INDIVIDUAL-LEVEL RESEARCH

At the individual level, we gain important insight on how people experience work–life balance from research on gendered selves and expectations for work–family arrangements (for example, Damaske 2011a, Gerson 2009, Pedulla and Thébaud 2015, Schweitzer et al. 2011). Research on changing gender ideologies is also useful here (Cotter, Hermsen, and Vanneman 2011; Scott, Alwin, and Braun 1996; Sullivan 2015).

Gendered Selves and Expectations for Work–Family Arrangements

At the individual level, it is important to consider how gendered selves shape individuals' expectations for their share of work and family responsibilities, which influence later experiences of work–life balance. Scholarship in the past 20 years suggests that gendered self-perceptions continue to shape men's and women's different expectations regarding the competing demands of work and family, even decades after the gender revolution began (England 2010). However, recent literature also presents evidence of progress toward gender egalitarianism in terms of both individual beliefs and behaviors.

Gender scholarship has shown that personal career aspirations and expectations for work–family arrangements begin prior to family formation, and that gender continues to be salient in these expectations. Most young adult women think, plan for, and adjust their career goals in anticipation of future work–family conflict to a much greater degree than men (Bass 2014; Crabb and Ekberg 2014; Fetterolf and Eagly 2011; Schweitzer et al. 2011; Stone and McKee 2000; Weisgram, Bigler, and Liben 2010; Weisgram, Dinella, and Fulcher 2011). At the dawn of the new millennium, an interview study of American men and women college students found that nearly all of the women, but none of the men, planned to pause or cease their career once they had children (Stone and McKee 2000). Young adult women and men continued to draw on traditional gendered cultural notions of mothers as the best caregivers for children and fathers as best suited for breadwinning. A decade later, scholars found persistent gender differences in pre-career expectations (Schweitzer et al. 2011) and anticipation of parenthood (Bass 2014). In a sample of over 23,000 Canadian undergraduate women and men, Schweitzer et al. (2011) finds that women were more likely to prefer 'beta' career priorities (for example, work–life balance) while men preferred 'alpha' career priorities (for example, building a sound financial base). Bass (2014) demonstrates that women thought about becoming parents and scaled back their stated career goals more than men when considering the responsibilities that they expect to accompany parenthood. An important exception in the gendered expectations literature is Cech (2015), who finds that neither women nor men undergraduates report deliberate consideration of future family plans in their choice or either college major or career aspirations.

In a study of career and relationship aspirations among the U.S. children of the gender revolution, Gerson (2009) finds important evidence of change regarding expectations for work–life balance: young adult women and men both aspired to committed relationships characterized by flexibility in sharing of household labor and childcare. However, in light of the potential social and economic barriers to their ideal relationship, a gender divide emerges: women prefer to 'fall back' on self-reliance, while men prefer a neotraditional relationship in which they are the primary breadwinners and involved fathers, with wives employed part-time so that they do not have to share equally in domestic work. Pedulla and Thébaud (2015) replicate and extend Gerson's findings using a survey experiment to assess young, unmarried men's and women's work–family role preferences. Consistent with Gerson (2009), Pedulla and Thébaud (2015) find that when the option is available, both men and women prefer an egalitarian relationship, regardless of education level. Faced with constraint to the achievement of the egalitarian ideal, men's and women's fallback options revealed distinct social class differences. While highly educated men and women both opted for a neotraditional arrangement, those with lower education followed the patterns first established by Gerson (2009): women fell back on self-reliance, while men preferred to be the primary breadwinner.

In a study of mostly married adult American women, Damaske (2011a) finds that gender, race, and class intersected to influence women's future work expectations. While middle-class women, regardless of race, and Black working-class women expected continual workforce participation, white and Latina working-class women considered both full- and part-time work, with half expecting to work continuously and the other half intermittently. Middle-class women's families had the resources to prepare them for professional employment, and thus they formed an early expectation of full workforce participation and were able to 'delay the consideration of work–family conflict' (Damaske 2011a, p. 424). White and Latina working-class women's upbringings, on the other hand, were marked by structural constraints on parents' work opportunities and gender division inside the home, making these women more aware of work–family conflict and making part-time work a more viable option.

Once they became working wives/mothers, Damaske (2011b) reports that both middle- and working-class women justify their decisions to stay or leave work as 'for the family', rather than employing a discourse of personal fulfillment or disliking their work. Nonetheless, the steadily employed women in Damaske's (2011b) study discussed rewarding jobs, financial incentives, and family support for their work, suggesting reasons of personal fulfillment are present, if not at the forefront of women's accounts. Tichenor (2005) demonstrates that when wives earn more, they often still attempt to compensate for their unconventional status through domestic labor to achieve the statuses of 'good wife/mother'. Further, among 'highly quali-fied' professionals (that is, those with a graduate, professional, or high-honors undergraduate degree), women, especially mothers, are more likely than their male counterparts to leave the career 'fast lane' (37 percent of women and 43 percent of mothers, compared to 24 percent of men), and more likely to do so in order to spend more time on family (Hewlett and Luce 2005). Literature on professional working women reveals that while most women plan to work and need to work, and many find work rewarding, at the individual level women often still hold gendered beliefs about women as selflessly devoted to family and the best caregivers for children.

Yet, some heterosexual households have established more egalitarian practices within the household. In a small interview study of egalitarian couples, Risman (1999) found that heterosexual married partners in the United States who were actually successful at sharing the work of raising their children and earning shared several characteristics. They held strong ide-ological commitments to gender equality, had spouses with equal earning power, and the men had flexible jobs. Schwartz (1995) reported similar findings, but in addition, suggested that the couples most likely to be successfully in 'peer marriages' were couples in which neither partner had a very elite, high-pressure position.

Overall, the literature at the individual level suggests that women continue to face a disproportionate share of work–family conflict. They still struggle to achieve work–life balance as their identification with work and their family roles remain, in many instances, difficult to reconcile. This uncertainty and shifting between gender egalitarianism and tradition is reflected in Risman's recent research (2018b), which finds that some millennials are now straddlers of the gender structure, internalizing some elements of traditional gender socialization while rejecting other aspects. In their expectations for work–family arrangements, Risman (2018b) finds that while straddlers have abandoned 'separate spheres' and do not expect a male breadwinner/female caregiver arrangement, many retain elements of traditional gendered identities that conflict with egalitarian strategies. However, recent research on individual gender ideologies and contributions to housework offers evidence that individuals across many countries are moving in the direction of gender-egalitarian attitudes about household labor.

Gender Ideologies and Contribution to Housework

Multinational public opinion data shows progress in men's gender ideologies toward more egalitarian beliefs. Further, there is evidence of between- and within-cohort change, indicating that not only are more egalitarian young men replacing traditional, older cohorts, but men are also evolving their views during their lifetimes (Sullivan 2015). Data on gender attitudes in the United States and several European countries shows a clear trend toward rejection of traditional gender beliefs, though there is variation by country, with a slowdown in the 1990s, but further progress toward gender-egalitarian attitudes in the 2000s (Cotter et al. 2011; Scott et al. 1996; Scarborough, Sin and Risman 2019). While men's attitudes are changing, so too have they increased their contributions to housework and childcare, while women have reduced their housework hours and slightly increased their childcare time (Sullivan 2015, 2018). Sullivan (2015) argues that the co-incidence of change in gender ideologies and changing gender practices within households 'is our strongest argument for change in the direction of gender equality' (p. 621).

A small body of qualitative research also links men's gender ideologies with their contributions to housework. In a study of politically conservative, married heterosexual spouses, men who were laid off (and whose wives went to work) resisted taking on a greater share of housework. Housework appeared to be a threat to their identity and conflicted with cultural gender ideologies, and so there was little undoing of the gendered division of housework among these couples (Legerski and Cornwall 2010). However, in a study of more diverse men who became unemployed during the 'mancession' of 2007–2010, Myers and Demantas (2015) found that the men revised their concept of providing for the family to include their greater share of housework and childcare. In essence, the men decoupled masculinity from breadwinning, and found masculine pride in the work of taking care of the family at home.

3.   INTERACTIONAL-LEVEL RESEARCH

At the interactional level of analysis, there are important bodies of research on the household and workplace as key sites where the gender structure shapes the experience and potential for work–life balance. Regarding the household, scholars have investigated couples' strategies to negotiate work–life conflict and attempt work–life balance (see Cha 2010, Moen and Yu 2000). Research has also focused on documenting changes in the gender division of contributions to housework and care work within countries and cross-nationally (Altintas and Sullivan 2016; Bianchi et al. 2012; Bianchi, Robinson, and Milkie 2006; Sullivan 2018). In the workplace, research at the interactional level examines how cognitive bias and stereotypes disadvantage mothers in paid work (as the motherhood penalty) (Benard and Correll 2010; Correll, Benard, and Paik 2007; England et al. 2016). Another strand of inquiry explores how flexibility stigma and bias inhibit workers from seeking work–life balance through flexible work arrangements, and penalize those who do (see Munsch, Ridgeway, and Williams 2014; Williams, Blair-Loy, and Berdahl 2013).

Couples' Strategies to Negotiate Work–Life Conflict and Balance

At the level of household interaction, the body of work by Phyllis Moen and colleagues advances our understanding of couples' strategies to meet the competing demands of work and family (Becker and Moen 1999, Han and Moen 1999, Moen and Yu 2000, Clarkberg and Moen 2001, Moen 2003). Moen and colleagues emphasize the agency of subjects who actively negotiate the dual demands of work and home, and attempt to reconcile their preferences with structural constraints. Most couples attempt to scale back their work commitment to achieve balance (Becker and Moen 1999). However, couples' strategies are highly gendered, with wives doing most of the scaling back (Becker and Moen 1999) and most couples adopting a 'neotraditional' arrangement in which husbands have a greater commitment to paid, professional work (Moen and Yu 2000, Clarkberg and Moen 2001). This body of work also reveals gendered effects of work–life balance strategies on well-being. Women in dual-earner couples report lower quality of life, more stress and overload, and lower levels of coping and mastery (Moen and Yu 2000). Further, among dual-earners, caregiving has been associated with well-being declines for women, and well-being improvements for men (Chesley and Moen 2006). Moen and colleagues' work on couples' strategies demonstrates the structural lag (Han and Moen 1999), in which the institutions of family and work have not adequately restructured to account for the societal transformation of women's dramatically increased labor force participation over the last several decades.

Much recent research on professional couples facing high work-time demands reveals similar findings as the earlier work by Moen and colleagues. Research suggests that increased time demands in professional careers, particularly the 'greedy professions' (those that require long hours and personal commitment), are working to reproduce old patterns of gender inequality in the workplace and home (Cha 2010, 2013; Cha and Weeden 2014; Weeden, Cha, and Bucca 2016). The increase in long hours, and rising compensation for those hours, in the 1990s and 2000s is a significant factor driving the continuing gender gap in wages, as men more frequently worked over 50 hours a week (Cha and Weeden 2014). Notably, when comparing the likelihood of long work hours among men and women who are parents or childless, fathers are most likely to work long hours and mothers are least likely (Weeden et al. 2016). Within male-dominated occupations, mothers who overwork (more than 50 hours per week) are more likely to leave their jobs, and the workforce entirely, compared to men and childless women (Cha 2013). Overwork influences the family work dynamics of couples and has led some highly educated couples to adopt a neotraditional household arrangement where men work long hours and women scale back their careers to spend more time on caregiving (as found in earlier work by Moen and colleagues). Cha (2010) found that having a husband who works long hours significantly increased a women's chance of quitting her job, particularly for mothers, while the reverse scenario did not increase men's likelihood of quitting.

Thus, for spouses in professional and managerial jobs, the strain of overwork leads some dual-earner couples to adopt a 'separate sphere' arrangement. The body of research by Cha, Weeden, and colleagues demonstrates that overwork is a pernicious factor in the persistence of gender inequality both at work and home, as mothers are 'structurally less able' to meet work-time demands given that 'their time is subject to family demands more than is men's time' (Cha 2013, p. 158), thus driving some professional women out of the workplace and into primary caregiving.

Gender and Contributions to Household Labor

Another arena key to understanding work–life balance arrangements is the gender division (or lack thereof) in contributions to household labor. During the 1990s, scholarship on the gender division of household labor was dominated by Hochschild's (1989) highly influential text *The Second Shift*, which argued that among dual-earner heterosexual spouses, men were resistant to shouldering an equal share of domestic work, leaving women with an extra unpaid shift in addition to their paid work. While an essential contribution to feminist scholarship with its evidence that women's paid work would not automatically 'buy' equality within the home, later scholars noted that Hochschild's use of outdated time-use data and qualitative study of 50 heterosexual married couples made the generalizability of the findings questionable (Milkie, Raley, and Bianchi 2009).

Recent, large-scale time-use data suggests a different long-term trend in the direction of slow, if not always steady, progress toward gender equality in the household. Over the past several decades, men have increased time spent on both housework and childcare, and women have decreased time on housework and spend about the same time on childcare as the previous generation (Bianchi et al. 2006; Kan, Sullivan, and Gershuny 2011; Sullivan 2015, 2018; Sullivan and Coltrane 2008). Several scholars argue that we have reached virtual gender equity in men's and women's total work contributions (including paid work, household work, and childcare) (Bianchi et al. 2006, 2012; Sullivan 2015), although not equality across work/family spheres of work. Further, there remains gender specialization in the types of domestic work that men/women and mothers/fathers do (Bianchi et al. 2006, Kan et al. 2011). While men have increased their time spent on housework and childcare, mothers still perform more routine care tasks (for example, feeding, bathing) while men do more non-routine chores (for example, repairs, shopping) (Kan et al. 2011), though men have increased their share of time on routine tasks over the past 40 years (Bianchi et al. 2006).

Examination of multinational time-use data has shown cross-national slow, sometimes stuttering, trends toward gender equality in domestic work, both housework and childcare (Altintas and Sullivan 2016; Kan et al. 2011; Sullivan 2018). Longitudinal study of 50 years of time-use surveys in 19 countries demonstrates progress toward gender equity in core housework (cleaning, cooking, and washing clothes), but with a slowing of the trend in the late 1980s in those countries where households were already closer to gender parity in time contributions to housework, and greater progress for those countries with more gender inequality in housework in the later years of the study (Altintas and Sullivan 2016). Furthermore, while men are doing more domestic work and women less than in the past, cross-national gender segregation in domestic work persists, with women doing more of the routine 'female-typed' housework such as cooking and cleaning (Kan et al. 2011). Fathers have also increased their time on childcare, but most of that increase is by men with higher levels of education attainment, and is part of a trend of highly educated parents spending more intensive time in children's development than in the past (Altintas and Sullivan 2016, Sullivan 2018).

Motherhood Penalty

The motherhood penalty is an important area of work–life balance research because it elucidates how cognitive stereotypes of mothers as primary caregivers impact their work potential and opportunities. The motherhood penalty refers to the fact that mothers are disadvantaged in the labor market in terms of both getting a job (Correll et al. 2007) and pay (Budig and Hodges 2010; England et al. 2016; Wilde, Batchelder, and Ellwood 2010). In a line of inquiry aimed at explaining why the motherhood penalty exists and persists, Shelley Correll and colleagues have demonstrated that cognitive biases are translated into status-based discrimination that stereotypes mothers as less competent and less committed than other workers (Benard, Paik, and Correll 2008; Correll et al. 2007). Even when mothers show indisputable evidence of their competence and commitment, they face normative discrimination, being rated as less likeable and less warm by evaluators (Benard and Correll 2010). Thus, Correll and colleagues argue that normative discrimination is another mechanism explaining the persistence of the motherhood penalty in wages and other work-related outcomes. This body of research establishing the role of cognitive biases and discrimination in the persistence of the motherhood penalty uses experimental lab and/or audit studies in which participants assess the qualifications of hypothetical or supposedly real job applicants or workers.

Other scholars demonstrate evidence of the motherhood penalty through analyses of panel data (Budig and Hodges 2010; England et al. 2016; Oesch, Lipps, and McDonald 2017; Wilde et al. 2010). England et al. (2016) shows that among white women, the most highly skilled and highly paid workers suffer the steepest motherhood penalties. While these women rarely leave the workforce, they pay the highest price, in the form of future wage growth, when they take short leaves for mothering (England et al. 2016). Importantly, researchers have demonstrated that women's work–life conflict is related to the motherhood penalty. Yu and Kuo (2017) show that job strain and work–family conflict explain a good deal of mothers' wage disadvantage. They reach this conclusion by demonstrating that mothers in jobs that require less teamwork, are less competitive, and have higher autonomy suffer a slighter motherhood penalty. The argument that job strain and work–family conflict explain some portion of the motherhood wage penalty is further supported by research demonstrating that the wage penalty is greatest for younger mothers and mothers with children at home (Oesch et al. 2017).

Flexibility Stigma/Bias

In the past decade, scholars have made the case for workplace flexibility as a key structural solution to the mismatch between the lives of the modern workforce and outmoded workplace norms (Christensen and Schneider 2010, 2011). Yet workplace flexibility arrangements and policies are still not universal, and their use is often fraught with stigma. A growing area of research examines the challenges associated with workplace flexibility, including flexibility stigma and bias (Rudman and Mescher 2013, Munsch et al. 2014, Williams et al. 2013) and pluralistic ignorance (Munsch et al. 2014; Mandeville, Halbesleben, and Whitman 2016; Miyajima and Yamaguchi 2017).

Even when workplace flexibility policies are 'on the books', research on workplace interactions illuminates how flexibility stigma and flexibility bias inhibit workers from utilizing policies aimed at supporting work–life balance (see Cech and O'Connor 2017, Dodson 2013, Munsch 2016, Munsch et al. 2014, Rudman and Mescher 2013, Stone and Hernandez 2013, Williams et al. 2013). Williams et al. (2013) posit a macro-level cultural explanation: the moral underpinnings of the United States, specifically the work-devotion schema and ideal worker norm. At the interactional level within the workplace, those unable to perform as ideal workers, either by seeking flexible arrangements, taking leave, or having interrupted career trajectories, are branded with flexibility stigma and consequently 'discredited; that is, seen as less than full professionals and less committed' (Stone and Hernandez 2013, p. 239). Once this group of workers is stigmatized, they are open to flexibility bias and stereotyping by members of the workplace in-group. It is unclear if or to what extent the cultural biases and stigma for flexibility exist in countries beyond the United States.

Flexibility stigma and bias operate differently for women and men given the divergent gendered cultural expectations that persist: for women, being a good mother and good worker are incompatible, while for men, being a good provider and good worker are synonymous, but caregiving is considered deviant (Williams et al. 2013). Research on men and the flexibility stigma (Coltrane et al. 2013, Rudman and Mescher 2013, Vandello et al. 2013) documents the 'backlash' (Brescoll, Glass, and Sedlovskaya 2013) against men who display gender-atypical behavior. Men seeking flexibility are perceived as more feminine (Rudman and Mescher 2013, Vandello et al. 2013) and suffer economic penalties (as lower evaluations and earnings) (Coltrane et al. 2013). Men are also more penalized in job searches for having worked part-time than are women, as women's flexible labor force participation can be pardoned by beliefs about women's responsibility for children, while men's is not (Pedulla 2016). These findings suggest that gendered cultural norms of men as the appropriate primary breadwinner remain a significant barrier to both women's and men's ability to achieve work–life balance.

For women, flexibility stigma and bias influence professional and working-class women differently, but can push both out of their careers or jobs (Dodson 2013, Stone and Hernandez 2013). Mothers who 'opted out' of their professional careers discuss flexibility stigma and bias as relevant to their decisions, yet do not necessarily perceive these forces as prejudice, but rather accept the legitimacy of traditional workplace time norms of required intensive devotion to career (Stone and Hernandez 2013). Dodson (2013) finds that employers of low-wage mothers draw on cultural stereotypes of the poor to pathologize their work–family conflict (for example, poor mothers are irresponsible), rather than view it as a societal issue. Further, unlike middle-class mothers who may trade off career advancement for more time spent with families, low-wage mothers have no such cards to play and often face 'crisis decisions' where a job may be sacrificed, through quitting or dismissal, in order to attend to children's needs (Dodson 2013).

Pluralistic Ignorance

Recent research has investigated another potential explanatory mechanism for the low utilization of workplace flexibility resources: 'pluralistic ignorance' (Mandeville et al. 2016;

Miyajima and Yamaguchi 2017; Munsch et al. 2014). Pluralistic ignorance refers to situations in which 'individuals misperceive the attitudes of other group members and … in which those misperceived attitudes are misaligned with their own preferences' (Mandeville et al. 2016, p. 897). In a study of mostly male firefighters and mostly female nurses, misperception of family-friendly benefit utilization as socially unacceptable among peers had a stronger effect on individuals' benefit use than their personal views on such benefits. There was little variation in pluralistic ignorance by gender (Mandeville et al. 2016). Munsch et al. (2014) find evidence of pluralistic ignorance regarding both 'flextime' and 'flexplace' accommodations among U.S. workers: they believed that others held more discriminatory attitudes toward both types of accommodations than they personally did, although this was untrue. Similarly, in Japan men whose employers offer paternity leave policies overestimate their colleagues' negative attitudes toward such leave. Among men who held personal positive views toward paternity leave, those who assessed their colleagues as having negative attitudes were less likely to take leave than men who thought their colleagues shared their positive view (Miyajima and Yamaguchi 2017). This small but growing body of research suggests that misperceptions of group norms explain at least part of workers' persistent under-use of work–life balance benefits.

4.   MACRO-LEVEL RESEARCH: ORGANIZATIONAL RULES AND CULTURE LOGICS

It is important to examine how organizational structures and culture facilitate or constrain the potential for work–life balance among workers. Within organizations, both formal policies and workplace culture influence the potential and experience of work–life balance for workers. At the level of state policy, both material aspects, such as laws, and national culture shape work–life balance for citizens and workers.

Organizational Constraints and Cultural Logics

One key area of research on organizational structure examines formal initiatives to promote work–life balance. Moen and colleagues' work has shown that well-designed work–life balance initiatives can increase employee work–life balance, retention, job satisfaction, and well-being (Almeida et al. 2016; Kelly et al. 2014; Kelly, Moen, and Tranby 2011; Moen et al. 2011, 2016, 2017). Analysis of two formal workplace initiatives, ROWE and STAR (discussed below), reveal that schedule control (Kelly et al. 2011, Kelly et al. 2014, Moen et al. 2016, Moen et al. 2017), and formalized supervisory support for workers' personal lives (Kelly et al. 2014; Moen et al. 2016, 2017; Almeida et al. 2016) contribute to employee work–life balance, retention, and job satisfaction.

Work–Life Balance Initiatives

One example of such an initiative is worth discussion: a corporate initiative at the Best Buy headquarters, Results Oriented Work Environment (ROWE), involved participatory team trainings to move employees from time-oriented work measures (hours spent on a task) to exclusively results-oriented measures of productivity and achievement. (Best Buy is a major

American retail box store for electronic equipment.) The enhanced schedule control at the heart of ROWE reduces work–life conflict (time strains and negative work-to-family emotional spillover) and improves work–life fit (employees' sense of adequate time for personal and family activities and how well work schedules work for their family) (Kelly et al. 2011). The enhanced schedule control and resulting improvements in work–life balance are related to improved employee health and well-being, including almost an extra hour of sleep per night (Moen et al. 2011). Moen and colleagues argue that ROWE is effective because it is an organizational-level change in the structure of the workplace, shifting the entire organization to a standard of flexible work arrangements rather than granting flexibility as an exception to some workers (Moen et al. 2011).

A similar corporate work–life balance initiative, STAR (Support. Transform. Achieve. Results.), implemented in the IT department of a Fortune 500 company, was aimed at both schedule control and training supervisors to demonstrate support for workers' lives outside of work. STAR eased employees' work–family conflict and improved their sense of time adequacy (Kelly et al. 2014). The STAR initiative, mediated by increased schedule control and decreased work–family conflict, also significantly improved employee well-being, including reductions in burn-out, perceived stress, and psychological distress (Moen et al. 2016). STAR also has distinct gendered and classed effects on well-being: STAR benefits women more than men in terms of reduced perceived stress and psychological distress, and was related to increased job satisfaction for non-supervisory employees more than supervisors (Moen et al. 2016). Overall, Moen and colleagues demonstrate that well-designed organizational-level structural changes can affect individuals' work–life balance and well-being. Key to these two initiatives was not only broad changes in the structure of work, but changes that challenged assumptions and norms (as organizational culture) underlying that structure (Perlow and Kelly 2014). We discuss the importance of organizational culture further in the next section.

Organizational Culture: How Context Shapes Use/Effectiveness of Work–Life Balance Policies

Organizational culture is central to understanding both the use and effectiveness of work–life balance policies. Theoretically, work–life policies support families outside the workplace and gender equity within the workplace, by allowing workers time and flexibility to meet their commitments in both areas of life (Jacobs and Gerson 2004). As we have discussed in this chapter, this theory does not always translate into reality for workers and their families. The typical problem with implementing work–life balance policies is that organizations introduce alternative ways of working without confronting the organizational culture that only rewards the standard ways of working (Perlow 1995, 2012; Perlow and Kelly 2014). Workplace cultural norms of the 'ideal worker' (Acker 1990, Drago 2007, Williams 2001), 'career culture' (Gregory and Milner 2009), as well as norms of long hours and constant accessibility (particularly in the professions) (Cha and Weeden 2014, Epstein et al. 1999, Perlow 2012), inhibit workers from utilizing work–life policies for fear of punishment in terms of career advancement and pay (Jacobs and Gerson 2004). For example, 'time norms' in the legal profession force attorneys to sacrifice involvement in family life and make work–life balance out of reach (Epstein et al. 1999). Engineers face similar high demands on their time, with both long hours and an uninterrupted work trajectory required for career advancement (Perlow 1995, 2012). Up to now, most employers have followed the Accommodation Model (Perlow and Kelly 2014), viewing work–life policies as accommodating family needs and negotiated on an individual basis between employees and supervisors, rather than implemented broadly in order to challenge prevailing modes of working and workplace values.

A body of research from Sweden on organizational culture and parental leave offers evidence on how organizational culture constrains workers' behavior, and how culture can also be challenged through efforts at multiple levels of social process (Allard, Haas, and Hwang 2011; Haas, Allard, and Hwang 2002; Haas and Hwang 2009, 2016). Sweden was the first country to guarantee parental leave for fathers, and has a national culture supportive of women's paid work and men's involvement in housework and childcare; the country has been an interesting case for work–life balance scholars because Swedish policy makers have actively encouraged paternity leave to promote a more nurturant fatherhood and child well-being (Haas et al. 2002).

Despite progressive state-level structure and culture, Swedish fathers use a small proportion of leave time and work part-time much less than mothers (Haas et al. 2002, Haas and Hwang 2016). This is largely because workplace organizational cultures in Sweden remain generally rooted in a 'male model of work' that emphasizes male breadwinning and considers work and family separate spheres (Allard et al. 2011, Haas and Hwang 2016). However, companies have increased support for men's parental leave-taking over time, partly attributable to the greater representation of women in high-ranking managerial positions (Haas and Hwang 2009). There is evidence of a class divide in this progress, with white-collar Swedish men generally having more supportive workplace cultures and co-workers than blue-collar men (Haas and Hwang 2009). Haas and colleagues (2002) demonstrate that organizational culture powerfully constrains men's parental leave-taking, independent of household and individual-level effects. Nonetheless, there is evidence of independent effects on men's parental leave use at each level of the gender structure: men's advocacy for shared parenting, perception of their partner's preference for shared leave, and supportive workplace culture. These findings suggest that organizational culture can facilitate the enactment of fathers' egalitarian gender beliefs, and 'fathers can become agents of change within organizations' (Haas et al. 2002, p. 319). Overall, this area of research demonstrates the powerful effects of workplace culture, which can constrain use of work–life balance arrangements and limit gender equality even when individual workers hold gender-egalitarian ideologies and state-level policy provides gender-egalitarian policies and practices.

State-Level Structure: Work–Life Balance Laws Shape Individual Behavior

State-level policies aimed at supporting work–family balance, including parental leave, flexible or alternative work arrangements, and publicly-funded childcare, may facilitate or constrain worker behaviors such as mothers' labor force participation and parental leave-taking (Hegewisch and Gornick 2011). Countries vary dramatically in the policy designs of maternal leave (Gornick, Meyers, and Ross 1997), as well as the levels of generosity and gender equality in parental leave policies (Ray, Gornick, and Schmitt 2010). Scholars in these areas of research emphasize the material side of state policies and show that the provision and design of state-guaranteed parental leave shapes employment patterns and caretaking practices (Gornick, Meyers, and Ross 1998).

Across 14 industrialized nations, mothers with young children faced the largest decreases in employment in countries with the least-developed state policies to support mothers' employment; conversely, in countries with job protection and generous maternity leave, mothers of young children had similar employment rates to mothers with children aged 12 and over (Gornick et al. 1998). However, very extended maternal leave can also exacerbate existing gendered labor market inequalities. Comparing the employment effects of maternal leave policies across 17 countries, Jaumotte (2003) demonstrates that maternity leaves beyond four months have a depressive effect on mothers' employment.

In the UK and Europe, research suggests that state work–life policies, including leaves offered to fathers, increase men's use of parental leave but in gendered ways (Hegewisch and Pillinger 2006, Jónsdóttir and Aðalsteinsson 2008). While women take leave in one block, men are more likely to use leave intermittently and maintain a connection to work during leave (Jónsdóttir and Aðalsteinsson 2008). Further, in European countries that have introduced non-transferrable 'daddy days' in addition to leave that can be shared between parents (Eriksson 2005, Kluve and Tamm 2009), fathers have increased their leave use over time, but it is still mothers who take the vast majority of sharable leave (Jónsdóttir and Aðalsteinsson 2008). Overall, research on state-level policies that guarantee leave for parents demonstrates that policies influence individuals' leave-taking, but policy alone cannot create gender equality in contributions to parenting.

Cultural Logics: National Variations

In addition to state-level policy, cultural ideology matters. Cultural ideology shapes if and how family-friendly work policies improve employment outcomes for working mothers. Using international data from 22 countries, Boeckmann, Misra, and Budig (2015) demonstrate that ideological support for employed mothers amplifies the positive association between family-friendly work policies and mothers' employment outcomes. Specifically, in countries with cultural support for working mothers, moderate-length parental leave and publicly-funded childcare had the strongest positive relationships with mothers' earnings. In a similar study, Boeckmann, Misra, and Budig (2015) examined the influence of both cultural and institutional factors on mothers' employment levels in postindustrial countries. The authors compare employment participation of mothers and childless women in 19 postindustrial countries and find that well-paid leaves, publicly supported childcare, and cultural norms accepting of mothers' employment are all associated with smaller gaps in employment and working hours for mothers. Boeckmann, Misra, and Budig (2015) argue that the focus on the gender gap in employment outcomes obscures the inequalities faced by mothers specifically, compared to childless women. A key contribution of this strand of inquiry to the field of work–life balance is demonstrating that cultural ideology regarding mothers' employment interacts with work–family policy to influence employment outcomes for working mothers.

CONCLUSION: HIGHLIGHTING RESEARCH ACROSS THE GENDER STRUCTURE

In our conclusion, we highlight two recent research projects that exemplify the strength of taking the individual-level choices, the interactional expectations, and the macro structures and cultural logics into account in research on work–life balance. These projects show that an analysis that takes into account each level of the gender structure can be quantitative or qualitative, as well as comparative. We begin with a discussion of the work by Sullivan, Gershuny, and Robinson (2018) using longitudinal internationally comparative data, and end with a discussion of the new study by Collins (2019) on 'Making Motherhood Work' based on over 100 interviews with women in the United States, Italy, Sweden, and Germany.

Sullivan and colleagues' (2018) multilevel model of lagged generational change helps to explain the slow progress toward equality in the gender division of housework and care work. They argue that we should discard notions of a gender revolution and instead take a longer view of change in the gender structure, over generations rather than across decades. Their (2018) longitudinal theory of change links gendered processes at the individual level (for example, gender socialization in the family of origin) with interactional processes (peer and spousal interactions over housework and care work) and macro-level policy and ideology.

Using an example of a girl raised in her parents' home in the latter half of the 20th century, the authors note that the gendered practices in her household of origin are influenced, to an extent, by the gendered practices and ideologies of her grandparents, and she takes this socialization into her adult household. As she enters a labor market of greatly expanded opportunity for women, her paid work conflicts with the gendered expectations and ideologies that she and her partner bring to their household, which are negotiated through household interaction. These interactions create a gradual buildup of pressure for change at the institutional level in the form of policies such as paid parental leave and publicly- and employer-supported childcare. Thus, household interaction is recursively connected to macro-level policies influencing the ideologies and behaviors of individual working spouses and parents. There is also time lag at both ends of the model: at the start as individual gender ideologies take time to diffuse into the public discourse and at the end as policy changes and norms diffuse and become effective. Sullivan and colleagues (2018) provide a model to understand the slow change in the gender division of household labor that may appear stalled at times, but, taking the long view, continues in the direction of gender equality at multiple levels of social process.

Collins (2019) interviews working mothers in the capitals of four countries: Washington, DC; Rome; Stockholm; and both East and West Berlin. Her analysis reveals that the gendered socialization of men and women in three of these four countries (all but Sweden) creates male and female parents who feel differentially responsible for the care of their children, and therefore come to strategies for work–life balance quite differently. Even if that were not the case, the expectations of good mothering that haunt women, including in Sweden, are not constraining to fathers. The sexist responses of supervisors toward pregnancy again privilege husbands' careers. Yet it is Sweden, where government and work policies support working mothers and involved fathers, and fathers are largely committed to egalitarian parenting, in which Collins (2019) finds the 'most serene' mothers. But perhaps most interesting in Collins's (2019) interviews with employed mothers in the four countries is that even state-regulated progressive work/family supports do not help women balance work and family in cultures where women are considered 'bad mothers' or 'career whores' for having ambitious labor force plans. Thus, Collins (2019) effectively demonstrates that cultural ideology must change in tandem with state policies to support work–life balance for working mothers.

We conclude with a set of recommendations based on the evidence presented in this article. Based on our review of research at the individual level, we suggest that future research on work–life balance must take seriously the socialization of boys and girls in their families of origin. We cannot expect boys to grow up into committed caretaking fathers if we do not raise them to be nurturing and respect women as equals. All the policies in the world alone will not allow for working mothers' work–life balance unless men do their fair share. Research suggests, however, that individual egalitarian gender attitudes alone are not enough. We must have workplaces that presume that every worker has, or will have, caretaking responsibilities over the course of their lives, for children, for sick or disabled relatives, and/or for elders. Further, productivity measures must be based on accomplishments, not face-time. All workers must have the right, and the expected responsibility, to work part-time for short periods of intensive caregiving. State policies must enforce paid parental leave, preferably 'use it or lose it' for fathers. But the availability of leave alone will not be enough; it is up to social movement entrepreneurs to work to change the cultural logics of their own societies so that both women and men can imagine a gender-just world with work–life balance for all workers.

In addition, we recommend that scholars of work–life balance go farther to distinguish the material from the cultural aspects of work–life balance, and consider how these two parts of the gender structure work in tandem or in tension. For example, as we have discussed, research clearly indicates that workplace policies are often under-used and ineffective when organizational cultures remain committed to 'ideal worker' and traditional gender norms. Thus, in efforts aimed at improving work–life balance, it is crucial to assess how workplaces can effectively change both policy and culture. Moving forward, it is important that scholars identify the structural and cultural phenomena in their work, and the relationship between these two aspects of the gender structure, in order to assess how best to work toward a gender-equitable world where work–life balance is accessible to all workers and family members.

One of us has previously argued (Risman, 2018b) that a just world must be post-gender, a world where being assigned male or female at birth does not predict one's destiny as responsible for caregiving (or not) or as an economically autonomous individual. We suggest that what the world needs now is what Collins (2019) refers to as 'radical hope'. Work–life balance struggles are not inevitable, as they vary tremendously across postindustrial societies. What we need now is the will to use the excellent body of knowledge covered in this review to change households, workplaces, and the entire gender structure to create a more just world in which work–life balance is possible for all of us. We need radical hope to give us the strength to work toward such a future.

REFERENCES

Acker, Joan (1990), 'Hierarchies, Jobs, Bodies: A Theory of Gendered Organizations', *Gender & Society*, 4(2), 139–58.
Allard, Karin, Linda Haas, and C. Philip Hwang (2011), 'Family-Supportive Organizational Culture and Fathers' Experiences of Work-Family Conflict in Sweden', *Gender, Work and Organization* 18(2), 141–57.
Almeida, David M., Kelly D. Davis, Soomi Lee, Katie M. Lawson, Kimberly N. Walter, and Phyllis Moen (2016), 'Supervisor Support Buffers Daily Psychological and Physiological Reactivity to Work-to-Family Conflict', *Journal of Marriage and Family*, 78(1), 165–79.
Altintas, Evrim, and Oriel Sullivan (2016), 'Fifty Years of Change Updated: Cross-National Gender Convergence in Housework', *Demographic Research*, 35, 455–69.
Bass, Brooke Conroy (2014), 'Preparing for Parenthood? Gender, Aspirations, and the Reproduction of Labor Market Inequality', *Gender & Society*, 29(3), 362–85.
Becker, Penny Edgell, and Phyllis Moen (1999), 'Scaling Back: Dual-Earner Couples' Work-Family Strategies', *Journal of Marriage and the Family*, 61(4), 995–1007.
Benard, Stephen, and Shelley J. Correll (2010), 'Normative Discrimination and the Motherhood Penalty', *Gender & Society*, 24(5), 616–46.

Benard, Stephen, In Paik, and Shelley J. Correll (2008), 'Cognitive Bias and the Motherhood Penalty', *Hastings Law Journal*, **59**, 1359.

Bianchi, Suzanne M., John P. Robinson, and Melissa A. Milkie (2006), *The Changing Rhythms of American Family Life*. Russell Sage Foundation, New York, NY.

Bianchi, Suzanne M., Liana C. Sayer, Melissa A. Milkie, and John P. Robinson (2012), 'Housework: Who Did, Does or Will Do It, and How Much Does It Matter?', *Social Forces*, **91**(1), 55–63.

Blackstone, Amy, and Amy Greenleaf (2015), 'Childfree Families', in *Families as They Really Are*, edited by Barbara J. Risman and Virginia Rutter. W.W. Norton, New York, NY, pp. 137–44.

Boeckmann, Irene, Joya Misra, and Michelle J. Budig (2015), 'Cultural and Institutional Factors Shaping Mothers' Employment and Working Hours in Postindustrial Countries', *Social Forces*, **93**(4), 1301–33.

Brescoll, Victoria L., Jennifer Glass, and Alexandra Sedlovskaya (2013), 'Ask and Ye Shall Receive? The Dynamics of Employer-Provided Flexible Work Options and the Need for Public Policy', *Journal of Social Issues*, **69**(2), 367–88.

Bruni, Attila, Silvia Gherardi, and Barbara Poggio (2004), *Gender and Entrepreneurship: An Ethnographic Approach*. Routledge, London.

Budig, Michelle J., and Melissa J. Hodges (2010), 'Differences in Disadvantage: Variation in the Motherhood Penalty across White Women's Earnings Distribution', *American Sociological Review*, **75**(5), 705–28.

Cech, Erin A. (2015), 'Mechanism or Myth?', *Gender & Society*, **30**(2), 265–88.

Cech, Erin A., and Lindsey Trimble O'Connor (2017), '"Like Second-Hand Smoke": The Toxic Effect of Workplace Flexibility Bias for Workers' Health', *Community, Work & Family*, **20**(5), 543–72.

Cha, Youngjoo (2010), 'Reinforcing Separate Spheres: The Effect of Spousal Overwork on Men's and Women's Employment in Dual-Earner Households', *American Sociological Review*, **75**(2), 303–29.

Cha, Youngjoo (2013), 'Overwork and the Persistence of Gender Segregation in Occupations', *Gender & Society*, **27**(2), 158–84.

Cha, Youngjoo, and Kim A. Weeden (2014), 'Overwork and the Slow Convergence in the Gender Gap in Wages', *American Sociological Review*, **79**(3), 457–84.

Chesley, Noelle, and Phyllis Moen (2006), 'When Workers Care: Dual-Earner Couples' Adult Caregiving, Benefit Use, and Psychological Well-Being', *American Behavioral Scientist*, **49**, 1–22.

Christensen, Kathleen, and Barbara Schneider, eds (2010), *Workplace Flexibility*. Cornell University Press, Ithaca, NY.

Christensen, Kathleen, and Barbara Schneider (2011) 'Making a Case for Workplace Flexibility', *Annals of the American Academy of Political and Social Science*, **638**(1), 6–20.

Clarkberg, Marin, and Phyllis Moen (2001), 'Understanding the Time-Squeeze: Married Couples' Preferred and Actual Work-Hour Strategies', *American Behavioral Scientist*, **44**(7), 1115–36.

Cohen, Philip N., and Matt L. Huffman (2007), 'Working for the Woman? Female Managers and the Gender Wage Gap', *American Sociological Review*, **72**(5), 681–704.

Collins, Caitlyn (2019), *Making Motherhood Work: How Women Manage Careers and Caregiving*. Princeton University Press, Princeton, NJ.

Coltrane, Scott, Elizabeth C. Miller, Tracy Dehaan, and Lauren Stewart (2013), 'Fathers and the Flexibility Stigma', *Journal of Social Issues*, **69**(2), 279–302.

Cook, Alison, and Christy Glass (2014), 'Women and Top Leadership Positions: Towards an Institutional Analysis', *Gender, Work & Organization*, **21**(1), 91–103.

Cook, Alison, and Christy Glass (2015), 'Diversity Begets Diversity? The Effects of Board Composition on the Appointment and Success of Women CEOs', *Social Science Research*, **53**, 137–47.

Correll, Shelley J., Stephen Benard, and In Paik (2007), 'Getting a Job: Is There a Motherhood Penalty?' *American Journal of Sociology*, **112**(5), 1297–1338.

Cotter, David, Joan M. Hermsen, and Reeve Vanneman (2011), 'The End of the Gender Revolution? Gender Role Attitudes from 1977 to 2008', *American Journal of Sociology*, **117**(1), 259–89.

Crabb, Shona, and Stuart Ekberg (2014), 'Retaining Female Postgraduates in Academia: The Role of Gender and Prospective Parenthood', *Higher Education Research & Development*, **33**(6), 1099–1112.

Damaske, Sarah (2011a), 'A "Major Career Woman"? How Women Develop Early Expectations about Work', *Gender & Society*, **25**(4), 409–30.

Damaske, Sarah (2011b), *For the Family? How Class and Gender Shape Women's Work*. Oxford University Press, Oxford.

David, Autor, and Melanie Wasserman (2013), 'Wayward Sons: The Emerging Gender Gap in Labor Markets and Education', Third Way Report.

Dodson, Lisa (2013), 'Stereotyping Low-Wage Mothers Who Have Work and Family Conflicts', *Journal of Social Issues*, **69**(2), 257–78.

Drago, Robert William (2007), *Striking a Balance: Work, Family, Life*. Dollars & Sense, Boston, MA.

England, Paula (2010), 'The Gender Revolution: Uneven and Stalled', *Gender & Society*, **24**(2), 149–66.

England, Paula, Jonathan Bearak, Michelle J. Budig, and Melissa J. Hodges (2016), 'Do Highly Paid, Highly Skilled Women Experience the Largest Motherhood Penalty?', *American Sociological Review*, **81**(6), 1161–89.

Epstein, Cynthia Fuchs, Carroll Seron, Bonnie Oglensky, and Robert Saute (1999), *The Part-Time Paradox: Time Norms, Professional Life, Family and Gender*. Routledge, Abingdon.

Eriksson, Rickard (2005), *Parental Leave in Sweden: The Effects of the Second Daddy Month*, Working Paper Series 9, Stockholm University, Swedish Institute for Social Research.

Ferree, Myra Marx (2010), 'Filling the Glass: Gender Perspectives on Families', *Journal of Marriage and Family*, **72**(3), 420–39.

Fetterolf, Janell C., and Alice H. Eagly (2011), 'Do Young Women Expect Gender Equality in Their Future Lives? An Answer from a Possible Selves Experiment', *Sex Roles*, **65**(1), 83–93.

Gerson, Kathleen (2009), *The Unfinished Revolution: Coming of Age in a New Era of Gender, Work, and Family*. Oxford University Press, Oxford.

Giddens, Anthony (1984), *The Constitution of Society*. University of California Press, Berkeley, CA.

Gornick, Janet C., Marcia K. Meyers, and Katherin E. Ross (1997), 'Supporting the Employment of Mothers: Policy Defining Employment-Supporting Policies', *Journal of European Social Policy*, **7**(1), 45–70.

Gornick, Janet C., Marcia K. Meyers, and Katherin E. Ross (1998), 'Public Policies and the Employment of Mothers: A Cross-National Study', *Social Science Quarterly*, **79**(1), 35–54.

Green, Robert-Jay (2015), 'From Outlaws to In-Laws: Gay and Lesbian Couples in Contemporary Society', in *Families as They Really Are*, edited by Barbara J. Risman and Virginia Rutter. W. W. Norton, New York, NY, pp. 197–213.

Gregory, Abigail, and Susan Milner (2009), 'Work–Life Balance: A Matter of Choice?', *Gender, Work and Organization*, **16**(1), 1–19.

Haas, Linda, Karin Allard, and Philip Hwang (2002), 'The Impact of Organizational Culture on Men's Use of Parental Leave in Sweden', *Community, Work & Family*, **5**(3), 319–42.

Haas, Linda, and C. Philip Hwang (2009), 'Is Fatherhood Becoming More Visible at Work? Trends in Corporate Support for Fathers Taking Parental Leave in Sweden', *Fathering: A Journal of Theory, Research, and Practice about Men as Fathers*, **7**(3), 303–21.

Haas, Linda, and C. Philip Hwang (2016), '"It's About Time!": Company Support for Fathers' Entitlement to Reduced Work Hours in Sweden', *Social Politics*, **23**(1), 142–67.

Han, Shin Kap, and Phyllis Moen (1999), 'Work and Family Over Time: A Life Course Approach', *Annals of the American Academy of Political and Social Science*, **562**(1), 98–110.

Hartsock, Nancy (1987), 'The Feminist Standpoint: Developing a Ground for a Specifically Feminist Historical Materialism', in *Feminism and Methodology: Social Science Issues*, edited by S. Harding. Indiana University Press, Bloomington, IN, pp. 157–80.

Hegewisch, Ariane, and Janet C. Gornick (2011), 'The Impact of Work-Family Policies on Women's Employment: A Review of Research from OECD Countries', *Community, Work and Family*, **14**(2), 119–38.

Hegewisch, Ariane, and Jane Pillinger (2006), 'Out of Time: Why Britain Needs a New Approach to Working-Time Flexibility', research paper for the Trades Union Congress, London.

Hewlett, Sylvia Ann, and Carolyn Buck Luce (2005), 'Off-Ramps and On-Ramps: Keeping Talented Women on the Road to Success', *Harvard Business Review*, **83**(3), 43–6, 48, 50–4 passim.

Hochschild, Arlie Russell (1989), *The Second Shift*. Penguin, New York, NY.

Huffman, Matt L., Philip N. Cohen, and Jessica Pearlman (2010), 'Engendering Change: Organizational Dynamics and Workplace Gender Desegregation, 1975–2005', *Administrative Science Quarterly*, **55**(2), 255–77.

Jacobs, Jerry A., and Kathleen Gerson (2004), *The Time Divide*. Harvard University Press, Cambridge, MA.

Jaumotte, Florence (2003), 'Female Labour Force Participation: Past Trends and Main Determinants in OECD Countries', *OECD Working Papers*, **376.**

Jónsdóttir, Bryndís, and G. Dalmann Aðalsteinsson (2008), 'Icelandic Parents' Perception of Parental Leave', in *Equal Rights to Earn and Care: Parental Leave in Iceland*, edited by G. B. Eydal and I. V. Gíslason. Reykjavik: Félagsvısindastofnun Háskóli Íslands, pp. 65–86.

Kan, Man Yee, Oriel Sullivan, and Jonathan Gershuny (2011), 'Gender Convergence in Domestic Work: Discerning the Effects of Interactional and Institutional Barriers from Large-Scale Data', *Sociology*, **45**(2), 234–51.

Kelly, Erin L., Phyllis Moen, J. Michael Oakes, Wen Fan, Cassandra Okechukwu, Kelly D. Davis, Leslie B. Hammer, Ellen Ernst Kossek, Rosalind Berkowitz King, Ginger C. Hanson, Frank Mierzwa, and Lynne M. Casper (2014), 'Changing Work and Work-Family Conflict: Evidence from the Work, Family, and Health Network', *American Sociological Review*, **79**(3), 485–516.

Kelly, Erin L., Phyllis Moen, and Eric Tranby (2011), 'Changing Workplaces to Reduce Work-Family Conflict: Schedule Control in a White-Collar Organization', *American Sociological Review*, **76**(2), 265–90.

Kluve, Jochen, and Marcus Tamm (2009), 'Now Daddy's Changing Diapers and Mommy's Making Her Career: Evaluating a Generous Parental Leave Regulation Using a Natural Experiment', SSRN.

Legerski, Elizabeth Miklya, and Marie Cornwall (2010), 'Working-Class Job Loss, Gender, and the Negotiation of Household Labor', *Gender & Society*, **24**(4), 447–74.

Mandeville, Ashley, Jonathon Halbesleben, and Marilyn Whitman (2016), 'Misalignment and Misperception in Preferences to Utilize Family-Friendly Benefits: Implications for Benefit Utilization and Work–Family Conflict', *Personnel Psychology*, **69**(4), 895–929.

Milkie, Melissa A., Sara B. Raley, and Suzanne M. Bianchi (2009), 'Taking on the Second Shift: Time Allocations and Time Pressures of U.S. Parents with Preschoolers', *Social Forces*, **88**(2), 487–517.

Miyajima, Takeru, and Hiroyuki Yamaguchi (2017), 'I Want to But I Won't': Pluralistic Ignorance Inhibits Intentions to Take Paternity Leave in Japan', *Frontiers in Psychology*, **8**:1508.

Moen, Phyllis (2003), *It's About Time: Couples and Careers*. ILR Press, Ithaca, NY.

Moen, Phyllis, Erin L. Kelly, Wen Fan, Shi Rong Lee, David Almeida, Ellen Ernst Kossek, and Orfeu M. Buxton (2016), 'Does a Flexibility/Support Organizational Initiative Improve High-Tech Employees' Well-Being? Evidence from the Work, Family, and Health Network', *American Sociological Review*, **81**(1), 177–217.

Moen, Phyllis, Erin L. Kelly, Shi Rong Lee, J. Michael Oakes, Wen Fan, Jeremy Bray, David Almeida, Leslie Hammer, David Hurtado, and Orfeu Buxton (2017), 'Can a Flexibility/Support Initiative Reduce Turnover Intentions and Exits? Results from the Work, Family, and Health Network', *Social Problems*, **64**(1), 53–85.

Moen, Phyllis, Erin L. Kelly, Eric Tranby, and Qinlei Huang (2011), 'Changing Work, Changing Health: Can Real Work-Time Flexibility Promote Health Behaviors and Well-Being?', *Journal of Health and Social Behavior*, **52**(4), 404–29.

Moen, Phyllis, and Yan Yu (2000), 'Effective Work/Life Strategies: Working Couples, Work Conditions, Gender, and Life Quality', *Social Problems*, **47**(3), 291–326.

Munsch, Christin L. (2016), 'Flexible Work, Flexible Penalties: The Effect of Gender, Childcare, and Type of Request on the Flexibility Bias', *Social Forces*, **94**(4), 1567–91.

Munsch, Christin L., Cecilia L. Ridgeway, and Joan C. Williams (2014), 'Pluralistic Ignorance and the Flexibility Bias: Understanding and Mitigating Flextime and Flexplace Bias at Work', *Work and Occupations*, **41**(1), 40–62.

Myers, Kristen, and Ilana Demantas (2015), 'Being 'The Man' without a Job And/Or: Providing Care Instead of "Bread"', in *Families as They Really Are*, edited by Barbara J. Risman and Virginia Rutter. W. W. Norton, New York, NY, pp. 632–47.

Oesch, Daniel, Oliver Lipps, and Patrick McDonald (2017), 'The Wage Penalty for Motherhood: Evidence on Discrimination from Panel Data and a Survey Experiment for Switzerland', *Demographic Research*, **37**, 1793–1824.

Pedulla, David S. (2016), 'Penalized or Protected? Gender and the Consequences of Nonstandard and Mismatched Employment Histories', *American Sociological Review*, **81**(2), 262–89.

Pedulla, David S., and Sarah Thébaud (2015), 'Can We Finish the Revolution? Gender, Work-Family Ideals, and Institutional Constraint', *American Sociological Review*, **80**(1), 116–39.

Perlow, Leslie A. (1995), 'Putting the Work Back into Work/Family', *Group & Organization Management*, **20**(2), 227–39.

Perlow, Leslie A. (2012), *Sleeping with Your Smartphone: How to Break the 24/7 Habit and Change the Way You Work*. Harvard Business Review Press, Boston, MA.

Perlow, Leslie A., and Erin L. Kelly (2014), 'Toward a Model of Work Redesign for Better Work and Better Life', *Work and Occupations*, **41**(1), 111–34.

Ray, Rebecca, Janet C. Gornick, and John Schmitt (2010), 'Who Cares? Assessing Generosity and Gender Equality in Parental Leave Policy Designs in 21 Countries', *Journal of European Social Policy*, **20**(3), 196–216.

Ridgeway, Cecilia L. (2011), *Framed by Gender: How Gender Inequality Persists in the Modern World*. Oxford University Press, New York, NY.

Ridgeway, Cecilia L., and Shelley J. Correll (2004), 'Unpacking the Gender System: A Theoretical Perspective on Gender Beliefs and Social Relations', *Gender & Society*, **18**(4), 510–31.

Risman, Barbara J. (1999), *Gender Vertigo: American Families in Transition*. Yale University Press, London.

Risman, Barbara J. (2017), '2016 Southern Sociological Society Presidential Address: Are Millennials Cracking the Gender Structure?', *Social Currents*, **4**(3), 208–27.

Risman, Barbara J. (2018a), 'Gender as a Social Structure', in *Handbook of the Sociology of Gender*, edited by Barbara J. Risman, Carissa M. Froyum, and William J. Scarborough. Springer, Cham, pp. 19–43.

Risman, Barbara J. (2018b), *Where the Millennials Will Take Us: A New Generation Wrestles with the Gender Structure*, Oxford University Press.

Rudman, Laurie A., and Kris Mescher (2013), 'Penalizing Men Who Request a Family Leave: Is Flexibility Stigma a Femininity Stigma?', *Journal of Social Issues*, **69**(2), 322–40.

Sawhill, Isabel, and Joanna Venator (2015), 'Is There a Shortage of Marriageable Men?', Center on Children and Families.

Scarborough, William, Ray Sin, and Barbara J. Risman (2019), 'Attitudes and the Stalled Gender Revolution: Egalitarianism, Traditionalism, and Ambivalence from 1977 through 2016', *Gender & Society*, **33**(2), 173–200.

Schwartz, Pepper (1995), *Love between Equals: How Peer Marriage Really Works*. Simon and Schuster, New York, NY.

Schweitzer, Linda, Eddy Ng, Sean Lyons, and Lisa Kuron (2011), 'Exploring the Career Pipeline: Gender Differences in Pre-Career Expectations', *Industrial Relations*, **66**(3), 422–44.

Scott, Jacqueline, Duane F. Alwin, and Michael Braun (1996), 'Generational Changes in Gender-Role Attitudes: Britain in a Cross-National Perspective', *Sociology*, **30**(3), 471–92.

Skaggs, Sheryl, Kevin Stainback, and Phyllis Duncan (2012), 'Shaking Things up or Business as Usual? The Influence of Female Corporate Executives and Board of Directors on Women's Managerial Representation', *Social Science Research*, **41**(4), 936–48.

Smock, Pamela J., and Wendy D. Manning (2015), 'New Couples, New Families: The Cohabitation Revolution in the United States', in *Families as They Really Are*, edited by Barbara J. Risman and Virginia Rutter. W. W. Norton, New York, NY, pp. 131–39.

Stainback, Kevin, Sibyl Kleiner, and Sheryl Skaggs (2016), 'Women in Power: Undoing or Redoing the Gendered Organization?', *Gender & Society*, **30**(1), 109–35.

Stone, Linda, and Nancy P. McKee (2000), 'Gendered Futures: Student Visions of Career and Family on a College Campus', *Anthropology & Education Quarterly*, **31**(1), 67–89.

Stone, Pamela, and Lisa Ackerly Hernandez (2013), 'The All-or-Nothing Workplace: Flexibility Stigma and 'Opting out' among Professional-Managerial Women', *Journal of Social Issues*, **69**(2), 235–56.

Sullivan, Oriel (2015), 'Men's Changing Contribution to Family Work', in *Families as They Really Are*, edited by Barbara J. Risman and Virginia Rutter. New York, NY, W. W. Norton, New York, NY, pp. 617–28.

Sullivan, Oriel (2018), 'The Gendered Division of Household Labor', in *Handbook of the Sociology of Gender*, edited by Barbara J. Risman, Carissa M. Froyum, and William J. Scarborough. Springer, Cham, pp. 377–92.

Sullivan, Oriel, and Scott Coltrane (2008), 'Men's Changing Contribution to Housework and Childcare', Council on Contemporary Families Brief Report, April 25.

Sullivan, Oriel, Jonathan Gershuny, and John P. Robinson (2018), 'Stalled or Uneven Gender Revolution? A Long-Term Processual Framework for Understanding Why Change Is Slow', *Journal of Family Theory and Review*, **10**(1), 263–79.

Tichenor, Veronica (2005), 'Maintaining Men's Dominance: Negotiating Identity and Power When She Earns More', *Sex Roles*, **53**(3–4), 191–205.

Townsend, Nicholas W. (2002), *Package Deal: Marriage, Work and Fatherhood in Men's Lives*. Temple University Press, Philadelphia, PA.

Vandello, Joseph A., Vanessa E. Hettinger, Jennifer K. Bosson, and Jasmine Siddiqi (2013), 'When Equal Isn't Really Equal: The Masculine Dilemma of Seeking Work Flexibility', *Journal of Social Issues*, **69**(2), 303–21.

Weeden, Kim A., Youngjoo Cha, and Mauricio Bucca (2016), 'Long Work Hours, Part-Time Work, and Trends in the Gender Gap in Pay, the Motherhood Wage Penalty, and the Fatherhood Wage Premium', *RSF: The Russell Sage Foundation Journal of the Social Sciences*, **2**(4), 71–102.

Weisgram, Erica S., Rebecca S. Bigler, and Lynn S. Liben (2010), 'Gender, Values, and Occupational Interests among Children, Adolescents, and Adults', *Child Development*, **81**(3), 778–96.

Weisgram, Erica S., Lisa M. Dinella, and Megan Fulcher (2011), 'The Role of Masculinity/Femininity, Values, and Occupational Value Affordances in Shaping Young Men's and Women's Occupational Choices', *Sex Roles*, **65**(3–4), 243–58.

West, Candace, and Don Zimmerman (1987), 'Doing Gender', *Gender & Society*, **1**(2), 125–51.

Wilde, Elizabeth Ty, Lily Batchelder, and David T. Ellwood (2010), 'The Mommy Track Divides: The Impact of Childbearing on Wages of Women of Differing Skill Levels', National Bureau of Economic Research.

Williams, Joan (2001), *Unbending Gender: Why Family and Work Conflict and What to Do about It*. Oxford University Press, New York, NY.

Williams, Joan C., Mary Blair-Loy, and Jennifer L. Berdahl (2013), 'Cultural Schemas, Social Class, and the Flexibility Stigma', *Journal of Social Issues*, **69**(2), 209–34.

Wood, Robert G. (1995) 'Marriage Rates and Marriageable Men: A Test of the Wilson Hypothesis', *Journal of Human Resources*, **30**(1), 163–93.

Yu, Wei Hsin, and Janet Chen Lan Kuo (2017), 'The Motherhood Wage Penalty by Work Conditions: How Do Occupational Characteristics Hinder or Empower Mothers?', *American Sociological Review*, **82**(4), 744–69.

5. Work–life balance through the life course

Jeanne Ganault and Ariane Pailhé

INTRODUCTION

Most of the literature on reconciling professional and private life has been cross-sectional. Work–life conflict is generally studied at a specific point in people's lives and approached from a short-term (or medium-term) perspective. Studies also mainly focus on single events; for instance, the effect of parenthood or marriage on work and family trade-offs. While a considerable body of literature has incorporated the effect of age, fewer studies have investigated work–life conflict through a life-course approach (Moen and Sweet, 2004).

Yet, work–family balance evolves according to the stages of the life cycle, and some events can have long-lasting effects. The timing of transitions also differs across individuals. It is thus important to integrate the allocation of time over the entire life course and to focus on trajectories, not only on transitions (or changes in role) at a particular moment in time. The life-course perspective highlights the importance of going beyond singular events or single domains and of incorporating the whole life course (Elder, 1985).

As Elder defines it (2000), "the life course refers to a pattern of age-graded events and social roles that is embedded in social structures and subject to historical change". As such, it appears intrinsically linked to the core questions of work–life research, from the gendered structure of the division of labor between partners to increasing work demands impeding on family life. Life-course theorists have identified five paradigms (Elder et al., 2003), which could enrich work–life research and have marginally begun to do so: the "principle of life-span development" can foster interrogations on potential benefits of work and caregiving roles in later life (Marks et al., 2002); the "time and place" paradigm, investigating the evolution of social norms and practices across different societies, could serve as a theoretical background for comparative research on work–life conflict over the last decades and across Western countries (Bühlmann et al., 2009); another paradigm explores "agency" over the course of individuals' lives and could help researchers better understand individual and couple strategies in work–life arrangements (Becker and Moen, 1999); "the principle of timing" can be applied to the effect of family events (such as first births) on work outcomes (Florian, 2018); finally, the "linked lives" paradigm aims at acknowledging between-individual and within-household variation and how a partner's work–life conflict might be dependent on the other's work characteristics (Fagan and Press, 2008).

Beyond theoretical considerations, reconciliation of life-course and work–life research is constrained by methodological concerns and data availability: longitudinal studies remain a minority compared to cross-sectional ones – which are more cost-effective – and are exposed to greater risk of weak statistical significance due to high attrition rates. Still, research on panel data is growing and the methods used are expanding (Allison, 1994; Johnson, 2005), while researchers working on cross-sectional data have found ways to incorporate the life course in a one-off survey (Anxo et al., 2011) and improve the quality of retrospective data (Drasch and Matthes, 2013).

Up to now, few literature reviews combining work–life and life-course research have been conducted, and they focused on a small number of studies. In their seminal review of work–life research, Bianchi and Milkie (2010) identify only 11 papers integrating these two perspectives. Their review covers articles published mostly in the 1990s and early 2000s. This chapter reviews more recent work on issues in reconciling work life and private life over the life course by focusing on papers published after 2000 in peer-reviewed journals that adopted a life-course approach or differentiated different life stages within cross-sectional analysis. It focuses on methodological issues, especially on measures of work–life conflict over the life course. Objective and subjective measures are used to examine work–life reconciliation over the life course. The former, mostly used by quantitative sociologists, demographers and economists, rely on individuals' actual trade-offs between work time and private time throughout their life course. A large range of studies analyzes work–life trajectories; others focus on paid and unpaid work throughout the life course or work–life strategies. Subjective measures, mostly used by psychologists, focus on perceived conflict between the two domains and how it evolves depending on the life stage.

WORK–LIFE TRAJECTORIES

The main approach adopted to measure work–family conflict throughout the life course is to study work–life trajectories – that is, individuals' employment status over time and how it relates to family configuration – by focusing either on employment after specific family events or on multidimensional trajectories combining work and family. This is made possible (and thus simultaneously limited) by longitudinal data, providing information for individuals over the course of several years. These can be panel surveys, following an initial sample of respondents through different waves; surveys providing retrospective information on work and family histories; or combining panel data and retrospective work and family histories. These studies identify typical paths and illustrate the diverse ways women (mostly), but also men or couples, negotiate work and family roles over the life course.

Employment Outcomes after Specific Family Events

A large body of literature focuses on employment trajectories after specific family events, and mostly on the effect of parenthood. Most studies analyze short-term effects; we review here studies focusing on effects in the medium and long run. Most of these rely on panel data, using random- or fixed-effects models – or other econometric methods such as group-based trajectory methods and latent-class analysis – to identify the effect of specific life events (parenthood, eldercare) on employment. Outcomes investigated are labor force participation, the number of hours worked or the degree of work commitment. Another strand of this literature explores this issue through qualitative analyses, conducting one-off interviews with women, men or couples at various stages of their life course.

The Transition to and through Parenthood

Panel studies have overall found transition to parenthood to have a negative impact on female labor force participation, full-time employment and weekly paid work hours (Killewald and

García-Manglano, 2016; Scheiner, 2016). Although longitudinal results on fathers are scarcer, a rare study using panel data on British fathers found parenthood to have no impact on weekly work hours (Dermott, 2006), which is consolidated by cross-sectional studies (Jacobs and Gerson, 2001; Anxo et al., 2011). Motherhood also has a negative impact on work commitment for women still employed; women who gave birth in Sweden between 1999 and 2013 were less committed to work than those who did not (Evertsson, 2013). In qualitative studies, motherhood is found to instigate a "redistribution of priorities" (op cit.), in which women tend to "scale back" from work demands (Becker and Moen, 1999; Blair-Loy, 2001; Emslie and Hunt, 2009; Murray and Cutcher, 2012) and their goals become more family-oriented than "achievement-related" (Salmela-Aro et al., 2000). As a result, a "motherhood penalty" in terms of income is identified in several countries (Damaske and Gerson, 2008; Gangl and Ziefle, 2009; Sefton et al., 2011; Killewald and García-Manglano, 2016). Using fixed-effect models on large panel surveys, which control for unobserved heterogeneity in time-invariant individual characteristics, researchers find the magnitude of this penalty to vary with age, cohort and the number of children (Gangl and Ziefle, 2009; Sefton et al., 2011; Kahn et al., 2014). For instance, early parenthood is more often associated with a transition out of employment or a weaker attachment to the labor market (Macmillan and Copher, 2005; Florian, 2018). Age at first birth is decisive in being "continuously out" of employment or in "low intermittent employment" (Hynes and Clarkberg, 2005).

These patterns are two out of a diversity of female employment patterns following childbearing (Hynes and Clarkberg, 2005). Using the US National Longitudinal Survey of Youth (NLSY79) and applying a group-based trajectory method, they identify six typical paths after the first and second births: continuously out of employment, low intermittent employment, hiatus at birth, exit at birth, declining employment or continuously employed. Based on the *German Socio-Economic Panel* and the *British Household Panel Survey* (BHPS), Zagel (2014) also investigates work patterns based on employment status during and after single motherhood. This research provides information on labor market attachment throughout single motherhood using sequence analysis and optimal matching analysis (OMA), modeled by eight clusters: full-timers, employment-oriented, leavers, part-timers, part-time returners, gradual returners, casually employed and inactive. While the first have only one or two brief interruptions, "gradual returners" go through phases of inactivity before working part-time and then full-time, while "casually employed" remain mostly inactive with occasional instances of part- or full-time work.

Other works focusing on the length of the effect of family events on women's employment trajectory find that as they reach their forties and fifties, the effect of children on female employment status diminishes (Kahn et al., 2014). Shifting focus to the effect of parenthood on later life, Stafford et al. (2018) find that both men and women have a higher likelihood of working in their sixties, compared to childless individuals.

The Transition to Informal Caregiving

While childcare has been extensively incorporated in work–life research, other forms of care work have been largely overlooked. As early as 1994, Doress-Worters insisted on the relevance of integrating multiple caregiving roles in addition to childcare when studying work–life conflict, while Moen et al. (1994) showed the growing importance of informal caregiving as women age and through time periods. A small literature on "informal caregiving" has emerged and has mainly focused on the effect of and impact on employment histories.

Several studies found no link between employment status and "informal" caregiving, meaning that individuals tend to take up caregiving regardless of their employment status and thus, of their workload (Ettner, 1995; Wolf and Soldo, 1995; Henz, 2006). Moen et al. (1994), using the *Women's Roles Survey* (United States, small sample – 1956 to 1986), concluded that the likelihood of becoming a caregiver was irrespective of employment. Using Australian longitudinal data, Berecki-Gisolf et al. (2008) found no significant statistical association between entry into caregiving in 2001 or 2004 and employment status in 2004, as did Alpass et al. (2017) in their study based on the *Health, Work and Retirement* survey conducted in New Zealand from 2010 to 2014. Other evidence suggests that schedule flexibility and the ability to reduce working hours are associated with more hours of informal care and that this association is due to a selection process, as future caregivers preemptively (re)direct themselves towards more flexible sectors (Bryan, 2012). Furthermore, caregiving is more likely for men and women with a history of lower levels of employment (Young and Grundy, 2008) or with lower attachment (part-time or unemployment) to work (Henz, 2010). Yet several studies found gendered patterns. In Australia, women working full-time in the years prior are less likely to provide *residing* or *intensive* care, while men, either working full- or part-time, are less likely to provide intensive care (Nguyen and Connelly, 2017).

Another set of studies focuses on the effect of caregiving on employment. Caregiving responsibility was found not to be related to labor force participation for men in the United States, according to a study conducted on data from the *Health and Retirement Study*, yet women caregivers for parents and/or grandchildren were less likely to be in the labor force, suggesting a more complex interaction between work and informal caregiving (Lee and Tang, 2015). Indeed, taking into consideration time spent in caregiving paints a different picture. Based on data from the *Survey of Health, Ageing and Retirement*, Fontaine (2009) found a drop from a 63 percent employment rate for caregivers allocating one hour to informal care a day to a 5 percent employment rate for those spending over eight hours a day on such activities. This corroborates Bolin et al.'s (2008) findings on the same data, as they find informal care to have a negative and significant effect on employment probability, both for men and women, as well as a significant and negative effect on work hours, more so for women. These results differ, however, depending on care recipients. Caregiving for a disabled spouse, more specifically, would lead to early retirement and financial instability for women (Pavalko and Artis, 1997) and delayed retirement and lower job satisfaction for men (Dentinger and Clarkberg, 2002).

MULTIDIMENSIONAL TRAJECTORIES COMBINING WORK AND FAMILY

Another strand of research incorporates both work and family trajectories in pattern determination. In doing so, they conceptualize work trajectories and family trajectories as interlocked multidimensional life-course processes. These studies paying attention to both the career path and subsequent family events usually identify trajectories by sequence analysis and OMA or multichannel sequence analysis and cluster analysis, widely accepted as a useful tool for life-course scholars (Aisenbrey and Fasang, 2010). Sequence analysis aims to describe, explain and understand multidimensional trajectories and allows the taking into account of the timing, sequence and order of events (Abbott and Forrest, 1986; Abbott, 1995).

Family and working lives are simultaneously defined as individuals get older. An example is provided by Aassve et al. (2007) in their study based on a *BHPS* sample of 578 young British women born in 1960 and 1969, in which they use dichotomous variables for employment and union formation as well as a continuous variable for the number of children women have had. Nine trajectories are identified: four clusters are work-driven, and among them, three are characterized by early entry into the labor market while the other is defined by a long period of time spent on education; for the five remaining clusters, fertility events are a prominent feature, and these clusters are much more heterogeneous.

A more elaborate typology is established by Macmillan and Copher (2005), who use data from the NLSY79 and combined marital status (either never married, married, separated, divorced or widowed), parenthood status (with or without children), employment status (not employed, less than 35 hours of work a week, or 35 hours or more a week) and schooling (in or out of school) to establish typical work–life "pathways" throughout the life course, distinguishing between "rapid school-to-parent transition", "extended schooling-to-delayed work transition" or "school-to-work-to-work and family transition". Integrating not only parenthood status but the number and timing of children, García-Manglano (2015) identifies four trajectories for mothers, using the *National Longitudinal Survey of Young Women*, a sample of women aged 14 to 24 first interviewed in 1968: those consistently detached from the labor force, those who gradually increased their labor market attachment, those who worked intensely in young adulthood but dropped out of the workforce after midlife and those who were steadily employed across midlife. Most recently, Aisenbrey and Fasang (2017) compare work–life trajectories based on the NLSY79 sample, as well as the German *National Education Panel Study*. They build a seven-cluster typology, incorporating occupational prestige, marital status and presence and number of children. Similar methods were applied to a British survey, the *National Survey of Health and Development*, by Lacey et al. (2016), who establish 11 ideal types of work–family configurations over the life course: "work, early family", "work, early family, retired", "work, later family", "work, later family, retired", "work, marriage, non-parent", "work, no family", "later family, work break", "early family, work break", "part-time work, early family" (the modal type for women), "no paid work, early family" and "teen parent". Examining the effect of work–life trajectories on late-life employment, Stafford et al. (2018) apply standard sequence analysis to the same data and develop an eight-cluster typology, very similar to the former, with the exclusion of retirement stages.

Pailhé et al. (2013) focus on linked lives and investigate couple trajectories. Using retrospective data from the French cross-sectional *Family and Employers Survey* (Institut national d'études démographiques, 2004–2005), they establish an 11-category typology of trajectories for 950 long-lasting couples, depending on female and male employment path (full- or part-time employment, short-term job, unemployment, inactivity), number of children and timing of childbearing. Nearly half of their sample are couples with full-time working mothers and fathers and belong to either "work-oriented, 1 child", "0 or 1 postponed child", "spaced births", "2 children and full-time employment" or "3 children and full-time employment" clusters; 13 percent are couples with part-time working mothers, while almost one in four couples are characterized by mothers shifting to inactivity.

Finally, a study based on data from the BHPS *Understanding Society* sample from 1991 to 2001 has used similar methods yet with a different type of information, focusing no longer on family configuration but on time spent on informal caregiving (Carmichael and Ercolani, 2016). Depending on employment status (full-time, part-time or not employed), the presence of young children and the amount of time spent in informal caregiving, they distinguish five "employment-caregiving pathways": full-time careers, evolving careers, part-time careers, caring-intensive and decaying careers.

PAID AND UNPAID WORK THROUGHOUT THE LIFE COURSE

A prolific literature incorporates time use rather than formal employment or family statuses in objectifying work–life arrangements. It mostly focuses on the private life; that is, on time dedicated to housework and/or leisure and on the division of labor between men and women and among partners.

A first group of studies uses panel data and men and women's reports on either the distribution of domestic tasks between spouses or their hours of unpaid work throughout the life course. Grunow et al. (2012) measure the division of labor between partners using the *Bamberg Panel Study of Married Couples* (a 14-year panel study conducted in Germany from 1988 to 2002) by constructing a "Task Participation Index". Using questions on whether the respondent or their partner takes up specific chores, they identify four types of division of labor: "strongly traditional", "traditional", "egalitarian" and "role reversal". Using event-history models, they investigate its evolution depending on marriage duration and presence and age of children. Focusing on same-sex couples, Bauer (2016) uses similar items present in the *Generations and Gender Survey* from 2002 to 2013 and constructs an "equality index" (ratio of number of tasks shared to overall number of tasks), a "segregation index" (number and extensiveness of tasks always or usually done by one partner) and a "balance index" (ratio of both partners' engagement in all chores), studying their evolution depending on partnership duration and children in the household. These studies offer a relative measure of work–life arrangements, focusing on the share of housework which falls to each member of a couple. Yet these measures seem to rely on implicit assumptions regarding housework and care work which might misrepresent couples' experience, as they overlook the total burden of domestic work and are limited to "a set of repetitive physical tasks", excluding various forms of affective or administrative work (Eichler and Albanese, 2007).

Other studies use absolute numbers rather than relative measures, often relying on declared weekly hours. Baxter et al. (2008) use random-effect models on data from an Australian panel survey, *Negotiating the Life Course*, and observe the variation in weekly hours spent on housework (limited to preparing meals, doing dishes, shopping, laundry, vacuuming and cleaning) when transitioning from cohabitation to marriage, marriage to cohabitation, and marriage to separation, as well as transitions to first- or second-order parenthood. Killewald and García-Manglano (2016) apply similar methods to American data using the *Panel Study of Income Dynamics* from 1984 to 2013. Gjerdingen and Center (2005) have elaborated a longitudinal survey design, including questions on the number of hours spent on housework or paid work, but on a very limited sample of 128 couples residing in Minnesota and over a limited period (during pregnancy and six months after childbirth).

Another group of studies uses cross-sectional data and constitutes life-cycle stages based on the main family situations. Large-scale cross-sectional surveys permit several robust analyses which, even though not longitudinal, incorporate the life course in work–life considerations.

Bühlmann et al. (2009) capture work–life arrangements through measures of declared hours spent in paid and unpaid work, available in the 2004 *European Social Survey*, and distinguish between five "biographical stages" : "no child, no child plan", "expecting child" (according to at least one member of the couple), "first child aged 0 to 2", "children between 2 and 5" and "last child over 5". Although this categorization provides an overview of various *parenting* stages, it remains limited in terms of *life course* stages.

Time spent in daily activities is also measured through time-use data in which people keep a time diary on randomly selected days, which avoids bias in reporting time. Focusing on leisure, Degenne and Lebeaux (2003) establish daily timetables for individuals throughout the life course and identify specific patterns for each type of household configuration. A more comprehensive approach is provided by Anxo et al. (2011), as they examine the evolution of time use through nine life stages based on living situation, age, presence and age of children and employment status: single individuals under 36 living with their parents; single individuals under 36 living on their own; couples in which women are under 46 and without children; couples with children whose mean age is under 6; couples with children whose mean age is between 6 and 15; couples with children whose mean age is between 16 and 25; midlife "empty nest" couples without resident children, where women are 45 to 59; older retired couples without resident children, both members over 60; older retired singles without resident children over 60. In addition to their more extensive life-course measure, they rely on time-use diaries from national time-use surveys rather than questionnaire information, which was found to be more accurate. Work–life arrangements are measured through time spent on paid work, unpaid work (housework and care activities) and leisure time.

Different approaches to the evolution of time use over the life course have been adopted. Using diary data from the German *Mobility Panel* from 1994 to 2014, Scheiner (2016) studies the effect of key life events on the change in time use: the birth of a first child, of another child, a child moving out, household formation *or* separation from a partner, entry into or exit from the labor market and retirement. As was found using employment patterns, transition to parenthood is associated with stronger gendered division of unpaid work (Baxter et al., 2015). Time spent in unpaid work considerably rises for women after childbirth (Gjerdingen and Center, 2005; Baxter et al., 2008; Bühlmann et al., 2009; Dribe and Stanfors, 2009; Anxo et al., 2011). Evidence also finds that women spend more time and men less time on domestic work after the transition to marriage, and that this gender gap widens throughout the relationship (Grunow et al., 2012). The result holds even for same-sex couples (Bauer, 2016). The retirement stage has been associated with a less traditional division of labor, as each spouse spends more time in housework, both in their own chores domain (female or male) and their spouse's, and both husbands and wives benefit from a relief in females' chores when their partner retires (Szinovacz, 2000). Widowhood, however, yields different results for men and women, resulting in an increase in domestic chores for men and a decrease for women.

WORK–LIFE STRATEGIES

The quantitative studies of work–life arrangements presented so far have been largely dominant in sociological and economics studies integrating a life-course approach. Yet they offer limited insights into how individuals operate everyday trade-offs and how they choose (or declare choosing) to do so (Gregory and Milner, 2009). Grunow and Evertsson (2016) advocate for a qualitative approach to work–life issues, focusing on expecting, well-educated, dual-earner couples. A previous study conducted by Becker and Moen (1999) consisting of 117 interviews with a similar population of interest but at various points in their life course leads to a better understanding of agency in reconciling work and private life. By comparing four different life stages, which they refer to as "anticipatory", "launching", "establishment" and "shifting gears", they identify three types of work–life strategies, all relying on a "scaling back" attitude following parenthood: "placing limits" is a strategy elaborated as a couple or by the wife and consists of limiting work commitments; "having a one-job, one-career" marriage is mostly described as an individual strategy and consists of designating one partner (most often, the male partner) as primary breadwinner and the other as primary caregiver; finally, the "trading off" strategy is presented as a couple strategy, in which both partners alternate roles depending on opportunities or life-course-related events. Similar arrangements have been identified for an Austrian sample of 22 educated mothers and fathers (Schmidt, 2017): strategies ranged from "shared breadwinning" to "sole breadwinning" (systematically fathers) and included "supplemented breadwinning" (in which fathers were also considered as carers) and "reluctant breadwinning" (in which fathers were dissatisfied with their sole-breadwinner status).

Combining qualitative interviews with quantitative analysis, Pixley (2008) also establishes a typology of work–life strategies among heterosexual couples, incorporating more distinctly relations of power between both partners: he defines five clusters of "career hierarchy patterns", including the "equal gains" cluster, the "taking turns cluster" and the "husband large gains cluster", based on several decisions that were made along the life course and identified as "career-prioritizing".

These studies examine work–life strategies as joint decisions between members of a couple regarding paid work. Yet, work–life strategies entail various decisions along the life course, notably regarding care work rather than paid work. Loder (2005) sheds light on various "life course strategies" adopted by her sample of 31 women administrators in the United States, at different life stages, which can differ in the types of care arrangements: while Black women much rely on extended women-kinship ties for help in housework and childcare, White women rely primarily on their spouse. In a rare study focusing on men, Halrynjo (2009) discerns four adaptation strategies depending on whether a high or a low amount of time is spent on work and care. Da Roit and Naldini (2010) explore strategies in another type of care work, conducting 27 interviews with Italian workers (at least 20 hours a week; 22 of the workers were female) providing care for a dependent relative. The researchers objectify care strategies according to four types of care arrangement, which can be used in turn by interviewees: "patchworking" when no constant presence is needed; "outsourcing" care work to paid help (specifically, to migrants); "recohabitation", perceived as "unrealistic"; and "institutionalization" as a "last resort". Most interviewees go from patchworking to outsourcing, eventually leading to institutionalization. Although this study does not adopt a life-course approach, it sheds light on a specific life stage often discarded in work–life research, when informal care is provided to sick or disabled relatives.

PERCEPTION OF WORK–LIFE CONFLICT OVER THE LIFE COURSE

Intertwinement between work and home and impediment of one sphere over the other have been largely studied, mostly through quantitative analysis relying on subjective measures of "conflict", "balance" or "spillover". Psychologists and management researchers have abundantly written about *perceived* conflict over the life course using subjective – and quantitative – measures. These subjective measures can be divided into three categories, following their chronological development: measures of conflict from work to family, measures of conflict from family to work, and measures of positive enrichment from one domain to the other. Those three types of measures have so far been independently reviewed (see Byron, 2005 for a review of work-to-family conflict; Bellavia and Frone, 2005 for a review of family-to-work conflict; Crain and Hammer, 2013 for a review of work–life enrichment; and Greenhaus and Allen, 2011 for a general review), but have yet to be presented altogether in regard to their life-course approach. Relying on several theoretical paradigms such as "border theory" (Clark, 2000) or "ecological systems theory" (Voydanoff, 2002; Moen and Chesley, 2008; Moen et al., 2008; Perry-Jenkins et al., 2013) or "demand and resources theory" (Demerouti et al., 2012), this literature explores interconnections between work and family spheres and measures how one imprints on the other.

Even though the longitudinal and life-course approaches are widely referred to in psychological work, few papers adopt the former, and much fewer adopt the latter. Darcy et al. (2012) conduct a cross-sectional study over a sample of 729 employees in 15 organizations in the Republic of Ireland. They take into account the effects of career stages defined by age – that is, "early career stage" (age 18–29), "developing career" (age 30–39), "consolidating career stage" (age 40–49) and "pre-retirement stage" (age 50 and more) – on conflict from work to family.

More papers focus on family–work conflict at specific life stages. First-order parenthood is, in that sense, a source of subjective work–life conflict for both mothers and fathers (Lin and Burgard, 2018) and workers with children are found to experience more family–work conflict than non-parents (Hill et al., 2008), yet mothers would experience it more so than fathers (Dilworth, 2004). Grunow and Evertsson (2016) also found in their sample of expecting couples that fathers did not express concern regarding juggling work and care, unlike mothers. Effects of parenthood, however, vary as children get older and parity gets higher. Mothers with preschool-age children were found to report especially high work–family and family–work conflict (Moen and Roehling, 2005). Conflicting results are found regarding school-age children, women experiencing either less work–family conflict (Roehling et al., 2003) or more family–work spillover when their youngest child is in elementary school, or a teenager (Martinengo et al., 2010), although these differences might reflect variations in measures. Based on the *European Working Conditions Survey*, Anxo et al. (2013) found the impact of parenthood on work–life conflict to be indeed limited to young children in pre-school, but only for men – the impact for women extended to "the whole parenting period". This prolonged effect of parenthood for women seems corroborated by a qualitative study on Scottish men and women in midlife, conducted by Emslie and Hunt (2009), in which men declared having experienced conflict when their children were young, while women referred to their work–life conflict as a current issue. In addition to children's ages, their number also stirs towards more or less work–life conflict and varying work–life arrangements. Dilworth (2004) finds that having several children rather than one diminishes negative spillover from family to work. Union formation can also have an impact on work–life conflict in other ways: emotional support from a spouse, for instance, can alleviate work–life conflict (Loder, 2005; Thorstad, 2006).

Papers that adopt a more comprehensive approach to work and family roles as having both a negative and positive influence on one another (Hanson et al., 2006; Carlson et al., 2006; Zimmerman and Hammer, 2010) *do not* attempt to measure such "enrichment" throughout the life course, and authors who have, used different measures to do so. Using the *Mid-Life in the United States* study, Lin and Burgard (2018) have developed quite resilient measures of positive spillover, two four-item scales (from work to family and from family to work). They observe a limited significant change in negative *and* positive home–work spillover up until children reach adolescence, and a decline in negative home–work and work–home spillover as they reach young adulthood. First-order parenthood leads to an increase in positive work–home spillover for men and a decrease for women. However, these results rely on a limited sample of 16 new fathers and 11 new mothers.

Research on other life events suggests that the life stage associated with informal caregiving leads to increased reported conflict, especially for women and even more so if care recipients are impaired (Kwak et al., 2012). However, based on a literature review, Demerouti et al. (2012) describe late adulthood as a period of low conflict and high facilitation between work and life and high resources and low demands in terms of work and family. Grzywacz et al. (2002) also find a curvilinear relationship between negative work–family positive spillover and age, net of family structure, identifying a specific age effect on work–life conflict in which conflict would diminish for senior workers. Yet, the lack of questions regarding informal care work often leads to identifying midlife and later life with an alleviation of work–life conflict, as children move out and parents enter the "empty nest stage" (Hill et al., 2008; Erickson et al., 2010; Martinengo et al., 2010). Moreover, eldercare providers might adapt their work schedules and commitment to facilitate care work, as suggested by Barrah et al. (2004), leading to no effect of time spent providing eldercare per week on family–work conflict. This mixed evidence suggests that further research is needed to shed light on the additional constraints weighing on contemporary senior workers, too often neglected so far.

While such subjective measures, from work to family or family to work, positive or negative, often have the advantage of being available in longitudinal surveys, thus facilitating a life-course approach, they also present a set of inconveniences which ought not to be overlooked. Mainly, the lack of consensus around specific phrasings has led to inconsistent results between studies (Allen et al., 2000). Most often, items used to identify determinants of conflict implicitly feature the most probable causes, making the results tautological (Pichler, 2009). Other subjective measures have been used by sociologists to study the evolution of work–life conflict over the life course, but do not avoid risks of inconsistency and do not discern the source of the conflict (between work and family). For instance, Laurijssen and Glorieux (2013) measure "work–life *balance*" by feeling more or less time pressure, with an eight-item index constructed with data from the longitudinal Flemish SONAR survey (Study Group from Education to the Labor Market). Comparing cross-lagged and synchronous-effects models, they conclude that it takes time for people to adapt their work to their family conditions. Milkie et al. (2004) use retrospective time diaries and subjective indicators. They adopt a more specific measure, feelings about time spent with children ("Do you think you spend about the right amount of time with your youngest/oldest child in a typical week, too much, or too little?"), available in the *National Survey of Parents* 1999–2000. Parents of young children report feeling more time deficit with children than parents of adolescents. Overall, fathers feel more time-constrained than mothers, due to their higher time devoted to paid work. This result highlights the relevance of combining subjective and objective indicators of work–life conflict.

CONCLUSION

The life-course approach provides a dynamic conceptualization of women and men's behaviors that captures the changes families experience over time. This overview of research explored work–life reconciliation issues over the life course, including both life-stage-specific research and longitudinal approaches and quantitative as well as qualitative work. This prolific literature mostly relies on objective measurements of work–life trade-offs (either on a daily basis at various points in life, or throughout the life course). Studies focusing on subjective work–life conflict less frequently adopt a life-course perspective and indicators are insufficiently harmonized. We find that research attempting to connect objective work–life arrangements to reported work–life conflict is strikingly lacking. A more comprehensive and inductive approach to work–life conflict, combining both subjective and objective measures and integrating its various sources, has yet to be incorporated in this burgeoning literature to expand our knowledge of workers' and individuals' everyday lives and life trajectories, how they are shaped and how early life conditions relates to later work–life conflict. Such a program is in line with gaps in life-course sociology, which "needs to answer satisfactorily the question of what kind of mechanisms operate to relate early conditions in life to later outcomes" (Mayer, 2009, p.423). This would lead to a better understanding of the impact of work–life conflict on different outcomes and especially on health (Kinnunen et al., 2004; Perry-Jenkins et al., 2007; Cullati, 2014; Westrupp et al., 2016).

Most studies investigating social inequalities in relation to work–life issues have pondered on how pre-existing inequalities might shape heterogeneous life trajectories and reported work–life conflict and how inequalities, especially gender inequalities, *deepen* over the life course (Anxo et al., 2011; Grunow et al., 2012; Aisenbrey and Fasang, 2017). Adopting a life-course perspective when considering work–life issues that takes into consideration differences in work–life conflict both throughout life stages and *within* each life stage could further our knowledge on how inequalities are reproduced, and therefore could pave the way for more egalitarian and inclusive social policies (Moen and Sweet, 2004; Bovenberg, 2005, 2008).

REFERENCES

Aassve, Arnstein, Billari, Francesco C., and Piccarreta, Raffaella (2007), "Strings of Adulthood: A Sequence Analysis of Young British Women's Work-Family Trajectories". *European Journal of Population*, **23** (3–4), 369–88.

Abbott, Andrew (1995), "Sequence Analysis: New Methods for Old Ideas". *Annual Review of Sociology*, **21**, 93–113.

Abbott, Andrew, and Forrest, John (1986), "Optimal Matching Methods for Historical Sequences". *Journal of Interdisciplinary History*, **16** (3), 471–94.

Aisenbrey, Silke, and Fasang, Anette (2010), "New Life for Old Ideas: The "Second Wave" of Sequence Analysis Bringing the "Course" Back into the Life Course". *Sociological Methods and Research*, **38**, 420–62.

Aisenbrey, Silke, and Fasang, Anette (2017), "The Interplay of Work and Family Trajectories over the Life Course: Germany and the United States in Comparison". *American Journal of Sociology*, **122** (5), 1448–84.

Allen, Tammy, Herst, David E. L., Bruck, Carly S., and Sutton, Martha (2000), "Consequences Associated with Work-to-Family Conflict: A Review and Agenda for Future Research". *Journal of Occupational Health Psychology*, **5** (2), 278–308.

Allison, Paul (1994), "Using Panel Data to Estimate the Effects of Events". *Sociological Methods & Research*, **23**, 174–99.

Alpass, Fiona, Keeling, Sally, Allen, Joanne, Stevenson, Brendan and Stephens, Christine (2017), "Reconciling Work and Caregiving Responsibilities among Older Workers in New Zealand". *Journal of Cross-Cultural Gerontology*, **32** (3), 323–37.

Anxo, Dominique, Franz, Christina, and Kümmerling, Angelika (2013), "Working Time and Work–Life Balance in a Life Course Perspective: A Report Based on the Fifth European Working Conditions Survey". Eurofound.

Anxo, Dominique, Mencarini, Letizia, Pailhé, Ariane, Solaz, Anne, Tanturri, Maria Letizia and Flood, Lennart (2011), "Gender Differences in Time Use over the Life Course in France, Italy, Sweden and the US". *Feminist Economics*, **17** (3), 159–95.

Barrah, Jaime, Shultz, Kenneth, Baltes, Boris and Stolz, Heidi (2004), "Men's and Women's Eldercare-Based Work-Family Conflict: Antecedents and Work-Related Outcomes". *Fathering: A Journal of Theory, Research and Practice about Men as Fathers*, **2** (3), 305–30.

Bauer, Gerrit (2016), "Gender Roles, Comparative Advantages and the Life Course: The Division of Domestic Labor in Same-Sex and Different-Sex Couples". *European Journal of Population*, **32** (1), 99–128.

Baxter, Janeen, Buchler, Sandra, Perales, Francisco and Western, Mark (2015), "A Life-Changing Event: First Births and Men's and Women's Attitudes to Mothering and Gender Divisions of Labor". *Social Forces*, **93** (3), 989–1014.

Baxter, Janeen, Hewitt, Belinda and Haynes, Michele (2008), "Life Course Transitions and Housework: Marriage, Parenthood and Time on Housework". *Journal of Marriage and Family*, **70** (2), 259–72.

Becker, Penny Edgell, and Moen, Phyllis (1999), "Scaling Back: Dual-Earner Couples' Work-Family Strategies". *Journal of Marriage and Family*, **61** (4), 995–1007.

Bellavia, Gina, and Frone, Michael (2005), "Work-Family Conflict". In Barling, Julian, Kelloway, Kevin, and Frone, Michael (eds), *Handbook of Work Stress*, Thousand Oaks, CA: SAGE, 113–147.

Berecki-Gisolf, Janneke, Lucke, Jayne, Hockey, Richard and Dobson, Annette (2008), "Transitions into Informal Caregiving and out of Paid Employment of Women in Their 50s". *Social Science & Medicine*, **67** (1), 122–127.

Bianchi, Suzanne M., and Milkie, Melissa A. (2010), "Work and Family Research in the First Decade of the 21st Century". *Journal of Marriage and Family*, **72** (3), 705–25.

Blair-Loy, Mary (2001), "Cultural Constructions of Family Schemas: The Case of Women Finance Executives". *Gender and Society*, **15** (5), 687–709.

Bolin, Kristian, Lindgren, Björn and Lundborg, Petter (2008), "Your Next of Kin or Your Own Career?" *Journal of Health Economics*, **27** (3), 718–38.

Bovenberg, A. Lans (2005), "Balancing Work and Family Life during the Life Course". *The Economist*, **153** (4), 399–423.

Bovenberg, A. Lans (2008), "The Life-Course Perspective and Social Policies: An Overview of the Issues". *CESifo Economic Studies*, **54** (4), 593–641.

Bryan, Mark L. (2012), "Access to Flexible Working and Informal Care". *Scottish Journal of Political Economy*, **59** (4), 361–89.

Bühlmann, Felix, Elcheroth, Guy and Tettamanti, Manuel (2009), "The Division of Labour among European Couples: The Effects of Life Course and Welfare Policy on Value–Practice Configurations". *European Sociological Review*, **26**, 49–66.

Byron, Kris (2005), "A Meta-Analytic Review of Work-Family Conflict and Its Antecedents". *Journal of Vocational Behavior*, **67**, 169–98.

Carlson, Dawn S., Kacmar, K. Michele, Wayne, Julie Holliday and Grzywacz, Joseph G. (2006), "Measuring the Positive Side of the Work–Family Interface: Development and Validation of a Work–Family Enrichment Scale". *Journal of Vocational Behavior*, **68** (1), 131–64.

Carmichael, Fiona, and Ercolani, Marco G. (2016), "Unpaid Caregiving and Paid Work over Life-Courses: Different Pathways, Diverging Outcomes". *Social Science & Medicine*, **156**, 1–11.

Clark, Sue Campbell (2000), "Work/Family Border Theory: A New Theory of Work/Family Balance". *Human Relations*, **53** (6), 747–70.

Crain, Tori L., and Hammer, Leslie B. (2013), "Work-Family Enrichment: A Systematic Review of Antecedents, Outcomes and Mechanisms". *Advances in Positive Organizational Psychology*, **1**, 303–28.

Cullati, Stéphane (2014), "The Influence of Work-Family Conflict Trajectories on Self-Rated Health Trajectories in Switzerland: A Life Course Approach". *Social Science & Medicine*, **113**, 23–33.

Da Roit, Barbara, and Naldini, Manuela (2010), "Should I Stay or Should I Go? Combining Work and Care for an Older Parent in Italy". *South European Society and Politics*, **15** (4), 531–51.

Damaske, Sarah, and Gerson, Kathleen (2008), "Viewing 21st Century Motherhood through a Work-Family Lens". in Korabik, Karen, Lero, Donna, and Whitehead, Denise (eds), *Handbook of Work-Family Integration*, New York, NY: Academic Press, 233–48.

Darcy, Colette, McCarthy, Alma, Hill, Jimmy and Grady, Geraldine (2012), "Work–Life Balance: One Size Fits All? An Exploratory Analysis of the Differential Effects of Career Stage". *European Management Journal*, **30**, 111–20.

Degenne, Alain, and Lebeaux, Marie-Odile (2003), "Le Temps Des Loisirs, Le Cycle de Vie et Ses Contraintes". In Donnat, Olivier (ed.), *Regards Croisés Sur Les Pratiques Culturelles*, Paris: Documentation française, 83–105.

Demerouti, Evangelia, Peeters, Maria C. W., and van der Heijden, Beatrice I. J. M. (2012), "Work-Family Interface from a Life and Career Stage Perspective: The Role of Demands and Resources". *International Journal of Psychology*, **47** (4), 241–58.

Dentinger, Emma, and Clarkberg, Marin (2002), "Informal Caregiving and Retirement Timing among Men and Women: Gender and Caregiving Relationships in Late Midlife". *Journal of Family Issues*, **23** (7), 857–79.

Dermott, Esther (2006), "What's Parenthood Got to Do with It? Men's Hours of Paid Work". *British Journal of Sociology*, **57** (4), 619–34.

Dilworth, Jennie E. Long (2004), "Predictors of Negative Spillover from Family to Work". *Journal of Family Issues*, **25** (2), 241–61.

Doress-Worters, Paula B. (1994), "Adding Elder Care to Women's Multiple Roles: A Critical Review of the Caregiver Stress and Multiple Roles Literatures". *Sex Roles*, **31** (9–10), 597–616.

Drasch, Katrin, and Matthes, Britta (2013), "Improving Retrospective Life Course Data by Combining Modularized Self-Reports and Event History Calendars: Experiences from a Large Scale Survey". *Quality & Quantity*, **47** (2), 817–38.

Dribe, Martin, and Stanfors, Maria (2009), "Does Parenthood Strengthen a Traditional Household Division of Labor? Evidence From Sweden". *Journal of Marriage and Family*, **71** (1), 33–45.

Eichler, Margrit, and Albanese, Patrizia (2007), "What Is Household Work? A Critique of Assumptions Underlying Empirical Studies of Housework and an Alternative Approach". *Canadian Journal of Sociology*, **32** (2), 227–58.

Elder, Glen H., Jr (1985), *Life Course Dynamics: Trajectories and Transitions 1968–1980*, Ithaca, NY: Cornell University Press.

Elder, Glen H., Jr (2000), "The Life Course", in Borgatta, Edgar F., and Montgomery, Rhonda J. V. (eds), *Encyclopedia of Sociology*, 2nd ed., New York, NY: Macmillan, 1614–22.

Elder, Glen H., Jr, Johnson, Monica Kirkpatrick, and Crosnoe, Robert (2003), "The Emergence and Development of Life Course Theory". In Mortimer, J.T., and Shanahan, M.J. (eds), *Handbook of the Life Course*, Boston, MA: Springer, 3–19.

Emslie, Carol, and Hunt, Kate (2009), "'Live to Work' or 'Work to Live'? A Qualitative Study of Gender and Work–Life Balance among Men and Women in Mid-Life". *Gender, Work & Organization*, **16** (1), 151–72.

Erickson, Jenet Jacob, Martinengo, Giuseppe, and Hill, E. Jeffrey (2010), "Putting Work and Family Experiences in Context: Differences by Family Life Stage". *Human Relations*, **63** (7), 955–79.

Ettner, Susan L. (1995), "The Impact of 'Parent Care' on Female Labor Supply Decisions". *Demography*, **32** (1), 63–80.

Evertsson, Marie (2013), "The Importance of Work: Changing Work Commitment Following the Transition to Motherhood". *Acta Sociologica*, **56** (2), 139–53.

Fagan, Jay, and Press, Julie (2008), "Father Influences on Employed Mothers' Work–Family Balance". *Journal of Family Issues*, **29** (9), 1136–60.

Florian, Sandra M. (2018), "Motherhood and Employment Among Whites, Hispanics and Blacks: A Life Course Approach". *Journal of Marriage and Family*, **80** (1), 134–49.

Fontaine, Roméo (2009), "Aider Un Parent Âgé Se Fait-Il Au Détriment de l'emploi ?" *Retraite et Société*, **58** (2), 31–61.

Gangl, Markus, and Ziefle, Andrea (2009), "Motherhood, Labor Force Behavior and Women's Careers: An Empirical Assessment of the Wage Penalty for Motherhood in Britain, Germany and the United States". *Demography*, **46** (2), 341–69.

García-Manglano, Javier (2015), "Opting Out and Leaning In: The Life Course Employment Profiles of Early Baby Boom Women in the United States". *Demography*, **52** (6), 1961–93.

Gerson, Kathleen (2008), "Viewing 21st Century Motherhood through a Work-Family Lens". In Korabik, Karen, Lero, Donna S., and Whitehead, Denise L. (eds), *Handbook of Work-Family Integration*, Cambridge, MA: Academic Press, 233–48.

Gjerdingen, Dwenda K., and Center, Bruce A. (2005), "First-Time Parents' Postpartum Changes in Employment, Childcare and Housework Responsibilities". *Social Science Research*, **34** (1), 103–16.

Greenhaus, Jeffrey H., and Allen, Tammy D. (2011), "Work–Family Balance: A Review and Extension of the Literature". In Campbell Quick, James, and Tetrick, Lois E. (eds), *Handbook of Occupational Health Psychology*, 2nd ed., Washington, DC: American Psychological Association, 165–83.

Gregory, Abigail, and Milner, Susan (2009), "Editorial: Work–Life Balance: A Matter of Choice?" *Gender, Work & Organization*, **16** (1), 1–13.

Grunow, Daniel, and Evertsson, Marie (2016), *Couples' Transitions to Parenthood: Analyzing Gender and Work in Europe*, Cheltenham, UK and Northampton, MA, US: Edward Elgar Publishing.

Grunow, Daniela, Schulz, Florian, and Blossfeld, Hans-Peter (2012), "What Determines Change in the Division of Housework over the Course of Marriage?" *International Sociology*, **27**, 289–307.

Grzywacz, Joseph G., Almeida, David M., and McDonald, Daniel A. (2002), "Work–Family Spillover and Daily Reports of Work and Family Stress in the Adult Labor Force". *Family Relations*, **51** (1), 28–36.

Halrynjo, Sigtona (2009), "Men's Work–Life Conflict: Career, Care and Self-Realization: Patterns of Privileges and Dilemmas". *Gender, Work & Organization*, **16** (1), 98–125.

Hanson, Ginger C., Hammer, Leslie B., and Colton, Cari L. (2006), "Development and Validation of a Multidimensional Scale of Perceived Work-Family Positive Spillover". *Journal of Occupational Health Psychology*, **11** (3), 249–65.

Henz, Ursula (2006), "Informal Caregiving at Working Age: Effects of Job Characteristics and Family Configuration". *Journal of Marriage and Family*, **68** (2), 411–29.

Henz, Ursula (2010), "Parent Care as Unpaid Family Labor: How Do Spouses Share?" *Journal of Marriage and Family*, **72** (1), 148–64.

Hill, E. Jeffrey, Jacob, Jenet I., Shannon, Laurie L., Brennan, Robert T., Blanchard, Victoria L., and Martinengo, Giuseppe (2008), "Exploring the Relationship of Workplace Flexibility, Gender and Life Stage to Family-to-Work Conflict and Stress and Burnout". *Community, Work & Family*, **11** (2), 165–81.

Hynes, Kathryn, and Clarkberg, Marin (2005), "Women's Employment Patterns during Early Parenthood: A Group-Based Trajectory Analysis". *Journal of Marriage and Family*, **67** (1), 222–39.

Jacobs, Jerry, and Gerson, Kathleen (2001), "Overworked Individuals or Overworked Families? Explaining Trends in Work, Leisure and Family Time". *Work and Occupations*, **28**, 40–63.

Johnson, David (2005), "Two-Wave Panel Analysis: Comparing Statistical Methods for Studying the Effects of Transitions". *Journal of Marriage and Family*, **67** (4), 1061–75.

Kahn, Joan R., García-Manglano, Javier, and Bianchi, Suzanne M. (2014), "The Motherhood Penalty at Midlife: Long-Term Effects of Children on Women's Careers". *Journal of Marriage and Family*, **76** (1), 56–72.

Killewald, Alexandra, and García-Manglano, Javier (2016), "Tethered Lives: A Couple-Based Perspective on the Consequences of Parenthood for Time Use, Occupation and Wages". *Social Science Research*, **60**, 266–82.

Kinnunen, Ulla, Geurts, Sabine, and Mauno, Saija (2004), "Work-to-Family Conflict and Its Relationship with Satisfaction and Well-Being: A One-Year Longitudinal Study on Gender Differences". *Work & Stress*, **18** (1), 1–22.

Kwak, Minyoung, Ingersoll-Dayton, Berit, and Kim, Jeungkun (2012), "Family Conflict from the Perspective of Adult Child Caregivers: The Influence of Gender". *Journal of Social and Personal Relationships*, **29** (4), 470–87.

Lacey, Rebecca, Stafford, Mai, Sacker, Amanda, and McMunn, Anne (2016), "Work-Family Life Courses and Subjective Wellbeing in the MRC National Survey of Health and Development (the 1946 British Birth Cohort Study)". *Journal of Population Ageing*, **9** (1–2), 69–89.

Laurijssen, Ilse, and Glorieux, Ignace (2013), "Balancing Work and Family: A Panel Analysis of the Impact of Part-Time Work on the Experience of Time Pressure". *Social Indicators Research*, **112** (1), 1–17.

Lee, Yeonjung, and Tang, Fengyan (2015), "More Caregiving, Less Working: Caregiving Roles and Gender Difference". *Journal of Applied Gerontology*, **34** (4), 465–83.

Lin, Katherine Y., and Burgard, Sarah A. (2018), "Working, Parenting and Work-Home Spillover: Gender Differences in the Work-Home Interface across the Life Course". *Advances in Life Course Research*, **35**, 24–36.

Loder, Tondra L. (2005), "Women Administrators Negotiate Work-Family Conflicts in Changing Times: An Intergenerational Perspective". *Educational Administration Quarterly*, **41** (5), 741–76.

Macmillan, Ross, and Copher, Ronda (2005), "Families in the Life Course: Interdependency of Roles, Role Configurations and Pathways". *Journal of Marriage and Family*, **67** (4), 858–79.

Marks, Nadine F., Lambert, James David and Choi, Heejeong (2002), "Transitions to Caregiving, Gender and Psychological Well-Being: A Prospective U.S. National Study". *Journal of Marriage and Family*, **64** (3), 657–67.

Martinengo, Giuseppe, Jacob, Jenet I., and Hill, E. Jeffrey (2010), "Gender and the Work-Family Interface: Exploring Differences Across the Family Life Course". *Journal of Family Issues*, **31** (10), 1363–90.

Mayer, Karl Ulrich (2009), "New Directions in Life Course Research". *Annual Review of Sociology*, **35**, 413.

Milkie, Melissa A., Mattingly, Marybeth J., Nomaguchi, Kei M., Bianchi, Suzanne M., and Robinson, John P. (2004), "The Time Squeeze: Parental Statuses and Feelings about Time with Children". *Journal of Marriage and Family*, **66** (3), 739–761.

Moen, Phyllis, and Chesley, Noelle (2008), "Toxic Job Ecologies, Time Convoys and Work-Family Conflict: Can Families (Re) Gain Control and Life-Course 'Fit'?" In Korabik, Karen, Lero, Donna S. and Whitehead, Denise L. (eds), *Handbook of Work-Family Integration*, San Diego, MA: Academic Press, 95–122.

Moen, Phyllis, Kelly, Erin, and Huang, Qinlei (2008), "Work, Family and Life-Course Fit: Does Control over Work Time Matter?", *Journal of Vocational Behavior*, **73** (3), 414–25.

Moen, Phyllis, Robison, Julie, and Fields, Vivian (1994), "Women's Work and Caregiving Roles: A Life Course Approach". *Journal of Gerontology*, **49** (4), S176–86.

Moen, Phyllis, and Roehling, Patricia (2005), *The Career Mystique: Cracks in the American Dream*, Lanham, MD: Rowman & Littlefield.

Moen, Phyllis, and Sweet, Stephen (2004), "From 'Work–Family' to 'Flexible Careers': A Life-Course Reframing". *Community, Work & Family*, **7** (2), 209–26.

Murray, John, and Cutcher, Leanne (2012), "Gendered Futures, Constrained Choices: Undergraduate Perceptions of Work and Family". *Journal of Population Research*, **29** (4), 315–28.

Nguyen, Ha Trong, and Connelly, Luke B. (2017), "The Dynamics of Informal Care Provision in an Australian Household Panel Survey: Previous Work Characteristics and Future Care Provision". *Economic Record*, **93** (302), 395–419.

Pailhé, Ariane, Robette, Nicolas, and Solaz, Anne (2013), "Work and Family over the Life-Course: A Typology of French Long-Lasting Couples Using Optimal Matching". *Longitudinal and Life Course Studies*, **4** (3), 196–217.

Pavalko, Eliza K., and Artis, Julie E. (1997), "Women's Caregiving and Paid Work: Causal Relationships in Late Midlife". *Journals of Gerontology Series B: Psychological Sciences and Social Sciences*, **52B** (4), S170–79.

Perry-Jenkins, Maureen, Goldberg, Abbie E., Pierce, Courtney P., and Sayer, Aline G. (2007), "Shift Work, Role Overload and the Transition to Parenthood". *Journal of Marriage and Family*, **69** (1), 123–38.

Perry-Jenkins, Maureen, Newkirk, Katie, and Ghunney, Aya K. (2013), "Family Work Through Time and Space: An Ecological Perspective". *Journal of Family Theory & Review*, **5** (2), 105.

Pichler, Florian (2009), "Determinants of Work-Life Balance: Shortcomings in the Contemporary Measurement of WLB in Large-Scale Surveys". *Social Indicators Research*, **92** (3), 449.

Pixley, Joy E. (2008), "Life Course Patterns of Career-Prioritizing Decisions and Occupational Attainment in Dual-Earner Couples". *Work and Occupations*, **35** (2), 127–63.

Roehling, Patricia, Moen, Phyllis, and Batt, Rosemary (2003), "When Work Spills Over into the Home and Home Spills Over into Work". In Moen, Phyllis (ed.), *It's About Time: Couples and Careers*, Ithaca, NY: ILR Press, 101–121.

Salmela-Aro, Katariina, Nurmi, Jari-Erik, Saisto, Terhi, and Halmesmäki, Erja (2000), "Women's and Men's Personal Goals during the Transition to Parenthood". *Journal of Family Psychology*, **14** (2), 171–186.

Scheiner, Joachim (2016), "Time Use and the Life Course: A Study of Key Events in the Lives of Men and Women Using Panel Data". *European Journal of Transport & Infrastructure Research*, **16** (4), 638.

Schmidt, Eva-Maria (2017), "Breadwinning as Care? The Meaning of Paid Work in Mothers' and Fathers' Constructions of Parenting". *Community, Work & Family*, **21** (4), 445–62.

Sefton, Tom, Evandrou, Maria, and Falkingham, Jane (2011), "Family Ties: Women's Work and Family Histories and Their Association with Incomes in Later Life in the UK". *Journal of Social Policy*, **40** (1), 41–69.

Stafford, Mai, Lacey, Rebecca, Murray, Emily, Carr, Ewan, Fleischmann, Maria, Stansfeld, Stephen, Xue, Baowen, et al. (2018), "Work–Family Life Course Patterns and Work Participation in Later Life". *European Journal of Ageing*, **16**, 83–94.

Szinovacz, Maximiliane E. (2000), "Changes in Housework After Retirement: A Panel Analysis". *Journal of Marriage and Family*, **62** (1), 78–92.

Thorstad, Roxane R., Anderson, Tamara L., Hall, M. Elizabeth Lewis, Willingham, Michele, and Carruthers, Lisa (2006), "Breaking the Mold: A Qualitative Exploration of Mothers in Christian Academia and Their Experiences of Spousal Support". *Journal of Family Issues*, **27** (2), 229–51.

Voydanoff, Patricia (2002), "Linkages Between the Work-Family Interface and Work, Family and Individual Outcomes: An Integrative Model". *Journal of Family Issues*, **23** (1), 138–64.

Westrupp, Elizabeth M., Strazdins, Lyndall, Martin, Angela, Cooklin, Amanda, Zubrick, Stephen R., and Nicholson, Jan M. (2016), "Maternal Work–Family Conflict and Psychological Distress: Reciprocal Relationships Over 8 Years". *Journal of Marriage and Family*, **78** (1), 107–26.

Wolf, Douglas, and Soldo, Beth J. (1995), "Married Women's Allocation of Time to Employment and Care of Elderly Parents". *Journal of Human Resources*, **29**, 1259–76.

Young, Harriet, and Grundy, Emily (2008), "Longitudinal Perspectives on Caregiving, Employment History and Marital Status in Midlife in England and Wales". *Health & Social Care in the Community*, **16** (4), 388–99.

Zagel, Hannah (2014), "Are All Single Mothers the Same? Evidence from British and West German Women's Employment Trajectories". *European Sociological Review*, **30** (1), 49.

Zimmerman, Kristi L., and Hammer, Leslie B. (2010), "Work–Family Positive Spillover: Where Have We Been and Where Are We Going?" In Houdmont, Jonathan, Leka, Stavroula, and Sinclair, Robert R. (eds), *Contemporary Occupational Health Psychology: Global Perspectives on Research, Education and Practice*, Volume 1, Chichester: Wiley-Blackwell, 272–95.

6.   Work-(later) life balance: shifting the temporal frame

Anne E. Barrett, Rachel Douglas and Jessica Noblitt

A reading of the literature on work–life balance could lead to the conclusion that this issue only faces those in young adulthood and early middle age. Across quantitative and qualitative methodological approaches, research tends to address the challenges confronting employed parents of young children, with few studies examining those faced by older adults (Bernard and Phillips 2007; Emslie and Hunt 2009; Loretto and Vickerstaff 2015; Sayer and Gornick 2009). Illustrating this pattern, a recent search of ProQuest's Sociological Abstracts database for peer-reviewed articles containing 'work–life balance' in the title revealed approximately 200 articles – fewer than 10 of which included 'older adults,' 'elderly' or 'later life' anywhere in the text. Closer inspection of this subset of articles revealed that the references to aging were limited in nearly all to brief mentions of the possibility of younger family members caring for older ones (Ackers 2003; Fernandez-Crehuet, Gimenez-Nadal and Reyes Recio 2016). This approach leaves many questions unanswered about work–life balance in the second half of life; however, the existing literature, focusing on earlier adulthood, provides a starting point for the development of these questions.

Prior studies tend to focus on examining either the factors influencing work–life balance (or imbalance) or the consequences of it. Numerous studies have identified individual char-acteristics shaping work–life balance, with gender, socioeconomic status and household structure receiving much attention (Byron 2005; Ford, Heinen and Langkamer 2007; Kasearu 2009; Milkie et al. 2010; Roehling, Jarvis and Swope 2005). Structural factors have also been identified, including work intensification, job stressors, social support and state or workplace policies permitting flexible schedules (Abendroth and den Dulk 2011; Haar et al. 2019; Ruppanner 2013; Yu 2014). Like its antecedents, the consequences of work–family balance are found at micro and macro levels. Studies find that work–life balance not only influences individuals' emotional and physical well-being and the quality of their relationships with their children and spouses or partners (Allen and Armstrong 2006; Gassman-Pines 2011; Gisler et al. 2018; Haar et al. 2014; Shafer et al. 2018; Symoens and Bracke 2015) but also impacts women's employment and fertility rates (Fernandez-Crehuet, Gimenez-Nadal and del Valle 2017; Luci-Greulich and Thévenon 2013).

While some findings are likely to extrapolate to the second half of life, others may not – given shifting investments in and orientations toward paid and unpaid work and other activ-ities. Perhaps most notably, middle-aged and older adults, especially women, often engage in other types of care work, namely care for older family members, spouses or partners and grandchildren – activities less often addressed by private or public policies (Biggs, Carr and Haapala 2015; Saraceno and Keck 2011). Further, changes accompanying aging – including physiological, psychological and social ones – can constrain or expand options and shift prior-ities regarding investments in various life domains, including paid and unpaid work, volunteer activities, leisure and social relationships.

This chapter discusses three issues raised by shifting the temporal frame on work–life balance to middle and later life. First, it examines the long-term effect of work–life balance in early adulthood, suggesting research directions that would illuminate a fuller range of its consequences. Second, the chapter addresses the issue of balancing paid work with care work for older family members, spouses or partners and grandchildren, pointing to the theoretical utility of research comparing role combinations and types of care work that vary in their prevalence across adulthood. Third, it discusses leisure – a domain receiving limited attention in the work–life balance literature. Leisure is brought into focus by employing an aging lens, as later life is often viewed in Western cultures as devoted to its pursuit (though far from universally experienced as such). We argue that motivating research on these issues would not only enrich the conceptual and theoretical underpinnings of work–life balance but also illuminate individuals' experiences across their increasingly longer lives.

DEMOGRAPHIC, ECONOMIC AND POLITICAL CONTEXT OF WORK–LIFE BALANCE IN LATER LIFE

The aging of most of the world's populations underscores the importance of considering work–life balance in later life. Although the timing of population aging varies across regions of the world, with the process beginning over a century ago in more developed nations, the fastest growing age group globally is older adults. According to a United Nations report, the number of adults aged 60 or over is projected to double between 2015 and 2030, with the number of those aged 80 or over (that is, the 'oldest-old') tripling. Also projected by 2030 is the outnumbering of children younger than 10 by those 60 or over (United Nations 2015). This shift is driven by two demographic trends – shrinking family size and increasing life expectancy. Women's average fertility rate globally has fallen from over five children in 1950 to 2.5 in 2015 (United Nations 2015). While families are getting smaller, lives are getting longer, with much of the recent expansion of life expectancy driven by improvements in later-life survival. Global estimates indicate that 60-year-olds can anticipate living another two decades, on average (United Nations 2015). These patterns yield decades of life – extending well beyond the care of (fewer) young children – during which individuals seek work–life balance.

Paid work is a central activity across many of these years, a reality made possible by improvements in health across cohorts and encouraged by policies aimed at reducing pension payouts. The United States provides an example. Later-life disability has been declining since the 1980s, due to medical and socioeconomic advances, including higher educational attainment (Schoeni, Freedman and Martin 2008). Also lengthening Americans' years of paid work was legislation passed in the 1980s, allowing individuals to retain full Social Security benefits and remain employed (Alley and Crimmins 2007). Moreover, the age for receipt of full Social Security benefits is higher for younger cohorts – 67 for those born in 1960 or later, compared with 65 for those born before 1940 (Social Security Administration 2019). The lengthening of paid work lives, a trend mirrored in many other Western nations, points to the importance of considering work–life balance in the second half of life.

Whether spent in employment or retirement, some portion of these years may involve declining health. The World Health Organization (2014) estimates that life expectancy at birth globally averages 71, while 'healthy life expectancy' – the number of years lived free of disease and disability – averages 62. These figures suggest that the work–life balance equation shifts across middle and later life, as health-related changes create new demands on time and energy. This issue, however, receives limited attention in the work–life balance literature, given its focus on younger (presumably healthy) working-age adults.

Colliding with these demographic and health trends are economic ones that further shape work–life balance in later life. In short, while the expansion of life expectancy and postponement of disability create new possibilities for achieving work–life balance across adulthood, economic trends restrict such options for many people. Rising economic inequality has intensified the pressure to remain in the paid labor force. Over the past four decades, income inequality has risen in nearly every world region (Alvaredo et al. 2018). As illustrations, the share of income received by the top 10 percent of earners in the United States and Canada increased from 34 percent in 1980 to more than 47 percent in 2016, while even more striking increases were observed in Russia (21 to more than 46 percent) and India (31 to 56 percent). These patterns hint at a reality experienced by a growing number of older adults – they lack the resources to exit the paid labor force even though poor health may limit their ability to work.

Driving these shifts is the rise of neoliberal political economies aimed at increasing profits of corporations, a goal ideologically based on an emphasis on individual rather than state responsibility for populace well-being (Polivka and Luo 2015). This goal has been sought through policies centering on low taxes, deregulation and privatization that together have eroded the social safety net for older adults. Illustrating this shift is the declining prevalence of defined benefit pension plans and the increase in defined contribution ones – a transition well underway in many Western nations (Ebbinghaus 2011). This transfer of risk from the collective to the individual has implications for work–life balance, as it requires more years of paid work for a growing segment of older adults globally. Adding to the economic pressures are moral ones, generated by the current emphasis on 'productive ageing' that leads to a view of 'additional years of healthy ageing [as] an economic resource not to be wasted' – with work offered 'as a legitimizing role for a long life' (Biggs et al. 2017, pp. 1477–78).

These demographic, economic and political shifts point to a need for researchers to give greater attention to work–life balance issues in middle and later life. They draw into question whether the existing literature applies to these life stages, when work–life balance often becomes work–life–health balance and pressures intensify to fill lives to their end with activities of economic value (Biggs et al. 2017; Vickerstaff 2010). With these concerns as a backdrop, we discuss three broad areas for further research on work–family balance in middle and later life: (1) long-term effects of early work–life balance, (2) work–life balance among older care providers and (3) leisure in later life.

LONG-TERM EFFECTS OF EARLY WORK–LIFE BALANCE

While the literature reveals numerous consequences of inadequate work–life balance, including greater stress, lower marital and parent–child relationship quality, lower life (and work) satisfaction and worse mental and physical health (Allen and Armstrong 2006; Gassman-Pines 2011; Gisler et al. 2018; Haar et al. 2014; Shafer et al. 2018; Symoens and Bracke 2015), the timeframe of analysis often is fairly short, leaving unanswered questions about possible long-term effects. Studies tend to examine work–family balance and the hypothesized outcomes either contemporaneously (Allen and Armstrong 2006; Haar et al. 2014) or over a short timespan (Peter, March and du Prel 2016; van Hooff et al. 2005). As an illustration, a study of over 3000 German employees examined the effect of work–family conflict on depressive symptoms but only over a three-year period (Peter et al. 2016). The study with the longest timeframe that we were able to identify in this literature examined the effect of work–family spillover on chronic conditions over a nine-year span (Lee et al. 2015). Little is known about the effect of work–life balance on individuals' well-being across the often three to five decades in the paid labor force.

Taking a longer-range view of the known short-term consequences of work–life balance raises avenues for both quantitative and qualitative studies. Using panel data following individuals over long timespans, quantitative research could address two voids in this literature: It could not only examine possible long-range consequences of early work–life balance but also describe changes in work–life balance across adulthood. An illustration is provided by parent–child relationships – a topic of interest to work–life balance researchers (Dinh et al. 2017; Milkie et al. 2010), as well as gerontologists (Suitor et al. 2016; Ward, Spitze and Deane 2009). Integrating and extending these literatures, research could illuminate how the interface of parenthood and paid work shapes the well-being of both generations across their lives, which may overlap for six or more decades. Further insight could be gained from qualitative work examining how individuals alter meanings of work–life balance across the life course, along with their strategies to achieve it. Such work could include further development of the concept of 'biographical work–life balance' that takes a long-range view of individuals' distribution of time across life domains and their satisfaction with it (Schilling 2015, p. 475).

Other directions for research on long-term effects of work–life balance are suggested by a closer consideration of the context of later life, including its health and social dimensions. Although studies examine health effects of work–life balance, we are aware of none examining effects on either the more negative health experiences of later life, like cognitive and functional decline, or the positive ones, like greater psychological well-being and wisdom. Turning to later life's social dimension, studies could examine whether achieving greater work–life balance in early or middle adulthood sets the stage for better social relationships in later life, with not only spouses and adult children but also siblings, friends and grandchildren. Related questions that remain unexamined include the potential effects of early work–life balance on living arrangements in later life, as well as the provision and receipt of care work. In short, more research is needed to examine how work–life balance, including institutional supports to encourage it, shapes the 'social convoys' accompanying individuals over their lives (Kahn and Antonucci 1980). Such studies may reveal that the benefits of work–life balance are more wide-ranging – over time and across life domains – than the current literature suggests.

Further research questions are raised by studies revealing work–life balance's effects manifesting at more macro levels, like fertility and employment rates (Fernandez-Crehuet et al. 2017; Luci-Greulich and Thévenon 2013). As an illustration, a study developing an international index capturing variation in conditions shaping fertility decisions, including perceived work–family balance and state policies addressing it, found that nations with the highest index values also have the highest fertility (see Denmark and the Netherlands; Fernandez-Crehuet et al. 2017). Looking beyond the years of child-bearing and child-rearing raises other macro-level phenomena to be examined. For example, cross-national research could examine the effect of state or workplace policies facilitating care for spouses or partners and older family members (as examples, paid leave or flexible hours) on a range of possible outcomes, such as the quality of intergenerational relationships and the proportion of older adults living in institutions versus the community. Other possibilities stem from women's more intensive investment in unpaid care work across their lives. In particular, work–life balance may impact women's employment rates across middle and later life and, consequently, their economic security in retirement.

WORK–LIFE BALANCE AMONG OLDER CARE PROVIDERS

With its focus on young parents with small children, the work–life balance literature leaves other realms of care work less explored, including care for grandchildren, spouses or partners, older family members, friends and neighbors. The limited attention is surprising, given the prevalence, intensity and duration of many of these care activities. For example, an estimated 17 percent of Americans provide unpaid care for someone 50 years or older, most often a parent or spouse (National Alliance for Caregiving and AARP Public Policy Institute 2015). The typical care provider is a 50-year-old adult daughter, who has cared for her 69-year-old mother for four years and currently provides approximately 24 hours of care per week. Some care providers' investments are even greater. For example, 12 percent have occupied this role for a decade or more, and nearly a quarter spend more than 41 hours weekly providing care (National Alliance for Caregiving and AARP Public Policy Institute 2015). Moreover, about half of Americans currently providing care for an older adult expect that they will be a caregiver (either for the current recipient or another) five years in the future (National Alliance for Caregiving and AARP Public Policy Institute 2015). Also prevalent, and often intensive, is care for grandchildren. An estimated 1 in 4 American preschool children is cared for by a grandparent, typically a grandmother (Laughlin 2013). Care by grandparents also is increasing, as suggested by research revealing that approximately 6 percent of American households in 2014 contained a grandparent and grandchild, up from 3 percent in 1970 (Ellis and Simmons 2014).

This care work raises work–life balance issues whether combined with paid work or not – and it frequently is. As an illustration, a survey of American caregivers found that 60 percent were employed, working an average of 35 hours a week (National Alliance for Caregiving and AARP Public Policy Institute 2015). Providing further evidence of care providers' juggling of roles, a survey of two public service organizations in the United Kingdom found that about 10 percent of employees were caregivers for someone over the age of 60 – one-third of whom were part of the 'sandwich generation' also caring for children (Bernard and Phillips 2007). Like other forms of unpaid care, grandchild care is frequently combined with paid work. Research finds that employed grandparents are as likely to provide care as those who are retired – with those clocking many hours in the paid labor force providing as much grandchild care as those working fewer hours (Harrington Meyer 2014). These patterns point to directions for further research, focusing on the many possible interfaces between types of paid and unpaid work in later life (for example, grandchild care and volunteering) – as well as their links with other life domains, such as leisure and social relationships. Such examinations could draw on concepts employed in the work–life balance literature (for example, work–family spillover), developing similar ones to more fully investigate the interplay between roles often held in later life (for example, grandchild care–spousal care spillover). These investigations would facilitate comparisons across role combinations experienced in different life stages that would illuminate work–life balance issues, along with yielding broader insight on constructions of work, family and the life course.

A comparative perspective on work–life balance across adulthood draws into focus an issue yet to be fully articulated by work–life balance scholars – similarities and differences in caring for children versus older adults. While sharing some challenges and rewards, they differ in ways that limit the extrapolation of much of the work–life balance literature to later life. Compared with childcare, care for older family members can be, on a day-to-day basis, more intense and less predictable – and last longer than was planned (Bernard and Phillips 2007; Dugan et al. 2016). An even more fundamental difference, however, stems from sociocultural constructions of the two life stages during which care needs are greatest – at life's beginning and its end. The much more positive view of infancy and childhood than 'deep old age,' when daily care needs arise, is reflected in the conditions encountered by care providers at each stage. The transition to parenthood is often a highly anticipated, visible and celebrated one, accompanied by advice and support from family members and friends – and workplace and state policies to accommodate care work. In contrast, acquiring the role of care provider for an older family member is not marked by celebration. Rather it is entered with some degree of apprehension and is rarely facilitated by workplace or state policies. It is invisible work performed by the 'shadow workforce' (Bookman and Harrington 2007). Yet another difference is the change in care demands over time: They decrease as children 'grow up' but increase as older adults grow frailer.

These differences in the content and conditions of care work are likely to have implications for work–life balance, and research could further examine them. Quantitative studies could systematically compare care for children versus older adults along several dimensions, including their challenges and rewards, the experience of combining them with paid work and institutional supports to facilitate this care work. Adding texture to our understanding of care work, qualitative studies could illuminate the shared and divergent meanings attached to care for children (and grandchildren) versus older adults. Such research also could examine shifting meanings of care work as individuals age through various roles involving care for younger and older family members (as well as similarly-aged spouses or partners), including their influence on meaning-making as care providers, perhaps become care recipients.

LEISURE IN LATER LIFE

Viewing work–life balance through an aging lens brings into focus a domain receiving limited attention in this literature – leisure. After all, later life is often viewed, in Western cultures, as a stage devoted to it. However, time-use data reveal fewer differences across age groups than this view would suggest. According to the American Time Use Survey, adults aged 65 or older spend more than seven hours a day in leisure and sports – compared with about five hours for younger adults (Bureau of Labor Statistics 2019). While these figures point to age differences, they also illustrate the substantial time that individuals, of all ages, spend in leisure pursuits – an amount that exceeds that of all other categories, except personal care (which includes sleep). It also exceeds time spent working for pay for all age groups except those between 25 and 54 – who spend only about one more hour working than engaging in leisure. These observations make the limited focus on leisure in studies of work–life balance particularly striking.

In many work–life balance studies, leisure receives either no mention or only a brief one (Kasearu 2009; Roehling et al. 2005). This observation resonates with a broader critique of work–life measures made by Pichler (2009, p. 461) who notes that studies 'partly put "life" into a black box: life means everything else than work, from cleaning, care work, leisure, family, to social life.' Exceptions can be found, such as Warren's (2004) quantitative study examining the effect of work–life balance on women's leisure, and Hilbrecht and colleagues' (2008) qualitative study examining teleworking mothers' constrained leisure opportunities. But this literature's focus on younger workers with children limits our understanding of the interface between work (paid and unpaid) and leisure among older adults. Exceptions also are found in studies examining the effect of work–life balance on an aspect of leisure – physical activity. These studies, however, view it as a health-related behavior, illustrated by its frequent examination along with others, such as alcohol consumption, smoking and sleep (Allen and Armstrong 2006; Lee et al. 2015; Moen, Fan and Kelly 2013). This framing treats leisure as a consequence of work (namely as constrained by it), rather than exploring more nuanced interconnections between these domains that involve preferences and meanings that shift across the life course.

A similar critique could be made of a related literature – gerontological studies of leisure's health effects. Many studies document leisure's positive effects on health and well-being (for a review see Adams, Leibbrandt and Moon 2011). Providing an illustration, a panel survey of older Taiwanese found that those engaging in more leisure activities, whether physical or sedentary, reported higher well-being eight years later (Ku, Fox and Chen 2016). This study also illustrates the typical framing of research on leisure in later life around gerontology's 'activity theory,' hinging on the straightforward assertion that higher levels of activity (social, physical, mental) enhance well-being. While such studies yield insight on how and why leisure impacts well-being, another avenue for research is suggested by an alternate framing of leisure. Derived from the work–life balance literature, it focuses on 'balance' rather than 'activity,' including its evolving meaning across adulthood.

Studies could give greater attention to these shifting meanings, and their implications for work–life balance, by examining their patterning by age as well as cohort. Such studies would extend the small literature addressing this issue – for example, Twenge and colleagues' (2010) study following three cohorts across 15 years. Comparing baby boomers, Generation X and Generation Y, the study found that each successive cohort valued leisure more highly – and paid work less highly – than did the previous cohort. But age differences also may operate, generated by social psychological processes unfolding as individuals grow older. Providing an example are shifts in goals based on perceived future time horizons – which lead older adults to prioritize emotionally meaningful and satisfying activities in the present over longer-term future rewards or achievement (Carstensen, Fung and Charles 2003). These age and cohort patterns point to an increasing valuation of leisure over time and across adulthood, an observation with implied but relatively unexplored implications for work–life balance.

IMPLICATIONS FOR WORK–LIFE BALANCE RESEARCH

Our analysis of the work–life balance literature through an aging lens revealed many unanswered questions that offer opportunities to researchers. Central among them is theoretical development of constructs central to this literature, indeed to much social science research – including work, care and family. For example, integrating research on later-life care work into the work–life balance literature could clarify the concept of unpaid work and facilitate research on its shifting interface with paid work across the life course. Greater focus on the second half of life also would aid efforts to unpack 'life' in the work–life balance by drawing attention not only to leisure, as a central but underexamined component of it, but also to individuals' changing investment in this realm, and others, as they age. Along with its benefits to theory, expanding the temporal scope of this research could have the practical consequence of bringing greater awareness among policymakers and the public to work–life balance's relevance across the life course and the need for structural changes that help individuals create it in their own lives.

Pursuing these research directions, however, is not without challenges. Among the most substantial is the tendency of researchers – along with the agencies funding their work and journals publishing it – to focus on particular life stages. For example, the mission of the National Institute on Aging, the primary funding agency for U.S. research on middle and later life, is 'to understand the nature of aging and the aging process, and diseases and conditions associated with growing older, in order to extend the healthy, active years of life' (National Institute on Aging 2020). This focus yields rich datasets describing the experience of later life but does not lend itself to research questions about large swaths of adulthood, such as two we suggested – the long-term consequences of work–life balance in early adulthood and shifting meanings of care work as individuals age through various care-provider, and perhaps care-recipient, roles. A related challenge stems from data collection decisions that reflect cultural assumptions about the relevance of various life domains across the life course and complicate attempts to fully examine work–life balance issues and to make comparisons across life stages. For example, large datasets collected through surveys with young adults tend to examine paid work and family roles, while those collected from older adults often focus on care work, health and (to a lesser extent) leisure. Drawing attention to these shortcomings of some of the existing data, however, may spark creative solutions to them, such as incorporating more retrospective accounts of paid and unpaid work into surveys of older adults.

In summary, our chapter makes the case for more work–life balance research that takes into account issues faced in the second half of life. To stimulate research in this direction, we outline three themes raised by examining work–life balance through an aging lens – the long-term effects of early work–life balance, work–life balance among older care providers and leisure in later life. However, numerous other themes could be explored. For example, many research questions are raised by considering how work–life balance in middle and later life is shaped by dimensions of inequality known to be important in earlier adulthood. Gender is perhaps the most salient, but others to explore include socioeconomic status, race-ethnicity and sexual minority status. Our broader goal, however, has been to underscore the value of making age more explicit in work–life balance research. To this end, we urge researchers to examine their own assumptions about various life stages and the activities filling them and to consider their research findings' applicability to other ages, stages or cohorts – exercises certain to enrich scholarship on work–life balance.

REFERENCES

Abendroth, Anja-Kristin, and Laura den Dulk (2011) 'Support for the Work-Life Balance in Europe: The Impact of State, Workplace and Family Support on Work-Life Balance Satisfaction.' *Work, Employment and Society* 25(2): 234–256.

Ackers, Peter (2003) 'The Work-Life Balance from the Perspective of Economic Policy Actors.' *Social Policy & Society* 2(3): 221–229.

Adams, Kathryn Betts, Sylvia Leibbrandt, and Heehyul Moon (2011) 'A Critical Review of the Literature on Social and Leisure Activity and Wellbeing in Later Life.' *Ageing & Society* 31(4): 683–712.

Allen, Tammy D., and Jeremy Armstrong (2006) 'Further Examination of the Link Between Work-Family Conflict and Physical Health: The Role of Health-Related Behaviors.' *American Behavioral Scientist* 49(9): 1204–1221.

Alley, Dawn, and Eileen Crimmins (2007) 'The Demography of Aging and Work,' in *Aging and Work in the 21st Century*, edited by Kenneth S. Shultz and Gary A. Adams. Mahwah, NJ: Lawrence Erlbaum, pp. 7–23.

Alvaredo, Facundo, Lucas Chancel, Thomas Piketty, Emmanuel Saez and Gabriel Zucman (2018) 'World Inequality Report: Executive Summary.' World Inequality Lab. Retrieved May 1, 2019 (https://wir2018.wid.world/files/download/wir2018-summary-english.pdf).

Bernard, Miriam, and Judith E. Phillips (2007) 'Working Careers of Older Adults? What Helps and What Hinders in Juggling Work and Care?' *Community, Work and Family* 10(2): 139–160.

Biggs, Simon, Ashley Carr and Irja Haapala (2015) 'Work, Aging, and Risks to Family Life: The Case of Australia.' *Canadian Journal on Aging/LaRevue Canadienne du Vieillissement* 34(3): 321–330.

Biggs, Simon, Michael McGann, Dina Bowman and Helen Kimberley (2017) 'Work, Health and the Commodification of Life's Time: Reframing Work–Life Balance and the Promise of a Long Life.' *Ageing & Society* 37(7): 1458–1483.

Bookman, Ann, and Mona Harrington (2007) 'Family Caregivers: A Shadow Workforce in the Geriatric Health Care System?' *Journal of Health Politics, Policy and Law* 32(6): 1005–1041.

Bureau of Labor Statistics (2019) 'Average Hours Per Day Spent in Selected Activities by Age.' Bureau of Labor Statistics. Retrieved May 1, 2019 (www.bls.gov/charts/american-time-use/activity-by-age.htm).

Byron, Kristin (2005) 'A Meta-Analytic Review of Work–Family Conflict and Its Antecedents.' *Journal of Vocational Behavior* 67(2): 169–198.

Carstensen, Laura L., Helene H. Fung and Susan T. Charles (2003) 'Socioemotional Selectivity Theory and the Regulation of Emotion in the Second Half of Life.' *Motivation and Emotion* 27(2): 103–123.

Dinh, Huong, Amanda R. Cooklin, Liana S. Leach, Elizabeth M. Westrupp, Jan M. Nicholson and Lyndall Strazdins (2017) 'Parents' Transitions into and out of Work-Family Conflict and Children's Mental Health: Longitudinal Influence via Family Functioning.' *Social Science & Medicine* 194: 42–50.

Dugan, Alicia G., Richard H. Fortinsky, Janet L. Barnes-Farrell, Anne M. Kenny, Julie T. Robison, Nicholas Warren and Martin G. Cherniack (2016) 'Associations of Eldercare and Competing Demands with Health and Work Outcomes among Manufacturing Workers.' *Community, Work & Family* 19(5): 569–587.

Ebbinghaus, Berhard, ed. (2011) *The Varieties of Pension Governance: Pension Privatization in Europe.* Oxford: Oxford University Press.

Ellis, Renee R., and Tavia Simmons (2014) 'Coresident Grandparents and their Grandchildren: 2012 – Population Characteristics: Current Population Reports, P20–576.' Washington, DC: U.S. Census Bureau.

Emslie, Carol, and Kate Hunt (2009) '"Live to Work" or "Work to Live"? A Qualitative Study of Gender and Work–Life Balance among Men and Women in Mid-Life.' *Gender, Work and Organization* 16(1): 151–172.

Fernandez-Crehuet, Jose Maria, J. Ignacio Gimenez-Nadal and Ignacio Danvila del Valle (2017) 'The International Multidimensional Fertility Index: The European Case.' *Social Indicators Research* 132(3): 1331–1358.

Fernandez-Crehuet, Jose Maria, J. Ignacio Gimenez-Nadal and Luisa Eugenia Reyes Recio (2016) 'The National Work–Life Balance Index: The European Case.' *Social Indicators Research* 128(1): 341–359.

Ford, Michael T., Beth A. Heinen and Krista L. Langkamer (2007) 'Work and Family Satisfaction and Conflict: A Meta-Analysis of Cross-Domain Relations.' *Journal of Applied Psychology* 92(1): 57–80.

Gassman-Pines, Anna (2011) 'Associations of Low-Income Working Mothers' Daily Interactions with Supervisors and Mother-Child Interactions.' *Journal of Marriage and Family* 73(1): 67–76.

Gisler, Stefanie, Rachel Omansky, Paige R. Alenick, Alexandra M. Tumminia, Erin M. Eatough and Ryan C. Johnson (2018) 'Work-Life Conflict and Employee Health: A Review.' *Journal of Applied Biobehavioral Research* 23(4): e12157.

Haar, Jarrod M., Marcello Russo, Albert Suñe and Ariane Ollier-Malaterre (2014) 'Outcomes of Work-Life Balance on Job Satisfaction, Life Satisfaction and Mental Health: A Study Across Seven Cultures.' *Journal of Vocational Behavior* 85(3): 361–373.

Haar, Jarrod M., Albert Suñe, Marcello Russo and Ariane Ollier-Malaterre (2019) 'A Cross-National Study on the Antecedents of Work–Life Balance from the Fit and Balance Perspective.' *Social Indicators Research* 142(1): 261–282.

Harrington Meyer, Madonna (2014) *Grandmothers at Work: Juggling Families and Jobs.* New York, NY: NYU Press.

Hilbrecht, Margo, Susan M. Shaw, Laura C. Johnson and Jean Andrey (2008) '"I'm Home for the Kids": Contradictory Implications for Work–Life Balance of Teleworking Mothers.' *Gender, Work and Organizations* 15(5): 454–476.

Kahn, Robert L., and Toni C. Antonucci (1980) 'Convoys over the Life Course: Attachment, Roles, and Social Support.' *Life-Span Development and Behavior* 3(1): 253–286.

Kasearu, Kairi (2009) 'The Effect of Union Type on Work-Life Conflict in Five European Countries.' *Social Indicators Research* 93(3): 549–567.

Ku, Po-Wen, Kenneth R. Fox and Li-Jung Chen (2016) 'Leisure-Time Physical Activity, Sedentary Behaviors and Subjective Well-Being in Older Adults: An Eight-Year Longitudinal Research.' *Social Indicators Research* 127(3): 1349–1361.

Laughlin, Lynda (2013) 'Who's Minding the Kids? Child Care Arrangements: Spring 2011. Current Population Reports, P70-135.' Washington, DC: U.S. Census Bureau.

Lee, Bora, Katie M. Lawson, Po-Ju Chang, Claudia Neuendorf, Natalia O. Dmitrieva and David M. Almeida (2015) 'Leisure-Time Physical Activity Moderates the Longitudinal Associations Between Work-Family Spillover and Physical Health.' *Journal of Leisure Research* 47(4): 444–466.

Loretto, Wendy, and Sarah Vickerstaff (2015) 'Gender, Age and Flexible Working in Later Life.' *Work, Employment and Society* 29(2): 233–249.

Luci-Greulich, Angela, and Olivier Thévenon (2013) 'The Impact of Family Policies on Fertility Trends in Developed Countries.' *European Journal of Population* 29(4): 387–416.

Milkie, Melissa A., Sarah M. Kendig, Kei M. Nomaguchi and Kathleen E. Denny (2010) 'Time with Children, Children's Well-Being, and Work-Family Balance Among Employed Parents.' *Journal of Marriage and Family* 72(5): 1329–1343.

Moen, Phyllis, Wen Fan and Erin L. Kelly (2013) 'Team-Level Flexibility, Work-Home Spillover, and Health Behavior.' *Social Science & Medicine* 84: 69–79.

National Alliance for Caregiving and AARP Public Policy Institute (2015) 'Caregiving in the U.S. 2015: Executive Summary.' Retrieved September 13, 2020 (www.aarp.org/content/dam/aarp/ppi/2015/caregiving-in-the-united-states-2015-executive-summary-revised.pdf).

National Institute on Aging (2020) 'Mission: Overview.' Retrieved September 13, 2020 (www.nia.nih.gov/about/mission).

Peter, Richard, Stefanie March and Jean-Baptist du Prel (2016) 'Are Status Inconsistency, Work Stress and Work-Family Conflict Associated with Depressive Symptoms? Testing Prospective Evidence in the LidA Study.' *Social Science & Medicine* 151: 100–109.

Pichler, Florian (2009) 'Determinants of Work-Life Balance: Shortcomings in the Contemporary Measurement of WLB in Large-Scale Surveys.' *Social Indicators Research* 92(3): 449–469.

Polivka, Larry, and Baozhen Luo (2015) 'The Neoliberal Political Economy and Erosion of Retirement Security.' *The Gerontologist* 55(2): 183–190.

Roehling, Patricia V., Lorna Hernandez Jarvis and Heather E. Swope (2005) 'Variations in Negative Work-Family Spillover Among White, Black, and Hispanic American Men and Women: Does Ethnicity Matter?' *Journal of Family Issues* 26(6): 840–865.

Ruppanner, Leah (2013) 'Conflict Between Work and Family: An Investigation of Four Policy Measures.' *Social Indicators Research* 110(1): 327–347.

Saraceno, Chiara, and Wolfgang Keck (2011) 'Towards an Integrated Approach for the Analysis of Gender Equity in Policies Supporting Paid Work and Care Responsibilities.' *Demographic Research* 25(11): 371–406.

Sayer, Liana C., and Janet C. Gornick (2009) 'Older Adults: International Differences in Housework and Leisure.' *Social Indicators Research* 93(1): 215–218.

Schilling, Elisabeth (2015) '"Success is Satisfaction with What You Have"? Biographical Work–Life Balance of Older Female Employees in Public Administration.' *Gender, Work and Organization* 22(5): 474–494.

Schoeni, Robert F., Vicki A. Freedman and Linda G. Martin (2008) 'Why Is Late-Life Disability Declining?' *Milbank Quarterly* 86(1): 47–89.

Shafer, Emily Fitzgibbons, Erin L. Kelly, Orfeau M. Buxton and Lisa F. Berkman (2018) 'Partners' Overwork and Individuals' Wellbeing and Experienced Relationship Quality.' *Community, Work and Family* 21(4): 410–428.

Social Security Administration (2019) 'Full Retirement Age.' Retrieved May 1, 2019 (www.ssa.gov/planners/retire/retirechart.html).

Suitor, J. Jill, Megan Gilligan, Siyun Peng, Gulcin Con, Marissa Rurka and Karl Pillemer (2016) 'My Pride and Joy? Predicting Favoritism and Disfavoritism in Mother-Adult Child Relations.' *Journal of Marriage and Family* 78(4): 908–925.

Symoens, Sara, and Piet Bracke (2015) 'Work-Family Conflict and Mental Health in Newlywed and Recently Cohabiting Couples: A Couple Perspective.' *Health Sociology Review* 24(1): 48–63.

Twenge, Jean M., Stacy M. Campbell, Brian J. Hoffman and Charles E. Lance (2010) 'Generational Differences in Work Values: Leisure and Extrinsic Values Increasing, Social and Intrinsic Values Decreasing.' *Journal of Management* 36(5): 1117–1142.

United Nations (2015) 'World Population Ageing 2015 (ST/ESA/SER.A/390).' Retrieved May 1, 2019 (www.un.org/en/development/desa/population/publications/pdf/ageing/WPA2015_Report.pdf).

Van Hooff, Madelon L.M., Sabine A.E. Geurts, Toon W. Taris, Michiel A.J. Kompier, Josje S.E. Dikkers, Irene L.D. Houtman and Floor M.M. van den Heuvel (2005) 'Disentangling the Causal Relationships Between Work-Home Interference and Employee Health.' *Scandinavian Journal of Work and Environmental Health* 31(1): 15–29.

Vickerstaff, Sarah (2010) 'Older Workers: The "Unavoidable Obligation" of Extending Our Working Lives?' *Sociology Compass* 4(10): 869–879.

Ward, Russell A., Glenna Spitze and Glenn Deane (2009) 'The More the Merrier? Multiple Parent-Adult Child Relations.' *Journal of Marriage and Family* 71(1): 161–173.

Warren, Tracey (2004) 'Working Part-Time: Achieving a Successful "Work-Life" Balance?' *British Journal of Sociology* 55(1): 99–122.

World Health Organization (2014) 'World Health Statistics 2014: Part III – Global Health Indicators.' Retrieved May 1, 2019 (www.who.int/gho/publications/world_health_statistics/EN_WHS2014_Part3.pdf?ua=1).

Yu, Serena (2014) 'Work–Life Balance: Work Intensification and Job Insecurity as Job Stressors.' *Labour and Industry* 24(3): 203–216.

PART III

COMPARATIVE RESEARCH (APPROACHES AND STUDIES)

7. The household division of labour in Europe: a multilevel perspective

Dirk Hofäcker and Simone Braun

1. INTRODUCTION

Gender equality represents one of the key social aims of the European Union (EU). In its recent Gender Equality Strategy for the period 2020–2025, the European Commission (2020) has highlighted the importance of equality between the sexes as a cross-cutting field. Following recent policy advances, the EU indeed can be considered as a "global leader" in gender equality, with 14 out of the top 20 countries with the highest gender-equality levels originating from the EU-28 (ibid.: p. 1). Yet, despite these undoubtable advances, full gender equality has yet not been achieved. Even though in all EU member states women have overtaken men in the attainment of tertiary education (Eurostat 2020a), this educational advantage frequently does not translate into labour market outcomes: while the overall employment rate of men and women has converged throughout the last decade, there remains a difference in double figures as 79 per cent of men aged 20–64, but only 67.4 per cent of women in the same age group are employed (Eurostat 2019: 9). Moreover, women are disproportionately found in atypical work forms, such as part-time work, where around a third of women in EU countries are currently employed, while this applies to less than 10 per cent of men (Eurostat 2020b). Together with the persistent gender pay gap (European Commission 2018), this leads to inequalities not only in current labour market outcomes, but also in future social security outcomes (European Parliament 2019).

This inequality in labour market outcomes – that is, in "paid work" – is paralleled by persistent inequalities in unpaid work, where women still carry a disproportionate burden (European Commission 2020: 11). Even though a large number of both men and women nowadays participate in household and family care activities, women's daily participation time in such activities clearly surpasses that of men (Eurostat 2020c). Within couples, the share of household duties often is initially equal in the beginning of their relationship; yet it traditionalizes over time, notably irrespective of the working hours of the spouses (Grunow et al. 2012: 89).

Different explanations for this surprising yet persistent inequality in the division of unpaid work have been put forward. On the individual level, reference has been made to individual (economic) resources that make a certain division of work among spouses economically rational. In contrast, proponents of so-called "doing gender" theories have explained the persistence by the adherence of spouses to traditional gender norms within society, which constantly reproduces individual gender identities. At the same time, previous research has pointed to the fact that such gendered norms vary between countries and thus differentially shape the lives of men and women in different societies.

In this chapter, we aim to link both levels of explanation – the micro and the macro level – using recent survey data on gender-specific time spent on housework tasks. In doing so, our chapter aims to contribute to ongoing discussions on the gendered division of unpaid labour where such micro–macro linkages have been considered only more recently. At the same time, we aim to provide an example of how advanced methods of multilevel regression models can be used to empirically explore such relationships.

To this end, this chapter is structured as follows. In a first step, we will give a concise overview of existing theories in the field of the gendered division of housework, particularly looking at economic and "doing gender" explanations at the micro level, and theories of different gender cultures at the macro level (Section 2). Based on these theories, we will derive hypotheses, both for the micro and macro level as well as for possible interactions between the two levels (Section 3). Section 4 subsequently describes the data used and the International Social Survey Programme (ISSP) module "Family and Changing Gender Roles" fielded in 2012, as well as the multilevel methods applied in the subsequent analyses (Section 5). Finally, Section 6 summarizes the results and draws conclusions for further research.

2.   THEORETICAL BACKGROUND: EXPLAINING THE DIVISION OF HOUSEWORK

The explanation of the surprising persistence of the traditional division of labour between couples has been the focal point of scientific discussions in both economic and social sciences. In the following, we will outline three selected explanations, locating the cause for the asymmetric division either on the micro level of individuals or the macro level of societal cultures. These explanations will be tested subsequently in the empirical part.

2.1   Micro-Level Theories

A classical explanation of the traditional division of household work has been provided by Gary S. Becker based on the idea of "economic specialization" (Becker 1998). According to this approach, partners divide up the share of paid and unpaid work in such a way that they specialize in one of these two fields: the partner with higher labour market capital consequently would specialize in paid work activities while the other will specialize in household duties. It is assumed that through means of specialization, an economically optimal outcome for the couple as a whole is achieved. In its most basic form, this theory is gender-neutral as it does not explicitly postulate which partner specializes in which activity, but makes it dependent on their market income (Gupta 2007: 401). However, it is assumed that men and women have "intrinsically different comparative advantages" in childbearing and childcare which determine the "direction of the sexual differences by task and hence sexual differences in the accumulation of specific human capital that reinforce the intrinsic differences" (Becker 1985: 41). Through this self-reinforcing mechanism, the gender-specific division of labour would become more and more irreversible over time.

While Becker considers the division of household labour to arise from (biologically or socially) predetermined intrinsic differences, "economic bargaining" theory regards the division of household labour as the outcome of permanent negotiation processes between partners about who does the household work (Ott 1992). Negotiation power within these processes is determined by labour markets and the consequent earnings potential of the partners. Those with higher earnings potential will be better able to pursue their interests in negotiations and to avoid the negatively perceived household work. As labour market chances change, negotiation power will change accordingly and allow for a recalibration of the division of household labour. While the bargaining approach is less deterministic and more dynamic, it is, however, also individual labour market capital that determines the gendered division of labour.

While the argument behind the economic approaches appears to be compelling, their explanatory power has recently been called into question: recent advances of women in educational and labour market capital should have led to lesser gains in the specialization into household- and employment-related tasks and thereby should have improved the negotiation power of women. Yet, as outlined, the gendered division of labour has remained largely stable. Attention in research has thus increasingly shifted to "doing gender" approaches. According to these theories, the relative stability of households can be explained by traditional perceptions of "wifely and husbandly" roles that are constantly being produced and reproduced through respective behaviour in the private sphere (West and Zimmerman 1987: 144). These normative foundations explain not only the persistence of such behaviour but also the observation by Berk (1985) that such asymmetric modes of labour division often are considered as being "fair" by both spouses, even among employed women. Engagement in gender-specific tasks leads to further identification with respective gender norms, thus contributing to a reinforcement of the gender-specific behavioural pattern (Bielby and Bielby 1989). In cases of deviations from traditional models in the employment sphere (for example, through joblessness of the husband), couples even tend to adopt compensation behaviour in private life – that is, reverting to even more traditional gender norms – as a means of reclaiming their gender identities (Brines 1994). Using the "doing gender" approach, the surprising stability of gender-specific norms can be explained by the constant reinforcement of traditional gender roles, even in the case of changes in partners' resources. Empirical studies indeed seem to suggest that such traditional gender norms effectively "seem to trump earnings" in determining outcomes in household labour (Grunow et al. 2012: 289).

2.2   Macro-Level Theories and Micro–Macro Interactions

Brines (1994) highlights that the strength of gender norms is inherently connected to institutional structures that reinforce them. Such institutional structures may be reflected in labour market or family policies that promote certain types of household-related behaviour. On the national level, there appears to be a close relationship between gender cultures and gender policies that jointly define a gender arrangement (Pfau-Effinger 1998). There have been various attempts to categorize such institutional patterns; for example, by differentiating between strong, moderate and weak male-breadwinner states (Lewis and Ostner 1994) or between different family-cultural models (ranging from traditional family economy models to more egalitarian to dual-breadwinner/dual-carer models; Pfau-Effinger 2005). Germany, the Netherlands or Great Britain were frequently regarded as proponents of more traditional gender arrangements, while modern dual-earner/weak-breadwinner models are thought to be best represented by Scandinavian models. Empirical studies using cross-national data frequently have confirmed the normative significance of such institutional structures for both women (for example, Hofäcker and Lück 2004, Lück and Hofäcker 2008) and men (Hofäcker 2007).

Following this line of thinking, it seems reasonable to assume that different institutional patterns will shape the respective gender norms and thus the behavioural patterns in the division of labour within the household; that is, there are context-specific variations in the bindingness of traditional gender norms for actual behaviour within the household. This means that there are interactions between the micro level (gender) and the macro level (gender arrangements), a perspective that has only recently become the focus of empirical research (Grunow 2019): in countries where most traditional gender arrangements prevail at institutional and respectively cultural levels, gender differences in the takeover of household-related tasks can be expected to be most pronounced. Vice versa, in countries where gender arrangements are less traditional, the gender-specific division of household-related tasks will be less pronounced.

3. HYPOTHESES

In the previous section, we outlined key theoretical approaches aiming to explain the gendered division of household labour, including micro- and macro-level theories, as well as cross-level interactions. In the following, we will test these theoretical explanations in analysis of the gender-specific time investment in household-related tasks within European countries, using data from the "Family and Changing Gender Roles IV" module of the ISSP. For this analysis, we derive the following hypotheses from the previous theoretical discussion.

From the perspective of the economic theory of the household, we assume that a higher engagement of the spouse in employment will practically restrict the time available to take care of the household. At the same time such specialization will reinforce itself, both through cumulative gains in specialization but also through an increased bargaining power in negotiations about the division of housework. We thus assume that the lower the working hours in employment, the higher the working hours for housework.

In addition to these labour market capital differences, we assume that within all countries considered, the prevalence of gender-specific role models and norms will promote a gender-specific division of labour within the household ("doing gender"). Due to such gender-related role models and expectations, we assume that women spend more time on housework than men.

We also assume that on a national level, dominant cultural values and norms should have an effect on the amount of hours spent on housework. In countries with more traditional attitudes towards the division of labour, women should invest more time into household-related tasks than in less traditional countries. Moreover, in such countries the difference in the household-related time investment between the genders should be higher (interaction between cultural context and individual gender).

The hypotheses as well as the respective variables that are described in more detail in Section 4 are summarized in Table 7.1.

4. DATA AND METHODS

In order to test our hypotheses, we use data from the ISSP; more precisely, the rotating module "Family and Changing Gender Roles IV" for the year 2012. For reasons of comparability we merely focus on European countries, which reduces the data set to 24 countries in total.[1] In addition, we restrict the survey sample to the working-age population as usually defined in comparative statistics; that is, people aged between 18 and 64. As a result, the data contains 23,171 cases, including 12,774 women and 10,397 men.

Our dependent variable is the number of weekly hours spent on housework, reflected by the question "On average, how many hours a week do you personally spend on household work, not including childcare and leisure time activities?" (GESIS 2016: 128). Possible values range from a minimum of zero to 85 hours per week.

Table 7.1   Hypotheses

Variable	Assumed general effect
Country level	
Country itself	Country-specific (latent/diffuse) characteristics play a role
Average of Breadwinner Model proponents	The more the number of traditional supporters, the more time is used for housework
Individual level	
Gender	Females perform more hours than their male counterparts
Employment status	The lower the working hours in employment, the higher the working hours for housework
Interaction effect	
Average support and gender	In traditional countries the difference between men and women is greater. Or: the more the number of traditional supporters, the greater the difference in household working hours between males and females

In our analyses, we consider various aspects, which influence the weekly routine of housework activities of men and women. In doing so, we classify the independent variables into different levels of analysis: one group of covariates represents the *individual* characteristics like gender (men/women) and employment status (not employed, part-time, full-time), while the other group depicts a proxy for *cultural* context in terms of support of the Breadwinner Model. The question of agreement to the statement "A man's job is to earn money; a woman's job is to look after the home and family" could be answered using a five-point scale, where strong agreement is coded with lower values (GESIS 2016: 52).[2] In order to pick the proponents of the Breadwinner Model, we aggregate this individual measure to a percentage of supporters in a country (meaning the percentage of respondents who agree or strongly agree with this statement). This level-two covariate was centred at its Grand Mean (see discussion in Enders and Tofighi 2007, as well as Paccagnella 2006).

The data is structured in a hierarchical manner, so it permits different kinds of multivariate regression analyses, primarily a hierarchical method like multilevel regression analysis. In the following sections, we test our hypotheses using the following strategy.[3]

First, we present descriptive results on the distribution of housework hours in the European countries. This allows us to observe country-specific patterns in general, and to compare them descriptively to our proxy variable for cultural context.

Second, we apply linear multilevel regression analysis to decompose the different levels of influence, namely the country-specific context (level 2) and individual-level factors (level 1). Due to the expected differences in effect sizes within and between groups, statistical analysis requires one more level of analysis which accounts for aggregation present in the data. Disregarding such hierarchy in the data means conventional regression analyses will be biased, not only with regard to country differences but also regarding the effects of explanatory variables (see Gill and Womack 2013). This method presents an appropriate way to examine the nested data structure of respondents living in contexts and is recommended by several authors (see Snijders and Bosker 2012; Hox et al. 2018). To estimate the hierarchical models we use the software Stata (StataCorp 2019).

5.   RESULTS

5.1   Descriptive Results

As already mentioned, previous research indicates that there is still a gender gap concerning the commitment in household tasks. Even in modern societies with well-developed family-friendly policies, women tend to spend more time on housework than men. Yet it seems sensible to assume that the respective gender difference varies between countries, different kinds of (family) policies or cultural frames.

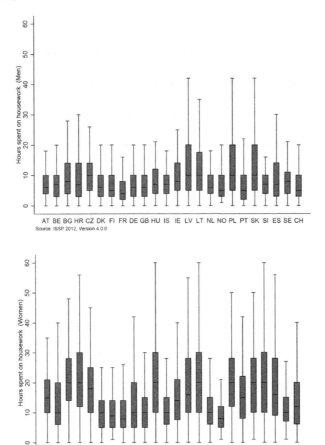

Figure 7.1   *Boxplots of hours spent on housework for men (top) and women (bottom)*

To illustrate these cross-country differences, Figure 7.1 shows the boxplots of hours spent on housework for every country in our analysis, separated by gender. Visual examination reveals a remarkable variation between countries and additionally between genders. Particularly in Nordic and Central European countries, median values of weekly housework are rather low and vary only modestly across respondents. In contrast, the reverse picture can be observed in Eastern and Mediterranean countries where both median values and inter-individual variations are higher. Overall, variations in weekly housework appear to be clearly more pronounced for women, while the distribution among men seems to be much more concentrated around lower median values. Yet in countries where women exhibit longer working hours, men show greater values as well (for example, in Latvia, Poland or Slovakia).

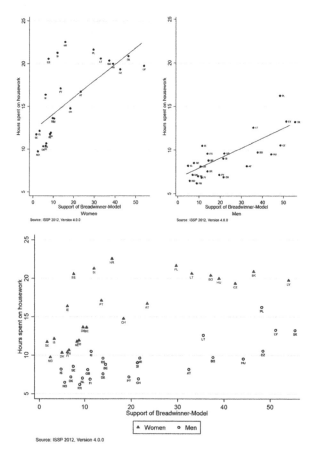

Figure 7.2a and 7.2b   Hours spent on housework (average) and support of Breadwinner Model (percentage) per country, separated by gender

At the macro level, a key question would be what drives these cross-national differences. In order to test for a possible linkage between working hours and the nation-specific cultural background, we contrast time spent on housework (displayed by mean hours in a country) and support of the Breadwinner Model (indicated by the country-specific share of supporters) in a two-dimensional scatterplot with a linear fit for both genders (Figure 7.2). Results indeed seem to confirm the idea of a link between cultural norms and individual housework hours. With few exceptional cases, the more respondents support a traditional division of labour, the higher their investment into housework hours.

As demonstrated in the univariate distributions, averaged housework hours are clearly higher for women (see the y-axis in Figure 7.2a). Yet this gender-related difference varies between countries: while 37 per cent of men and women in Bulgaria reveal traditional attitudes, women invest about 11 hours more than men into housework. In Norway, only around 6 per cent of male and 2 per cent of female respondents still strongly agree with a male-breadwinner model. With around three hours, the gender difference in household time is clearly smaller, yet still women engage in it to a larger extent. On the other hand, countries with lower support of traditional values may also reveal a huge amount of housework hours and vice versa. In Slovenia, for example, only around 21 per cent of men and 12 per cent of women support a breadwinner model, yet gender differences in housework differ profoundly (nine hours for men, 21 for women). At the same time, 55 per cent of men and 46 per cent of women in Slovakia support traditional values while displaying a more similar amount of hours (21 for women and 13 for men). Figure 7.2b reveals that relationship in a different manner: with increasing rates of traditional values, the housework hours of women rise more steeply than those of men. We come back to that descriptive finding at a later stage of our regression analysis.

5.2   Multilevel Analyses

The complex interplay of gender-related time spent on housework and the country-specific context of gender role attitudes restricts the use of conventional simple regression analysis and requires a second level of hierarchy. We thus employ multilevel regression models for further analyses.

Multilevel regression analysis consists of several analytical steps, which are refined step by step. Table 7.2 shows the successive results of every analytical step, presented in columns. The first part, displayed in rows, is similar to the results of simple regression outputs, with its fixed effects and intercept (or Grand Mean), and is referred to as Fixed Part. The part in the middle includes the error terms and co-variances, labelled as Random Part. These random effects shed light on the differences between the levels. The last section of the table shows some information about model fit and level-specific coefficients of determination.

First of all, an empty model (random-intercept-only model, RIOM) without any covariates has to be estimated to consider context dependencies; that is, country-specific differences in averaged hours spent on housework. The likelihood-ratio-chi^2 test statistic (LR test) – which tests for cross-state variation – and the estimated intra-class correlation (ICC) – which shows the percentage of variance due to such cross-state differences (see Hox et al. 2018: p. 36) – both suggest that multilevel modelling seems to be the appropriate method (significant test statistic). About 8 per cent of the variance can be explained by the nested data structure (see Model 1 in Table 7.2). Furthermore, the RIOM estimates an average of 13.01 hours of household hours per week for all respondents, irrespective of their belonging (Grand Mean) and the variances components for the intercept and residuals.

Figure 7.3 shows the country-specific deviation from this Grand Mean in a Caterpillar Plot. Countries where the 95 per cent confidence interval overlaps with this baseline (zero on the y-axis) do not differ significantly from the Grand Mean (in this case: Portugal and Austria). Countries where the confidence interval falls below the baseline show significantly lower values in averaged hours spent on housework. As shown in our earlier descriptions, this applies mostly to Northern and Central European countries. Reversely, countries where the confidence interval falls above the Grand Mean baseline show significantly higher than average values. In line with earlier results, these are mostly Eastern European countries.

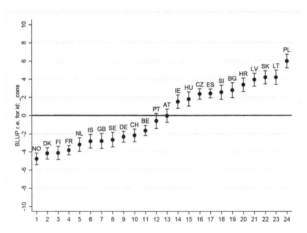

Figure 7.3   *Caterpillar plot of hours spent on housework for countries, empty model*

The second and third models show the results of a random-intercept model (RIM), where effects of the covariates are the same for all countries, meaning that these models are based on fixed effects (or, graphically speaking, parallel regression lines). Only the intercept is allowed to vary between countries (random intercepts), meaning that countries differ in their "starting points" of housework hours. In a first step (Model 2), only level-one covariates at the individual level are controlled for, while Model 3 additionally considers explanatory variables at the second (national) level.

The intercepts in Models 2 and 3 show the averaged hours spent on housework, and the fixed effects show an averaged change in hours performed for a one-unit change in the explanatory variable on condition that other variables are held fixed. Results from the two models confirm the expected gender gap: in contrast to men, women spend about 6.5 hours more on household tasks. Furthermore, housework time appears to be negatively related with working hours: respondents who are not in employment spend around three hours more on housework compared to full-time employed respondents, whereas part-time employed persons still deviate by around two hours from the same reference group. Notably, both effects appear to be independent from one another, meaning that neither can the working-time effect be reduced to gender differences in working hours, nor can the gender effect be fully explained through gender-specific working-time differences.

Table 7.2   Contextual dependencies of time use for housework (FML)

	(1) Empty model	Random intercept (RI)		Random slope (RS)		
		(2) Individual level	(3) + Macro-variables	(4) Individual level	(5) + Macro-variables	(6) + Interaction
Fixed Part						
Gender: female		6.515***	6.515***	6.520***	6.519***	6.428***
Not employed		3.290***	3.291***	3.285***	3.286***	3.287***
Part-time employed		1.994***	1.998***	2.249***	2.248***	2.253***
Support of Breadwinner Model			0.159***		0.122***	0.112***
Cross-level interaction: Breadwinner * gender						0.087*
Intercept (constant)	13.011***	8.241***	8.069***	8.235***	8.104***	8.113***
Random Part						
Intercept variance var()	10.428***	9.845***	3.640***	5.343***	2.296***	2.269***
Residual variance var()	119.103***	105.083***	105.083***	103.017***	103.018***	103.018***
Slope variance var()				8.614***	8.583*	6.740*
Covariance (Slope, Intercept)				1.795	-0.775	-0.563
Correlation (Slope, Intercept)				0.265	-0.175	-0.144
Model fit						
ICC	0.081					
Prob > chi2	.	0.000	0.000	0.000	0.000	0.000
p-value deviance test	0.000	0.000	0.000	0.000	0.000	0.000
deviance test	1802.163	1944.128	797.111	2346.951	1195.2791	1118.921
Akaike information criterion	176625.25	173730.93	173709.48	173332.11	173315.31	173311.83
R^2 Maddala		0.080	0.034	0.096	0.050	0.047
R^2 (Snijders und Bosker) L1		0.113	0.161	0.113	0.161	0.163
R^2 (Snijders und Bosker) L2		0.057	0.644	0.057	0.644	0.643
R^2 (Bryk und Raudenbush) L1		0.118	0.118	0.118	0.118	0.121
R^2 (Bryk und Raudenbush) L2		0.056	0.651	0.056	0.651	0.650

Notes: 24 countries with on average 965.5 respondents (minimum 626, maximum 1933). Full-Maximum-Likelihood (FML) estimation method. $+ p<0.1$, $* p<0.05$, $** p<0.01$, $*** p<0.001$. N (Level 1): 23171; N (Level 2): 24.
Source: ISSP 2012, Version 4.0.0. Own calculation with Stata 13.1.

Adding the level-two variable of proportion of the Breadwinner Model proponents as an indicator for division of gender roles in a country (see Model 3 in Table 7.2), one can state that with higher male-breadwinner support, individual hours spent on housework rise as well. The Random Part of the table reveals lower values for the variance components on both analytical levels.

The LR test points out if the inclusion of covariates improves the model fit (see p-values in the lower part of Table 7.2). As a standard measure for model fit, the Akaike information criterion serves as an estimator for model quality as well and deals with parsimonious modelling (see Hox et al. 2018: p. 38). In our case, the respective values indeed indicate a better model fit.

To find out how much of the variance our covariates explain, we compute level-specific coefficients of determination. The most common versions of Snijders and Bosker and Bryk and Raudenbush show the reduction in variance by introducing explanatory variables; that is, the proportional reduction in error. An overall R^2 using deviance measures is provided by Maddala's Pseudo-R^2, which expresses the improvement in explained variance in per cent (see Langer 2010: p. 755; Snijders and Bosker 2012: p. 109; Hox et al. 2018: p. 64). Initially, the values of level-one-R^2 are still comparatively low; yet, after introducing a level-two covariate the explained variance increases up to about 65 per cent. The average rate of support in a country thus explains up to 65 per cent of country differences. Figure 7.4 shows the variation of intercepts for the final RIM, considering all covariates (Model 3). Under these conditions, France exhibits the lowest, while Spain displays the largest intercept.

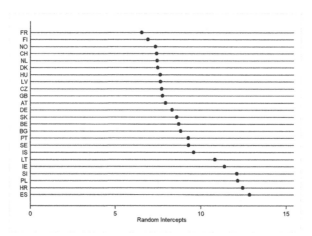

Note: Own calculation
Source: ISSP 2012, version 4.0.0

Figure 7.4   *Country-specific variation of intercepts (RIM)*

However, these estimates consider only between-country differences in the intercept, while single variable effects are assumed to be constant across countries. Our descriptive contrast of gender differences already suggest that this assumption cannot be considered as realistic. Instead, the effects of gender can also be considered to vary across countries.

To allow for country differences in the effects of level-one variables, we have to allow for random slopes, or, graphically speaking, country-specific regression lines with non-parallel slopes. We thus estimate a random-intercept-random-slope model (RIRSM). As in the RIM, we first have a look at level-one covariates and subsequently add the level-two variable in a second step, and only keep significant effects in the RIRSM. Concerning the fixed effects part, there are only minor differences compared to the RIM. The goodness of fit and test statistic confirm a further improvement in the model; that is, the RIRSM allows for country-specific variation of the gender gap and thus fits the data better than a model with fixed slopes.

The Random Part in the RIRSM model adds the information about the residual variance term for the gender slopes as well as the covariance between intercept and slope. The country-specific variation of the gender-gap effect (equivalent to random slope) becomes apparent in this residual variance term, which indicates the deviation of country-specific gender gaps from the mean gender gap. Figure 7.5 depicts these differences in slopes for the single countries. Holding other model variables fixed, the gender gap in Croatia seems to be the biggest, while in Norway we find the lowest gender differences. These findings statistically reaffirm the descriptive results already evident in our earlier descriptive findings: Northern and Central European countries exhibit lower starting points (intercepts) in household-related work, but at the same time flat slopes with regard to gender, whereas in Southern and Eastern European countries the opposite is the case.

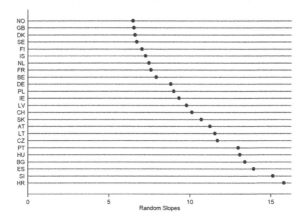

Note: Own calculation
Source: ISSP 2012, version 4.0.0

Figure 7.5   *Country-specific variation of slopes (RIRSM)*

To interpret the parameter for covariance, we have to consider the signs of the main effects of gender and support of the Breadwinner Model (see Langer 2010: p. 752). Making use of the correlation estimates simplifies the interpretation if the country-specific slopes are diverging or converging. Model 4 reveals positive signs, so regression lines will fan out, meaning narrow starting points (intercepts – that is, average housework hours for men – are closely spaced), but wider country-specific variation for women. This result is in line with the graphical presentation in the first part of this section, where we showed that housework hours vary more widely for women than for men. However, Models 5 and 6 in Table 7.2 indicate a reversal of the correlation sign: now regression lines will converge. In other words, the addition of a level-two covariate causes a change in the effect of gender (random slope). This clearly indicates an interaction effect between gender and cultural context.

To complete our analyses we explicitly model the mentioned interaction effect in terms of a moderation, in multilevel analyses known as cross-level interaction (CLI). In this step, the assumption of independent effects of covariates at different analytical levels is dropped in favour of the CLI: the effect of a level-one variable (here the gender gap) is moderated by a level-two variable (here the cultural context). In other words, the country-specific gender gap is partly due to country-specific characteristics like norms and values shared within society.[4] Model 6 (see Table 7.2) shows significant positive effects of the covariates and their interaction term. Our initial assumption thus can be confirmed: the gender effect on working hours will be stronger the greater the proportion of conservative attitudes in a country – women spend more hours per week than men on housework, most notably in countries with above-average proportions of traditional role attitudes.

6.   DISCUSSION

In the previous analyses we have investigated the division of household-related work in European societies, based on ISSP 2012 data. The descriptive analyses of our dependent variable, the hourly investment into household work, provided evidence of a considerable cross-national variation of household-related work across European countries, but also between the genders. Notably, not only the overall hourly investment into housework but also the country-specific gender differences in the variation of labour appeared to vary between countries. We took these results as a starting point for the estimation of a multilevel regression model to investigate these differences in more detail.

Our findings show that there is a negative correlation between the amount of working hours and the engagement in household-related work: the more individuals are engaged in paid work activities, the less they are engaged in household-related duties. While this pattern may be due to time constraints, it may also reflect differences in labour market capital and related negotiation power in partnerships, as postulated by economic theory. Individuals in full-time employment may also possess better opportunities to externalize household-related tasks to service providers outside their household. Further inclusion of respective control variables would help to investigate these potential explanations in more detail.

Our results further showed that irrespective of the country considered, and even when controlling for working hours, women spend more time than men on housework. This finding can be interpreted as an indication of the still-persistent strong influence of gender-specific norms on the household division of labour, as postulated in "doing gender" theories. Even though women have outperformed men in the attainment of higher educational degrees and despite the continuous convergence in employment rates, it is still predominantly women that invest the lion's share of their time into household-related duties, even when gender-specific differences in working hours are being considered. These persistent cultural influences need to be taken into account when further promoting gender equality within the labour market through public policies. If such initiatives are not accompanied by respective changes in the normative landscape, or buffered by respective support policies, there is a potential risk that women will be faced with a double burden of increasing work engagement and a persistent responsibility for household duties.

At the same time, our results indicate that both the amount of work as well as the gender-specific imbalance deviates between different gender-cultural arrangements. Including the overall nation-specific support for a traditional division of labour shows that in countries with higher male-breadwinner support, individual hours spent on housework are comparatively higher, and vice versa. It may be argued that countries with a low breadwinner orientation – particularly the dual-earner societies of Scandinavia – are better able to "shield" their citizens from housework; for example, by better opportunities to externalize household-related tasks.

The consideration of interaction effects also revealed that it is not only the amount of housework that differs between gender-cultural models, but also the gender-specific imbalance in its distribution. In countries with above-average values of support, the gender gap in housework is higher, and vice versa. Apparently, societies largely rejecting a traditional male-breadwinner model provide both a supportive normative framework and institutionalized support for a more equal division of labour between the sexes, as reflected in the reconciliation-oriented policies of Scandinavian countries. From a political perspective this means that even though gender equality in housework has been achieved in no European country up to now, policies may be effective in approaching it to a higher degree. Alternative multilevel analyses with concrete institutional indicators may be a means to better identify such policies.

From a more methodological perspective, our results have also shown that it is not only important to look at individual- and institutional-level determinants but also to consider interactions between the levels. Single variable effects, such as that of gender in our analyses, may have differential effects depending on the respective national context. We have demonstrated that the differential use of multilevel models is one effective means to consider such differentiated effects in one joint model. For the clarity of demonstration of such effects, our model was kept possibly parsimonious. More explanatory variables and other possible interactions will need to be considered in future research on the topic to further explore the gendered division of household labour.

NOTES

1. Countries in the final dataset: Austria (AT), Belgium (BE), Bulgaria (BG), Croatia (HR), Czech Republic (CZ), Denmark (DK), Finland (FI), France (FR), Germany (DE), Great Britain (GB), Hungary (HU), Iceland (IS), Ireland (IE), Latvia (LV), Lithuania (LT), Netherlands (NL), Norway (NO), Poland (PL), Portugal (PT), Slovakia (SK), Slovenia (SI), Spain (ES), Sweden (SE), Switzerland (CH).
2. The five-point-scale ranges from (1) strongly agree, (2) agree, (3) neither agree nor disagree), (4) disagree, to (5) strongly disagree. An exceptional case is Spain, where a four-point-scale was used without a middle category. Nonetheless, to present one more Mediterranean case in our analyses, we include this country. As for our indicator of male breadwinner support at the national level, we focus on proponents of the Breadwinner Model only, we neglect the difference in scales.
3. A more detailed discussion of the results and the methodology applied (in German) can be found in the textbook by Hofäcker and Stegl (forthcoming).
4. This interaction effect should only be interpreted in consideration of the corresponding main effects.

REFERENCES

Becker, G.S. (1998) *A Treatise on the Family*, 4th ed. Cambridge, MA: Harvard University Press.
Becker, G.S. (1985) Human Capital, Effort, and the Sexual Division of Labor, *Journal of Labor Economics*, Vol. 3, No. 1, Part 2: Trends in Women's Work, Education, and Family Building, pp. S33–S58.
Berk, S.F. (1985) *The Gender Factory: The Apportionment of Work in American Households*. New York, NY: Plenum.
Bielby, W.T., and Bielby, D.D. (1989) Family Ties: Balancing Commitments to Work and Family in Dual Earner Households, *American Sociological Review*, Vol. 54, pp. 776–789.
Brines, J. (1994) Economic Dependency, Gender, and the Division of Labor at Home, *American Journal of Sociology*, Vol. 100, No. 3, pp. 652–688.
Enders, C.K., and Tofighi, D. (2007) Centering Predictor Variables in Cross-Sectional Multilevel Models: A New Look on an Old Issue, *Psychological Methods*, Vol. 12, No. 2, pp. 121–138.
European Commission (2020) *A Union of Equality: Gender Equality Strategy 2020–2025*, COM(2020) 152 final, Brussels: European Commission.
European Commission (2018) *Gender Pay Gap in EU Countries Based on SES (2014)*. Luxembourg: Publications Office of the European Union.
European Parliament (2019) The gender gap in pensions in the EU. www.europarl.europa.eu/RegData/etudes/BRIE/2019/631033/IPOL_BRI(2019)631033_EN.pdf (retrieved December 4, 2020).
Eurostat (2020a) Gender statistics: statistics explained. https://ec.europa.eu/eurostat/statistics-explained/index.php/Gender_statistics#Education (retrieved December 4, 2020).
Eurostat (2020b) Part-time employment as percentage of the total employment, by sex, age and citizenship (%). https://appsso.eurostat.ec.europa.eu/nui/show.do?dataset=lfsa_eppgan&lang=en (retrieved December 4, 2020).
Eurostat (2020c) How do women and men use their time: statistics – gender statistics. Statistics explained. https://ec.europa.eu/eurostat/statistics-explained/index.php?title=How_do_women_and_men_use_their_time_-_statistics&oldid=463738 (retrieved December 4, 2020).
Eurostat (2019) *Smarter, Greener, More Inclusive? Indicators to Support the Europe 2020 Strategy*. Luxembourg: Publications Office of the European Union.
GESIS – Leibniz Institute for the Social Sciences (2016) International Social Survey Programme: ISSP 2012 – Family and Changing Gender Roles IV. Variable Report No. 2016/12. https://doi.org/10.4232/1.12661.
Gill, J., and Womack, A.J. (2013) The Multilevel Model Framework, in M.A. Scott, J.S. Simonoff and B.D. Marx (eds) *The SAGE Handbook of Multilevel Modeling*. London: SAGE, pp. 3–21.
Grunow, D. (2019) Comparative Analyses of Housework and Its Relation to Paid Work: Institutional Contexts and Individual Agency, *Kölner Zeitschrift für Soziologie*, Vol. 71, pp. 247–284. https://doi.org/10.1007/s11577-019-00601-1.
Grunow, D., Schulz, F. and Blossfeld, H.-P. (2012) What Determines Change in the Division of Housework over the Course of Marriage? *International Sociology*, Vol. 27, No. 3, pp. 289–307.
Gupta, S. (2007) Autonomy, Dependence, or Display? The Relationship between Married Women's Earnings and Housework, *Journal of Marriage and Family*, Vol. 69, No. 2, pp. 399–417.
Hofäcker, D. (2007) Väter im internationalen Vergleich, in T. Mühling and H. Rost (eds) *Väter im Blickpunkt: Perspektiven der Familienforschung*, Opladen: Barbara Budrich, pp. 161–204.
Hofäcker, D., and Lück, D. (2004) Angleichung nationaler Einstellungsmuster in Richtung eines liberaleren Rollenmodells? Einstellungen von Frauen zur geschlechtsspezifischen Arbeitsteilung im internationalen Vergleich, *Informationssystem Soziale Indikatoren*, Vol. 32, pp. 12–15.
Hofäcker, D., and Stegl, M. (forthcoming) Statistik und quantitative Forschungsmethoden: Lehr- und Arbeitsbuch für die Soziale Arbeit und (Sozial-)Pädagogik. Göttingen: Vandenhoeck & Ruprecht.
Hox, J.J., Moerbeek, M., and van de Schoot, R. (2018) *Multilevel Analysis: Techniques and Applications*, 3rd ed. New York, NY: Taylor & Francis.
Langer, W. (2010) Mehrebenenanalyse mit Querschnittsdaten, in C. Wolf and H. Best (eds) *Handbuch der sozialwissenschaftlichen Datenanalyse*. Wiesbaden: VS Verlag für Sozialwissenschaften/Springer Fachmedien, pp. 741–774.

Lewis, J., and Ostner, I. (1994) *Gender and the Evolution of European Social Policies*. Arbeitspapier No. 4 des Zentrums für Sozialpolitik, Bremen: ZeS.

Lück, D., and Hofäcker, D. (2008) The Values of Work and Care among Women in Modern Societies, in W. van Oorschot, M. Opielka and B. Pfau-Effinger (eds) *Culture and Welfare State: Values of Social Policy from a Comparative Perspective*. Cheltenham, UK and Northampton, MA, USA: Edward Elgar Publishing, pp. 289–313.

Ott, N. (1992) *Intrafamily Bargaining and Household Decisions*. Berlin: Springer.

Paccagnella, O. (2006) Centering or Not Centering in Multilevel Modes? The Role of the Group Mean and the Assessment of Group Effects, *Evaluation Review*, Vol. 30, No. 1, pp. 66–85. https://doi.org/10.1177%2F0193841X05275649.

Pfau-Effinger, B. (2005) Welfare State Policies and the Development of Care Arrangements, *European Societies*, Vol. 7, No. 2, pp. 321–347.

Pfau-Effinger, B. (1998) Gender Cultures and the Gender arrangement: A Theoretical Framework for Cross-National Comparisons on Gender, *Innovation: the European Journal of Social Sciences*, Vol. 11, No. 2, pp. 147–166.

Snijders, T.A.B., and Bosker, R.J. (2012) *Multilevel Analysis: An Introduction to Basic and Advanced Multilevel Modeling*, 2nd ed. London: SAGE.

StataCorp (2019) *Stata Statistical Software: Release 16*. College Station, TX: StataCorp.

West, C., and Zimmerman, DH. (1987) Doing Gender, *Gender and Society*, Vol. 1, pp. 125–151.

8. Subjective work–family conflicts: the challenge of studying self-employed workers[1]

Rossella Bozzon and Annalisa Murgia

1. INTRODUCTION

The aim of this chapter is to place the debate on the transformation of self-employment within the Job Demands and Resources (JD-R) framework and analyse how different types of self-employed workers perceive different levels of work–family conflict. Firstly, we introduce the JD-R framework and how this theoretical approach can be applied to the heterogeneous working conditions that characterize self-employment, which range from genuine entrepreneurial positions to forms of independent jobs that hide dependent job positions. Secondly, we use the European Working Conditions Survey (2015) (EWCS; Eurofound, 2017) to develop an empirical exercise aimed at analysing how subjective work-to-family (WtFC) and family-to-work (FtWC) conflicts vary across different types of self-employment, dependent employment and informal work; and how different distributions of job-related demands and resources across working arrangements mediate subjective work–family conflict(s). In the last section we discuss our findings, considering advantages and disadvantages of the JD-R approach and possible developments and directions for future research.

2. SUBJECTIVE WORK–FAMILY CONFLICT AND THE JD-R PERSPECTIVE

Subjective work–family conflict can be defined as 'a form of inter-role conflict' (Greenhaus and Beutell, 1985, p. 77) that manifests itself when the energies and the expectations connected with work struggle with pressures and duties from family domains (Kossek and Lee, 2017). Conflict can move from work to the family role and vice versa. Indeed, both occupational and family conditions can affect the perception of work–family conflict.

Originally designed to explain job-related well-being, the JD-R framework aims at identifying occupational and family conditions that either contribute to difficulties or solve problems that affect the equilibria between work and private life (Bakker and Demerouti, 2007; Bakker et al., 2011). In the JD-R framework, the excess of demands, pressures from job or household, and the lack of (job) resources are mechanisms that foster the conflict between work and family roles (Bakker and Demerouti, 2007; Bianchi and Milkie, 2010).

'Demands' refer to individual or organizational factors that imply efforts (physical or mental) that subtract energies for other life spheres (Bakker and Demerouti, 2007). They are usually distinguished between time- and strain-based demands. 'Time-based demands' refer to the amount of time devoted to work and family roles. 'Strain-based demands' relate to insecurity and psychological pressure, which can spill over from work to family or from family to work (Voydanoff, 2005). Time-based work demands are usually measured considering working hours and the quality of their distribution (that is, work overtime or at short notice), while strain-based work demands are measured through indicators of job intensity, emotional and cognitive pressures, and job instability. Time-based and strain-based family demands are usually connected to the household structure (living with a partner, having dependent children in the household) and measured by time devoted to care for children and the elderly, partner support and household/partner agreement regarding time and economic issues, the level of labour market attachment of family members and economic hardship (Fahlén, 2014).

'Resources' are individual and structural factors that support workers to cope with job and family demands. Job-related resources are usually captured by different forms of control of the working-time schedule (flexibility), autonomy and control over job tasks, and supportive working conditions and environments, and are usually analysed as job resources. Household/family resources are usually measured by forms of support to deal with family and private duties. They can be instrumental support, like having a partner or receiving paid and informal help with domestic or care tasks, or emotional support, like having good relations with partner(s) and relatives or having an active social life (Abendroth and den Dulk, 2011).

Typically, high levels of demands, from both work and family, fuel the conflict (Gallie and Russell, 2009; Nordenmark, Vinberg and Strandh, 2012). While differences and changes in work organization have a greater effect on the subjective WtFC, FtWC is more connected with family-related demands (Crompton and Lyonette, 2006; Fahlén, 2012; König and Cesinger, 2015; Kossek and Lee, 2017). However, there is less agreement in the literature on the role of job resources. On the one hand, resources are associated with less interference between work and family (Parasuraman and Simmers, 2001; Bakker and Demerouti, 2007; Schieman, Glavin and Milkie, 2009). Individual temporal, spatial and organizational control over the work sphere should buffer demands, reducing work–family conflict (Russell, O'Connell and McGinnity, 2009; Chung, 2011). On the other hand, other empirical studies stress the ambivalent role of job resources. Schieman and colleagues (2009) found that while resources like high autonomy and social support reduce work–family conflict, this is not the case for workers with more authority, decision-making latitude, skills and economic rewards, who report higher levels of interference. From their perspective, as suggested by the work–family border theory, some job resources may increase border permeability between work and private roles, therefore favouring work-to-non-work interference (Clark, 2000; Glavin and Schieman, 2012). The same mechanism is also identified for the conflict that flows from family to work (Ashforth, Kreiner and Fugate, 2000). Thus, the issue is to understand under which conditions the interrelationship between job or family resources and job or family demands favours the balance between work and family roles and vice versa.

3.   SELF-EMPLOYMENT AND SUBJECTIVE WORK–FAMILY CONFLICT IN THE JD-R FRAMEWORK

Much of the research on subjective work–family conflict focuses on dependent employment in large organizations (Annink and den Dulk, 2012; Glavin and Schieman, 2012). Self-employment tends to be overlooked by the literature, even if the recent growth of self-employed workers, especially without employees, and the diffusion of hybrid job positions that challenge the boundaries between dependent and independent employment have generated interest in bringing back the situations of self-employed workers within the JD-R framework.

The scholars that adapt the JD-R framework to self-employment subjective work–family conflict can be grouped into two main positions. The first defines self-employment as a job resource (König and Cesinger, 2015). According to this position, self-employment offers forms and levels of autonomy, control and flexibility that should allow a better balance between work and family duties, enjoying high working-time flexibility, breaking free from bureaucratic control typical of dependent positions and deciding when, where and how to work. Thus, job resources allow for the reduction of interferences that flow from work to family. But this is not the case for FtWC. On the contrary, higher autonomy and flexibility may make the boundaries between work and private life more permeable, favouring a higher pressure of family demands on the work sphere, fuelling family-to-work interferences (Clark, 2000; Reynolds and Renzulli, 2005; Glavin and Schieman, 2012). Adopting this perspective, Reynolds and Renzulli (2005) found that in the US context, working-time flexibility and autonomy are the mechanisms through which self-employment reduces subjective WtFC, preventing work roles from interfering with family roles. Moreover, they find that because women experience a higher increase in control than men, when they move from a dependent to a self-employed position, self-employment has more benefits for women. König and Cesinger (2015), analysing subjective WtFC among highly skilled workers, show that working-time flexibility and job autonomy allow for a reduction in time-based WtFC for the self-employed, but they have no effect on the strain-based WtFC, which is higher for self-employed workers than for employees. Annink and den Dulk (2012) show that the self-employed who experience economic dependence from clients and few possibilities to adapt working hours and workload face higher levels of WtFC than the self-employed with low dependency on clients and high autonomy. The FtWC is instead less explored in the empirical literature. However, Reynolds and Renzulli (2005) found that FtWC is higher among the self-employed, therefore supporting the perspective that sees typical self-employed resources as a way to make the temporal and physical boundaries of work more tenuous.

The second position understands self-employment as a source of job-related demands. Working conditions of the self-employed are often characterized by a higher workload and working hours per week than the average for employees, especially among men (Hagqvist, Toivanen and Vinberg, 2015). Entrepreneurial activities request levels of job involvement and time commitment that can favour the conflict between work and family spheres in both directions (Parasuraman and Simmers, 2001; Gallie and Russell, 2009; Annink and den Dulk, 2012; König and Cesinger, 2015; Annink, den Dulk and Steijn, 2016; Hagqvist, Toivanen and Bernhard-Oettel, 2018). Overall, self-employment job demands are more likely to invade all other spheres of life, resulting in blurred temporal, spatial and mental boundaries that increase both WtFC and FtWC. Empirical studies largely confirm that self-employed workers face higher WtFC and that the association between working arrangements and WtFC is mainly mediated by both time and strain-based job demands (König and Cesinger, 2015; Annink, den Dulk and Steijn, 2016; Hagqvist, Toivanen and Bernhard-Oettel, 2018). In relation to the FtWC, Hagqvist and colleagues (2018) show that time-related job demands significantly increase the risk of the self-employed perceiving higher FtWC, while strain-based job demands seem to have no effect, just like family-related demands.

To sum up, according to the perspective that stresses the role of job resources connected to self-employment, self-employed workers should be able to lower WtFC but face higher FtWC.

The perspective that focuses on job-related demands instead sees self-employment as a source of conflict in both directions.

4.   SELF-EMPLOYMENT HETEROGENEITY AND SUBJECTIVE WORK–FAMILY CONFLICT IN THE JD-R FRAMEWORK

Comparing studies on subjective work–family conflict is often problematic because of the extreme variation in the analytical design and measurement of work–family conflict (Kossek and Lee, 2017). However, the divergent results of the studies on work–family conflict for the self-employed are largely connected to the fact that the available data does not support an analysis of the heterogeneity of positions within self-employment (Bozzon and Murgia, 2021). Self-employed workers are, in fact, analysed as a single group or simply divided considering the presence (or absence) of employees, paying little attention to differences between business characteristics that define different types of independent jobs (Reynolds and Renzulli, 2005; Nordenmark, Vinberg and Strandh, 2012; König and Cesinger, 2015; Annink, den Dulk and Steijn, 2016; Hagqvist, Toivanen and Bernhard-Oettel, 2018). Such lack of evidence is mainly due to the lack of large-scale surveys that simultaneously collect detailed information on both self-employment business and subjective work–family conflicts.

In the empirical exercise proposed in this chapter, we use the detailed information on self-employment available in the last EWCS (Eurofound, 2017) to show how the perceptions of work–family conflicts change when a wider typology of self-employment is considered (Bozzon and Murgia, 2021). More precisely, leveraging the work of Williams and Horodnic (2018) and using the same dataset, we distinguish three types of self-employment: self-employed with employees, genuine solo self-employed and dependent solo self-employed. The distinction between 'genuine' and 'dependent' solo self-employed workers allows us to identify a hybrid category of independent workers who are formally described as self-employed, but who own characteristics that place them closer to wage workers because they do not have employees, economic autonomy or authority and/or control over how to run their business (Williams and Horodnic, 2018; Bozzon and Murgia, 2021).

The different business characteristics that define each group of self-employed workers lead us to ask how they balance job and family demands and job resources, and which scenario – self-employment as job-related resource vs self-employment as job-related demands – prevails in explaining their perceptions of WtFC and FtWC. Thus, the final objective of this exercise is to analyse how different types of self-employed workers perceive WtFC and FtWC in comparison with employees – both permanent and fixed-term – and informal workers, and to understand how differences in the perception of conflict are mediated by job-related demands and resources associated with different job positions.

If the perspective that stresses that the role of job resources connected to self-employment prevails, self-employed workers should be able to lower subjective WtFC only when they are characterized by high levels of flexibility, control and autonomy on their business activities, which are resources usually more available among 'genuine' types of independent jobs. By contrast, high flexibility control and autonomy could make the boundaries between work and private life more permeable, favouring the FtWC. Thus, hybrid self-employed types, with characteristics closer to dependent workers, should be more able to reduce their subjective FtWC than genuine forms of self-employment.

If the approach that stresses the role of job demands prevails, self-employed workers with a genuine entrepreneurial ethos and with a high involvement and commitment in their own business should be a type of the self-employed exposed to a higher subjective WtFC and FtWC. On the contrary, in this perspective, dependent self-employed workers that are defined by a low economic commitment and lower authority on their business should be able to lower their perception of conflict in both directions.

5.   SELF-EMPLOYMENT TYPES AND SUBJECTIVE WORK–FAMILY CONFLICT: AN EMPIRICAL EXERCISE

The empirical exercise proposed in this chapter is based on the EWCS 2015 (Eurofound, 2017). This survey allows us to overcome limitations in the data of previous research because it simultaneously includes: (1) a section on subjective work–family conflict; (2) several measures of job-related demands and resources and for the household domain; and, most important, (3) an ad hoc module on self-employment business characteristics. The main limit is that this information is available for only one point in time. Thus, no changes over time or causal relations can be explored, and mediation and moderation effects cannot be evaluated in a proper way in our analysis.

In the following, we briefly describe the step-by-step process of analysis. More precisely, we define the sample selection, the measures of work–family conflict, the main independent variables employed and the strategy of analysis adopted in the empirical exercise.

5.1   Sample Selection

The analysis focuses on men and women aged 25–59 from the EU28 countries who declared that they had a job at the time of the interview. The age selection should allow us to restrict the analysis to a set of respondents who are in a central phase of their life-cycle, when requests from work and private sphere should be higher, and the career trajectories are more consolidated but sufficiently far from the moment of retirement. The final sample includes 13,427 men and 14,571 women. In relation to countries, sample sizes range from N = 717 (339 men and 378 women) in the Netherlands to N = 2,807 (1,417 men and 1,390 women) in Spain.

5.2   Measuring Subjective Work-to-Family Conflict and Family-to-Work Conflict

Subjective work–life conflict is measured through five questions that register different forms of time- and strain-based work-to-family interferences and vice versa. Using these five items we create two additive indexes, which measure respectively subjective WtFC and FtWC.

The WtFC index is a sum of three items which measure on a five-point scale (from never to always) time- and strain-based conflicts that flow from work to family. The three items capture how often the respondents: (1) found that their job prevented them from giving the time they wanted to their family, (2) kept worrying about work when they were not working and (3) felt too tired after work to do some of the household jobs that needed to be done, in the last 12 months (Cronbach's Alpha of 0.69).

The FtWC index is the sum of two items which measure on a five-point scale how often the respondents: (1) found that their family responsibilities prevented them from giving the time they wanted to their job and (2) felt difficulty concentrating on their job because of their family responsibilities, in the last 12 months (scale reliability coefficient 0.72).

The final indexes were re-scaled in order to range from 0 to 10. A higher score indicates a higher level of conflict. Figure 8.1 summarizes the distribution of the WtFC and the FtWC by working arrangements in our sample selection.

5.3   Independent Variables

According to the discussion in the first part of the chapter, the main factors under examination in the proposed analyses are: (1) the type of self-employment, (2) a selection of job-related demands and resources that define each job condition and (3) family/household demands and resources. The survey contains detailed information on job quality and everyday working lives. Some of the questions focus only on employees and others only on self-employed workers. This implies that only a part of the questionnaire allows for a comparison between the working conditions of dependent and independent workers. Finally, since the survey aims at measuring differences in working conditions, the part on private lives is less developed.

5.3.1   Work arrangements

Workers are distinguished between self-employed workers (with and without employees), employees (permanent or fixed-term) and informal workers (no employment contract). Among the self-employed without employees – namely solo self-employed workers (SSE) – we differentiated between 'genuine' and 'dependent' SSE, applying to the data the operationalization proposed by Williams and Horodnic (2018). More precisely, dependent SSE have at least two of these three characteristics: they only work for one client (or more than 75 per cent of their income comes from the same client), they do not have the authority to hire staff if necessary and they do not have the authority to make important strategic decisions about how to run their business. Table 8.1 summarizes the main distribution of the work arrangements for men and women in our sample selection.

Table 8.1   Work arrangements: men and women aged 25–59, EU28

Work arrangement	Male	Female	Total
Self-employed with employees	6.2%	3.0%	4.6%
Genuine SSE	5.1%	3.1%	4.1%
Dependent SSE	5.8%	4.3%	5.1%
Permanent	71.1%	74.2%	72.6%
Fixed-term	9.3%	12.2%	10.7%
Informal	2.5%	3.2%	2.9%
N.	13,427	14,571	27,998

Source: Own elaboration on EWCS, 2015

5.3.2   Job-related demands and resources

Within the frame of the demands and resources approach, we have identified a set of indicators of JD-R which characterize both self-employment and dependent employment. As job-related demands, we consider working-time demands (weekly working hours and quality of working hours' distribution), indexes of job intensity or pace demands, emotional demands and cognitive demands. Finally, as a proxy of job instability, we consider the perceived risk of losing a job in the next six months.

As job-related resources, we use a variable that measures forms of working-time flexibility and the level of control over the working-time schedule, an indicator that measures who works from home, and an index that summarizes the level of job autonomy and discretion. Moreover, as a proxy of job rewards, we use an indicator of self-perception of being adequately paid for the work done. Table 8.2 contains details of each index included in the analysis.

Table 8.2   *List of the job-related demands and resources indicators included in the analysis*

Job demands	
Weekly working hours	Usual number of hours worked per week. Weekly work hours were recoded into five categories: 1 = less than 30 h; 2 = 30–39 h; 3 = 40 h; 4 = 41–49 h; 5 = 50 h and more.
Working-time pressures index	Standardized index based on six items that capture the frequency of working unsocial hours (Sunday and Saturday work, night work), overtime work (more than 10 hours per shift), and work at short notice (Cronbach's Alpha = 0.6818). High values mean low quality in the distribution of the working hours and a high exposure to non-standard work rhythms.
Pace demands (or job intensity)	Standardized index based on three items: the extent to which respondents declared working at high speed (five-point scale), having to meet tight deadlines (five-point scale) or not having enough time to complete the tasks assigned to them (five-point scale) (Alpha C= 0.6746). Higher values imply higher job intensity.
Emotional demands	Standardized index that summarized how often the job required working with people external to the organization (customers, service-users, and so on) (five-point scale); handling angry clients, customers, patients, pupils, and so on (five-point scale); and being in situations that are emotionally disturbing or mean having to hide feelings (Alpha C = 0.6565). Higher values imply higher emotional demands/pressures.
Cognitive demands	Standardized index measuring the extent to which respondents have 'to perform complex tasks', 'to solve unforeseen problems on their own', 'meet precise quality standards' and 'learn new things' (often or quite often) (Alpha C = 0.7131). Higher values imply higher cognitive demands/pressures.
Job insecurity	Dummy indicator which measures how likely a respondent thinks they might lose their job in the next six months. 1 = agree/strongly agree.
Job resources	
Control on working-schedule arrangement	Categorical variable which distinguishes who does not have any control over their working schedule and who has some forms of flexible working-time arrangements: (1) flexibility fixed by the organization, (2) possibility to choose among different forms of working time (flextime), (3) complete control over their working time.
Working from home	Dummy indicator which measures if the respondent works from home every day or several days every week or per month.
Job discretion/autonomy	Standardized index based on six items: the extent to which respondents declared they had influence over decisions at work (five-point scale); apply their ideas at work (five-point scale); contribute to improve the organization of work (five-point scale); control tasks (dummy); method of work (dummy); and pace of work (dummy) (Alpha C = 0.8023). Higher values imply higher job discretion/autonomy.
Perception to be adequately paid	Dummy indicator which measures how likely the respondent thinks it is that considering all their efforts and achievement in their job they feel they are adequately paid (1 = agree/strongly agree).

5.3.3   Household/family-related demands and resources

Focusing on the private sphere, in the available data there are few questions that allow us to identify pressures and support connected to family roles and duties. In this case we use five dummy indicators that identify: (1) who lives with a partner who works, (2) who lives with a partner without a job, (3) who lives with children, (4) who has dependent children (aged 0–15) in the household and (5) who cares for children, grandchildren, elderly or disabled relatives daily or several times a week. Moreover, as a proxy of the household economic situation we use a dummy measure of subjective income insecurity of the household, which identifies who answered that their household income is able to make ends meet 'with difficulty' or 'with great difficulty'. As socio-demographics characteristics we consider age and level of education.

5.4   Analytical Strategy

In order to determine how different self-employed workers perceive WtFC and FtWC, the analysis has been organized in two main steps.

Firstly, we describe how job-related resources and demands and household demands are distributed across different working arrangements for men and women. In this way we explore – on a descriptive basis – how different types of self-employed workers – that is, self-employed with employees, genuine SSE and dependent SSE – balance demands and resources, and how their situations differ from employees and informal workers.

Secondly, we analyse differences in the levels of subjective WtFC and FtWC reported by different types of self-employed in comparison to employees and informal workers, and how these differences are mediated by job demands and resources indicators. To this aim, we estimate a series of multilevel models (with individuals nested in countries) on the WtFC and FtWC indexes. The control variables are entered stepwise to investigate the role of household/family characteristics, job-related resources and demands in explaining the differences between the different types of self-employment and other job positions. We have also considered interactions between work arrangements and job-related demands and resources to test if and how their average effect on the measures of work–family conflict varies among different work arrangements.

Since we suppose that job-related demands and resources, as well as household circumstances, play different roles for men and women, we estimate separate models by sex.

6.   FINDINGS

6.1   Self-Employment and JD-R Indicators

Before deepening the relation between work arrangements – employment, self-employment, informal work – and subjective work–family conflict, this section briefly describes how the three types of self-employment differ according to the main JD-R indicators and family demands.

The comparison of the distribution of job-related demands (Table 8.3) and resources among different self-employment types highlights considerable differences between self-employed workers with employees and genuine SSE, on the one side, and dependent SSE on the other.

As far as job-related demands are concerned (Table 8.4), self-employed with employees and genuine SSE are the most demanding job positions both in terms of time demands and pace, emotional and cognitive pressures. Differently from other self-employed types, dependent SSE are polarized between part-time work (less than 30 hours per week) and overtime (working more than 50 hours per week) – especially among women – and pace, emotional and cognitive requests are generally lower. However, they share with the other self-employed the low quality of their working-time distribution. Thus, differently from employees and informal workers, they more frequently work unsocial hours, overtime or at short notice. Job resources are instead generally more available among all types of the self-employed. Even for dependent SSE, the level of resources is lower than other self-employed workers; they experience higher levels of autonomy and control over their everyday working lives and working schedule than employees. Therefore, while the self-employed with employees and genuine SSE combine wider margins of control, autonomy and discretion on their everyday working life with high job pressures, the profile of dependent SSE is positioned almost halfway between the other self-employed and the employees.

Finally, focusing on household and family characteristics by working arrangements, there is no clear pattern (Table 8.5). Generally, the self-employed with employees and genuine SSE are defined by higher levels of family demands connected to the presence of children and the time involved in care activities for children, elderly and disabled relatives than dependent SSE. On average, care activities are more common among women independent of work arrangement. With respect to the indicator of household economic difficulties, the self-employed with employees are less likely to face this situation. Dependent SSE and genuine SSE experience levels of economic uncertainty in the household similar to those of permanent employees, and less often than fixed-term employees and informal workers.

6.2   Self-Employment and Work–Family Conflict: The Role of Job Demands and Resources

After having briefly examined the differences between the three self-employment types in terms of job-related resources and demands and family situations, we move to the core of our empirical exercise, which aims to understand how subjective WtFC and FtWC is experienced by different groups of self-employed workers.

Figure 8.1 shows the average level of WtFC and FtWC by work arrangement and sex. Focusing on WtFC, the self-employed with employees and genuine SSE show the highest level of conflict, while dependent SSE show a mean level of conflict closer to employees. Among women, dependent SSE perceive similar levels of conflict to employees. Among men, even if the subjective conflict progressively decreases, moving from the self-employed with employees to dependent SSE, the average conflict is always significantly higher than for employees (both permanent and fixed-term) and informal workers. The picture changes for FtWC. On average, FtWC is less common than WtFC (Kossek and Lee, 2017). In this case, all types of self-employed workers perceive more conflict than dependent and informal workers. There are no substantial differences in the average levels of conflict across self-employed types. The only exception is genuine SSE women, who are the group with the highest level of FtWC.

Table 8.3 Job-related demands by working arrangements: men and women aged 25–59, EU28

Men

	Self-employed with employees	Genuine SSE	Dependent SSE	Permanent	Fixed-term	Informal	Total
Weekly working hours							
– less than 30 h	4.7%	10.6%	15.6%	4.2%	13.9%	26.1%	6.7%
– 30–39 h	8.0%	12.7%	23.7%	28.9%	25.9%	25.9%	26.1%
– 40 h	18.2%	20.7%	20.1%	37.6%	36.5%	18.3%	34.0%
– 41–49 h	13.8%	13.7%	10.1%	14.7%	11.2%	9.2%	13.8%
– 50 h and more	55.1%	42.2%	30.6%	14.6%	12.6%	20.6%	19.4%
Working-schedule demands (std index)	0.487	0.354	0.303	0.001	0.030	0.200	0.074
Pace demands (std index)	0.142	-0.042	-0.031	0.123	0.112	0.071	0.105
Emotional demands (std index)	0.130	0.010	-0.073	-0.130	-0.213	-0.217	-0.114
Cognitive demands (std index)	0.283	0.295	0.072	0.147	-0.011	-0.249	0.134
Work instability (%)	7.6%	10.4%	14.1%	10.8%	40.9%	26.0%	14.0%
N.	874	716	751	9,174	1,339	573	13,427

Women

	Self-employed with employees	Genuine SSE	Dependent SSE	Permanent	Fixed-term	Informal	Total
Weekly working hours							
– less than 30 h	7.8%	17.8%	32.4%	25.1%	36.0%	55.7%	27.3%
– 30–39 h	16.9%	22.6%	21.1%	32.3%	25.6%	23.0%	29.9%
– 40 h	20.7%	14.4%	15.7%	28.6%	25.3%	10.7%	26.3%
– 41–49 h	13.9%	16.6%	7.9%	9.2%	6.5%	4.0%	9.0%
– 50 h and more	40.7%	28.5%	22.9%	4.8%	6.6%	6.5%	7.6%
Working-schedule demands (std index)	0.274	0.213	0.154	-0.157	-0.074	-0.103	-0.108
Pace demands (std index)	0.007	-0.278	-0.130	0.033	0.052	-0.239	0.009
Emotional demands (std index)	0.215	0.169	-0.094	0.111	0.067	-0.219	0.091
Cognitive demands (std index)	0.278	0.118	-0.025	0.065	-0.180	-0.488	0.021
Work instability (%)	7.2%	11.3%	13.3%	9.0%	42.3%	20.9%	13.6%
N.	407	499	599	10,703	1,716	647	14,571

Source: Own elaboration on EWCS, 2015

Table 8.4   Job-related resources by working arrangements: men and women aged 25–59, EU28

Men

	Self-employed with employees	Genuine SSE	Dependent SSE	Permanent	Fixed-term	Informal	Total
Working-schedule control/flexibility							
– Flexibility fixed by the organization	3.3%	3.7%	4.3%	9.0%	6.0%	4.9%	7.7%
– Worker can choose (flextime)	9.9%	11.8%	15.9%	21.0%	14.9%	15.3%	18.8%
– Complete control	76.5%	81.0%	64.4%	5.8%	3.7%	16.5%	17.5%
Work from home (%)	38.6%	40.8%	40.5%	12.9%	8.5%	13.7%	17.1%
Job discretion/autonomy (std index)	0.675	0.621	0.290	-0.053	-0.283	-0.215	0.021
Well-paid job (perception) (%)	56.0%	45.4%	47.7%	51.5%	44.1%	36.8%	50.2%
	874	716	751	9,174	1,339	573	13,427

Women

	Self-employed with employees	Genuine SSE	Dependent SSE	Permanent	Fixed-term	Informal	Total
Working-schedule control/flexibility							
– Flexibility fixed by the organization	3.9%	2.5%	5.2%	10.7%	10.1%	3.9%	9.7%
– Worker can choose (flextime)	10.4%	10.7%	17.6%	20.9%	14.2%	22.8%	19.3%
– Complete control	69.2%	80.2%	67.3%	4.3%	5.4%	19.0%	11.9%
Work from home (%)	34.9%	44.1%	52.0%	13.7%	13.2%	18.3%	17.0%
Job discretion/autonomy (std index)	0.618	0.612	0.345	-0.034	-0.297	-0.134	-0.014
Well-paid job (perception) (%)	54.8%	48.6%	41.6%	49.8%	44.4%	41.9%	48.6%
	407	499	599	10,703	1,716	647	14,571

Source: Own elaboration on EWCS, 2015

Table 8.5   Household/family-related demands and resources by working arrangements: men and women aged 25–59, EU28

	Self-employed with employees	Genuine SSE	Dependent SSE	Permanent	Fixed-term	Informal	Total
Men							
Single	19.3%	24.8%	32.7%	22.8%	42.3%	41.9%	25.6%
Living with a partner with a paid job	61.1%	50.4%	44.6%	58.4%	34.8%	29.5%	54.5%
Living with a partner out of a job	19.6%	24.9%	22.7%	18.7%	22.9%	28.7%	20.0%
Living with children	57.7%	56.6%	46.6%	51.2%	33.9%	39.5%	49.7%
Living with dependent children (0–15)	40.4%	43.2%	34.2%	37.5%	26.7%	27.9%	36.5%
Care activities on daily/weekly basis	47.8%	53.7%	41.7%	45.5%	32.7%	29.0%	44.2%
Household economic insecurity	22.7%	41.6%	37.4%	29.9%	54.6%	63.4%	33.6%
N.	874	716	751	9,174	1,339	573	13,427
Women							
Single	19.9%	26.4%	23.5%	26.5%	32.1%	25.1%	26.8%
Living with a partner with a paid job	72.5%	64.2%	67.9%	64.4%	58.2%	61.6%	64.0%
Living with a partner out of a job	7.6%	9.5%	8.6%	9.1%	9.7%	13.2%	9.2%
Living with children	63.7%	64.6%	60.4%	58.4%	54.5%	67.6%	58.7%
Living with dependent children (0–15)	40.1%	40.0%	38.0%	39.6%	41.2%	44.1%	39.9%
Care duties on daily/weekly basis	61.3%	66.5%	54.8%	56.7%	53.8%	66.5%	57.0%
Household economic insecurity	18.7%	36.9%	37.6%	33.4%	51.8%	60.5%	36.4%
N.	407	499	599	10,703	1,716	647	14,571

Source: Own elaboration on EWCS, 2015

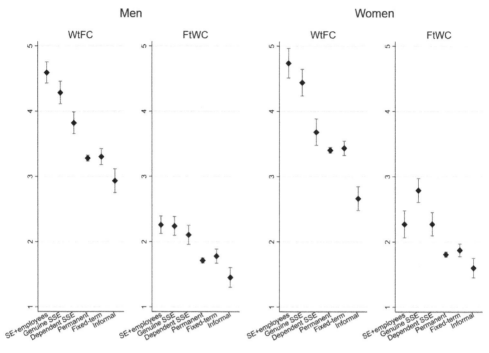

Source: Own elaboration on EWCS, 2015

Figure 8.1   *Work-to-family conflict index and family-to-work conflict index by sex and work arrangements*

In order to detect if and how the differences in subjective WtFC and FtWC shown in Figure 8.1 are mediated by household demands and job-related resources and demands, we estimated multilevel linear models for individuals nested in countries separated for men and women. Country effects are modelled as random. The preliminary inspection of the empty model – the model with no variable included – shows that the unconditional interclass correlation due to country differences accounts for only 2.8 per cent and 3.7 per cent of the whole variance of WtFC and 2.2 per cent and 2.7 per cent of the whole variance of FtWC, for men and for women respectively. Thus, as shown in other empirical works (Chung, 2011), only a small amount of the variance in WtFC and FtWC can be attributed to national-level features, and most of it is due to within-country variations in job-related demands and resources and household demands.

Tables 8.6 and 8.7 show the estimated models – separated for men and women – that analyse respectively the WtFC and FtWC for work arrangements and three groups of variables: (1) family-related demands, (2) job-related resources and (3) job-related demands. Assuming that the effect of demands and resources could differ for different working arrangements, we tested interactions between work arrangements and all job-related demands and resources, and family demands variables, included in the analyses. This exercise points out significant differences across working arrangements only for individuals working from home and for the working-schedule demands index. These significant parameters are summarized in Table 8.8.

Table 8.6   *Work-to-family conflict: multilevel models*

	Men					Women				
	M1	M2	M3	M4	M5	M1	M2	M3	M4	M5
Work arrangement										
(Ref: permanent)										
Self-employed with employees	1.312***	1.342***	0.958***	0.544***	0.336***	1.320***	1.380***	1.509***	0.516***	0.618***
Genuine SSE	0.895***	0.857***	0.368*	0.489***	0.2	0.943***	0.927***	1.003***	0.622***	0.675***
Dependent SSE	0.445***	0.459***	0.035	0.332**	0.081	0.250	0.228	0.143	0.156	0.117
Fixed-term	-0.087	-0.133	-0.119	-0.046	-0.04	-0.051	-0.110	-0.130	-0.101	-0.095
Informal	-0.513*	-0.558*	-0.681**	-0.428*	-0.504**	-0.901***	-0.936***	-0.957***	-0.332**	-0.366***
Job demands										
Weekly working hours										
(Ref: less than 30 h)										
– 30–39 h				0.243	0.237				0.466***	0.450***
– 40 h				0.298	0.321				0.618***	0.599***
– 41–49 h				0.615***	0.582***				0.969***	0.930***
– 50 h and more				1.063***	1.026***				1.540***	1.467***
Working-schedule demands				0.550***	0.534***				0.556***	0.524***
Pace demands				0.844***	0.823***				0.855***	0.831***
Emotional demands				0.579***	0.560***				0.530***	0.520***
Cognitive demands				0.166***	0.158***				0.211***	0.195***
Job insecurity (perception)				0.353***	0.359***				0.284***	0.270***
Job resources										
Control over working time										
(Ref: defined by the company)										
– Choose between fixed working schedule			0.445***		0.216***			0.088		0.026
– Adapt working hours			0.331***		0.309***			0.017		0.084
– Entirely determined by self			0.474***		0.310**			-0.380**		-0.242**
Working from home			0.616***		0.298***			0.701***		0.396***
Job autonomy			-0.050		0.000			-0.010		0.055
Well-paid job (perception)			-0.622***		-0.389***			-0.761***		-0.380***
Household/family conditions										
Living with (Ref: single)										
– A partner with a job	0.386***	0.386***	0.394***	0.337***	0.341***	0.091	0.091	0.063	0.121*	0.105

	Men					Women				
	M1	M2	M3	M4	M5	M1	M2	M3	M4	M5
– A partner jobless		0.315***	0.362***	0.340***	0.365***		0.017	0.027	0.148	0.149*
Children living in the household		-0.004	-0.013	-0.138	-0.136		-0.005	0.016	0.022	0.031
Dependent children in the household		0.084	0.071	0.221*	0.207*		0.1	0.111	0.209	0.21
Care activities on daily/weekly basis		0.227**	0.220**	0.223**	0.217**		0.238*	0.236*	0.263**	0.257**
Household economic insecurity		0.702***	0.564***	0.478***	0.409***		0.619***	0.423***	0.412***	0.334***
Age		-0.009**	-0.011**	0.002	0.000		0.002	-0.001	0.009*	0.007*
Age squared		-0.001***	-0.001***	0.000	0.000		0.000	0.000	0.001	0.001
Tertiary education		0.378***	0.233*	0.190**	0.103		0.633***	0.506***	0.362***	0.277***
Constant	3.290***	2.593***	2.798***	2.226***	2.349***	3.477***	2.708***	3.105***	2.206***	2.417***
Random part										
Var level 2 (Country)	0.136	0.124	0.118	0.072	0.07	0.196	0.162	0.144	0.096	0.088
Var level 1 (Workers)	4.679	4.488	4.325	3.292	3.233	4.718	4.555	4.361	3.273	3.22
N.	13427	13427	13427	13427	13427	14571	14571	14571	14571	14571
Country	28	28	28	28	28	28	28	28	28	28
BIC	63315.2	62798.8	62321.8	58409.8	58158.4	60797.4	60392.3	59848.2	55910.0	55690.9
LL	-31619.59	-31318.61	-31051.60	-29081.33	-28950.86	-30360.34	-30114.68	-29813.86	-27830.75	-27716.01
df	8	17	23	26	32	8	17	23	26	32

Note: * $p<0.05$, ** $p<0.01$, *** $p<0.001$
Source: Own elaboration on EWCS, 2015

Table 8.7 Family-to-work conflict: multilevel models

	Men					Women				
	M1	M2	M3	M4	M5	M1	M2	M3	M4	M5
Work arrangement										
(Ref: permanent)										
Self-employed with employees	0.535***	0.545***	0.329***	0.198**	0.047	0.427**	0.473**	0.494**	0.221	0.190
Genuine SSE	0.461***	0.419***	0.14	0.302***	0.099	0.919***	0.888***	0.863***	0.884***	0.797***
Dependent SSE	0.289***	0.284***	0.036	0.260**	0.079	0.357*	0.356*	0.238	0.429*	0.294
Fixed-term	-0.025	-0.027	-0.007	-0.006	0.012	-0.071	-0.097	-0.147	-0.149	-0.040
Informal	-0.382**	-0.403**	-0.460***	-0.330**	-0.367**	-0.438**	-0.472***	-0.146	-0.188*	-0.504**
Job demands										
Weekly working hours										
(Ref: less than 30 h)										
– 30–39 h				0.11	0.123				0.163	0.168
– 40 h				0.108	0.13				0.187***	0.196***
– 41–49 h				0.226***	0.218***				0.382***	0.368***
– 50 h and more				0.388***	0.363***				0.511***	0.457***
Working-schedule demands				0.205***	0.193***				0.078	0.056
Pace demands				0.542***	0.542***				0.523***	0.512***
Emotional demands				0.411***	0.391***				0.364***	0.364***
Cognitive demands				0.055	0.033				0.043	0.038
Job insecurity (perception)				0.297**	0.298*				0.370***	0.360***
Job resources										
Control over working time										
(Ref: defined by the company)										
– Choose between fixed working schedule			0.599***		0.466***			0.245*		0.215
– Adapt working hours			0.247***		0.246***			0.062		0.104
– Entirely determined by self			0.268**		0.213*			-0.054		0.045
Working from home			0.466***		0.306***			0.435***		0.326***
Job autonomy			-0.041		0.009			-0.077		-0.01
Well-paid job (perception)			-0.231***		-0.091			-0.334***		-0.142**
Household/family conditions										
Living with (Ref: single)										
– A partner with a job		0.165**	0.170***	0.146**	0.148***		0.006	-0.011	0.011	-0.002

	Men					Women				
	M1	M2	M3	M4	M5	M1	M2	M3	M4	M5
– A partner jobless		0.201**	0.222**	0.218***	0.224***		0.069	0.072	0.137	0.138
Children living in the household		0.017	0.015	-0.043	-0.037		0.087	0.101	0.097	0.107
Dependent children in the household		0.105	0.094	0.176*	0.163*		0.371**	0.370**	0.416***	0.409***
Care activities on daily/weekly basis		0.223**	0.210**	0.221**	0.207**		0.265**	0.266**	0.270**	0.268**
Household economic insecurity		0.480***	0.434***	0.333***	0.332***		0.432***	0.340***	0.314***	0.289***
Age		-0.003	-0.004	0.003	0.002		-0.003	-0.004	0	-0.001
Age squared		-0.001***	-0.001***	-0.001***	-0.001***		0.000	0.000	0.000	0.000
Tertiary education		0.248**	0.124	0.126	0.026		0.366***	0.300***	0.226***	0.163**
Constant	1.680***	1.251***	1.256***	1.132***	1.076***	1.776***	1.108***	1.236***	0.915***	0.934***
Random part										
Var level 2 (Country)	0.083	0.101	0.095	0.08	0.078	0.092	0.101	0.102	0.085	0.089
Var level 1 (Workers)	3.57	3.423	3.357	3.039	3.006	3.73	3.554	3.5	3.215	3.194
N.	13427	13427	13427	13427	13427	14571	14571	14571	14571	14571
Country	28	28	28	28	28	28	28	28	28	28
BIC	59276.6	58895.5	58670	57257.9	57110.7	57537.4	56959.8	56805.8	55657.9	55578.6
LL	-29666.4	-29366.9	-29225.7	-28505.4	-28427.04	-28730.4	-28398.4	-28292.7	-27704.3	-27569.9
df	8	17	23	26	32	8	17	23	26	32

Note: * p<0.05, ** p<0.01, *** p<0.001
Source: Own elaboration on EWCS, 2015

Table 8.8   *Multilevel models: relevant interactions between working arrangements and job-related demands and resources (working from home and working-schedule demands)*

	WtFC		FtWC	
	Men	Women	Men	Women
Working arrangement (Ref: permanent)				
Self-employed with employees	0.604***	0.747***	0.124	0.187
Genuine SSE	0.314	1.037***	0.158	0.858***
Dependent SSE	0.258	0.321	0.081	0.414
Fixed-term	-0.073	-0.068	0.040	-0.159
Informal	-0.382**	-0.243	-0.361**	-0.246**
Working from home	0.482***	0.567***	0.364***	0.328***
Working arrangement × Working from home				
Self-employed with employees × home	-0.777**	-0.460	-0.216	0.018
Genuine SSE × home	-0.367	-0.924***	-0.160	-.127
Dependent SSE × home	-0.539*	-0.515*	-0.024	-0.232
Fixed-term × home	0.430	-0.197*	-0.279	0.083
Informal × home	-0.876*	-0.689***	-0.041	0.328
Constant	2.317***	2.402***	1.064***	0.929***
N.	13427	14571	13427	14571
Country	28	28	28	28
BIC	58182.72	55735.47	57194.69	55665.44
LL	-28920.27	-27695.17	-28426.25	-27660.16
df	36	36	36	36
	WtFC		FtWC	
	Men	Women	Men	Women
Working arrangement (Ref: permanent)				
Self-employed with employees	0.253*	0.699***	0.031	0.258
Genuine SSE	0.157	0.612***	0.087	0.788***
Dependent SSE	0.076	0.067	0.067	0.230
Fixed-term	-0.041	-0.070	0.013	-0.123
Informal	-0.396**	-0306**	-0.349**	-0.170*
Working-schedule demands	0.501***	0.431***	0.172**	-0.015
Working arrangement × Working-schedule demands				
Self-employed with employees × Working-schedule demands (std index)	0.203	-0.122	0.050	-0.125
Genuine SSE × Working-schedule demands (std index)	0.153	0.460*	0.050	0.170
Dependent SSE × Working-schedule demands (std index)	0.047	0.626***	0.060	0.543***
Fixed-term × Working-schedule demands (std index)	0.182	0.216*	0.106	0.275*
Informal × Working-schedule demands (std index)	-0.478*	0.521***	-0.048	0.116
Constant	2.345***	2.406***	1.070***	0.923***
N.	13427	14571	13427	14571
Country	28	28	28	28
BIC	58217.37	55722.62	57197.33	55635.67

	WtFC		FtWC	
	Men	Women	Men	Women
LL	-28937.6	-27688.75	-28427.58	-27645.27
Df	36	36	36	36

Notes: All models control for all the variable included in Model M5 in Tables 8.6 and 8.7. * p<0.05, ** p<0.01, *** p<0.001
Source: Own elaboration on EWCS, 2015

Starting from the role of household demands, our models in Tables 8.6 and 8.7 show that economic constraints and care pressures are more relevant than the household structure in affecting the level of WtFC and FtWC. For both men and women, the high involvement in care activities with children and the elderly, and experiences of economic insecurity in the household, are positively associated with WtFC and FtWC among adults aged 25–59. By contrast, the presence of a partner accounts for differences among men, but not among women. For men living with a partner, it is positively associated with both subjective WtFC and FtWC, independent of the partner's job condition. Finally, overall household demands do not change the parameters associated with the different work arrangements in affecting WtFC and FtWC (compare models M1 and M2 in Tables 8.6 and 8.7). This suggests that differences across work arrangements are mainly due to working conditions.

Models M3, M4 and M5 in Tables 8.6 and 8.7 progressively control for information on job-related resources and demands.

Starting from WtFC (Table 8.6), models confirm that the highest level of conflict experienced by the self-employed with employees and genuine SSE are largely due to differences in job-related demands and job-related resources (Chung, 2011; Henz and Mills, 2015).

For men, controlling for JD-R almost nullifies the coefficients related to SSE positions: M5 in Table 8.6 shows only a small positive effect associated with the self-employed with employees among men. The higher conflict displayed by the self-employed with employees, genuine SSE and dependent SSE in Figure 8.1 is connected both to their more demanding job conditions in terms of time, pace of work and emotional and cognitive pressures, and to their job-related resources, especially their control over their working time and working from home. While it is not surprising that long working hours and a demanding working-schedule distribution – that is, working unsocial or long hours, and at short notice – fuels the perception of conflict, the parameters associated with resources, such as the level of control of the working schedule and job intensity, indicate that working-time flexibility does not help men to reduce the perception of conflict, which rather increases. This is also the case for working from home, even if the interaction terms displayed in Table 8.8 suggest that this effect varies across work arrangements. In fact, it fuels the WtFC experienced by employees, but its effect is substantially null for self-employed and informal workers.

For women, demands and resources considered are not able to nullify the differences in the perception of WtFC across work arrangements. In fact, model 5 in Table 8.6 shows that – after controlling for household demands and job demands and resources – the self-employed with employees and genuine SSE continue to face significantly higher WtFC than dependent SSE, employees (both permanent and fixed-term) and informal workers. Thus, among women, forms of business that imply higher economic commitment and responsibilities towards employees and/or clients are more exposed to high levels of work–family conflict. As for men, the role of time- and strain-based job demands is prevalent in capturing the level of subjective conflict. On the contrary, resources like autonomy and working-time flexibility do not affect WtFC.

The only exception is having complete control over the working schedule, which – different to men – decreases the level of conflict. Working from home positively affects WtFC but, again, the interactions in Table 8.8 suggest that this effect is significant only for employees and not for self-employed or informal workers.

Focusing on FtWC (Table 8.7), the models show that both job-related resources and demands moderate the perception of conflict, but with different dynamics for different types of self-employment. The greater resources associated with autonomous positions seem to be associated with the greater conflict perceived by dependent SSE, and in the case of men only, also by genuine SSE. For the self-employed with employees, the higher levels of conflict are mainly due to the higher job-related demands associated with these positions.

For men, the higher conflict displayed by the self-employed with employees, genuine SSE and dependent SSE is connected both to their higher job-related resources (control over the working schedule and working from home) and to their more demanding job conditions in terms of time, pace of work and emotional pressures. Forms of flexibility and control over working schedules and working from home nullify the higher conflict displayed by genuine and dependent SSE workers. For the self-employed with employees both job resources and job demands play a role in capturing variations in their FtWC.

For women, demands and resources considered in the models nullify the differences in the perception of FtWC associated with the self-employed with employees and dependent SSE, but has no effect on genuine SSE, who experience levels of FtWC higher than all other work arrangements. Job resources have limited or no effects on FtWC, with the exception, on the one side, of working from home, which fuels the conflict especially for dependent SSE, and, on the other, of the perception of being adequately paid, which allows the perception of conflict among all workers to be reduced. Working time, pace and emotional demands are positively associated with the perception of FtWC and mainly affect the higher conflict recorded by the self-employed with employees. Differently from WtFC, only the total number of hours worked per week plays a role in fuelling the conflict between family and work, while the quality of the working-schedule distribution does not seem to have a role in this dynamic.

7.   DISCUSSION

The empirical exercise proposed in this chapter contributes to the debate on how the heterogeneous category of self-employed workers experiences work–family conflict. The adoption of a more detailed classification of self-employment – based on the level of economic independence in managing the business – within the frame of the JD-R approach allows us to address the heterogeneity within the wide category of self-employment as well as to identify differences in the subjective WtFC and FtWC.

In the case of WtFC, the differences across self-employment types and other work arrangements are mainly connected to variations in the levels of job-related demands associated with different positions, while job-related resources have a limited role in the perception of conflict. Despite having the highest availability of autonomy and control over their job conditions, the self-employed with employees and the genuine SSE share such overwhelming job demands (job pressures, responsibilities and commitment over their business) that they end up increasing the perception of work–family conflict. Only dependent SSE, with job-related demands closer to those of employees, perceive a lower conflict, reaching levels of subjective WtFC similar to those of employees.

Our findings for WtFC are in line with the body of the literature that stresses the role of the demands related to self-employment – mainly high job involvement and time commitment – which favour a perception of conflict that is not counter-balanced by the available job resources (Annink and den Dulk, 2012; König and Cesinger, 2015; Parasuraman and Simmers, 2001). The role of job-related resources is in fact ambivalent: resources such as job autonomy and working-schedule flexibility or control have limited (or no) power in counteracting job-related time, task and workload pressures. Job resources are therefore, in many cases, a source of conflict. This means that higher control, autonomy and flexibility over a job position do not mitigate the experience of conflict that flows from work to the private sphere as expected by those scholars who understand self-employment mainly as a resource. An interesting exception is the effect associated with having complete control over the working schedule. In the case of women, it helps to reduce the perception of conflict, while for men all types of working-schedule flexibilities fuel the subjective perceptions of conflict that flow from work to family as well as from family to work. This could be connected to the fact that it is still uncommon among men to challenge hegemonic masculinity practices at work by dedicating time to family responsibilities (Murgia and Poggio, 2013; Musumeci and Santero, 2018).

As far as the FtWC is concerned, while descriptive statistics do not point out significant differences across self-employed types, the estimated models show that job-related resources and demands play different roles according to the type of self-employment. In the case of self-employed workers with employees, the higher levels of FtWC are substantially connected to their higher job-related demands. In the case of SSE workers, both dependent and genuine, the higher perception of conflict is connected to job-related resources – mainly working from home and a flexible working schedule – which make the boundaries between work and private life more permeable, favouring a spill-over effect of home pressures in the work sphere. An interesting exception to this picture is represented by genuine SSE women, for whom job-related resources and demands do not affect the levels of FtWC, which remain the highest, independent of job conditions. This could be related to a lack of support in the management of their activity, which is not as demanding as for self-employed women with employees, but which nevertheless probably implies a higher level of commitment than for dependent SSE women.

To summarize, in the case of FtWC, the perspective that understands self-employment as a job demand fits with the higher conflict experienced by self-employed workers with employees, while the perspective that stresses the role of job resources better fits the situation of the SSE, both dependent and genuine, with the exception of genuine SSE women. Moreover, different from what was expected by both perspectives, the dependent self-employed – who are defined by a low economic commitment and lower authority and autonomy over their business – do not have a lower perception of FtWC than other types of self-employed workers.

8.   CONCLUSIONS: ADVANTAGES AND DISADVANTAGES OF THE JD-R FRAMEWORK APPLIED TO SELF-EMPLOYMENT

The JD-R model has become highly popular with researchers over the last 20 years. It has its roots in the psychological debate that studies how job conditions of dependent workers in big companies predict well-being, burnout and performance at work (Bakker and Demerouti, 2007; Schaufeli and Taris, 2014). It has then also successfully entered into the sociological debate on work–life balance to analyse how the ongoing transformations of work (that is, the proliferation of non-standard and flexible work arrangements) and family (that is, the growth of dual-earner households) are challenging the boundaries between work and private spheres, and the interaction between work and family roles (Schieman, Glavin and Milkie, 2009; Drobnic and Guillén, 2011; Glavin and Schieman, 2012).

As highlighted by Schaufeli and Taris (2014), the reason for this success lies in the broad scope and flexibility of the JD-R framework. The basic assumption of this approach – according to which (im)balance between any positive (resources) and any negative (demands) job or family characteristics may affect health well-being and other work and life conditions – can, in fact, be applied to a wide variety of work settings, including self-employment.

The broad scope and flexibility of the JD-R framework has two main implications. Firstly, although this approach allows us to develop a fair description of the way demands and resources are associated with different kinds of outcomes (work–family conflict, well-being, and so on), it provides limited insights about the mechanisms behind such relations (Schaufeli and Taris, 2014). Thus, on the one side the JD-R approach has the advantage of explaining how demands and resources are related to relevant outcomes, but on the other side it does not help to explain why this happens. Secondly, due to its broad scope and flexibility, the JD-R framework can be easily combined with other theoretical frameworks in order to overcome its lack of explanatory power. For example, it has been combined with the person–environment fit theory to analyse how the societal constraints affect preferences and options about work–life interferences (Voydanoff, 2005; Glavin and Schieman, 2012; Riva, Lucchini and Russo, 2019). A further example is its combination with the border theory to investigate how job-related demands and resources are connected with work–family conflict (Clark, 2000; Glavin and Schieman, 2012). The combination of the JD-R framework and border theory has also been employed, as in the case of this chapter, to explain the relations between self-employment and work–family conflict (Reynolds and Renzulli, 2005).

From a methodological point of view, the application of the JD-R framework faces three main limits that represent a challenge for future researchers. Firstly, different empirical research has operationalized the main outcomes in different ways (Schaufeli and Taris, 2014; Kossek and Lee, 2017). In the specific case of the literature that analyses work–family conflict, for example, some studies measure work–family conflict as a composite index that summarizes every form of conflict, while others, as in the case study presented in this chapter, distinguish the direction of the conflict – from work to family and from family to work (Reynolds and Renzulli, 2005) – and also further distinguish the type of conflict (time-based vs strain-based) (König and Cesinger, 2015). The lack of consistency in the operationalization of work–family conflict across studies challenges and limits the effective comparability of different studies as well as the generalizability of results (Schaufeli and Taris, 2014; Kossek and Lee, 2017).

Secondly, the conceptual difference between job demands and job resources is not as neat as it might seem at first glance. In many studies, the identification and configuration of demands and resources are bound to the specific research case study and to different research outcomes. In the empirical exercise proposed in this chapter, for example, we considered as resources different forms of control and flexibility on the working schedule and working from home, because they are job conditions that should allow workers to be attached to the labour market and integrate them in the workplace. However, according to our findings, they produce negative consequences on the balance between work and family roles. Thus, they can hardly be considered as a 'resource' for work–life balance. From this perspective, an important effort in future research is to improve the definition and measurement of demand and resources, as well as our understanding about the cases in which specific job and family conditions can be considered to be resources or demands, and/or produce different consequences for different outcomes, such as the level of perceived work–family conflict (Schaufeli and Taris, 2014; Kossek and Lee, 2017).

Finally, the cross-sectional nature of the available data limits the quality of the analysis. The main implication is that research has to rely only on theory to establish causal relations (Glavin and Schieman, 2012). Therefore, longitudinal data is required to lead a more accurate analysis of the mechanisms hypothesized within the JD-R framework (Schaufeli and Taris, 2014; Kossek and Lee, 2017).

The empirical exercise proposed in this chapter shows that the limitations related to the data are even more serious when the focus of the study is on self-employment. Firstly, there is a lack of surveys that allow us to analyse the heterogeneity of working conditions within self-employment. Secondly, while the dimensions that define dependent job positions are more consolidated in the literature, the analyses on self-employment working conditions are less developed. For instance, while for employees it is possible to rely on information on the support they receive in the work environment and in managing their activity, this is not the case for self-employment. Finally, the sets of variables that describe working conditions are in many cases targeted only on dependent or on independent workers, and this reduces the dimensions on which experiences of self-employed workers and employees can be effectively compared.

NOTE

1.   This chapter is part of the SHARE project, which has received funding from the European Research Council (ERC) under the European Union's Horizon 2020 research and innovation programme (Grant Agreement N. 715950).

REFERENCES

Abendroth, A. K., and L. den Dulk (2011) 'Support for the work-life balance in Europe: the impact of state, workplace and family support on work-life balance satisfaction', *Work, Employment and Society*, **25**(2), 234–256.
Annink, A., and L. den Dulk (2012) 'Autonomy: the panacea for self-employed women's work-life balance?', *Community, Work and Family*, **15**(4), 383–402.
Annink, A., L. den Dulk and B. Steijn (2016) 'Work–family conflict among employees and the self-employed across Europe', *Social Indicators Research*, **126**(2), 571–593.
Ashforth, B. E., G. E. Kreiner and M. Fugate (2000) 'All in a day's work: boundaries and micro role transitions', *Academy of Management Review*, **25**(3), 472–491.
Bakker, A. B., and E. Demerouti (2007) 'The job demands-resources model: state of the art', *Journal of Managerial Psychology*, **22**(3), 309–328.
Bakker, A. B., L. L. ten Brummelhuis, J. T. Prins and F. M. M. A. va. der Heijden (2011) 'Applying the job demands–resources model to the work–home interface: a study among medical residents and their partners', *Journal of Vocational Behavior*, **79**(1), 170–180.

Bianchi, S. M., and M. A. Milkie (2010) 'Work and family research in the first decade of the 21st century', *Journal of Marriage and Family*, **72**(3), 705–725.

Bozzon, R., and A. Murgia (2021) 'Work-family conflict in Europe: a focus on the heterogeneity of self-employment', *Community, Work and Family*, **24**(1), 93–113.

Chung, H. (2011) 'Work-Family Conflict across 28 European Countries: A Multi-Level Approach', in S. Drobnic and A. M. Guillén (eds), *Work-Life Balance in Europe*. London: Palgrave Macmillan, pp. 42–68.

Clark, S. C. (2000) 'Work/family border theory: a new theory of work/family balance', *Human Relations*, **53**(6), 747–770.

Crompton, R., and C. Lyonette (2006) 'Work-life "balance" in Europe', *Acta Sociologica*, **49**(4), 379–393.

Drobnic, S., and A. M. Guillén (eds) (2011) *Work-Life Balance in Europe*. London: Palgrave Macmillan.

Eurofound (2017) *European Working Conditions Survey, 2015*. [Data collection]. 4th Edition. UK Data Service. SN: 8098, accessed 14 January 2021 at https://beta.ukdataservice.ac.uk/datacatalogue/studies/study?id=8098.

Fahlén, S. (2012) *Facets of Work–Life Balance across Europe: How the Interplay of Institutional Contexts, Work Arrangements and Individual Resources Affect Capabilities for Having a Family, and for Being Involved in Family Life*. Stockholm University, Department of Sociology, accessed 14 January 2021 at http://su.diva-portal.org/smash/record.jsf?pid=diva2%3A555515&dswid=-4325.

Fahlén, S. (2014) 'Does gender matter? Policies, norms and the gender gap in work-to-home and home-to-work conflict across Europe', *Community, Work and Family*, **17**(4), 371–391.

Gallie, D., and H. Russell (2009) 'Work-family conflict and working conditions in Western Europe', *Social Indicators Research*, **93**(3), 445–467.

Glavin, P., and S. Schieman (2012) 'Work–family role blurring and work–family conflict: the moderating influence of job resources and job demands', *Work and Occupations*, **39**(1), 71–98.

Greenhaus, J. H., and N. J. Beutell (1985) 'Sources of conflict between work and family roles', *Academy of Management Review*, **10**(1), 76–88.

Hagqvist, E., S. Toivanen and C. Bernhard-Oettel (2018) 'Balancing work and life when self-employed: the role of business characteristics, time demands, and gender contexts', *Social Sciences*, **7**(8), 1–20.

Hagqvist, E., S. Toivanen and S. Vinberg (2015) 'Time strain among employed and self-employed women and men in Sweden', *Society, Health & Vulnerability*, **6**(1), 29183.

Henz, U., and M. Mills (2015) 'Work-life conflict in Britain: job demands and resources', *European Sociological Review*, **31**(1), 1–13.

König, S., and B. Cesinger (2015) 'Gendered work–family conflict in Germany: do self-employment and flexibility matter?', *Work, Employment and Society*, **29**(4), 531–549.

Kossek, E. E., and K. H. Lee (2017) 'Work-family conflict and work-life conflict', *Oxford Research Encyclopedia, Business and Management*, accessed 14 January 2021 at https://doi.org/10.1093/acrefore/9780190224851.013.52.

Murgia, A., and B. Poggio (2013). 'Fathers' stories of resistance and hegemony in organizational cultures', *Gender, Work and Organization*, **20**(4), 413–424.

Musumeci, R., and A. Santero (eds) (2018) *Fathers, Childcare and Work: Cultures, Practices and Policies*. Bingley: Emerald.

Nordenmark, M., S. Vinberg and M. Strandh (2012) 'Job control and demands, work-life balance and wellbeing among self-employed men and women in Europe', *Vulnerable Groups & Inclusion*, **3**(1), 18896.

Parasuraman, S., and C. A. Simmers (2001) 'Type of employment, work-family conflict and well-being: a comparative study', *Journal of Organizational Behavior*, **22**(5), 551–568.

Reynolds, J., and L. A. Renzulli (2005) 'Economic Freedom or Self-imposed Strife: Work-Life Conflict, Gender, and Self-Employment', in L. Keister (ed.) *Entrepreneurship* (Research in the Sociology of Work. Vol. 15). Bingley: Emerald, pp. 33–60.

Riva, E., Lucchini, M., and M. Russo (2019) 'Societal gender inequality as moderator of the relationship between work–life fit and subjective well-being: a multilevel analysis across European countries', *Social Indicators Research*, **143**(2), 657–691.

Russell, H., P. J. O'Connell and F. McGinnity (2009) 'The impact of flexible working arrangements on work–life conflict and work pressure in Ireland', *Gender, Work and Organization*, **16**(1), 73–97.

Schaufeli, W. B., and T. W. Taris (2014) 'A Critical Review of the Job Demands-Resources Model: Implications for Improving Work and Health', in G. F. Bauer and O. Hamming (eds), *Bridging Occupational, Organizational and Public Health*. Dordrecht: Springer Netherlands, pp. 43–68.

Schieman, S., P. Glavin and M. A. Milkie (2009) 'When work interferes with life: work-nonwork interference and the influence of work-related demands and resources', *American Sociological Review*, **74**(6), 966–988.

Voydanoff, P. (2005) 'Toward a conceptualization of perceived work-family fit and balance: a demands and resources approach', *Journal of Marriage and Family*, **67**(4), 822–836.

Williams, C., and I. A. Horodnic (2018) 'Evaluating the prevalence and distribution of dependent self-employment: some lessons from the European Working Conditions Survey', *Industrial Relations Journal*, **49**(2), 109–127.

PART IV

LONGITUDINAL, DISCURSIVE AND NARRATIVE ANALYSIS

9. Qualitative longitudinal research for studying work–family balance (before and after childbirth)

Manuela Naldini

1. INTRODUCTION

In the dynamic of the relationship between families and social change, the transition to parenthood is a crucial phase, when the previous gender division of paid and unpaid work and the existing work–family balance within the couple must be re-examined from the ground up. In all Western countries, the social and cultural meaning of "parenthood" has changed profoundly (Furedi 2002; Daly 2015; Faircloth et al. 2015). Three major transformations have taken place (Long et al. 2018). The first concerns *if* one becomes a parent; that is, becoming a parent is no longer taken for granted, as it was in the past, but is the result of a "choice", of a "wish". Likewise, not becoming a parent, staying "child-free", is also a choice.

Second, *when* people become parents for the first time has changed. Postponing, and having fewer children, is one of the main characteristics of becoming parents nowadays.

Third, *how* people become parents, and child–parent relationships, have changed. This transformation is two-fold. The rise of conjugal instability, on the one hand, and the spread of assisted reproductive technologies, on the other hand, have increased the ways of (and the opportunities for) becoming parents or experiencing parenthood over the life course. In addition, what has changed is the "how", in terms of the essence (or the substance) of being parents, the cultural and social meaning of becoming a parent, or the "stuff" of parenthood, as La Rossa and La Rossa (1981) phrased it. This process has brought about what is called the new "culture of intensive parenthood" (Hays 1996; Faircloth et al. 2015), which mirrors the "new childhood" culture (Qvortrup 2005; Lister 2006). Nowadays, parents are expected to do much more than just raise their children and take care of them. How parents nurse or feed their children; what time they put them to bed; what they read to them or how they play with them; what rules they set; if, when and for how long they let them go out to play or leave them with grandparents or a baby-sitter: everything is thought out, pondered and discussed; everything comes under the precise – but often contrasting – guidance of the experts (Musumeci and Naldini 2017).

This new "culture of parenthood" not only calls for "intensity", but it operates at different levels, and it throws light on stark cultural and social contrasts, affecting women in particular (Naldini 2015b). On the employment side, motherhood and work have become two life experiences that women must balance and hold together. Women are expected to be in paid work and to reconcile work and family, and both women and men are requested to conform to the "unconditional adult worker" model (Lewis 2006). As argued by Hays (1996, p. xiii) the relationship between "intensive mothering" and work outside of the home is not easy; limited access to parental leaves, not enough flexible working hours, shortage of daycare centers and a lack of control over their workload may make it harder for mothers and fathers to respond to the changing needs of their families and the demands coming from being parents (Gornick and Meyers 2003).

To sum up, the changes in if, when and how to become parents, and above all the substance of becoming parents, take place as part of a social construction of parenthood that is permeated by the economic, cultural and institutional context where it concretely unfolds. And these contexts have undergone equally significant changes. The experiences and life courses of young men and women before the arrival of the first child have also changed, with a degree of convergence between the two genders that has never been seen before, in terms of the time and resources invested in education, sexual relations and intimacy, and training and work experience. Yet it seems that to become first-time parents marks a difference in the balance of work and family life. Timely, contemporary qualitative longitudinal research has become more widely available and an increasingly fruitful area of research, especially when it comes to understanding and to assessing change and persistence of separate gender spheres in a life-course perspective.

In this chapter, after analyzing the literature on the relation between the transition to parenthood and work–family balance (Section 2), I illustrate the theoretical and methodological challenges of a qualitative longitudinal study (QLS) of the transition to parenthood and work–family balance in the Italian context (Section 3). Throughout the discussion of the main framework, the research design, results, and practices involved in data analysis, the chapter will address two different broad issues (Section 4).

2. TRANSITION TO PARENTHOOD AND WORK–FAMILY LIFE: WHAT DO WE KNOW?

International studies on the changes in gender relations, between family and work, often speak of these changes as being a revolution, but one that is "incomplete" (Gerson 2010) or "stalled" (Hochschild 1989): a revolution that has stopped short at the threshold of the family home, since most of the changes have taken place in women's participation in paid work, but not in men's participation in unpaid household work. In addition, international studies on work–family gender differences have pointed to a major gap between attitudes and actual behaviors (Grunow and Evertsson 2016). Men and women would like greater equity in both the family and the job market, at least at the level of social desirability, than they are in fact able to achieve. This gap, which in a certain sense holds out hope for change as well as providing fertile ground for contradictions, would also appear to emerge for men in the new models of fatherhood, an "intimate fatherhood" that calls for "involved fathers" and "caring fathers", but which is more often announced and desired than actually practiced, while mothers continue to shoulder most of the childcare – and most of the housework (Dermott 2003; Miller 2005, 2011).

Though there is an extensive literature on the representations, the "discourses" and the experiences of motherhood and fatherhood at the international level (Hobson and Morgan 2002; Miller 2010, 2011; Neale 2011), and, more recently, in Italy (Ruspini 2006; Murgia and Poggio 2011; Magaraggia 2013, 2015), few scholars have focused on how crucial the transition to parenthood is, not only because of the major symbolic and material redefinition it entails in men's and women's life courses, but also because of the macro-level implications for demographic and economic equilibrium that have been emphasized in the literature (Ferrera 2008; Esping-Andersen 2009), and its repercussions on inequality, and on gender disparity in particular. However, as a number of international studies (Fox 2009, Grunow and Evertsson 2016) have pointed out, this move towards convergence slows and stops at a certain point in the life course, and specifically when the first child is born. Pronounced asymmetries between men and women come to the surface or are reinforced upon the arrival of the first child. This, indeed, is a major decision that calls for an intense, continuous process of adaptation: a redefinition of the priorities assigned to work and the family. Though the scenario doubtless differs from that faced by past generations, becoming parents in Western societies today still means different things for men and women, because the investments that they make – or that are expected of them – in paid work, housework and childcare are still different. As several international studies have shown (Fox 2009; Grunow et al. 2012; Grunow and Evertsson 2016, 2019), it is in the period between expecting a baby and the first years of the child's life that gender expectations show their full force, and some of the most significant processes in the social reproduction of gender inequalities come into play. This is the period when new models can be tried out, "undoing gender" and making room for change, since it is during this life phase that previous gender division of paid and unpaid work and the existing work–family balance within the couple must be re-examined from the ground up. Precisely because this period is so crucial, the focus must be on the dynamic and on the development of what happens in the couple before and after childbirth in terms of work and family life. In order to understand the dynamic and the change over time we need to collect and analyze longitudinal data (Naldini 2015a, 2015b).

3.   THE QUALITATIVE LONGITUDINAL STUDY OF COUPLES IN ITALY: THEORETICAL AND METHODOLOGICAL CHALLENGES

Against the backdrop of change and continuity described in studies of the transition to parenthood and in studies on gender division in balancing work and family, the study that I use in this chapter as the basis of a number of theoretical and methodological reflections has been conducted in a specific institutional context which has been labeled "familism by default" (Saraceno and Keck 2010). This context is far from being family-friendly (Fine-Davis et al. 2004, Naldini and Saraceno 2011), not only for mothers but also for fathers (Murgia and Poggio 2011, Magaraggia 2013, Musumeci and Santero, 2018). Italy is a social and cultural context defined by norms, values and orientations that support specific ways of representing, thinking about and "staging" motherhood and fatherhood, encouraging gender-specific expectations and practices (Naldini 2015b, Bertolini et al. 2016). Within this institutional and cultural context, and despite the fact that the life courses of young women and men are becoming more similar, two main questions were raised.

First, how does the arrival of a child contribute to reproducing gendered divisions of labor, and when are these divisions undone?

Second, why do more democratic and egalitarian models of relationships in the couple and the family fail to translate into a more equal division of housework and parenting practices, and thus more of a gender balance between work and family life? What kind of study and which type of methodology are more suitable to answer these questions?

3.1   Project and Research Design

The study I am going to discuss in this chapter stems from a wider research project which focused on the transition to parenthood in dual-earner couples in order to understand how male and female gender models are "done" and "undone" (Naldini 2015a). To do so, it employed different analytical lenses (those of the sociology of the family and of the sociology of work, developmental and psychodynamic psychology, and, lastly, demographics) and both quantitative and qualitative investigative tools. The transition to parenthood was the primary object of the research project, with a focus on the changes in what is expected by and from future parents and new parents, as well as the interdependence between the spheres of family and work, and between the gender "convergences" – or lack thereof – between men and women, fathers and mothers, family and work. The research design sought to establish a dialog between qualitative and quantitative research as well as between different theoretical and disciplinary perspectives.[1]

3.2   Theoretical Frameworks: Gender Approach and a Life-Course Perspective

Given the complex nature of the phenomenon, and given the characteristics of the research group, the study could not draw on a single, uniform theoretical corpus (Naldini 2015b).[2] However, certain perspectives undoubtedly came to the fore in guiding our work, and were used to explain the production and reproduction of gendered divisions of family and work responsibilities.

First, we used a life-course perspective which combines the micro dimension of the paths taken by the individuals and the couple with the macro dimension of the surrounding contexts. Analyzing the transition to parenthood with a life-course approach (Elder 1985; Saraceno 2001, Elder 2003) means going beyond "individualist" paradigms. The multidimensional approach to the life course helps in capturing the notion of time implied in social change, and in bridging the micro and the macro and the complex relationship between economic and institutional systems of life courses of individuals and families. Social change, as seen from the life-course perspective, implies the notion of time and lies at the intersection of three axes: individual time, generational time and historical time. Conceptualizing and measuring the life course as a bundle of interdependent trajectories, marked by events and turning points, whose development is intertwined with the trajectories of other "linked" individuals, is very important when the unit of analysis is couples' "trajectories" during a transition.

Second, we adopt a gender approach. The category of gender, as is well known, is applied in many areas of study. Seen as both a "social construction" (Piccone Stella and Saraceno 1996) and as a structure centering on the reproductive arena which is constructed in relationships and everyday practices by "doing gender" (Connell 1987, West and Zimmerman 2002), it is central to any discussion of motherhood and fatherhood.

The transition to parenthood is a particularly important area for investigating how gender roles change – or do not change – in contemporary societies, which in other respects show many similarities in what men and women experience along the long road to adulthood (Deutsch 1999, Grunow et al. 2012).

It is in this stage of the life course, with the arrival of the first child, that women and men find themselves having to redefine not only their own identities as women who are about to become mothers and men who are about to become fathers, but also their priorities as regards work and the family in an institutional and cultural context that assigns different roles to mothers and fathers.

In the attempt to adopt an integrated theoretical framework inspired by the life-course and gender perspectives while drawing together all of the various micro and macro factors and cultural, institutional and material factors, we anchored our efforts in the work of the scholars who have focused on integrative approaches (Connell 1987, Risman 2004).

Specifically, we took the analytical tack suggested by Barbara Risman (2004), who argues that gender should be considered as a social structure, on the same plane as politics and economics. According to Risman, gender is thus embedded in every aspect of society, and is multidimensional in nature, though analytically we can distinguish between three different levels at which it operates. These are also the levels at which gender inequalities are "done" and "undone".

The "gender as social structure" approach helps to explain that the gender structure has consequences on three dimensions: (1) at the individual level, for the development of gendered selves; (2) at the interactional level, as men and women face different cultural expectations; (3) at the institutional level, where both cultural norms and regulations regarding resource distribution and material goods are gender-specific. These three levels must be considered in conjunction, both in trying to explain the mechanisms that produce and reproduce gender, and – above all – when the goal is also a greater "gender parity", which means redressing the imbalance in power between men and women in society. Gender, in fact, structures and differentiates opportunities and presents different constraints for men and women.

Using Giddens' first formulation (Giddens 1984) and Connell's (1987) application of it, Risman argues that the concern should be with social structure as both constraint and created by action. "We must pay attention both to how structure shapes individual choice and social interaction and how human agency creates, sustains, and modifies current structure. Action itself may change the immediate and future context" (Risman and Davis, 2013, p. 12).

In other words, we blend the integrative "gender as social structure" perspective proposed by Risman (2004; Risman and Davis 2013), which focuses on social processes that may explain the gender structure, with the time-sensitive life-course approach (Elder 1995, 2003).

3.3   Methodology: Qualitative Longitudinal Study

In order to understand change over time, it has become more widespread to collect and analyze longitudinal qualitative data. As recently reported by Thomson and McLeod (2015) there has been considerable investment in QLS, both in substantive research projects and in investigating its methodological innovations and challenges – but only in some countries, mainly the United Kingdom (Corden and Millar 2007b, Miller 2011) – and published literature reviews and mappings of the field (Holland et al. 2006, Corden and Millar 2007a). National funding commitments have given rise to a stream of work that is both qualitative and longitudinal (Elliott, Holland and Thomson 2007; Shirani and Henwood 2011; Timescapes 2011; Neale 2011). There are other important national traditions which include biographical research in Germany (Rosenthal 1998, Heinz and Krüger 2001) and France (Bertaux 1981, Bertaux and Thompson 1997), longitudinal youth studies in Australia (McLeod and Yates 2006, Woodman and Wyn 2015) and educational and social work research in Norway (Helgeland 2010). In the same stream of research, to gain insights in couple processes, the collection of qualitative longitudinal interview data on both partners of couples at (at least) two points in time becomes crucial (Miller 2011). This approach enables researchers to analyze how interviewees nested in couples experience, anticipate and respond to changes. The comparison of different couples who face similar changes in their lives allows us to identify similarities and differences in ways of reacting to a similar situation and to find reasons for these similarities and differences.

3.3.1 The Italian qualitative longitudinal study

The QLS reconstructs the first transition to parenthood of 22 Italian middle-class dual-earner couples living in Turin and the surrounding area. A total of 88 in-depth antenatal and postnatal interviews were conducted between 2010 and 2013. In terms of sample strategy, we followed the transPARENT project strategy;[3] that is, we used a theory-based sampling approach, since previous research suggests that in many Western countries couples initially have an egalitarian division of paid and unpaid work. Therefore, the sample was intentionally biased towards "gender oriented" couples. Both partners were interviewed separately, the first time before their baby's arrival and the second when the child was aged 1 year and 6 months. The four interviews per couple allowed us to get information on different topics: (1) the pre-pregnancy period, which was reconstructed retrospectively during the antenatal interview; (2) pregnancy; and finally (3) when the son/daughter was about a year and a half old.[4]

The couples had been identified through a sampling strategy that started with contacts and formal requests for collaboration with different organizations and institutions of the Turin area (hospital birth centers, counseling services, centers of midwives and gynecologists). All interviewees were born in Italy. The majority of respondents (23 out 44 interviewees) were university graduates (five of these respondents also had a PhD), and this was most common among the women in the sample. Female and male respondents in dual-earner couples had fairly similar employment positions in terms of "power resources". Most women enjoyed a similar or higher position than their male partner in terms of education and standing in the labor market. Despite this, men tended to earn more than their partners (with a few exceptions).

3.3.2 Interviews analyses and analytic strategy

Transcription of the taped interviews conducted during pregnancy (the first wave) and after birth (the second wave) forms the basis for the analyses of couples' "transition to parenthood" in Italy. The in-depth interviews were analyzed using a content-analysis approach (Smith 2000), which identified issues relating to work and care balance, couples' gender ideology and the sharing of childcare, over time and between and within couples. After creating a code book shared by the research team (consisting of four sociologists and two psychologists), the interviews were coded using Atlas.ti software and subjected to content analysis. The analysis of these data is complex, because time and couple dimensions need to be compared separately and in their interaction (change is within couples and over time).

The work was carried out in two stages. In the first stage, we drafted a synopsis for each couple. The synopsis was a sort of "short summary" of the main issues emerging for the different topics (for instance, it was summarizing how housework was shared before the baby's birth, and plans for the first year after the birth). In the second stage, we identified men's and women's arguments concerning "doing gender" (gender ideology) in different areas; for instance, sharing housework, preparing for the baby's birth, and planning childcare. Using Atlas.ti7, the research team encoded recurrent themes and narratives about work, couples' history, care arrangements as planned (the first wave) and implemented (the second wave), and motivations. The coding style became more intersubjective and uniform within the research group by coding the same interview first individually, then in pairs of researchers and then in the entire research group. The research team defined codes, primary document families and procedures.

The interview coding process consisted of: (1) assigning codes to quotations; (2) classifying analytical categories for entire interviews into primary document families; (3) creating 22 longitudinal synopses ("case profiles"), one for each interviewed couple, in order to summarize individual stories and make comparisons between men's and women's narratives and between the first and second waves; (4) creating a file containing the information from the time-use diaries (first-wave interviews), the batteries of questions about the couples' lives and their use and assessment of services (second-wave interviews), the interviewees' sociodemographic characteristics, the aliases and the interview dates.

The list of codes and primary document families, the structure of the synopses, the working descriptions of each analytical category used and the general coding procedures to be followed were tested and defined intersubjectively (see the Methodological Appendix in Naldini 2015a).

The method used to define the codes was developed through a theoretical and methodological exchange with the research group of the Italian team and then confronted with the other research groups involved in the transPARENT project. A code book was prepared to keep track of all analytical and methodological decisions.

Qualitative longitudinal data on couples offer huge potential but also demand a complex strategy of analysis in order to take into consideration the various levels of interest. However, as we will discuss later, the analysis of these data is complex, because the couple and time dimensions need to be compared separately and in their interaction (change within couples over time). In the analysis we have considered the unfolding of individual stories over time, with two specific points in time (before and after the baby's birth, even though with retrospective information). Nevertheless, the guideline of the interviews is structured around the reconstruction of the couple's life during that time with a retrospective approach, and a prospective approach as far as the first-wave interviews is concerned. Following participants as they journey through time can provide a more dynamic sense of their changing identifications and the emergence of new influences on their thoughts and actions. But many analytical challenges emerge when you have to analyze and compare data within and between couples over time. In the next paragraph, the main results of the study are presented and relevant methodological issues discussed.

3.4   Main Results[5]

A life-course perspective sheds light on the importance of time, change and continuity within individual lives as well as the interrelationship of individual experience (and/or couples' and families' experiences) and their social context. It emphasizes the micro–macro links, highlighting the ways in which particular historical periods and locations shape the experiences of age cohorts as well as differences and inequalities between individuals (couples/families). This is why before discussing the main findings at the micro level, to understand the transition to parenthood as "the subjective experience of personal change" of these parents we need to put couples' narratives in their institutional context.

3.4.1   The Italian institutional context

The transition to parenthood structures women's and men's lives differently according to the institutional contexts – specifically the cultural, labor market and family-policy contexts – in which the parents find themselves and which are particularly influential for balancing work and family. In recent decades, Italian families have changed hugely: young people tend to stay longer in the parental home, postpone marriage, have their first child later in life and have fewer children (Aassve et al. 2002, Sobotka and Toulemon 2008, Olàh 2015). In the early 1990s, Italy (together with Spain) was one of the first European countries to drop to lowest-low fertility rates (Kohler et al. 2002), a level where Italy remains today.[6] As regards women's participation in the workforce, Italy is still below the European average, though dual-earner families prevail in the northern regions of the country, where 60 to 70 percent of mothers with very young children are in the labor market (Istat 2011). There are several circumstances related to the institutional context which make it difficult for young Italian couples in the transition to parenthood to combine family and work and to embrace gender equality in doing so. First, the increase in the numbers of working women has not resulted in a more balanced division of household responsibilities and childcare between men and women (Eurostat 2009). In other words, women's growing involvement in the world of paid work does not seem to have changed the expectations and obligations connected with their role as caregivers, particularly for small children. In this "traditional" model of complementary roles and separate spheres, we have a gender culture that sees fathers primarily as earners and mothers primarily as carers. Second, all Italian research points to the centrality of the family in taking care of small children (Istat 2011). Attitudinal data show that in Italy mothers and fathers are still subject to very different expectations as regards childcare. For example, in the various cross-country surveys such as the European Social Survey, International Social Survey Panel and World Value Study, some of which are also comparable across time, Italy is the country with the highest percentage of respondents who state that they agree that pre-school children are likely to suffer if their mother works, even though Italy also has one of the highest rates of nursery school attendance (for ages 3–6). Third, labor market changes during a time of economic recession have resulted in an increasing number of young adults (and women) who are employed in non-standard jobs, especially in part-time and temporary employment (Bertolini et al. 2016).

Fourth, Italy is an example of the Mediterranean welfare model, where in the absence of strong state involvement the family (and the women within the family) is seen as the main provider of care. This "unsupported familism" (Saraceno and Keck 2010) means that there are few services such as childcare facilities, and little effort has gone into developing work–family balance policies. Though Law 53/2000 on parental leave has brought about a major policy shift in the latter area by defining childcare as a parental, rather than solely maternal, responsibility, it has several shortcomings, especially for parents-to-be or for parents who have an unstable job trajectory. The parental leave replacement rate is only 30 percent of pay for a maximum of six months for each parent. Moreover, although the new law introduces a "use it or lose it" quota for the father, the rate of take-up by fathers remains very low (Koslowski, Blum and Moss 2016). Non-standard work contracts, which mainly affect men and women of reproductive age, are excluded from some measures protecting motherhood or supporting work–family balance, and where entitlements do exist, they are difficult to implement (Bertolini 2006). Moreover, there are relatively few childcare services such as nursery schools for children under 3 years of age. Even in regions – for example, Northern Italy – and municipalities where coverage is higher, the figure remains well below the 33 percent "Barcelona target" (Istat 2014, Naldini and Santero 2019). Work–family balance policy in Italy is also inadequate at company level, where flexible work schedules, part-time work and "family-friendly" measures are not widespread and/or many employees are unable to take advantage of them. Hence, in Italy the dilemma of work versus family is still largely relegated to the private sphere, managing family and work is mostly left up to women, and the tensions between changes in women's lives, resistant institutions and the issues of gender imbalance are not addressed. The couples' narratives in our study must thus be set against the background of Italy's gender norms, welfare policies and maternal labor market attachment, which are grounded in the male-breadwinner family model and in the type of "unsupported familialism" which features the Italian welfare state.

Table 9.1   Childcare strategies and gender in practice before and after childbirth – an analytical framework

Type of couple Before	Plans for childcare arrangement Before	Childcare strategies in practices After	Gap between Before–after	Time dynamic of childcare arrangement	Why	How
(In)Equality in his/her attitudes and behaviors towards domestic and paid work	Who in terms of gender, and what – actors and institutions involved in the care When – timing of different phases of childcare arrangements	Who in terms of gender, and what – actors and institutions involved in the care When – timing of different phases of childcare arrangements	– Between plans and practices – Between values/ideals and practices	– Static – Dynamic (expected change for the future)	Motivations for the choices and the shift in the choice (what they think about)	Mechanisms (at couple and institutional level) explaining "doing" and "undoing" gender

3.4.2   The private, family-based and "de-politicized" conception of childcare

What are the main findings that emerge from our longitudinal analysis of work–life balance strategies before and after the birth of the first child? Are parents' childcare plans, strategies and ideals/values about care before the birth in line with childcare practices after childbirth? How do parents account for their choices? And what are the main mechanisms that contribute to "doing" or, alternatively, "undoing" gender? In Table 9.1 is one example of the analytical framework used to analyze changes over time in a before-and-after approach which emphasizes differences between "then" and "now". Specifically, the framework is applied to childcare strategies and gender practices before and after childbirth.

As for the substantial results, the first finding of the longitudinal study on the transition to parenthood is that the childcare arrangements that are expected, planned and put into practice are heavily influenced by the parents' ideas about what is "best for the baby" both before and after the birth.

Before birth

Expectant mothers and fathers plan for the future thinking about what is best for the baby. The mother's presence in the first 12 months is considered best. The prevailing model is that of the mother's indispensability (and irreplaceability): the mother must stay with the baby as much as possible, especially because the couples believe strongly in the importance of breastfeeding for as long as possible. The father's presence during the first 12 months is regarded as a support for the mother's role. The experts in this field are the mothers. This is the dominant discourse in the justifications advanced for planned or enacted work–life balance strategies, and which would appear to underlie the main mechanisms of dichotomous gender construction which result in an asymmetrical division of roles between mother and father (Bertolini et al. 2016).

After birth
Work–life balance practices are temporary and negotiated solutions to the childcare dilemma. In most cases, work–life balance practices after the child's birth correspond to those planned by the expectant couple. In the first year of the child's life, it is generally preferred that the mother and family be responsible for childcare. After the first 12–18 months, there is a shift towards work–life balance strategies that are more open to involving non-family members and the use of home-based mini daycare centers, occasional childcare services or nursery schools, and plans are made to enroll the child in kindergarten at 3 years of age (Musumeci et al. 2015).

3.4.3   Fathers' presence is "circumscribed"
A second finding is that future fathers, even before the child's birth, move away from the old male-breadwinner model. For example, they begin to show a great deal of emotional involvement during their partner's pregnancy.

After the birth, in any case, fathers' and mothers' narratives, like their care practices, indicate that the father's presence in daily childcare is "circumscribed", and that an "alternative" model of fatherhood struggles to take clear shape. On the fatherhood front, then, both the longitudinal interviews and the focus groups (Bertone et al. 2015) where fathers and mothers discussed fatherhood reveal areas of continuity and many breaks with the past, some of which are counter-normative (fathers who take the "breastfeeding leave", or fathers who cut back on their work schedules), as well as significant variability in motivations and behavior, and a group of fathers who are coming to grips with men's "dual presence" in the workplace and the domestic sphere.

There can be no doubt that fathers' counter-normative behavior is still heavily penalized, especially at the workplace, as shown by the analysis of the few cases of "innovator" fathers, both when the father's greater involvement in childcare stems from subjective reasons or bargaining between the couple, and when he finds himself at home with the child through no choice of his own and, at the end, finds it tiring but rewarding.

The "discourse" on the changing representations of fatherhood is blended with an unchanging "essence", where the differences between male and female are seen as "incarnate" and thus inscribed not only in the body and in the biological differences between men and women (as witnessed by the importance assigned to breastfeeding), but also in men's and women's differing experiences and lessons learned regarding the ability to deal with care and the emotions (Naldini and Torrioni 2015).

The study shows that expectations and antenatal practices bear heavily on the processes of "doing gender", both in orienting the couple's adaptation to co-parenthood and in whether childcare is shared more equally. Fathers' resistance to greater involvement tends to make mothers expect less of them in the long run, in a relational and institutional context where it would appear that greater participation cannot legitimately be expected.

3.4.4   De-traditionalization and naturalization: re-interpreting the constraints

A third finding of the study is that the material, institutional and cultural constraints typical of Italy have considerable weight, both in dissuading innovative behavior on the part of fathers, and in reinforcing the idea that mothers are irreplaceable and in encouraging a sort of "motherhood mystique" which pushes women – and men too – to rationalizations that draw on the repertories of "naturalization" to restore the equilibria of a couple that sees itself as egalitarian.

The idea of nature, the body, instinct – especially in connection with breastfeeding – is ever-present and powerful, as well as being a readily accessible explanation to justify her choices at home and his choices at work, and to justify the "natural" differences between men and women as regards work and the family in the first years of the child's life.

Though mothers expect more from their partners both before the child's birth and after its first year of life, they tend to justify the partner's limited participation, and consider themselves "lucky" if the partner does housework or takes care of the child. Women do not call for departures from male gender practices, as even those who start from non-conventional positions tend to imagine their partners' behavior as taking place within familiar boundaries. They do not object, or at least not much, if their partners do not take paternity leave (except for a few examples of counter-normative behavior), they do not expect their spouses to be better or at least as good at taking care of the child as they are, and they do not expect that their partners sacrifice working hours or their career in order to stay with the child.

In a life-course analysis, which deals less with the individual life course than with "linked lives", the constraints (the economic crisis, for instance) seem to be re-interpreted differently for men and women.

On the employment front, in a period marked by economic crisis and labor market reforms that have resulted in more atypical and unstable jobs, the arrival of a desired child would appear to reduce mothers' individual freedom on the labor market. On the other hand, however, it can be a resource that helps mothers, and future mothers in particular, to cope with the dissatisfaction that the workplace can bring. Thus, while for women the economic crisis seems to have aggravated gender divisions and pushed mothers to be more invested in the family sphere, for men it appears to have reduced fathers' freedom as regards their involvement in childcare (Naldini and Torrioni 2015).

3.4.5   Variability

Though the sample involved in the survey was quite uniform in terms of cultural resources and social status, the study reveals a number of signals of change, and thus of variability in behavior.

Among the mothers, we have on the one hand a group of women who during the transition to motherhood redefined their priorities in favor of the family, finding a balance by applying for part-time work or reducing their job commitments, and on the other hand a group who decided, despite the uncertainties and difficulties, to stay in the labor market, not simply out of need but also from strong personal motivations and a sense of identity rooted in their professional or non-domestic lives.

As for fatherhood, the study revealed areas of continuity and many breaks with the past, some of which are counter-normative (fathers who take the "breastfeeding leave"), as well as significant variability in motivations and behavior, including a group of fathers who struggle daily with combining work and care (Naldini and Torrioni, 2015).

4. POTENTIAL AND PITFALLS OF THE QUALITATIVE LONGITUDINAL STUDY

4.1 Potential

Collecting and analyzing qualitative longitudinal data is increasingly used to understand change over time (Brannen 2002, Saldaña 2003; Miller 2011, Thomson and McLeod 2015). The longitudinal study envisioned a great number of theoretical and methodological challenges, first of all because Italy, unlike the English-speaking world and several other nations, has no tradition of qualitative longitudinal studies. As a matter of fact, the study discussed here is the first longitudinal study of the transition to parenthood in Italy. Methodologically as well as theoretically, the study illustrated in this chapter attempts to adopt an approach that blends a gender perspective with a life-course one. The study is adopting a gender-sensitive approach, not only because men and women are seen in "action" and in the midst of change, but also because by studying exactly when a couple become parents we analyze a crucial phase in the creation of gender. Indeed, in-depth interviews with mothers and fathers before and after the arrival of the first child enabled us to make effective use of an approach based on continuous comparison over time between men and women in an effort to interpret the similarities and differences between the two genders in terms of desires, values, choices, relationships, feelings, practices and experiences.

The life-course perspective, and in particular one of the key principles in the analysis of transitions, that of linked lives (Elder 1995, 2003), proved useful in the longitudinal analysis of the interviews. This is especially useful in couples' narratives, where it is possible to see that the work–life balance strategies adopted in daily life are enacted at the level of the couple and the family. In other words, the notion of linked lives sheds light on the interconnections between the father's and the mother's work and childcare careers and the two partners' different trajectories, and to see how they relate to the biographies of their own parents (in the latter's role as grandparents). In addition, the life-course perspective makes it possible to set the couples' accounts and their narratives into their socio-economic, cultural and institutional context characterized by specific gender ideology, welfare state policies and maternal labor market attachment.

The Italian research team had the opportunity to discuss and develop coding and analysis processes in an innovative and flexible way.[7] Collecting four interviews per couple allowed the research team to analyze how interviewees experience, anticipate and/or respond to change during the transition to parenthood, within the changing Italian context during the period 2010–2013. In addition, comparing different couples who faced similar changes in their lives makes it possible to identify similarities and differences in ways of reacting to a similar situation and to find reasons for these similarities and differences. At the end of this research journey, it should be emphasized that qualitative longitudinal data on couples offer enormous potential but also call for a complex analysis strategy in order to account for the various levels of interest. One of the strong points of this study has been the flexibility and potential for continuous conceptual and theoretical development and innovation throughout the research process.

4.2   Limitations

Though the QLS of the transition to parenthood in Italy provided the research team with a valuable learning opportunity, it also presented a number of pitfalls and several limitations, some of which are typical of longitudinal research (Cotter et al. 2002, Ruspini 2002, Thomson and Holland 2003, Thomson and McLeod 2015), while other are challenges more specific of the complexity of the data collected. Typical limitations of a QLS include the large investments of time and money as well as the long waiting periods involved in conducting interviews; in this specific case the research team had to consider a "reasonable" time, before and after the birth of the child. Other common limitations of a QLS encountered in this study were the large numbers of personnel required and the research personnel turnover. Also, participation attrition and the difficulty of maintaining contact with participants were serious challenges (in the first wave we had 27 interviews, in the second 22 interviews). Beyond the limitations in qualitative data collection, what is most complex in QLS is data analysis. Typically, pitfalls of this analysis are found in the absence of analytical closure, because data might not reach "saturation" or because the analytical possibilities might seem endless (Thomson and McLeod 2015). Specifically, in the Italian QLS those shortfalls became even greater due to the multidimensionality and complexity of data collected. From the reading, it emerges that the stories told by the interviewees can vary among couples as well as by gender (mothers and fathers), and it is not always obvious whether more weight should be given to the couple-specific experience or to the gendered experience. In other words, one has various dimensions to take into account, since a sort of multi-perspective analysis is open to the researchers. One has individual cases that may be analyzed cross-sectionally (in the first and/or second wave), and individual cases that may be analyzed longitudinally. As a matter of fact, handling these data involves several complex tasks. One has the "relational unit" ("the couple" data), which facilitates in-depth, over-time and within-couple perspectives as well as in-depth, over-time and between-couple comparisons. Related to that, one has to take into account that single interviews are available as separate text files but they need to be matched during the analysis by both person ID and couple ID over time. One may analyze data for similar groups of respondents or for different "types" of respondents, cross-sectionally or longitudinally (cf. Vogl et al. 2018).

5.   CONCLUSION

Qualitative longitudinal interview data on couples have become more widely available in a variety of European countries (see Fox 2009; Miller 2011; Naldini 2015a; Grunow and Evertsson 2016, 2019; Dominguez-Folgueras, Jurado-Guerrero and Botia-Morillas 2018). Nevertheless, the challenges of collecting and analyzing such data systematically for an international scientific readership have rarely been addressed. The greatest challenges in studying the transition to parenthood, as in the case illustrated in this chapter, arise not only in designing research, fundraising and collecting data, but in analyzing the mass of complex, multidimensional data collected from the couples over time. Qualitative longitudinal data are extremely rich, and make it possible to study changes over time. This study, with a "before-and-after" approach, illustrates the process of change and detailing the complexities of the journey. Two broad issues emerge from this study. The first issue is the complexity and multidimensionality of handling these data. The possibilities for qualitative longitudinal interviews of couples might seem endless and data might not reach "saturation", the stories told by the interviewees can vary among couples as well as by gender and it is not always obvious whether more weight should be given to the couple-specific experience or to the gendered experience. The second important issue to be addressed is the following: how to foster conceptual and theoretical development that can open up opportunities for methodological innovation in cross-national/ transnational or cross-border comparisons of couples' interview data ("couple cases") from different institutional contexts (countries/languages). In this perspective, discussing the methodological and analytical issues involved in qualitative longitudinal interviews brings us back to the need to understand social change as contextual and multi-faceted. Social change, as Ryder put it in 1965, is possible because one cohort succeeds another, because people are born and people die. At the same time, we can say that social change over time takes place only when different cohorts of women and men have different life courses, different life stages and different ways of living their different ages and transitions, and different strategies in combining work and family before and after childbirth. The changes in the rules and demands of the job market, in legislation, so as in gender culture and ideology, in socialization models, in maternal attachment to the labor market, in social policies and in family obligations, all change the context in which the new cohorts of parents find themselves. Contexts also change because each cohort of parents tries out new routes and new events, and fields different strategies that call for new answers. To this end qualitative longitudinal data are increasingly a fruitful area of research, especially when it comes to understanding and to assessing change and persistence of separate gender spheres in a life-course perspective, but a more systematic reflection on how to deal with multi-perspective qualitative longitudinal interviews is needed.

NOTES

1. The project is entitled "Practices and Policies around Parenthood: Work–Family Balance and Childcare in Multicultural Contexts", and is funded by the University of Turin and the Fondazione Compagnia di San Paolo as part of the Progetti di Ricerca Ateneo 2011 framework; the Principal Investigator is Manuela Naldini). It is also part of the work of a European network, transPARENT – international research cooperation for studies on the transition to parenthood (www.transparent -project.com). Specifically, the qualitative investigation was based on two studies: (1) a qualitative longitudinal survey of the transition to the first motherhood and fatherhood with interviews of dual-earner couples carried out at two points in time, before and after the birth of the child (90 interviews with Italian couples and 28 with foreign-born couples); and (2) a qualitative study with "homosocial" focus groups (that is, five focus groups involving fathers and two focus groups involving mothers) with children aged 0–6. The study was carried out in Turin and its metropolitan area.
2. Rather, we opted to apply multiple theoretical perspectives that operate at several micro and macro levels of analysis. Essentially, we took a multidisciplinary approach (the study involved psychologists and a demographer, as well as sociologists) to the pursuit of multiple approaches.
3. See Grunow and Evertsson 2016.
4. For full information on the sample characteristics, see the section Methodological Appendix, pp. 229–243, in Naldini 2015a.
5. The main findings of the research have been published in Naldini 2015a. In this paragraph I summarize some of the main findings, relying on all the chapters of the volume. In particular, I rely on the chapters based on the qualitative longitudinal data: Chapters II, III, IV, V, VI and VII.
6. According to Kohler et al. (2002, p. 641), "in the early 1990s Italy and Spain were the first countries to attain and sustain lowest-low fertility levels", which the authors defined "as a level of the total fertility rate (TFR) at or below 1.3".

7.   The research process and practices are fully discussed in the final report on the QLS on transition to parenthood (see Methodological Appendix in Naldini 2015a, pp. 229–243).

REFERENCES

Aassve, A., Billari, F. C., Mazzuco, S., and Ongaro, F. (2002) "Leaving home: A comparative analysis of ECHP data", *Journal of European Social Policy*, 12(4), 259–276.

Bertaux, D. (ed.) (1981) *Biography and Society: The Life Historical Approach in the Social Sciences*. London: SAGE.

Bertaux, D., and Thompson, P. (eds) (1997) *Pathways to Social Class: A Qualitative Approach to Social Mobility*. Oxford: Clarendon Press.

Bertolini, S. (2006) "La conciliazione per le lavoratrici atipiche", *Economia e lavoro*, 40(1), 57–71.

Bertolini, S., Musumeci, R., Naldini, M., and Torrioni, P. M. (2016) "The best for the baby: Future fathers in the shadow of maternal care", in D. Grunow and M. Evertsson (eds) *Couples' Transitions to Parenthood: Analysing Gender and Work in Europe*. Cheltenham, UK and Northampton, MA, USA: Edward Elgar Publishing, pp. 173–195.

Bertolini S., Musumeci R., Naldini M., and Torrioni P. M. (2019) "Italian couples with non-normative work-care plans and practices", in D. Grunow and M. Evertsson (eds) *New Parents in Europe: Work-Care Practices, Gender Norms and Family Policies*. Cheltenham, UK and Northampton, MA, USA: Edward Elgar Publishing, pp. 148–168.

Bertone, C., Ferrero Camoletto, R., and Rollè, L. (2015) "I confini della presenza: riflessioni al maschile sulla paternità", in M. Naldini (ed.) *La transizione alla genitorialità. Da coppie moderne a famiglie tradizionali*. Bologna: Il Mulino, pp. 161–81.

Connell, R. W. (1987) *Gender and Power: Society, the Person, and Sexual Politics*. Palo Alto, CA: Stanford University Press.

Corden, A., and Millar, J. (2007a) "Qualitative longitudinal research for social policy: Introduction to themed section", *Social Policy and Society*, 6(4), 529–532.

Corden, A., and Millar, J. (2007b) "Time and change: A review of the qualitative longitudinal research literature for social policy", *Social Policy and Society*, 6(4), 583–592.

Cotter, R. B., Burke, J. D., Loeber, R., et al. (2002) "Innovative retention methods in longitudinal research: A case study of the developmental trends study", *Journal of Child and Family Studies*, 11, 485–498.

Daly, M. (2015) "Introduction: Parenting support in European countries – A complex development", *Social Policy & Society*, 14(4), 593–595.

Dermott, E. (2003) "The 'intimate father': Defining paternal involvement", *Sociological Research Online*, 8(4).

Deutsch, F. M. (1999) *Having It All: How Equally Shared Parenting Works*. Cambridge, MA: Harvard University Press.

Dominguez-Folgueras, M., Jurado-Guerrero, T., and Botia-Morillas, C. (2018) "Against the odds? Keeping a nontraditional division of domestic work after first parenthood in Spain", *Journal of Family Issues*, 39 (7), 1855–1879.

Elder, G. (1985) (ed.) *Life Course Dynamics: Trajectories and Transitions, 1968–1980*. Ithaca, NY: Cornell University Press.

Elder, G. (1995) "The life course paradigm: Social change and individual development", in P. Moen, G. H. Elder Jr and K. Luscher (eds), *Examining Lives in Context*. Washington DC: American Psychological Association.

Elder, G. (2003) "The life course in time and place", in W. R. Heinz and V. W. Marshall (eds) *Social Dynamics of the Life Course*. Weinheim: Deutscher Studien Verlag, pp. 57–71.

Elliott, J., Holland, J., and Thomson, R. (2007) "Qualitative and quantitative longitudinal research", in L. Bickman, J. Brannen and P. Alasuutari (eds) *Handbook of Social Research Methods*. London: SAGE, pp. 228–248.

Esping-Andersen, G. (2009) *The Incomplete Revolution: Adapting to Women's New Roles*. Cambridge: Polity Press.

Eurostat (2009) *Reconciliation of Work, Private and Family Life in the European Union*. Luxembourg: European Commission.

Faircloth, C., Hoffman, D. M., and Layne, L. L. (eds) (2015) *Parenting in Global Perspective: Negotiating Ideologies of Kinship, Self and Politics*. London: Routledge.

Ferrera, M. (2008) *Il fattore D: perché il lavoro delle donne farà crescere l'Italia*. Milan: Mondadori.

Fine-Davis, M., Fagnani, J., Giovannini, D., Højgaard, L., and Clarke, H. (2004) *Fathers and Mothers: Dilemmas of the Work–Life Balance – A Comparative Study in Four European Countries*. Dordrecht: Kluwer.

Fox, B. (2009) *When Couples Become Parents: The Creation of Gender in the Transition to Parenthood*. Toronto: University of Toronto Press.

Furedi, F. (2002) *Paranoid Parenting: Why Ignoring the Experts May Be Best for Your Child*. Chicago, IL: Chicago Review Press.

Gerson, K. (2010) *The Unfinished Revolution: How a New Generation Is Reshaping Family, Work and Gender in America*. Oxford: Oxford University Press.

Giddens, A. (1984) *The Constitution of Society: Outline of the Theory of Structuration*. Berkeley, CA: University of California Press.

Gornick, J., and Meyers, M. K. (2003) *Families that Work: Policies for Reconciling Parenthood and Employment*. New York, NY: Russell Sage Foundation.

Grunow, D., and Evertsson M. (eds) (2016) *Couples' Transitions to Parenthood: Analysing Gender and Work in Europe*, Cheltenham, UK and Northampton, MA, USA: Edward Elgar Publishing.

Grunow, D., and Evertsson, M. (2019) *New Parents in Europe: Work-Care Practices, Gender Norms and Family Policies*. Cheltenham, UK and Northampton, MA, USA: Edward Elgar Publishing.

Grunow , D., Schulz, F., and Blossfeld H. P. (2012) "What determines change in the division of housework over the course of marriage", *International Sociology*, 27(3). https://doi.org/10.1177/0268580911423056.

Hays, S. (1996) *The Cultural Contradictions of Motherhood*. New Haven, CT: Yale University Press.

Heinz, W. R., and Krüger, H. (2001) "The life course: Innovations and challenges for social research", *Current Sociology*, 49, 29–45.

Helgeland, I. M. (2010) "What works? A 15-year follow-up study of 85 young people with serious behavioral problems", *Children and Youth Services Review*, 32, 423–429. www.sciencedirect.com/science/article/pii/S0190740909002989.

Hobson, B., and Morgan, D. (2002) "Introduction", in B. Hobson (ed.) *Making Men into Fathers: Men, Masculinities and Social Politics of Fatherhood*. Cambridge: Cambridge University Press, pp. 1–24.

Hochschild, A. R. (1989) *The Second Shift: Working Parents and the Revolution at Home*. London: Piatkus.

Holland, J., Thompson, R., and Henderson, S. (2006) *Qualitative Longitudinal Research: A Discussion Paper*. Families and Social Capital ESRC Research Group (Working Paper No. 21).

Istat (2011) "La conciliazione fra lavoro e famiglia" (Statistiche Report, 28 December 2011). www.istat .it/it/archivio/48912.

Istat (2014) *L'offerta comunale di asili nido e altri servizi socio-educativi per la prima infanzia* (*The Municipal Offer of Childcare and Other Socioeducational Services for Early Childhood*). www.istat .it.

Kohler, H.-P., Billari, F. C., and Ortega, J. A. (2002) "The emergence of lowest low fertility in Europe during the 1990s", *Population and Development Review*, 28(4), 641–680.

La Rossa, R., and La Rossa, M. M. (1981) *Transition to Parenthood: How Infants Change Families*. Beverly Hills, CA: SAGE.

Lewis, J. (2006) "Employment and care: The policy problem, gender equality and the issue of choice", *Journal of Comparative Policy Analysis*, 8(2), 103–114.

Lister, R. (2006) "An agenda for children: Investing in the future or promoting wellbeing in the present?", in J. Lewis (ed.) *Children, Changing Families and Welfare State*. Cheltenham, UK and Northampton, MA, USA: Edward Elgar Publishing, pp. 51–66.

Long, J., Naldini, M., and Santero, A. (2018) "The role of reproductive rights and family policies in defining parenthood", in T. Knijn and M. Naldini (eds) *Gender and Generational Division in EU Citizenship*, Cheltenham, UK, and Northampton, MA, USA: Edward Elgar Publishing, pp. 87–110.

Magaraggia, S. (2013) "Di certo mio figlio non lo educo allo stesso modo dei miei. Relazioni intergener-azionali e trasformazione dei desideri paterni", *Studi Culturali*, X(2), 189–210.
Magaraggia, S. (2015) *Essere giovani e diventare genitori. Esperienze a confront*. Rome: Carocci.
McLeod, J., and Yates, L. (2006) *Making Modern Lives: Subjectivity, Schooling and Social Change*. Albany, NY: State University of New York Press.
Miller, T. (2005) *Making Sense of Motherhood: A Narrative Approach*. Cambridge: Cambridge University Press.
Miller, T. (2010) *Making Sense of Fatherhood: Gender, Caring and Work*. Cambridge: Cambridge University Press.
Miller T. (2011) "Falling back into gender? Men's narratives and practices around first-time fatherhood", *Sociology*, 45(6), 1094–1109.
Murgia, A., and Poggio, B. (eds) (2011) *Padri che cambiano. Sguardi interdisciplinari sulla paternità contemporanea tra rappresentazioni e pratiche quotidiane*. Firenze: ETS.
Musumeci, R., and Naldini, M. (2017) "Parenting in Italy: Exploring compliance and resistance to the expert-led parenting model during the transition to parenthood", *Italian Journal of Gender-Specific Medicine*, 3(3), 117–120.
Musumeci, R., Naldini, M., and Santero, S. (2015) "Strategie di conciliazione - tra congedi, servizi e nonni", in: M. Naldini (ed.) *La transizione alla genitorialità. Da coppie moderne a famiglie tradizion-ali*. Bologna: Il Mulino, pp. 113–136.
Musumeci, R., and Santero, A. (2018) "Introduction: Caring fathers in discouraging contexts? A multi-dimensional theoretical framework", in R. Musumeci and A. Santero (eds), *Fathers, Childcare and Work: Cultures, Practices and Policies*. Bingley: Emerald Group, pp. 1–14.
Naldini M. (ed.) (2015a) *La transizione alla genitorialità. Da coppie moderne a famiglie tradizionali*. Bologna: Il Mulino.
Naldini, M. (2015b) "Introduzione - La transizione alla genitorialità: per una prospettiva di studio multi-disciplinare e longitudinale", in M. Naldini (ed.) *La transizione alla genitorialità. Da coppie moderne a famiglie tradizionali*. Bologna: Il Mulino, pp. 9–32.
Naldini, M. (2016) "Diventare genitori tra divisioni e condivisioni", *Il Mulino*, 3, 485–492.
Naldini, M., and Long, J. (2017) "Geographies of families in the European Union: A legal and social policy analysis", *Int J Law Policy Family*, 31(1), 94–113.
Naldini, M., and Santero, A. (2019) "Le politiche di conciliazione famiglia-lavoro e le politiche per l'infanzia: L'Italia nel contesto europeo", in M. Naldini, T. Caponio and R. Ricucci (eds) *Politiche e pratiche di genitorialità in un contesto multiculturale*. Bologna: Il Mulino, pp. 19–42.
Naldini, M., and Saraceno, C. (2011), *Conciliare famiglia e lavoro. Vecchi e nuovi patti tra i sessi e tra le generazioni*. Bologna: Il Mulino.
Naldini, M., and Torrioni, M. P. (2015) "Modelli di maternità e di paternità in transizione", in: M. Naldini (ed.) *La transizione alla genitorialità. Da coppie moderne a famiglie tradizionali*. Bologna: Il Mulino, pp. 229–242.
Neale, B. (2011) "Journeys through time: Qualitative longitudinal research". Invited keynote address to International Expert Seminar: Times of Life in Times of Change. University of Bremen. February. www.timescapes.ac.uk.
Olàh, L. (2015) *Changing Families in the European Union: Trends and Policy Implications*, paper prepared for United Nations Experts Group Meeting, New York, May 2015.
Piccone Stella, S., and Saraceno, C. (eds) (1996) *Genere. La costruzione sociale del femminile e del maschile*. Bologna: Il Mulino.
Qvortrup, J. (2005) "Varieties of childhood", in J. Qvortrup (ed.) *Studies in Modern Childhood*. Basingstoke: Palgrave Macmillan, pp. 1–20.
Risman, B. (2004), "Gender as social structure: Theory wrestling with activism", *Gender & Society*, 18, 429–450.
Risman, B., and Davis, G. (2013), "From sex roles to gender structure", *Current Sociology*, 61(5–6), 733–755.
Rosenthal, G. (1998) *The Holocaust in Three Generations: Families of Victims and Perpetrators of the Nazi Regime*. London: Cassells.
Ruspini, E. (2002) *An Introduction to Longitudinal Research*. Abingdon: Routledge.

Ruspini, E. (2006) "All'ombra delle cure materne. La costruzione della paternità", in F. Bimbi and R. Trifiletti (eds) *Madri sole e nuove famiglie. Declinazioni inattese della genitorialità*. Rome: Edizioni Lavoro, pp. 257–278.

Ryder, N. B. (1965), "The cohort as a concept in the study of social change", *American Sociological Review*, 30, 843–861.

Saldaña, J. (2003) *Longitudinal Qualitative Research: Analyzing Change through Time*. Walnut Creek, CA: AltaMira.

Saraceno, C. (ed.) (2001) *Età e corso della vita*. Bologna: Il Mulino.

Saraceno, C., and Keck, W. (2010) "Can we identify intergenerational policy regimes in Europe?", *European Societies*, 12(5), 675–696.

Shirani, F., and Henwood, K. (2011) "Continuity and change in a qualitative longitudinal study of fatherhood: Relevance without responsibility", *International Journal of Social Research Methodology*, 14(1), 17–29.

Smith, C. (2000) "Content analysis and narrative analysis", in T. Reis and C. Judd (eds) *Handbook of Research Methods in Social and Personality Psychology*. Cambridge: Cambridge University Press, pp. 331–335.

Sobotka, T., and Toulemon, L. (2008) "Changing family and partnership behaviour: Common trends and persistent diversity across Europe", *Demographic Research*, 19, 85–138.

Thomson, R., and Holland, J. (2003) "Hindsight, foresight and insight: The challenges of longitudinal qualitative research", *International Journal of Social Research Methodology*, 6(3), 233–244.

Thomson, R., and McLeod, J. (2015) "New frontiers in qualitative longitudinal research: An agenda for research", *International Journal of Social Research Methodology*, 18(3), 243–250.

Vogl, S., Zartler, U., Schmidt, E.-M., and Rieder I. (2018) "Developing an analytical framework for multiple perspective, qualitative longitudinal interviews (MPQLI)", *International Journal of Social Research Methodology*, 21(2), 177–190.

West, C., and Zimmerman, D. H. (2002) "Doing gender", in S. Fenstermaker and C. West (eds) *Doing Gender, Doing Difference*. New York, NY: Routledge, pp. 3–24.

Woodman, D., and Wyn, J. (2015) *Youth and Generation: Rethinking Change and Inequality in the Lives of Young People*. London: SAGE.

10. Fathers in focus: two discursive analyses on addressing men, work and care

Suvi Heikkinen, Marjut Jyrkinen and Emilia Kangas

INTRODUCTION

In this chapter, we explore discourse analysis as a methodological tool for studying work–family issues, particularly those of men and fathers in work and care. Despite a proliferation of work–family literature over the past three decades, research employing quantitative methodologies significantly outweighs those employing qualitative (Casper et al., 2007; Beigi and Shirmohammadi, 2017). Many recent reviews make visible the fact that work–family research has been dominated by a positivistic paradigm with a focus on women (see Byron, 2005; Bochantin and Cowan, 2016; Beigi and Shirmohammadi, 2017; Allen et al., 2018). A typical type of study in this field is a cross-sectional, survey-based assessment that gathers single-source data on the perceived conflict effects of one domain on another (Poppleton et al., 2008). Yet recent debates have also taken seriously the rise of men's family involvement and their everyday reality with managing work and family with its complex processes, dynamics, and emotions, and that these interpretations are temporally and contextually changing (Heikkinen and Lämsä, 2017; Kangas et al., 2019).

The value of using methodological approaches which focus on language use is that they help us to understand how people interpret their experiences and what kinds of meanings and emotions they attribute to those experiences (Merriam, 2009). The emphasis on the meaning of a phenomenon enables discursive studies to provide insights that are difficult to produce, such as detailed descriptions of actions taken in real-life contexts that recover and preserve the actual meanings and feelings that actors ascribe to those actions and settings (Rynes and Gephart, 2004). Thus, these approaches have the potential to re-humanise work–family research and theory by highlighting the tunnelled human interactions and meanings that underlie the phenomena and relationships impacting the actual work–life and the challenges that people encounter (ibid.). The value of discourse analysis is that it focuses on the organisation of talk and texts as social practices, and on the resources that are drawn upon to enable such practices (Potter, 1996). Discourse analysis enables the study of language in the context of society and culture, and embedded power relations, and thereby exploration of the forms that language helps us to create, and how it even helps us to accomplish certain purposes (see Gee and Handford, 2012). As such, discourse analysis is both a branch of linguistics and contributes to the social sciences, although the field of studying discourses is not unitary and cannot be referred to as a singular method (ibid.).

Here, our understanding of onto-epistemological assumptions resides in social constructionism. The key understanding of social constructionism, as presented by Berger and Luckmann (1966), is that human beings together create and sustain all social phenomena through social practices. Societies and working life are socially constructed through the interactions of people, but at the same time they are experienced by people as if the nature of their world is pre-determined and fixed; we are all born into a social world that pre-dates us, and therefore the context may seem natural. Discourses can be understood as socially constructed as well as socially conditioned; thus, a discourse can consist of situations, objects of knowledge and the social identities of and relationships between people and groups of people (Wodak, 2011). Locke (2004, 5) describes discourse as a practice not just of representing the world, but of signifying the world, constituting and constructing the world in meaning. Thus, the everyday or mundane use of language can also be a site of political struggle. The value of using discourse analysis in work and family research lies in revealing the hidden motivations embedded in the texts as well as raising ontological and epistemological questions in work and family research (Cowan and Bochantin, 2011; Bochantin and Cowan, 2016). From postmodern perspectives, discourses live their own lives, but they can be important for societies and organisations at meta, meso and micro levels (Alvesson and Karreman, 2000).

Discourses in work and family research address the language of the ordinary and the everyday use of terms, and take into account the local context influencing linguistic terms (Moi, 1999). Our discourse-analytical approaches were inspired by Foucauldian emphasis on power as a central element in studying different levels of discourses. Another key aspect, as stated above, was the social constructivist understanding of discourses both as (re)constituting the reality of the working life and men's care, and as representing and reflecting the earlier and current realities. To contribute to the field of men, work and care, we present two empirical examples using discourse analysis to study work–family issues from a male gender perspective in a Finnish context. Further, we discuss the advantages of using discursive analytical perspectives in work–family research as well as what kinds of omissions this approach might entail. In the first analysis we applied Carla Willig's (2013) apparatus of six analytical stages to reveal the historically specific phases of fatherhood discourses. In the second analysis we applied a synthesis approach that combines both Foucauldian-inspired discourse analysis and discourse psychology, which addresses in particular the social acts employed during individual discussions (here, for example, interviews with fathers) and how individuals are engaging in such acts (Budds et al., 2014).

The structure of this chapter is as follows: first, we present an overview of studies on men and fathers in work and care and briefly introduce the Finnish context in which our two exemplary studies are situated. Secondly, we introduce the research scene and demonstrate our two case examples. In the last section, we discuss the examples and the implications of using discourse analysis in work–family research.

LOOKING AT MEN AND FATHERS IN WORK AND CARE

Fathers' work–family relationship is often unacknowledged in research and in practice, especially in comparison with that of mothers (Holter, 2007; Halrynjo, 2009; Tracy and Rivera, 2010; Burnett et al., 2013). Previous research contains examples of the generally negative workplace responses to men's attempts to be better fathers, and, for instance, make use of parental leave or flexible work schedules (Holter, 2007; Halrynjo, 2009; Gatrell and Cooper, 2016). Fathers who try to reduce their working hours to be more involved with their children and families often face a poor response at work (Gatrell and Cooper, 2016). Marsiglio and Roy (2012) note that men's involvement in work is the main cause of their emotional distance from their families. Hence, employed fathers have tended consistently to 'fall back' into the gendered roles expected of them (Miller, 2011; Gatrell and Cooper, 2016). These studies support the understanding that employers or societies do not see men as caregivers. This type of strong breadwinning discourse in many societies appears to remain a prevailing issue for many fathers and shapes their reality at work and with respect to family issues, while bearing in mind there have been some recent developments towards prioritising caregiving and involved fatherhood (Heikkinen and Lämsä, 2017; Kangas et al., 2017).

Care, caring work and unpaid care at home and work and in other sectors of life is still strongly gendered (Tronto, 1992; Bowlby et al., 2010). The gendered nature of care impacts the segregation of care, making it a 'woman's work area' and also an innate part of a woman's (and man's) private life, impacting decisions about how to spend time and energy, and affecting career prospects. However, increasingly an 'involved fatherhood' phenomenon has been emerging (Eräranta and Moisander, 2011), which challenges the traditional role of a man merely as a breadwinner. Involved fatherhood is described as a role wherein the man takes responsibility for care and nurturing. It depicts men as capable of co-parenting and engaging in active interaction with their spouses and children. Involved fatherhood also portrays fathers as spending more time with and being present for their children and being available to them on a daily basis (Wall and Arnold, 2007; Eräranta and Moisander, 2011). Often the traditional care roles exclude men from intimacy and caring. Discourses have begun to focus on men's care only quite recently – even though some men have cared for their children for ages and various societies have recognised different types of caring masculinities (Elliot, 2016). The involved fatherhood phenomenon offers a different portrayal of male care, one where the spouses are equal in working life as well; both careers are taken seriously and both parties 'do' care work within the family (Heikkinen and Lämsä, 2017). This phenomenon reforms the traditional role of a spouse and, for example, challenges the assumptions of many male professionals or managers regarding home and care by suggesting that there is no longer a (female) homemaker staying at home to take care of domestic responsibilities (Heikkinen, 2014). Therefore, the involved fatherhood phenomenon offers spouses an opportunity to share the domestic work and to participate in the work–family relationship on an equal footing, thus diminishing gender differences and fostering different modes of family involvement for women and men (ibid.).

Not only mothers but also fathers appear to be affected by intensified workplace cultures and the strains of family life. For example, men with a newborn infant usually work longer hours than at any other point in their careers. Yet, despite apparent pressures on men with families to work more intensively and for longer hours during such phases of increased costs and often during early- or mid-career stages, fathers often fade into the background in work–family discussions as well as in research (Burnett et al., 2013). While studies dealing with discourses on men's work, family and care have grown in number (Holter, 2007; Thébaud and Pedulla, 2016), it is important to evaluate what this body of knowledge can offer to theory and practice. We emphasise that a methodology with the ability to capture the intersections of and dynamics between men, work and care is of utmost importance, as such a focus allows for an analysis of significant but often neglected issues that are raised on a daily basis from a male gender perspective. The advantage of using discourse analysis is that it brings out the complexity of such issues and, as Locke and Yarwood (2017) note, calls attention to the fact that even fathers themselves state that they want to be more involved with the care of their children (Miller, 2011; Dermott and Miller, 2015). Thus, this kind of focus and method may reveal, for instance, differences between acceptable fatherhood practices and the level of fathers' actual involvement in parenting practices and care (Johansson and Klinth, 2008; Dermott and Miller, 2015).

The value of using discourse analysis lies in addressing fathers' experiences: many fathers can find themselves marginalised, enduring gender disparity and negative peer relations with respect to work–family issues (Burnett et al., 2013). To study work–family interface through discourse-analytical approaches can reveal the dominant discourses on men, masculinities and fathers' roles in care. This can enable challenging the current dominant discourses on fatherhood and masculinity in working life contexts (see Burr, 2015) and reformulating understanding of work–life 'balance' and its demands and power structures.

To summarise, discourse analysis offers an opportunity for further exploration of societal, organisational and individual factors that might hide the positive and negative reactions that men with domestic interests encounter; it is significant to explore these reactions to better understand the challenges impacting men's participation in family life and women's advancement in organisations. The societal or national culture and contexts shaping individuals' experiences of the work–family interface have often been unacknowledged in theories and research done on work–family balance (Powell et al., 2009). Importantly, this methodological approach may offer positive understandings of the prejudice against male employees using parental leave and suggest that traditional gender stereotypes still affect relationships, even if gender relations have become more complex.

In the following section, we introduce two empirical research examples using discourse analysis in work–family research, in particular those focusing on men, work and care. Both of the studies are made in the Finnish socio-cultural context, and understanding the context in discourse analytical approach is most important. In Finland, women are working full-time at labour markets without having a strong 'housewife' culture, but still they confront problems in career advancement. Despite the positive changes of involvement of men in family life, women still carry the main responsibility for housework and childcare. In a Nordic comparison, Finnish men are at the bottom of the list for using parental leaves (Cederström, 2019); in fact, one-fifth of fathers do not use any of the available family leave (Kela, 2021). Thus, a paradox exists: Finland has advanced policies, but fathers' readiness to use parental leave is lower than in other Nordic countries (ibid.). According to Närvi (2018) one reason for fathers' unwillingness to use longer parental leaves is the lack of organisational practices, and it is often the case that companies do not take substitutes for fathers who are on parental leave. The examples offer an opportunity to delve into the ways men invoke different aspects of fatherhood and masculinities within their talk about work–family concerns in a specific context. With these examples, we aim to highlight how men define their fatherhood amidst competing discourses on work and family.

THE FIRST CASE EXAMPLE: DISCOURSE ANALYSIS IN MEDIA TEXTS ON FATHERHOOD

The first example has to do with how media discourses on fatherhood have developed during the last two and a half decades in Finland. The original study was based on data gathered from business magazines and the most widely read daily newspaper in Finland (Kangas et al., 2019). According to the social constructivist epistemological premise of the study, the writers emphasised how the mass media importantly reflects social reality while at the same time (re) producing and modifying it. Thus, the media representations reflect people's values and understandings of, for instance, fatherhood and work–life 'balance', giving media an active role in shaping and challenging how fatherhood or the work–life interface are valued, understood and (re/de)constructed (Fairclough, 1998; McCullagh and Campling, 2002).

The writers collected the data systematically from three different Finnish media sources – the largest mainstream newspaper, *Helsingin Sanomat*, which regularly publishes articles on work and family issues, and the two leading business publications, *Kauppalehti* and *Talouselämä*. These reach a wide general audience in Finland, and they are also followed carefully by working professionals on a daily basis. The sample was gathered for the original study through the publications' electronic databases using particular keywords: *FATHER, FATHERHOOD, FAMILY, WORKLIFE* and *MANAGER*. The search resulted in a total of 531 articles. After careful readings, the writers chose 67 articles for further analysis. The main criteria for the in-depth reading and analysis was that the article discussed fatherhood from the viewpoint of male professionals or managers in the context of working life or organisations. The period 1990–2015 was chosen for the study, because during these years many remarkable changes took place in the Finnish parental leave system that increased opportunities for fathers to participate in family life. In 1991, fathers were given the possibility of six days' paternity leave; in 2003, a one-month paternity leave was introduced, which today is still the only non-transferable leave for fathers; finally, in early 2013 paternity leave and the father's quota were amalgamated, giving fathers the right to nine weeks of paternity leave (Kangas et al., 2019).

Researchers have begun applying a discourse-analytic approach because it reveals the contradictions within and between discourses (Jäger and Maier, 2009) on fatherhood in the context of work life. In other words, by using a discourse-analytic approach researchers can also unmask contradictory societal and/or organisational discourses on fatherhood. As such, the writers came to the conclusion that discourse analysis would be an appropriate method for studying media texts to better understand how fatherhood is represented and how this relates to men's work–family interface in a specific context. This study focused on media discourses pertaining to managers and professionals as fathers – men often viewed as role models within their own organisations and wider society (Weaver et al., 2005). They are in influential positions as regards changes in organisational cultures, such as the choice of whether to increase fathers' willingness to take family leave. Thus, it was interesting to analyse how the media represented the choices and behaviours of men in the role of managers and fathers. It was also intriguing to study discourses pertaining to this group of men because the assumptions and ideas on leadership and organising are still often masculine or masculinist in nature (Grint, 2011; Klenke, 2011; Katila and Eriksson, 2013; Powell, 2014).

The voices in the analysis were those of journalists and the experts and practitioners they interviewed or quoted as a means of constructing discourses on what takes place in organisations and how it relates to work–life balance. As discourse analysis is not a clear method and implies many epistemological and ontological viewpoints, the various approaches employed by, for instance, organisation and management studies differed in their criteria and level of discourse analysis (see Alvesson and Karreman, 2000). Thus, it was crucial to decide upon the measures by which to apply discourse analysis. The present study was inspired by Carla Willig's (2013) approach to (Foucauldian) discourse analysis, with separate stages that address discursive constructions, discourses, action orientation, positionings, practice and subjectivity. Therefore, the actual analysis which followed those six stages was conducted manually; however, the analytical process was iterative, and the different phases overlapped with each other.

In the first phase, the texts were carefully read and notes were made about the various ways in which the articles discussed managerial and professional men's work–family relationships (Willig, 2013, p. 131). We then placed the various constructions of the topic within wider contexts (ibid., p. 132), such as organisational and societal contexts. We also paid attention to potential topics and issues not discussed in the data. For instance, texts written in the 1990s largely failed to discuss the role of organisations in supporting work–family balance. When we reflected together on the preliminary observations, it was noticed that the data contained two recurring ways of talking about and constructing men's work–family interface: one had to do with the demands of work not being reconcilable with involved fatherhood, which refers to a father who has a close and caring relationship with his children (Wall and Arnold, 2007); the other talking point constructed involved fatherhood as a modern ideal that should be followed. As the result of the first phase of the readings of the data, two different discourses emerged. The first one implied that no change in gender relationships or the role of fathers is needed, which we named 'working fathers – no time for caring' discourse. The second discourse recognised from the data was that change takes place gradually and over a long period of time; we named this 'fatherhood in flux' discourse (Kangas et al., 2019).

In the next phase, the action orientations were investigated in the texts. We asked what could possibly be achieved by constructing men's work–family relationship in this particular way through this particular discourse (Willig, 2013, p. 132). 'Working fathers – no time for caring' discourse seeks to maintain the idea that men's work is incompatible with fatherhood, while 'fatherhood in flux' discourse aspires to advance involved fatherhood in the context of organisations. This was the moment to take a closer look at the subject positions that the discourses offered for the men – they were relatively narrow even in 'fatherhood in flux' discourse. The roles offered were very much based on a model of the white heterosexual male as exemplified by many business leaders and even politicians, such as the former Prime Minister of Finland. The analysis was continued by exploring the relationship between the two identified discourses and established practice within Finnish society and organisations. This was done by evaluating the opportunities and/or constraints for action produced by the discourses. In particular, 'working fathers – no time for caring' discourse produces traditional gender roles in organisational life and thus silences men's family concerns and responsibilities. In the final stage of the analysis, we concentrated on the subjectivities created by the discourses and addressed the question of what could be felt or experienced from the 'man's position' in the discourse (ibid., p. 133). For example, in 'fatherhood in flux' discourse in the 2010s young men feel that they are good fathers when they decide to be and are able to dedicate themselves to their children. Through discussions in the research group, we noted that the selected texts repeatedly addressed issues that either denied the need for fathers' involvement in family life because of the demands of working life or, contradictorily, hinted that men also have the right to care (see Bowlby et al., 2010).

In the analysis, the two major discourses differed from each other timewise and in continuity as well as in terms of how they addressed gender aspects. The stasis discourse, 'working fathers – no time for caring', was constructed around traditional notions of masculinity, or perhaps masculinist management and fatherhood roles. This discourse brought out how organisations are often reluctant to change and how many men in managerial positions have adapted such a perspective. For instance, despite the fact that 82 per cent of Finnish women work full-time, often the spouses of top managers are housewives – which is exceptional in

Finland – or else only work part-time (Hearn et al., 2008). The female spouses often carry the main responsibility for care at home.

The second identified discourse, 'fatherhood in flux', did not focus so much on 'wartime stories', traumatised masculinity and non-absent fathers, all of which are often present in traditional Finnish notions of masculinity (see Näre, 2008; Kivimäki, 2013). Instead, it constructed fatherhood in a more modern way, such as by discussing the notion of involved fatherhood (Wall and Arnold, 2007). This discourse was, however, present only in the later years of the analysis, namely after the year 2000. There has been a remarkable change in focus, which to a certain extent began with the Prime Minister, who at that time took paternal leave – even if for only for two weeks – which was big news in Finland as well as internationally. All in all, it seems that the change towards acceptance of involved fatherhood is slow and requires many more role models in different sectors of society as well as top managers. This supports Kvande's insights (2005), in which she proposes that the increased focus on paternity leave in the Nordic countries that has taken place during the last few decades can be seen as an important process of gendering and embodying men as fathers. Table 10.1 presents the analytical layers/phases and how they informed the two discourses.

As explained above, the present study has based its discursive analysis on social constructionism and an analysis of national media sources that at least indirectly impact workplaces and their leadership. The analysis highlighted how the discourses have changed over time. Overall, this discursive research on fatherhood discourses in the media brought out those organisational and societal discourses that might hinder men's opportunities or willingness to participate as more involved parents in the work–life context. Hence, discursive analysis also captures what can be said and how it is said in certain discourse (Jäger and Maier, 2009), and it can be used as a tool to challenge social understandings of the studied topic. By using discourse analysis, we point out that ideas can be interpreted in another way, that our common ways of categorising and ordering phenomena are reified and driven by personal interest rather than simply being reflections of 'reality' (Willig, 1999, p. 2).

Table 10.1   *The time span of the discourses and the analytical layers*

Discourses over time	'Working fathers – no time for caring' 1990–2015	'Fatherhood in flux'		
		1990–1999	2000–2009	2010–2015
Action orientation: what is achieved from the discourse?	Maintains the idea that men's work is incompatible with fatherhood	Shows that working men can participate in involved fatherhood	Highlights the idea of sharing parenting. Demands that organisations develop their work–family policies and practices to pay attention to men's viewpoints on work–family balance	Argues for the advantages of involved fatherhood for fathers themselves and for forward-looking organisations
Subject positions: how is the man positioned in relation to other actors in the discourse?	The man is a victim of the organisational culture, which ignores work–family balance. The man is a distant father to his children. The man is not responsible for the home – this is his spouse's (wife's) responsibility	Young men are signifiers of involved fatherhood before older male managers in organisations take it up. A famous male politician (the Prime Minister) sets an example of involved fatherhood for other men in society	Young men are trailblazers in organisations in combining work and family. They do it sooner than other men in organisational life. Visible politicians are examples of family men more often than other men in society. Women are more active agents than men in promoting involved fatherhood	Successful young working men are role models for combining work and family in practice sooner than other men in organisations. Forward-looking organisations promote men's work–family integration more than do other organisations. Young successful men share parental responsibilities with their spouses (wives)
Discourse and practice: what kinds of opportunities or constraints for action does the discourse produce?	Produces traditional gender roles in organisational life that silence men's family concerns and responsibilities	Produces exceptions to traditional gender roles in society and opens a door to public discussion of men's work–family issues	Produces the idea of sharing parenting and increases the opportunity for men to have a work–family balance, but this is demanded by women	Produces acceptance of shared parenting in forward-looking organisations and strengthens men's aspirations to and possibilities for involved fatherhood
Subjectivities: what is felt and experienced from within the man's position?	Men feel a sense of powerlessness in work–family issues	Involved fatherhood is an encouraging possibility for some men; involved fatherhood is resisted by older male managers	Young men come to participate in shared parenting, pushed by women	Young men feel that they are good fathers when they decide to be and are able to dedicate themselves to their children

Original source: Kangas et al., 2019

THE SECOND CASE EXAMPLE: STUDYING MALE EMPLOYEES' EMOTION TALK IN WORK–FAMILY INTERPLAY

The second case example is a study of the emotion talk of male employees (who are also fathers) with respect to work–family interplay. The study focused on the discursive ways in which male employees make sense of emotions in their daily experiences of work and family life. The research aim was therefore to broaden the understanding of the emotions that men construct around work–family interplay in their talk. Hence, the interest was in the social construction of emotions – the meanings behind the emotions constructed around men's talk of work–family interplay.

In this study, we used a critical discursive-psychology approach (see Wetherell, 1998; Edley, 2001; Budds et al., 2014), which represents a synthesis of two discourse-analysis approaches: Foucauldian discourse analysis (FDA) and discursive psychology (DP). FDA is concerned with the ways in which discourse constitutes versions of social life (Willig, 2013; see also Budds et al., 2014). The DP approach, in turn, treats language as performative – it holds a function for individuals in addition to having certain effects (Budds et al., 2014). Hence, FDA's interest is in available discourses, particularly the social context and the implications such discourses may have for individuals (Willig, 2013), whereas DP is interested in the social acts employed during individual discussions and how individuals are engaging in such acts (Budds et al., 2014). A synthesis approach that combines both FDA and DP focuses specifically on the dual role of discourse. Discourse is both constitutive, as it shapes, enables and constrains possibilities for identity and social activity, and it is also constructive, meaning that it can be a tool used by individuals within social interactions to achieve certain effects (Budds et al., 2014). Discourses have a great deal of power over individuals, but similarly individuals also draw from specific discourses and shape discourses for their own purposes. For instance, the emotions that men are employing in their talk concerning work–family interplay not only reflect their individual emotions, but also play a part in shaping and challenging social understandings of men's emotions in relation to work–family interplay. Hence, discourses constructed as a result of men's emotion talk regarding work–family interplay constrain and create identities and social activities for men, but they may also enable men to absorb or partly abuse these identities for their own benefits.

We collected the data used in the original study in the years 2016–2017. The data included 23 interviews in which we recruited male employees in their mid and late career who are fathers from five organisations in different fields. The criteria were designed to keep the group of research participants broad in order to reflect and make visible the diverse perspectives and experiences of male employees. The age of the interviewed men ranged from 29 to 61 years old. The men worked in various tasks and at various hierarchical levels, from the shop floor to top management. We conducted all of the interviews in an identical manner, with the interviews touching on a range of different issues pertinent to men's work and working styles, their family life and life outside the organisation and organisational habits and culture. The interviews lasted between 45 and 80 minutes; they were tape-recorded and later transcribed.

In this research, we utilised Edley's (2001, p. 189) analysis model of critical DP, which includes three key concepts: interpretative repertoires, ideological dilemmas and subject positions. Interpretative repertoires are different ways of talking about/constructing objects and events in the world (ibid.). According to Edley (ibid., p. 203), lived ideologies are not at all coherent; rather, they are often inconsistent, fragmentary and contradictory. Hence, interpretative repertoires or discourses do not always include only one ideology. They may include several lived, conflicting ideologies – creating ideological dilemmas. A subject position is a 'location' within conversation identity that is made relevant within discourse (ibid., p. 210).

In the analysis stage of this study, we first made notes about the various ways men discussed the work–family relationship in the data. Then, we located the emotion talk regarding men's work–family interplay in the data. In other words, we explored what kinds of emotions men chose to talk about in connection to their work–family interplay. The value of using the interview setting is that it offers the possibility to describe complex and asymmetric emotions, not just positive or negative, but emotions that are socially constructed and are limitless as they depend on new emerging social situations and their labelling. We also paid attention to any potential topics and emotions not addressed. As a result of this first round of analysis, we defined different interpretative repertoires of emotion talk; that is, emotion discourses regarding men's work–family relationship. They included discourses of adequacy, empowerment and autonomy. In a second analysis round, we looked for ideological tensions; that is, ideological dilemmas inside the interpreted discourses. Two of the interpreted discourses were rather fragmented and contradictory and included an ideological dilemma (ibid.), while a third emotion discourse appeared essentially coherent. In the third round of analysis, we took a closer look at the subject positions that the discourses offered, by analysing the 'ways of being' that were made available for participants within the discourses (Budds et al., 2014).

The first discourse was characterised by talk about adequacy in work–family interplay. The men reported that as fathers they experience emotions related to being both adequate and inadequate; however, most often the sense of adequacy was not related to work. In particular, such emotions had to do with being present for their children, but the men also mentioned a lack of time, thus including both negative and positive talk about a sense of adequacy. Hence, 'discourse of adequacy' invokes two contradictory subject positions: a successful father who manages to arrange enough time for his children, and an insufficient father who cannot give enough time to his children.

With the second discourse, 'discourse of empowerment', the male employees reflected on both a sense of empowerment and powerlessness with respect to work–family interplay. The key difference from the first discourse is the fact that the men's emotion talk was related to working life. The ideological dilemma in this discourse is that even though the men described fatherhood as a source of social capital, motivation and even skills, such feelings of empowerment with respect to work–family interplay are not valued in working life. Thus, this discourse also includes two conflicting subject positions. On the one hand, the discourse creates a subject position for the fathers as mature workers who are motivated by and proud of their roles as fathers, while on the other it constructs men as victims, operating under the pressures and demands of a workplace that stresses the importance of work over family and does not value their development as fathers.

The third discourse consisted of emotion talk regarding fathers' autonomy in relation to work–family interplay. In this 'discourse of autonomy in work–life interplay', the men described how they have themselves defined the boundaries or boundlessness of work–family interplay. Their emotion talk included talk of their own authority in constructing the boundaries or maintaining a sense of boundlessness between work and family. Many of the men mentioned the emotion of self-control when talking about either preferring work and family as separate spheres or deliberately constructing them as a seamless whole. Hence, the discourse helps construct the subject position of a person in self-control. Even though some of the men told about having strict boundaries between work and family, and others that they maintain a sense of boundlessness in their work–family relationship, both practices are described as being of their own choice. Table 10.2 summarises the content of the discourses, the ideological dilemmas and the subject positions.

Table 10.2   Emotion discourses and analytical layers

Emotion discourses	Emotion talk	Ideological dilemma	Subject position
Discourse of adequacy in work–family interplay	Men told about having feelings of being both adequate and inadequate. They talked about a sense of guilt due to working during family time, but also about the importance of giving time for family and children	Discourse is constructed from social understanding, where work and family appear as contradictory spheres of life	Insufficient father. Successful father
Discourse of empowerment in work–family interplay	Men described both how they feel empowered due to assuming care duties with the children, and how they are powerless in relating to the high demands of work	The men described fatherhood as a source of mental capital, motivation and even skills. However, such emotions of empowerment are not valued in working life	Mature workers. Victims of working life demands
Discourse of autonomy in work–family interplay	Men described how they have themselves defined the boundaries or boundlessness of work–family interplay	No dilemma Even though some of the men told about how they have strict boundaries between work and family and other parts of life, they also experience a boundlessness in their work–family relationship. They described both practices as their own choice	Exhibiting self-control

Taken together, the emotion discourses constructed in our original study are not unitary or straightforward, and the discourses embody conflicting emotion talk, and consequently bidi-rectional subject positions. Hence, the discourse analysis utilised here makes visible the fact that the work–family domain divide seems to be problematic also for male employees, as it may cause mixed emotions and identities, with men feeling oppressed by the current conditions of working life. The advantage of using discourse analysis in this study is to highlight the experiences of male employees in the context of their daily lives by showing the interconnected nature of work, organisation, working life and society. Yet, this study also highlights individual differences and complexities, with some male employees having the autonomy to maintain either strict boundaries or else no boundaries at all. This seems to be advantageous for their work–family interplay, suggesting that there are now straightforward solutions; for example, when male employees' work–family relationship and work–family policies are designed within the company organisations themselves or at the societal level.

DISCUSSION AND IMPLICATIONS

We suggest that discourse-analysis can offer a non-traditional and even more in-depth scrutiny of the intersections between work and family as a complex bundle of, and standing in relation to, societal policies, working-life conditions, organisational norms and gender. In particular, discourse analysis makes it possible to explore how the language, values, assumptions and ideas surrounding work and family create and situate male employees within working life and the existing gendered ordering of family life from a male gender perspective. We maintain that one advantage of using discourse analysis in work–family research is that it offers tools to systematically explore often opaque relationships between discursive practices, texts, events and broader social and cultural structures, relations and processes. When studying language use in work and family dynamics, it can offer representations of speakers' attitudes, beliefs, positions and ideas in terms of texts (Smithson and Stokoe, 2005). These texts may then convey meanings that often remain unexplored. Analysis of underlying meanings can assist in interpreting issues regarding the conditions and events of working life and family life from a male standpoint (Lorbiecki and Jack, 2000).

The two exemplar cases discussed above highlighted the historical nature of discourses on men and family care; secondly, they emphasised the discourse surrounding men as fathers and how it relates to their working life and experiences of fatherhood, their day-to-day activities and perceptions of their attempts to achieve a satisfactory work–family relationship in society. Our interest was to make the fathers and men more visible with respect to the paradoxical issues inherent to work and family care. We chose to approach this topic through two examples in which we (with colleagues) used discourse analysis as a method. We encountered challenges in the discourse analysis, such as in the first example, the agency of the text: with respect to the media texts, it would be beneficial to ask and analyse the questions, whose voices are we dealing with and what power does the media have in this particular society? On the other hand, we were not interested in single articles, but focused instead on the discourses that started to emerge from the data. Hence, discourse analysis suited this approach quite well – to analyse the texts on their own and their possible position(s) within society instead of in terms of single meanings or articles. The second example in the data could obviously be analysed, for instance, through thematic content analysis. But, as shown above, the discourse analysis applied reveals the multiple layers of meanings and the extent to which the voices can vary. The focus of the exemplary studies was on different levels of work–family balance: while the first example indicated the development of fatherhood in media texts during the past few decades (meta-level discourses), the second example focused on the individual level in daily life. This latter example brings to the forefront the complexity of combining fatherhood with work and organisational life (the meso-/micro-level focuses).

Of particular note is the fact that men reportedly also feel compelled to care and work just like women, and they would also benefit from challenging the underlying assumptions and binaries at home and in the workplace, as was highlighted in the discourses in both of our examples. The case examples presented here show how men are positioned within and respond to the discursive power of combining fatherhood and work and what it can tell us about the power of discourse to sustain gender inequalities in the spheres of paid labour and the private domain. However, if we focus only on individual differences and choices, we would gain an imperfect understanding of the norms and values related to the cultural meanings and enactments of work and family that have influenced the nature and strength of the relationship and attitudes as well as power relations in these two domains (Thébaud and Pedulla, 2016). Therefore, we suggest that discourse analysis may offer a fruitful point of departure for investigating mutually dependent individuals (that is, superior–subordinate, spouse–spouse, parent–child relations) who are in positions of systemic and structural power imbalances, or studies where emotional responses are reified as the 'appropriate' or 'expected' responses in certain existing power relationships (Bochantin and Cowan, 2016). The value of using discourse analysis is in its ability to connect language to broader social relations of power and inequality, particularly in terms of gender (Sunderland, 2004).

The use of discourse analysis in work–family research also has the advantage of offering a temporal and space-specific framework. Allen et al. (2018) claim that time is a critical element in work–family research, since the experience can be inherently dynamic – occurring and reoccurring, likely differently on different days and across one's life span. Discourses are dynamic and tend to reflect shifting contexts (Fleetwood, 2007; Tatli et al., 2012), and therefore they offer the possibility to adopt a contextual approach to research on work and family. Discourses shape the concepts used to frame work–family discussions in organisations and the assumptions embedded therein (Lewis et al., 2017). This is important because discourses not only reflect, but can also shape, organisational practices by what they emphasise (explicit messages) and what they de-emphasise or obscure (implicit messages) (Benschop and Doorewaard, 1998; Lewis et al., 2017). The use of words can also direct, assist and constrain men in work and family domains; a focus on language use and changing the discourses around work–family issues and gendered binaries may enhance the move towards a lasting cultural shift (Rapoport et al., 2002).

Based on our empirical examples, we outline three main lessons learnt from using discourse analysis in work and family research:

1. Given the complexity of work–family research, we contend that discourse analysis can offer time- and space-specific understandings of work–family discussions from a historical perspective.
2. Discourse analysis offers a means to investigate different layers and meanings from macro, meso and micro perspectives. To advance equality in the workplace and care at home, we need research from all these perspectives, but meso-level investigations in particular offer a tool for change in working life.
3. Discourse analysis in work–family research is a powerful way of challenging norms and underlying assumptions in families, organisations and societies, and ultimately it can be a tool for societal change.

Taken together, our empirical examples demonstrate the multiplicity of roles assigned to men with respect to work and family and challenge the portrayal of men as solely being focused on work and achievement. The discourses used in our examples are interwoven by many different contextual details, relationships and digressions from a focus solely on career and hierarchical career advancement. These types of data sets may offer a range of themes that can be addressed with different participants, which may in turn capture people's everyday language use and reflect societal change; thus, it is valuable to bear in mind that the data-gathering process also brought to light practices that might have an effect on what occurs during the interviews, and may lead to preventing the interactions from being swamped by the interviewer's own categories and constructions. Likewise, when media texts are being analysed for the purposes for work–family research, it would be beneficial to ask, whose voice are we dealing with and what is the power of the media in this particular society (McCullagh and Campling, 2002)?

To conclude, there is too little knowledge about men and fathers, their spouses (Heikkinen, 2015) and the circumstances wherein men make decisions about working life and family; that is, if they will take family leave. We know that the organisational policies and practices

– meso-level decisions and policies – are crucial for family-friendly policies. It is important to encourage such measures. We also want to emphasise that it would be important in future research to tackle the omissions in current studies, such as the changing forms of families, multiple genders being involved in parenting, same-sex families, families with children from current and former relationships, and single-parent families. The national-level surveys do not necessarily reach the groups and individuals whose lives differ from that of the nuclear family ideology present in many Western countries. Thus, it would be important to gather qualitative data on men, women, other genders and children with respect to each of these issues.

ACKNOWLEDGEMENTS

This research was part of the programme Equality in Society (WeAll project, 292883), supported by strategic research funding of the Academy of Finland. We gratefully acknowledge this support. We are also thankful for an excellent language revision by Erik Hieta.

REFERENCES

Allen, T.D., French, K.A., Braun, M.T., and Fletcher, K. (2018), 'The passage of time in work-family research: toward a more dynamic perspective', *Journal of Vocational Behavior*, 110, 245–257.

Alvesson, M., and Karreman, D. (2000), 'Varieties of discourse: on the study of organizations through discourse analysis', *Human Relations*, 53 (9), 1125–1149.

Beigi, M., and Shirmohammadi, M. (2017), 'Qualitative research on work–family in the management field: a review', *Applied Psychology*, 66 (3), 382–433.

Benschop, Y., and Doorewaard, H. (1998), 'Covered by equality: the gender subtext of organizations', *Organization Studies*, 19 (5), 787–805.

Berger, P.L., and Luckmann, T. (1966), *The Social Construction of Reality*. New York, NY: Anchor.

Bochantin, J.E., and Cowan, R.L. (2016), 'Focusing on emotion and work–family conflict research: an exploration through the paradigms', *Journal of Management Inquiry*, 25 (4), 367–381.

Bowlby, S., McKie, L., Gregory, S., and MacPhearson, I. (2010), *Interdependency and Care over the Lifecourse*. Abingdon: Routledge.

Budds, K., Locke, A., and Burr, V. (2014), 'Combining forms of discourse analysis: a critical discursive psychological approach to the study of "older" motherhood', SAGE Research Methods Cases. Available at: http://methods.sagepub.com/case/discourse-analysis-critical-discursive-psychological-older-motherhood (accessed 12.6.2019).

Burnett, S.B., Gatrell, C.J., Cooper, C.L., and Sparrow, P. (2013), 'Fathers at work: a ghost in the organizational machine', *Gender, Work & Organization*, 20 (6), 632–646.

Burr, V. (2015), *Social Constructionism*. London, Routledge.

Byron, K. (2005), 'A meta-analytic review of work-family conflict and its antecedents', *Journal of Vocational Behavior*, 67 (2), 169–198.

Casper, W.J., Eby, L.T., Bordeaux, C., Lockwood, A., and Lambert, D. (2007), 'A review of research methods in IO/OB work-family research', *Journal of Applied Psychology*, 92 (1), 28–43.

Cederström, C. (2019), State of Nordic fathers. Nordic Council of Ministers 2019. Copenhagen.

Cowan, R.L., and Bochantin, J.E. (2011), 'Blue-collar employees' work/life metaphors: tough similarities, imbalance, separation, and opposition', *Qualitative Research Reports in Communication*, 12 (1), 19–26.

Dermott, E., and Miller, T. (2015), 'More than the sum of its parts? Contemporary fatherhood policy, practice and discourse', *Families, Relationships and Societies*, 4, 183–195.

Edley, N. (2001), 'Analysing masculinity: interpretative repertoires, ideological dilemmas and subject positions', in M. Wetherell, S. Taylor and S. Yates (eds), *Discourse as Data: A Guide for Analysis*. London: SAGE, pp. 189–228.

Elliot, P. (2016), *Debates in Transgender, Queer, and Feminist Theory: Contested Sites*. London: Routledge.

Eräranta, K., and Moisander, J. (2011), 'Psychological regimes of truth and father identity: challenges for work/life integration', *Organization Studies*, **32** (4), 509–526.

Fairclough, N. (1998), *Discourse and Social Change*. Oxford: Polity Press.

Fleetwood, S. (2007), 'Why work–life balance now?', *International Journal of Human Resource Management*, **18** (3), 387–400.

Gatrell, C., and Cooper, C.L. (2016), 'A sense of entitlement? Fathers, mothers and organizational support for family and career', *Community, Work & Family*, **19** (2), 134–147.

Gee, J.P., and Handford, M. (2012), *The Routledge Handbook of Discourse Analysis*. London: Routledge.

Grint, K. (2011), 'A history of leadership', in A. Bryman, D. Collinson, K. Grint, B. Jackson and M. Uhl-Bien (eds), *The SAGE Handbook of Leadership*, London: SAGE, pp. 3–14.

Halrynjo, S. (2009), 'Men's work–life conflict: career, care and self-realization – patterns of privileges and dilemmas', *Gender, Work and Organization*, **16** (1), 98–125.

Hearn, J., Jyrkinen, M., Piekkari, R., and Oinonen, E. (2008), '"Women home and away": transnational managerial work and gender relations', *Journal of Business Ethics*, 83(1), 41–54.

Heikkinen, S. (2014), 'How do male managers narrate their female spouse's role in their career?', *Gender in Management: An International Journal*, **29** (1), 25–43.

Heikkinen, S. (2015), *(In) Significant Others: The Role of the Spouse in Women and Men Managers`Careers in Finland*. Academic dissertation. Jyväskylä Studies in Business and Economics, 158.

Heikkinen, S., and Lämsä, A.-M., (2017), 'Narratives of spousal support for the careers of men in managerial posts', *Gender, Work & Organization*, **24** (2), 171–193.

Holter, O.G. (2007), 'Men's work and family reconciliation in Europe', *Men and Masculinities*, **9** (4), 425–456.

Jäger, S., and Maier, F. (2009), 'Theoretical and methodological aspects of Foucauldian critical discourse analysis and dispositive analysis', *Methods of Critical Discourse Analysis*, 2, 34–61.

Johansson, T., and Klinth, R. (2008), 'Caring fathers: the ideology of gender equality and masculine positions', *Men and Masculinities*, **11** (1), 42–62.

Kangas, E., Lämsä, A.-M., and Heikkinen, S. (2017), 'Father managers (un)doing traditional masculinity', in A. Pilinska (eds), *Fatherhood in Contemporary Discourse: Focus on Fathers*. Newcastle upon Tyne: Cambridge Scholars, pp. 17–30.

Kangas, E., Lämsä, A.-M., and Jyrkinen, M. (2019), 'Is fatherhood allowed? Media discourses of fatherhood in organizational life', *Gender, Work and Organization*, **26** (10), 1433–1450.

Katila, S., and Eriksson, P. (2013), 'He is a firm, strong-minded and empowering leader, but is she? Gendered positioning of female and male CEOs', *Gender, Work & Organization*, **20** (1), 71–84.

Kela (2021), *Perhavapaiden tietopaketti*. Available at: www.kela.fi/perhevapaat-tietopaketti (accessed 14.9.2021).

Kivimäki, V. (2013), *Battled Nerves: Finnish Soldiers' War Experience, Trauma, and Military Psychiatry, 1941–44*. Turku: Åbo Akademi University.

Klenke, K. (2011), *Women in Leadership: Contextual Dynamics and Boundaries*. New York, NY: Springer.

Kvande, E. (2005), 'Embodying male workers as fathers in a flexible working life', in D. Morgan, B. Brandth and E. Kvande (eds), *Gender, Bodies and Work*. London: Ashgate, pp. 75–88.

Lewis, S., Anderson, D., Lyonette, C., Payne, N., and Wood, S. (2017), 'Public sector austerity cuts in Britain and the changing discourse of work–life balance', *Work, Employment and Society*, 31(4), 586–604.

Locke, A., and Yarwood, G. (2017), 'Exploring the depths of gender, parenting and "work": critical discursive psychology and the "missing voices" of involved fatherhood', *Community, Work & Family*, **20** (1), 4–18.

Locke, T. (2004), *Critical Discourse Analysis*. London: Bloomsbury.

Lorbiecki, A., and Jack, G. (2000), 'Critical turns in the evolution of diversity management', *British Journal of Management*, 11, 17–31.

Marsiglio, W., and Roy, K. (2012), *Nurturing Dads: Social Initiatives for Contemporary Fatherhood*, Vol. 13. New York, NY: Russell Sage Foundation.

McCullagh, C., and Campling, J. (2002), *Media Power: A Sociological Introduction*. New York, NY: Palgrave.

Merriam, S.B. (2009), *Qualitative Research: A Guide to Design and Implementation*. San Francisco, CA: Jossey-Bass.

Miller, T. (2011), *Making Sense of Fatherhood: Gender, Caring and Work*. Cambridge: Cambridge University Press.

Moi, T. (1999), 'What is a woman? Sex, gender, and the body in feminist theory', in T. Moi, *What Is a Woman? And Other Essays*. Oxford: Oxford University Press, pp. 3–121.

Näre, S. (2008), '"Kuin viimeistä päivää": Sota-ajan sukupuolikulttuuri ja seksuaalinen väkivalta', in S. Näre and J. Kirves (eds), *Ruma sota: Talvi – ja jatkosodan vaiettu historia*. Helsinki: Johnny Kniga, pp. 335–380.

Närvi, J. (2018), *Isä hoitaa vai hoitaako?* Helsinki: Finnish Institute for Health and Welfare.

Poppleton, S., Briner, R.B., and Kiefer, T. (2008), 'The roles of context and everyday experience in understanding work-non-work relationships: a qualitative diary study of white- and blue-collar workers', *Journal of Occupational and Organizational Psychology*, **81** (3), 481–502.

Potter, J. (1996), *Representing Reality: Discourse, Rhetoric and Social Construction*. London: SAGE.

Powell, G.N. (2014), 'Sex, gender, and leadership', in S. Kumra, R. Simpson and R. Burke (eds), *The Oxford Handbook of Gender in Organizations*. New York, NY: Oxford University Press, pp. 249–268.

Powell, G.N., Francesco, A.M., and Ling, Y. (2009), 'Toward culture-sensitive theories of the work–family interface', *Journal of Organizational Behavior*, **30** (5), 597–616.

Rapoport, R., Bailyn, L., Fletcher, J.K, and Pruit, B.H. (2002), *Beyond Work-Family Balance: Advancing Gender Equity and Performance*. San Francisco, CA: Jossey-Bass.

Rynes, S., and Gephart Jr, R.P. (2004), 'From the editors: qualitative research and the "Academy of Management Journal"', *Academy of Management Journal*, **47** (4), 454–462.

Smithson, J., and Stokoe, E.H. (2005), 'Discourses of work–life balance: negotiating "genderblind" terms in organizations', *Gender, Work & Organization*, **12** (2), 147–168.

Sunderland, J. (2004), *Gendered Discourses*. Basingstoke: Palgrave Macmillan.

Tatli, A., Vassilopoulou, J., Ariss, A.A., and Özbilgin, M. (2012), 'The role of regulatory and temporal context in the construction of diversity discourses: the case of the UK, France and Germany', *European Journal of Industrial Relations*, **18** (4), 293–308.

Thébaud, S., and Pedulla, D.S. (2016), 'Masculinity and the stalled revolution: how gender ideologies and norms shape young men's responses to work–family policies', *Gender & Society*, **30** (4), 590–617.

Tracy, S.J., and Rivera, K.D. (2010), 'Endorsing equity and applauding stay-at-home moms: how male voices on work-life reveal aversive sexism and flickers of transformation', *Management Communication Quarterly*, **24** (1), 3–43.

Tronto, J.C. (1992), 'Politics and revisions: the feminist project to change the boundaries of American political science', in S. Zalk and J. Gordon-Kelter (eds), *Revolutions in Knowledge*. Boulder, CO: Westview Press, pp. 91–110.

Wall, G., and Arnold, S. (2007), 'How involved is involved fathering? An exploration of the contemporary culture of fatherhood', *Gender & Society*, **21** (4), 508–527.

Weaver, G.R., Treviño, L.K., and Agle, B. (2005), '"Somebody I look up to": ethical role models in organizations', *Organizational Dynamics*, **34** (4), 313–330.

Wetherell, M. (1998), 'Positioning and interpretative repertoires: conversation analysis and post-structuralism in dialogue', *Discourse & Society*, **9** (3), 387–412.

Willig, C. (2013), *Introducing Qualitative Research in Psychology*. Maidenhead: McGraw–Hill Education.

Willig, C. (1999), 'Beyond appearances: a critical realist approach to social constructionist work', in D. Nightingale and J. Cromby (eds), *Social Constructionist Psychology: A Critical Analysis of Theory and Practice*, Buckingham: Open University Press, pp. 37–52.

Wodak, R. (2011), 'Complex texts: analysing, understanding, explaining and interpreting meanings', *Discourse Studies*, **13** (5), 623–633.

11. Work–life balance for fathers during paternal leave in Norway: a narrative approach

Kristine Warhuus Smeby and Ulla Forseth

INTRODUCTION

The aim of this chapter is to illustrate how narratives may represent a key resource in research on work–life balance (WLB). In particular, we want to summarize some features of narrative theory and narrative analysis and illustrate one way of performing a narrative inquiry.

The recent growth in research on work–family balance (WFB) in academic, political, professional and popular literature might give the impression that this is a new phenomenon (Lewis et al. 2007), but this is not the case. The dilemmas related to the management of coordinating work and life outside work have been in the limelight for several decades (Grzywacz and Carlson 2007, Rapoport and Rapoport 1965, Voydanoff 2005). However, cultural, social, economic and political changes and ideas open up for new questions and new combinations and arrangements. Mainstream research on WLB has mainly used surveys or interviews and focused on working mothers with children and/or middle-class dual-career parents (Gatrell et al. 2013, Seierstad and Kirton 2015). According to Chang et al. (2010, p. 2381) and Gatrell et al. (2013, p. 301) these sampling choices have led to inequity within the research and marginalized other groups. When it comes to fathers, however, there is a rich Nordic literature on paternal and parental leave and growing international interest in fathers as breadwinners *and* caregivers (Brandth and Kvande 2001, 2017, 2018, 2019, 2020; Farstad and Stefansen 2015; Halrynjo and Lyng 2017; Kvande and Brandth 2019).

In the literature, there has been a turn in terminology from "work–family" to "work–life" balance (Gatrell et al. 2013, Lewis et al. 2007). Other scholars prefer to talk about conflict (Crompton and Lyonette 2006) or tensions (Perrons 2017). Current literature on WFB/WLB is multi-disciplinary and embraces several theoretical perspectives, topics and methodologies. Consequently, there are many possibilities of combining different perspectives, research designs and methods when doing research in this field.

WLB is particularly interesting to study in relation to Norway, which has been celebrated along with the other Scandinavian countries as the most gender-equal countries with the most family-friendly welfare regimes in the world (Bungum et al. 2015; Seierstad and Kirton 2015; World Economic Forum 2020). Indeed, Norway was the first country to introduce a specific quota for paternal leave in 1993. Based on the experiences with having an individual, non-transferable leave for fathers as part of the parental leave system in Norway, we will analyse how this period works in order to promote WLB between responsibilities at work and home. Other interesting aspects, such as the mothers' narratives, negotiations between the partners concerning the third shift (taking on family responsibilities coordinating family activities and work) have previously been studied by the first author (Smeby 2013, 2017a, 2017b). In line with recent scholarship in this field (Brandth et al. 2017, Brandth and Kvande 2020), we illustrate the interplay between different logics, in particular how state-regulated welfare schemes impact on work organizations and individual fathers. We explore how a sample of working fathers, "pioneers" in having ten weeks of earmarked paternity leave, make sense of their experiences by analysing narratives elicited in in-depth interviews. Our results illustrate both work–life balance, tensions, imbalance and conflict. After introducing narrative analysis, the context and our research methodology, we present and discuss our findings, the advantages and disadvantages of our approach and the implications for future research. In the next part, we outline some key features of narrative theory and research design.

A NARRATIVE APPROACH

A narrative approach is a theory and a method where the researcher searches for and identifies basic stories. The story metaphor emphasizes that we create order and construct texts in particular contexts (Riessman 1993, p. 1). Lakoff and Johnson (1980, p. 3) argue that our conceptual systems are largely metaphorical, and narratives are often based on core metaphors evoking a given range of emotions (Hochschild 2019, p. 9). Narratives at the personal level can play an important role in the production of cultural knowledge, and even make power relations in the broader society visible (Poggio 2018). Although narratives are situated knowledge and context-dependent, they can also serve as an intake to broader social discourses. It is also important to underscore that multiple interpretations are possible because there is no "correct" reading of a narrative, whether it has been spoken or is written text or an image.

In the wake of the "narrative turn" in the human sciences, the interest in narratives was propelled to the humanities and the social sciences (Czarniawska 2004, 2011, p. 3) and further embraced in many other disciplines (Boje 2001). There is no single agreed-upon definition of what a narrative is, and it is employed in numerous ways (Chase 2005, Riessman 2008). Riessman (2008, p. 5) underscores that all talk and text is not narrative. In a qualitative interview, most of the talk will be question-and-answer exchanges, arguments and other forms of discourse (Riessman 1993, p. 3). Informants will often narrativize particular experiences in their lives in order to understand and make sense of their lifeworlds and to construct and reconstruct identity (Barthes 1977). According to Barthes (1977, p. 79) all social groups have their narratives and they can be found everywhere in myths, legends, fables, texts, visuals and so forth. In contrast to this wide approach, a narrow approach views a narrative as a story related to an event where someone re-tells what happened. A narrative in this basic form requires three elements: an original state of affairs, an action or an event, and the consequent state of affairs (Czarniawska 1998, 2004; Poggio 2004).

Riessman (2008) spells out three facets of narrative inquiry: storytelling (producing and sharing stories), narrative data (the empirical data material and object of analysis) and narrative analysis (the scrutiny of narrative data). Narratives can be elicited in many ways: while doing ethnographic observation, during interviews or scrutinizing different kinds of written "texts" or visuals. Events can be portrayed out of chronological order in a non-sequential or nonlinear narrative, and in such cases the researcher will have to construct narratives from the data material. The researcher might also be able to tease out if there is a grand narrative beyond a selection of different narratives. Having selected the most relevant narratives from the data material, which shed light on the research questions, the researcher can use standard interrogative techniques asking "what, how or why?" (Poggio 2004, p. 433). Each of them can be associated with different analytical strategies depending on the aim of the study in order to bring forth the content and what actors and objects are involved, how the narrative is organized and why the narrator develops the story in a particular way.

According to Riessman (2008), there are four types of narrative analysis for the human sciences: thematic, structural, dialogic/performative and visual. There are no absolute divisions between these categories, but it can be useful to highlight some of the differences between them. In a thematic-oriented analysis, the investigator will look at the content; *what* is said, written or visually shown rather than *how* the story was told (Riessman 2008, p. 73). This approach is probably the most common method of narrative analysis, and it often appeals to novice researchers. Data are interpreted in light of thematics developed by the researcher based on theory, the purpose of the study, the data themselves and discursive factors (p. 54). Previous research on thematic narrative analysis has contributed to unveiling gender and power issues, paradoxes, ambivalence and polysemy in many stories (Forseth 2005, Haug 1987, Poggio 2018). In a structural narrative analysis, there is a shift from the "told" towards the "telling" and from the experience of the narrator to the narrative itself (Riessman 2008, p. 77). Structural analysis is linked to narratology in literary analysis and the way in which literary texts are scrutinized searching for different devices used to affect or persuade the audience. "Structure" can refer to a genre, an overarching "storyline" or brief embedded moments that take a poetic form (p. 78). Structural and thematic narrative analyses may be carried out in combination. A dialogic/performance analysis is a broad and varied interpretive approach to oral narrative and departs from the detailed form of analysis related to the previous categories (Riessman 2008, p. 105). It draws on both thematic and structural narrative analysis and employs selective elements while also adding other dimensions. In this approach, the investigator seeks to find out *who* the utterance might be directed to, and for what purpose. Stories are social artefacts, and they are composed in contexts: interactional, historical, institutional and discursive, to mention a few. The particular words and styles of the narrator are not taken on face value but become important focal areas for interrogation. Within this approach, there is a relationship between the voice of the investigator and the informant's utterance (p. 137). In this way, intersubjectivity and reflexivity come to the fore, as there is a dialogue between text and reader, knower and known.

Narrative analysis has mainly relied on spoken and written discourse from interview transcripts, field notes from ethnographic observations, letters, documents and other language-based material. There are, however, other forms of communication beyond words, such as gesture, body movement, sound, images or aesthetic representations by artists (p. 141). Visual narrative analysis is a developing area building on "found images" (photographs, paintings, and drawings) and "made images" during the research process (self-portraits in collage and video diaries) (p. 179). The advent of high-quality digital cameras, even on cell phones, opens up new opportunities for visual data analysis. On the one hand, employing images can stimulate imagination, evoke emotions and thicken interpretation. On the other hand, ethical issues arise as persons and institutions become more vulnerable to recognition.

For our purpose, a narrow definition of narratives is sufficient as the prolongation of the quota for paternal leave can be seen as a natural intervention introducing a change in these fathers' lives. Our assertion is that the parental leave represents a turning point and a transition to a different phase in life and can be challenging for fathers' and mothers' balance between work and home. However, it also opens up a potential for narrowing a gender gap culturally enforced by this long, previously gendered break from paid work. It is interesting to explore how fathers combine the two different logics of work and home when they have to transform their main responsibilities from one logic to the next. Our point of departure is a combination of the thematic and the structural approach. We are genuinely interested in the content of the fathers' stories illustrating balance, tensions and imbalance in a specific situation. In addition, we have searched for metaphors and utterances used by the fathers to position themselves within a former female setting, thus re-constructing their identity as fathers.

NARRATING THE NORWEGIAN CONTEXT

State regulation and welfare schemes in the Nordic countries have been praised as a model for WLB (Brandth et al. 2017, Cousins and Tang 2004, Eydal and Rostgaard 2018) due to its enabling force. Among the core values in the Norwegian model of working life and welfare are liberty, democracy, equality, egalitarian gender norms, trust, participation and collaboration (Bungum et al. 2015, Dølvik et al. 2014). A central principle is to liberate individuals from subordination and dependencies, and the outcome is "statist individualism", as the state provides a safety net and offers services to the citizens from "cradle to grave". Another important political principle is that paid work should always be beneficial. To increase the share of full-time workers is encouraged by the state to ensure a sustainable welfare state (Ministry of Finance 2017). The Norwegian welfare state is based on universalism and decommodification of social rights in the pursuit of equality. This is called the social-democratic (Nordic) model in Esping-Andersen's (1990) typology of welfare state regimes.

Gender parity in labour force participation is an important indicator for gender equality, and the figures for Norway are 74 per cent for men and 68 per cent for women aged 15–74 (Statistics Norway 2018a). Partners equally sharing paid work is an increasing constellation in Norway (Kitterød and Rønsen 2012). In 2017 85 per cent of men and 63 per cent of women worked full-time (Statistics Norway 2018b). The influx of women into the labour market during the 1970s happened at the same time as the expansion of the welfare state and the service industry. Comparative research shows that Norway has a medium score on indexes for gender segregation in Europe (Bettio and Verashchagina 2009). Reisel and Teigen (2014) underscore that gender segregation of the labour force in a country that promotes gender equality is the outcome of policies for gender equality and not necessarily a gender-equality paradox (Forseth 2019). When it comes to division of domestic labour, Norway is less traditional than many other European countries (Vaage 2012). In particular, couples where both work full-time share domestic work more equally than couples where he works full-time and she works part-time (Kitterød and Rønsen 2017).

Norway has a generous parental leave scheme, and it was the first country in the world to introduce an earmarked father's quota in 1993. The father's quota has been extended from an initial four weeks to 15 weeks today. Previous statistics reveal an increase in the use of the father's quota each time the number of weeks has been extended (Fougner 2012).

From July 2018 the Norwegian parental leave was divided in three more equal parts (NAV 2018): 15 weeks for the mother, 15 weeks for the father and 16 weeks that parents can share between them. In addition to this, the mothers-to-be are entitled to three weeks prior to giving birth. This distribution is in force if the parents take out 100 per cent of their salary during the leave. If the parents choose an 80 per cent payment during the leave period, the time period will be extended to 19 weeks for the mother and 19 weeks for the father with 18 weeks to share (NAV 2018). The political argument for a more rigid division was to secure children and fathers more time together, and to contribute to more gender equality at the workplace (Ministry of Children and Equality 2018). The Norwegian experience with a special father's quota is that paternal leave has become a norm for what men do when they become fathers (Naz 2010). However, fathers may use this period in different flexible ways, managing the balance between the needs of greedy work organizations and being a modern and gender-equal father (Brandth and Kvande 2016, Smeby 2013).

It is worth noting that maternal and paternal leave depend on the position of the individual in the labour market. Both mothers and fathers individually earn their right to parental leave benefits if they have been in paid work for at least six of the last ten months prior to birth. The state provides for childcare when the parental leave period ends. A turning point in the Norwegian family policies took place in 2003 when all 1-year-old children were promised full Early Childhood Education and Care (ECEC) supply at a low maximum cost. The outcome is that 84.4 per cent of all 1- and 2-year-old children attend an ECEC institution (Statistics Norway 2020). These numbers suggest a strong culture for letting small children attend ECEC when the parents have to go back to work.

Table 11.1   Extensions in length of the father's quota 1993–2019

Year of change	Father's quota	Parental leave in all 100%/80% pay
April 1993	4 weeks (20 days)	42 weeks
July 2005	5 weeks (25 days)	43 weeks
July 2006	6 weeks (30 days)	44 weeks
July 2009	10 weeks (50 days)	46 weeks
July 2011	12 weeks (60 days)	47 weeks
July 2013	14 weeks (70 days)	49/59 weeks
July 2014	10 weeks (50 days)	49/59 weeks
July 2018	15 weeks (75 days)	49/59 weeks
Jan 2019	15 weeks (100% pay) (19 weeks 80% pay)	49/59 weeks

METHODOLOGY: CULTIVATING NARRATIVES

The research adopted an interpretative approach because we are interested in lived experiences (Ritchie et al. 2014, Silverman 2017). As with most narrative projects in the human sciences (Riessman 2008, p. 53), our research is based on interviews. The empirical data stem from a sample of 12 well-educated Norwegian heterosexual couples in different cities in Norway and were gathered in 2012–2013 by the first author for her doctoral thesis (Smeby 2017a). Smeby explored gender equality in a presumed third shift – a shift of family responsibilities, coordinating the first shift of paid work and the second shift of family work (see Hochschild 1989, 1997). To generate individual stories and gain a fuller picture of their collaborating partnership and how they managed to balance work, family work and family responsibilities, the researcher interviewed both spouses individually, each interview lasting approximately one hour (Smeby 2017a, 2017b). To gain substantial stories, the interview guide was semi-structured thematically. The researcher asked all informants about their involvement in all three shifts and for specific episodes. The paternal leave was one of these thematic situations, and the participants were invited to convey their experiences from this period. Encouraging informants to elaborate through re-telling examples and events is a fruitful approach in narrative interviewing (Czarniawska 2004, Brinkmann and Kvale 2014, Poggio 2004).

The couples were recruited from the researcher's extended network, and then the informants continued recruiting from their extended networks, and so on. This is often referred to as the snowball method. Both mothers and fathers in the sample went back to full-time work when their child attended ECEC. In most of our cases the mothers took the first part of the parental leave, and the fathers went on paternal leave just before or when the mothers returned to work. This chapter is based on a strategic sample of in-depth interviews with the fathers who had experienced the full length of the father's quota in one continuous period.

Table 11.2 shows that the fathers in this sample were aged 28–53 and employed in a variety of occupations. They were all working full-time and had just returned to work after staying at home with their child during parental leave. The informants had one to four children and at least one 1- to 2-year-old child who had just attended kindergarten. All names in the analysis are pseudonyms.

Table 11.2   Socio-demographic characteristics of the sample of fathers

Name	Occupation	Age
André	Physiotherapist, self-employed	28
Bernt	International adviser, state organization	35
Dag	Administrative adviser, state organization	41
Eric	Psychologist, state organization	36
Frank	Graduate engineer, private firm	31
Gard	Teacher/researcher, state organization	37
Henrik	Physician, state organization	32
Karl	Chief executive, private international firm	35
Ola	Adviser in business administration, self-employed	53
Paul	Economic adviser, private firm	47
Said	Chief executive, private international firm	45
Trond	Lawyer, private firm	41

The Norwegian Centre for Research Data approved the research design. An ethical issue regarding the descriptions generated is that narratives might include several actors, and the researcher needs to attend to the participants' integrity by leaving out unethical material. In this case, it was sometimes inevitable that the partner appeared in the stories because their stories were intertwined. Therefore, the partners were informed that they might recognize each other in the analysed narratives.

The narratives adopted for the current analysis are drawn from the fathers' elaborations on the period of life when the mother is back at work and the father is "in charge" of the baby. The analysis proceeds from transcribed raw interview data that we have coded searching for narratives where the fathers elaborate on their experiences of taking care of a little baby during ten weeks of paternal leave, and their commitments to the workplace. We were interested in intact stories, not coded segments (Riessman 2008, p. 74). We generated narratives across the fathers in the sample. We also looked for particular metaphors, recurring and distinct, in describing the transition and experiences. In doing this, we combined a thematic and structural narrative approach. A selection of quotes is presented verbatim in order to make the storytelling of the fathers come alive and, as raw data, it affords verisimilitude. In order to give space to the authentic experiences, we have chosen to elaborate on a selection of the fathers in order to present a comprehensive account of their stories. This technique brings about both transparency and depth. Analytically, we have categorized our findings in two units: home–work balance and work–home imbalance. This divide became evident as the fathers' two main narratives exploring the interplay of different logics.

ANALYSIS: APPLYING A NARRATIVE APPROACH

These fathers were "pioneers" as for the first time the Norwegian state provided men with the opportunity of taking ten weeks' earmarked paternal leave. For these fathers this was a transition to a new phase of life, taking care of a baby on their own.

Home–Work Balance during the Father's Quota

The fathers in this category assumed the main responsibility for the child as the mothers returned to their full-time jobs, and the children had not yet attended ECEC. For these fathers it was not a question of if they should take the father's quota, but rather how state intervention and work organizations made an impact on the fathers' experience of home–work balance during this period.

State intervention: fathers take what they get
As a rule, the fathers in our sample had taken approximately the state-provided ten weeks of leave. We were interested in knowing if they had reflected on the extension of the father's quota as these weeks will be lost if the fathers are prevented from taking them. Trond, father of 1-year-old twins, and a solicitor in a big company, did not have a solid answer: "Well, I guess I took … it was ten weeks at the time (…) I guess mainly because that was it. That was the father's quota." When asked if he could imagine taking more than the ten weeks offered, he said: "I think I really felt that I was long enough absent from work, being in the job I was. I felt responsible to be there. Being absent could have an economic impact on the firm." Trond took what was legally accepted and offered him as a father. At the same time, it is interesting to notice his argument knowing that his wife holds a similar high position in another firm. She took 39 weeks of parental leave. We can imagine taking care of twins is a handful. Nevertheless, Trond's story is not revealing an exhausted father; rather he tells us he "had a good time with the kids, and as long as it was legitimate, and so it was, I thought it was quite nice to be home". His thoughts suggest that the rest of the leave culturally belongs to the mother, and that asking for more is sending out the wrong signals as a career-oriented man. For Trond it seemed crucial that the father's quota is a legal right. If not, he would probably not take out ten weeks. "I felt responsible for work. I remember being quite a lot at work in that period." He said that he was present physically as well, but mostly working online from home. We wondered how he managed being physically at work caring for twins. He laughed and said:

Well, I went in on some meetings and things like that, and then it was [the women in] the administration who took care of the boys. (…) I called in and arranged for these meetings. However, there was no pressure from my employer saying I had to. However, I felt strongly obliged to do so towards my clients – that they needed me present.

Here a gendered subtext emerges: the women in lower, administrative positions stepped up to babysit while he was attending meetings at work (see also Poggio 2018, pp. 441–2).

Trond did not have anybody taking charge of his responsibilities at work while he cared for the twins. Still, he managed to combine work and care as the workload was not overwhelming. Being able to keep up with work through technology at home and by letting the administration take care of the twins creates a balance where Trond's work dedication is not cut off completely. His narrative is representative for several of the fathers. Choosing one of these narratives instead of displaying many fragmented stories allows for an in-depth understanding of the cultural picture. This story reveals how men in high-level jobs feel obliged to be on duty, even if they have become fathers. It reveals cultural norms saying that the child's mother is obliged to take care of the child, unless the state provides an exclusive right for fathers.

Physical replacement at work: going all in at home
A recurrent finding among the fathers on leave is the significance of having a stand-in during one's absence from work. Having a stand-in lifts a substantial burden off the father's shoulders. This might not have been needed when the father's quota was shorter and more in length with a holiday. With the extension to ten weeks, the loss of an employee's expertise will in fact offer some more challenges. At the time of his parental leave Gard was working as a teacher. After an eight-week summer holiday, he took ten weeks of parental leave as his wife went back to work. Having a substitute teacher take over his responsibilities at work opened the possibility for him to go all in for being a caring father. Work responsibilities were no obstacle for Gard's time with his son. In this case, the structure at work and the time of his father's quota fitted well. Gard also added that the given weeks were enough, and if he were to have another child in the future, "I don't think I will push for more weeks." Trond and Gard's stories reflect the statistics showing that fathers' usage increases and decreases according to the number of weeks given by the state (Fougner 2012). By exploring and comparing all the fathers' stories, we get a deeper understanding of the impact of the state policy on the fathers' practices.

Paternal responsibility: "alone with your child"
According to Gard, these ten weeks alone with his first child had given him "very much":

It is when you are alone with your child, it becomes … then you do it your own way, right? You get to do everything. The practical stuff; changing nappies, and you get to know him; how he wants things. I think this is very, very, very good. It would have been completely different if I had been working full-time all this time, and only been at home for a short period during the day, that's how it would have been because he was only awake three hours after work. I think this period [on leave] has been of vital importance, really. (…) To be alone together with the child, to get familiar with the daily routines and communication (…) Even though I have been with him all the time, the time being alone [with him] is still something different.

The time alone with his child was in contrast to the holidays when he and his partner shared the care, leaving him more like an assistant than a prime carer. By caring alone, Gard was given a genuine responsibility by the state. This experience has opened up a new dimension in the father–child relationship. "Slow" time together where the child is fully dependent on the father's care can be described as organic (Brandth and Kvande 2003, p. 108). Being alone with his son seems to have changed Gard as a human being. It has been a journey where he has experienced bonding with his son and his needs and reaching another level of understanding about the importance of taking this effort. If the state did not offer this lengthy paternal leave, there would be a greater gap between his responsibilities at work and his responsibilities at home. These responsibilities could then be harder to combine later on. Through this narrative, we view the re-construction of a new identity as a father. The narrative offers insight to what impact this period may have on the fathers' construction of varied masculine practices.

The greatest challenge for Gard was to find things to do, because at the time when his leave occurred, his son was becoming quite an active little boy. Gard experienced busy days. His son started walking at the age of 10 months and he did not sleep much. "It was a demanding period, but incredibly good at the same time." Taking care of an infant is demanding work, and the fathers alone on leave with all the responsibility experience this. It is necessary and demanding, but also meaningful and fulfilling. In Gard's story this ambivalence is evident. The weights are not in perfect equilibrium. It is dynamic – demanding and rewarding at the same time. Taking this paternal leave may be beyond reach unless fathers are given the pressure and the privilege to do so.

Through the narratives above, we understand the importance of state intervention in shaping modern gender practices, but also how work organizations can contribute in this respect by adapting to the idea that fathers also have parental responsibilities for their infants.

Pioneers extending the paternal leave

In addition to ten weeks of paternal leave, Frank, a graduate engineer in the oil industry, had added five weeks to his leave as compensation for overtime. Working overtime is quite common at his work, as he and several of his colleagues travel offshore from time to time. According to Frank, there is a culture at his workplace for taking out several weeks of overtime and extending the parental leave – this is common for both mothers and fathers: "When I will be absent for ten weeks and another person has taken charge of my duties, it gives me the opportunity to take five extra weeks." Being replaced eases the transition from work to home. When a substitute takes charge, it is easier to extend the paternal leave. However, Frank was working "day and night" before he went on leave, to prepare for a colleague to take on the responsibility to complete his ongoing mission during his absence. He finished just in time and told his colleagues and managers that he would be available for questions during his leave:

> They have called me several times because it is a big project. It cost a lot. Everything is expensive when it is offshore. It is mostly me who has the detailed knowledge about exactly this well. I have planned it for almost a year, so when someone comes in and takes over these 10 000 details, many things may be unclear, things that are very clear in my head. So, I told them before I left that if they have questions it is better that they call me for five minutes than spending a whole day on something I can explain at once. Therefore, they have called me a couple of times, and I think it is OK. I find my job really interesting and fun and getting small portions that [keep] me informed on what's going on with the operation, and I know things are going well, I think that is fine.

In his case, being in touch with work during parental leave seems to have a positive spillover effect from work to family (see Innstrand et al. 2009). The situation at work is under control and knowing this gives room for quality time when caring is his main business. Except for preparing for his absence from work, the only preparation he did before going on leave was to buy a *pulk* (a sort of sledge for the baby). For the first time in his life, Frank was going to be the main caretaker of his little boy for several weeks. "I realised quite early that this would be a full-time job," he says. It is interesting that he cleared his desk at work and opened the door to exploring adventures, shaping his identity towards the new period ahead. During the winter, he went on several skiing trips with his son. They explored nature and the neighbourhood together, joined open kindergartens, visited friends and even went on a trip to a cabin. As we interpret it, the *pulk* can be seen as a metaphor or symbol for his rite of passage to a new phase of life. Besides, the *pulk* is important in contextualizing the data material because it is an Arctic symbol. For many Nordics nature is important and available free of charge close to where you live. It is also an important example illustrating how fathers create their own practices in relation to care in public spaces, and an example of a particular type of masculinity. Previous literature has illustrated different masculine practices among Nordic fathers as care providers (Brandth and Kvande 2018, Farstad and Stefansen 2015), and how the child is brought into their worlds of interest spheres involving mobility and nature. In Italy, in comparison, a father in charge as caretaker of his child during daytime might have taken a stroll with the pram to the piazza in the city centre. In a Mediterranean welfare regime without earmarked paternal leave, he would qualify as an atypical father (Poggio 2018, p. 441).

Frank's time alone with his son turned out to be a positive experience. Prior to having the sole responsibility, he admitted that he was "a bit frightened" and "insecure" because he had "never been alone with a baby before". When his partner was present, it was "easy to lean on her". However, now he had taken on the task of caring and organizing days and adventures with his son, and in addition to adopting his wife's daily programme, he introduced the *pulk*.

> I've done this on my own. It is fine, but it involves quite a lot of equipment, so before a trip like that, I have to pack the car the night before. There is a lot of equipment and the skis must be waxed the evening before, so that we are ready when time is ripe, and everything must be packed in the car. Then I must prepare the *pulk* and set it up. It involves a lot of stress, actually, and I guess that is the reason why we don't do it more often.

The quote illustrates all the detailed work and organizing it takes to go on an adventure with a little baby. Doing it his way, deciding what the period on leave should involve for father and son, brings on experiences/adventures his partner is unfamiliar with. Being inexperienced as a father, Frank challenges himself and these challenges give him self-confidence. To go on outings like this and stay the night at a cabin with his son requires space where both partner and work obligations are absent.

Gard and Frank's stories represent situations where work organizations and the state play the same game. Work organizations arrange for fathering by providing a substitute worker. This opens up space for entering the father's quota on the child's terms rather than the terms of work. When the state's intentions meet goodwill from the work organizations, the fathers experience fewer obstacles. This interplay smoothens the WLB substantially. In these organizations, somebody had initiated a father-friendly practice, generating a more gender-neutral environment. However, being replaceable is not always possible, and in those cases research on elite professions finds that fathers' work obligations are often weighed more heavily than those of the mothers (Halrynjo 2017). For some fathers, the work organization challenges the norm of being a responsible and caring father during the relatively short period of the father's quota. In the following paragraphs, we will present Karl's story. He experienced how tough it may be to be torn in different directions in order to fulfil responsibilities both as a father on leave and as head of a department.

Work–Home Imbalance during the Father's Quota

Some of the fathers in this sample experienced a job-oriented practice during their father's quota (Smeby 2013, 2017a). This means that work restrains the content and forms the period on leave. Karl's experience falls into this category. Through his narrative, we understand some of the tensions that might arise when the father experiences discrepancy between formal regulated rights and the culture in a work organization.

Tension between state regulations and work obligations

Karl is head of department in an international company. For him, taking ten weeks of paternal leave when his wife went back to work turned out to be an exhausting experience.

> I knew it would be a demanding period. We lacked people at work and the management has a completely different understanding of what being on leave involves. The question was if they could buy me a housekeeper instead of me taking leave. It was not at all seen upon as any advantage for a father to stay at home. However, I had a strong wish to stay at home.

Karl did take out his father's quota but had to work almost full days on top. "I had a lot of administration and when someone quit, it became tough to handle the workload. I also have a boss in the United States who follows quite different rules of the game, or who operates in a different set of business rules than we do in Norway." It was up to Karl to juggle his work responsibilities and his baby simultaneously. The culture clash between the ideals of a career-oriented male worker expressed by the management overseas and the Norwegian ideal of being a responsible father is evident. There is a gap between a liberal welfare regime and a social-democratic welfare regime, not only in the structure and in politics, but also in how agents allow themselves to think and act. Fathering is culturally shaped by the accessible possibilities and regulations.

Tension between working and caring at home

Despite being aware of the demands from work, Karl had ideas for what his time at home could be like. For Karl there was more to it than just doing his share, as his wife went back to her full-time job. He strongly wanted to spend time with his daughter.

> I did have wishes [for the period on leave], it was winter and we did some indoor activities, but for me it quite simply became a disappointment because it was very much … child, bedtime, sleep, child, work. I did not get to do any activities with my child. As soon as she fell asleep, I had to work. Work stole my freedom to walk in the park, head downtown, visit the library or even the museum next door. Activities like that were out of the question because I had to sit by the phone or my email while she had her nap.

We asked him if it was too much, and he confirmed: "Yes, I was terribly exhausted. Terribly exhausted (…). It was double up, often working evenings as well because the management in the USA are six hours behind. In a way, my head was always on duty. It was awfully demanding." Karl had high expectations for this relatively short period in life where most Norwegian fathers stay home with their child. He wanted to fill this period with meaningful activities, not just fulfilling his daughter's basic needs. As this period expanded to ten weeks, it became harder to combine the leave with leading an office. No one else went in to do his job. It was impossible to dedicate himself completely to caring and devote himself to "the slow" time of just being in tune with his child (Brandth and Kvande 2003), as work constantly intervened into the father–child relationship. The baby's basic needs were always put first, but they were demanding to deal with during a workday:

> When Kaja started crying, I had to take care of her. I could not finish a meeting and take care of her after half an hour or an hour of screaming at the top of her voice. That would not work out well. So we [at work] needed some days where we could plan that I should be available for a longer period at a time.

As it turns out, Karl did not in fact take out a full ten weeks' father's quota. Every Monday he went to work, leaving his daughter behind with his mother-in-law or his wife, who correspondingly withdrew these days from her holiday. He did not manage to negotiate the loss of these days as weeks added to his leave, but he wished he could have. It is not uncommon in our sample that when the conflict between demands at work and home becomes unbearable, it becomes the mother's responsibility to manage the "holes" in the father's quota (cf. Smeby 2017a).

> I really like my job. It is a job I wish to keep. Nevertheless, I also wish for rights that are more formal. Being a start-up firm and having an American management leave its mark. I wish the rules were more rigid. Talking about the father's quota, I wish it was divided in two.

He went on to explain that in his experience there exists a difference between private and public companies. He has worked in several private companies. Last time he was on parental leave he was working for a public company where he did not have to negotiate when and how his father's quota should be, as he had to this time. Then he took out the state-provided five weeks in combination with the summer holidays. Even though the father's quota was not yet ten weeks "it felt like I had a longer period together with the child", he stated.

> As I see it, it is the child's leave. It is not the parents' leave, but rather an opportunity for the child to be at home with either Mum or Dad. However, today it has become an individualistic thing that fathers may claim ten weeks, and then mothers claim their share. And when you work in private business and wish for an arrangement that extends the standard or minimum, you get critical questions. If you don't get critical questions directly, there will be questions as you leave the room. It would mean that you are not as dedicated to your work. It would signal that he would rather stay at home than work, if he wished for six months of leave, for example. However, if it had been 50–50, it would have been much more difficult for the employer in private firms to say that the employee is misusing the arrangement.

In Karl's opinion the father's quota needs to be state-regulated; if not, it will be even harder to negotiate parental leave for fathers. His experience was that there exists a difference in culture between work organizations. Stronger state regulations might decrease these differences. Cultural differences are extra-visible in international business where the Norwegian model is hard to fulfil. It proves demanding to balance the demands of an international work logic where actual gender equality and culturally accepted duties and possibilities for fathers are unspoken. In this landscape, work obligations defeat the culturally accepted norms of Norwegian fatherhood. Nevertheless, in a Norwegian setting, paternal leave is something the workplace must take into account. However, Karl's story tells us this is not always the case, and the discrepancy between private business and state regulations in the social-democratic welfare state may stir up the WLB.

CONCLUDING REMARKS

In this chapter we have employed narrative theory and analysis to explore how a sample of fathers in Norway experienced a phase of their life being in charge of and caring for their infant. These fathers were "pioneers" when the Norwegian state provided men with the opportunity of taking ten weeks' earmarked paternal leave, consequently becoming outsiders within (Collins 1986) in a traditional feminine arena. The narrative approach has highlighted how individual experiences, at the micro level, relate to structures and cultures on meso and macro levels. The state and the work organizations became enabling or disabling forces; sometimes working favourably in tandem while at other times creating cross pressure and contradictions for the individual fathers. In the narratives of these fathers, both the state and the work organizations played an important part, shaping the experiences of the father's quota. Despite the state-implemented policy of the father's quota at the macro level, the work organization at the meso level may influence fathers' individual experience of managing to balance work obligations and family responsibilities during the paternal leave period.

Analysing a sample of narratives from these fathers in more depth brought out a fuller understanding of the interrelationship between these different logics and individual agency balancing work and family in a situation out of the ordinary. Indeed, we have illustrated some challenges and dilemmas resulting in work–life balance, tensions, imbalance and conflict. In line with these results, one can question the work–life balance metaphor, what this balance consists of and how it works.

In Norway, the father's quota is a fixed number of weeks, and it is evident from the analysis that the state-implemented policy regulates the fathers' possibilities and responsibilities at home. This finding is supported by previous research (Brandth and Kvande 2016, 2017, 2019, 2020). Our informants took what the state offered them, and this finding can suggest a cultural and gendered norm saying that the (rest of the) parental leave belongs to the mother. At the micro level, this expectation might be a question of negotiations between the parents, but this is not easily the case at the meso level in work organizations, particularly not in the private sector. Indeed, our analysis illustrates how the private sector plays a demanding and competitive role, not always compatible with family life, although offering attractive careers. The negotiation is challenged when the father struggles to combine the demands of an international, private work logic and the demands of fulfilling his role as a care-giving father in a gender-oriented society. It is hard to manage a reconciliation of the two spheres when they play by different and incompatible rules. This is a challenge the social-democratic welfare state logic meets in a globalized market where both work logics and gendered norms differ substantially compared to the liberal welfare state (Esping-Andersen 1990). Until there is a new way of thinking, especially in the still-male-dominated private sector, even within a Nordic welfare state context, obtaining WLB seems difficult. Discrepancy between state regulation and private work organizations' obstacles prevents the fathers' experience from having the full responsibility of one's child. Consequently, potential experiences of identity-shaping responsibilities, joys and tribulations at home remain unfulfilled. However, it liberated time for the mother to attend paid work even though the experience at home was somewhat unsatisfactory for the father.

The extension of the father's quota challenges cultural gendered norms as it invites fathers to spend more time at home and less time at work. This questions gendered norms concerning mothers' versus fathers' irreplaceability in both spheres. Here we face the gender division in the labour market in the gender-equal welfare state where a substantial share of the workers in the private sector is men. In elite professions, this distribution is even more gendered, and when work and family demands are incompatible, it is often women who reduce their commitment to work (Halrynjo 2017). In contrast to the narratives on family-unfriendly demands, other narratives showed work organizations internalizing gender-equal norms. Being physically replaced at work enabled a new dimension of fatherhood. The length of the father's quota is a caring push towards new arrangements formerly exclusively reserved for mothers. As illustrated in the analysis, new ways of thinking now exist also in elite professions.

Narratives are useful in highlighting the complexities and richness of lived experiences and how actors make sense of their situations. Besides, the narrative approach provides "thick descriptions" (Geertz 2017[1973]) – which are not detailed descriptions, but accounts of social actions and how the actors interpret the action and the context. It can also enable the researcher to tease out ambivalences, such as when one father talked about the fulfilling and demanding tasks of caring for his boy. By scrutinizing the narratives we were able to elaborate on symbols of the rite of passage to a new phase in the life of these fathers, such as in the case with the *pulk*. Analysing this metaphor in more detail drew our attention to context-specific gendered practices and mobility patterns. Fathers who take on the role of the prime caretaker during paternal leave develop care competence and integrate this competence into their masculine identities and practices promoting "caring masculinities" (cf. Brandth and Kvande 2020). Several narratives reveal fathers' growing practical and emotional involvement and understanding concerning their child. Elaborating on these particular experiences, the fathers emphasize the re-construction of their identities as fathers and reveal how this break from work has opened them up for new understandings and practices of masculinity.

One limitation of narrative analyses might be that the number of cases are restricted. In order to impart a deeper understanding of the personal lived experience these narratives offer, not all details nor stories can get the same amount of space. It is also a time-consuming effort to tease out the most relevant narratives and search for metaphors and symbols. Writing up the results, lack of space is a challenge when analysing several narratives in full detail. Nevertheless, narrative analysis is a fruitful way of teasing out more complex understanding (Czarniawska 2004, 2011), and the advantages of a narrative approach outweigh the limitations. A narrative analysis can be performed in several ways, and there is a growing literature in this field in different disciplines. Our choice was to highlight some of the literature that we have found interesting and useful as an introduction, and through this chapter we have tried to illustrate some options and possibilities in performing a narrative analysis. Our empirical focus was mainly on the content of the narratives of the fathers' possibilities and challenges balancing work and caring responsibilities during parental leave. We also provided a few illustrations about how the analysis of particular metaphors in these narratives can contribute to bringing forth underlying frames and patterns. We suggest that narrative analysis is an under-researched area within the field of WLB and parental leave. Based on our results there is a need for further narrative exploration of WLB topics, especially as the father's quota has now reached the historical length of 15 weeks in Norway. This may influence the fathers' stories on balance and imbalance. Performing a dialogic/performance or visual narrative analysis (Riessman 2008) could bring forth new aspects, including class and gender structures and gendering of work. It would also be interesting to compare the narratives of fathers and their efforts to integrate work and family across different welfare regimes.

REFERENCES

Barthes, R. (1977[1966]), "Introduction to the structural analysis of narratives", in R. Barthes, *Image Music Text* (pp. 79–124; S. Heat, trans.), Glasgow: William Collins.

Bettio, F., and A. Verashchagina (eds) (2009), *Gender Segregation in the Labour Market: Root Causes, Implications and Policy Responses in the EU*, Luxembourg: European Commission, Publications Office of the European Union.

Boje, D.M. (2001), *Narrative Methods for Organizational and Communication Research*, London: SAGE.

Brandth, B., S. Halrynjo and E. Kvande (eds) (2017), *Work-Family Dynamics: Competing Logics*, New York, NY: Routledge.

Brandth, B., and E. Kvande (2001), "Flexible work and flexible fathers", *Work Employment & Society*, 15(2): 251–267. https://doi.org/10.1177/09500170122118940.

Brandth, B., and E. Kvande (2003), *Fleksible fedre*, Oslo: Universitetsforlaget.

Brandth, B., and E. Kvande (2016), "Fathers and flexible parental leave", *Work, Employment and Society*, 30(2): 275–290. https://doi.org/10.1177/0950017015590749.

Brandth, B., and E. Kvande (2017), "Fathers integrating work and childcare: reconciling the logics?", in B. Brandth, S. Halrynjo and E. Kvande (eds), *Work-Family Dynamics: Competing Logics*, New York, NY: Routledge.

Brandth, B., and E. Kvande (2018), "Masculinity and fathering alone during parental leave", *Men and Masculinities*, 21(1): 72–90. https://doi.org/10.1177/1097184x16652659.

Brandth, B., and E. Kvande (2019), "Fathers' sense of entitlement to ear-marked and shared parental leave", *Sociological Review*, 67(5): 1154–1169. https://doi.org/10.1177/0038026118809002.

Brandth, B., and E. Kvande (2020), *Designing Parental Leave Policy: The Norway Model and the Changing Face of Fatherhood*. Bristol: Policy Press.

Brinkmann, S., and S. Kvale (2014), *InterViews: Learning the Craft of Qualitative Research Interviewing*, Thousand Oaks, CA: SAGE.

Bungum, B., U. Forseth and E. Kvande (eds) (2015), *Den norske modellen. Internasjonalisering som utfordring og vitalisering*, Bergen: Fagbokforlaget.

Chang, A., P. McDonald and P. Burton (2010), "Methodological choices in work-life balance research 1987 to 2006: a critical review", *International Journal of Human Resource Management*, 21(13): 2381–2413. https://doi.org/10.1080/09585192.2010.516592.

Chase, S.E. (2005), "Narrative inquiry: multiple lenses, approaches, voices", in N. K. Denzin and Y. S. Lincoln (eds), *Handbook of Qualitative Research* (3rd ed.), Thousand Oaks, CA: SAGE.

Collins, P.H. (1986), "Learning from the outsider within: the sociological significance of black feminist thought", *Social Problems*, 33(6): 14–32. https://doi.org/10.1525/sp.1986.33.6.03a00020.

Cousins, C., and N. Tang (2004), "Working time and family conflicts in the Netherlands, Sweden and the UK", *Work, Employment and Society*, 18(3): 531–549. https://doi.org/10.1177/0950017004045549.

Crompton, R., and C. Lyonette (2006) "Work-life 'balance' in Europe", *Acta Sociologica*, 49(4): 379–393. https://doi.org/10.1177/0001699306071680.

Czarniawska, B. (1998), *A Narrative Approach to Organization Studies*, London: SAGE.

Czarniawska, B. (2004), *Narratives in Social Science Research*, London: SAGE.

Czarniawska, B. (2011), "The 'narrative turn' in social studies", in B. Czarniawska, *Narratives in Social Science Research*, London: SAGE. Online edition.

Dølvik, J.E. et al. (2014), *The Nordic Model towards 2030: A New Chapter*, Oslo: FAFO. www.fafo.no/index.php/zoo-publikasjoner/fafo-rapporter/item/the-nordic-model-towards-2030-a-new-chapter.

Esping-Andersen, G. (1990), *The Three Worlds of Welfare Capitalism*, Cambridge: Polity Press.

Eydal, G.B., and T. Rostgaard (2018), "Policies promoting active fatherhood in five Nordic countries", in R. Musumeci and A. Santero (eds), *Fathers, Childcare and Work: Cultures, Practices and Politics*, Bingley: Emerald.

Farstad, G., and K. Stefansen (2015), "Involved fatherhood in the Nordic context: dominant narratives, divergent approaches", *NORMA*, **10**(1): 55–70. https://doi.org/10.1080/18902138.2015.1013348.

Forseth, U. (2005), "Gender matters? Exploring how gender is negotiated in service encounters", *Gender, Work and Organization*, **12**(5): 440–459. https://doi.org/10.1111/j.1468-0432.2005.00283.x.

Forseth, U. (2019), "Il paradosso norvegese non esiste", *Ingenere*, 3 October. www.ingenere.it.

Fougner, E. (2012), "Fedre tar ut hele fedrekvoten – også etter at den ble utvidet til ti uker", *Arbeid og Velferd*, 2. Oslo: Arbeids- og Velferdsdirektoratet.

Gatrell, C.J., S.B. Burnett, C.L. Cooper and P. Sparrow (2013), "Work–life balance and parenthood: a comparative review of definitions, equity and enrichment", *International Journal of Management Reviews*, **15**(3): 300–316. https://doi.org/10.1111/j.1468-2370.2012.00341.x.

Geertz, C. (2017[1973]), *The Interpretation of Cultures*, New York, NY: Basic Books.

Grzywacz, J.G., and D.S. Carlson (2007), "Conceptualizing work–family balance: implications for practice and research", *Advances in Developing Human Resources*, **9**(4): 455–471. https://doi.org/10.1177/1523422307305487.

Halrynjo, S. (2017), "Exploring the career logic within the Nordic work-family model", in B. Brandth, S. Halrynjo and E. Kvande (eds), *Work-Family Dynamics: Competing Logics of Regulation, Economy and Morals*, New York, NY: Routledge.

Halrynjo, S., and S.T. Lyng (2017), "Fathers' parental leave and work-family division in Norwegian elite professions", in B. Liebig and M. Oechsle (eds), *Fathers in Work Organizations*, Toronto: Barbara Budrich.

Haug, F. (1987), *Female Sexualization. A Collective Work of Memory* (E. Carter, trans.), London: Verso.

Hochschild, A.H. (1989), *The Second Shift*, London: Penguin.

Hochschild, A.H. (1997), *The Time Bind*, New York, NY: Holt.

Hochschild, A.R. (2019), "Emotions and society", *Emotions and Society*, **1**(1): 9–13. https://doi.org/10.1332/263168919x15580836411805.

Innstrand, S.T., E.M. Langballe, E. Falkum, G.A. Espnes and O.G. Aasland (2009), "Gender-specific perceptions of four dimensions of the work/family interaction", *Journal of Career Assessment*, **17**(4): 402–416. https://doi.org/10.1177/1069072709334238.

Kitterød, R.H., and M. Rønsen (2012), "Non-traditional dual earners in Norway: when does she work at least as much as he?", *Work, Employment and Society*, **26**(4): 657–675. https://doi.org/10.1177/0950017012445090.

Kitterød, R.H., and M. Rønsen (2017), "Does involved fathering produce a larger total workload for fathers than for mothers? Evidence from Norway", *Family Relations*, **66**(3): 468–483. https://doi.org/10.1111/fare.12264.

Kvande, E., and B. Brandth (2019), "Designing parental leave for fathers: promoting equality in working life", *International Journal of Sociology and Social Policy*, **40**(5/6): 465–477. https://doi.org/10.1108/ijssp-05-2019-0098.

Lakoff, G., and M. Johnson (1980), *Metaphors We Live By*, Chicago, IL: University of Chicago Press.

Lewis, S., R. Gambles and R. Rapoport (2007), "The constraints of a 'work–life balance' approach: an international perspective", *International Journal of Human Resource Management*, **18**(3): 360–373. https://doi.org/10.1080/09585190601165577.

Ministry of Children and Equality (2018), Prop. 74 L (2017-2018). Endringer i folketrygdloven og kontantstøtteloven (innfasing av tredeling av foreldrepenger mv.). Oslo. www.regjeringen.no/contentassets/b03aa88b52da486f9790644a6c9793b4/no/pdfs/prp201720180074000dddpdfs.pdf.

Ministry of Finance (2017). Meld. St. 29 (2016–2017). *Perspektivmeldingen*. www.regjeringen.no/contentassets/aefd9d12738d43078cbc647448bbeca1/no/pdfs/stm201620170029000dddpdfs.pdf.

NAV (2018), Parental benefit or lump-sum grant. https://familie.nav.no/veiviser.

Naz, G. (2010), "Usage of parental leave by fathers in Norway", *International Journal of Sociology and Social Policy*, **30**(5/6): 313–325. https://doi.org/10.1108/01443331011054262.

Perrons, D. (2017), "Managing work-life tensions in the neo-liberal UK", in B. Brandth, S. Halrynjo and E. Kvande (eds), *Work-Family Dynamics: Competing Logics of Regulation, Economy and Morals*, New York, NY: Routledge.

Poggio, B. (2004), *Mi racconti una storia? Il metodo narrativo nelle scienze sociali*, Rome: Carocci.

Poggio, B. (2018), "Deconstructing and challenging gender orders in organizations through narratives", in L.A.E. Booysen, R. Bendl and J.K. Pringle (eds), *Handbook of Research Methods in Diversity Management, Equality and Inclusion at Work*, Cheltenham, UK and Northampton, MA, USA: Edward Elgar Publishing.

Rapoport, R., and R.N. Rapoport (1965), "Work and family in contemporary society", *American Sociological Review*, **30**(3): 381–394.

Reisel, L., and M. Teigen (2014), *Kjønnsdeling og etniske skillelinjer på arbeidsmarkedet*, Oslo: Gyldendal akademisk.

Riessman, C.K. (1993), *Narrative Analysis*, Thousand Oaks, CA: SAGE.

Riessman, C.K. (2008), *Narrative Methods for the Human Sciences*, Thousand Oaks, CA: SAGE.

Ritchie, J., J. Lewis, C.M. Nicholls and R. Ormston (2014), *Qualitative Research Practice*, Los Angeles, CA: SAGE.

Seierstad, C., and G. Kirton (2015), "Having it all? Women in high commitment careers and work-life balance in Norway", *Gender, Work and Organization*, **22**(4): 390–404. https://doi.org/10.1111/gwao .12099.

Silverman, D. (2017), *Doing Qualitative Research*, Los Angeles, CA: SAGE.

Smeby, K.W. (2013), "Fedrekvoten – stykkevis og delt eller fullt og helt?", in B. Brandth and E. Kvande (eds), *Fedrekvoten og den farsvennlige velferdsstaten*, Oslo: Universitetsforlaget.

Smeby, K.W. (2017a), *Likestilling i det tredje skiftet?* PhD dissertation. Trondheim: Norwegian University of Science and Technology. http://hdl.handle.net/11250/2453772.

Smeby, K.W. (2017b), "When work meets childcare: the competing logics of mothering and gender equality", in B. Brandth, S. Halrynjo and E. Kvande (eds), *Work-Family Dynamics: Competing Logics of Regulation, Economy and Morals*, New York, NY: Routledge.

Statistics Norway (2018a), Likestilling. www.ssb.no/befolkning/faktaside/likestilling.

Statistics Norway (2018b), Women and men in Norway 2018. www.ssb.no/en/befolkning/artikler-og -publikasjoner/women-and-men-in-norway-2018.

Statistics Norway (2020), Barnehager. www.ssb.no/barnehager.

Utdanningsdirektoratet (2019), *Utdanningsspeilet 2019*, Oslo. www.udir.no/tall-og-forskning/finn -forskning/tema/utdanningsspeilet-2019/barnehage/#barn-i-barnehage.

Vaage, O.F. (2012). *Tidene skifter. Tidsbruk 1971-2010*, Oslo: Statistics Norway.

Voydanoff, P. (2005), "Toward a conceptualization of perceived work-family fit and balance: A demands and resources approach", *Journal of Marriage and Family*, **67**(4): 822–836. https://doi.org/10.1111/j .1741-3737.2005.00178.x.

World Economic Forum (2020), The Global Gender Gap Report. Geneva. www.weforum.org/reports/ gender-gap-2020-report-100-years-pay-equality.

PART V

MIXED AND MULTIMETHOD RESEARCH

12. Beyond the lines: gender, work, and care in the new economy – a view from the U.S.

Kathleen Gerson and Mauro Migliavacca

1. INTRODUCTION

Over the last several decades, shifting socioeconomic and politico-cultural landscapes have brought sweeping changes in gender relations as well as in demographic and family dynamics, all of which have had a significant impact on the trade-offs between family and work. These transformations have occurred amid a set of economic developments, especially in the context of Western capitalism, that has changed the meaning of "work" and the ways Western nations regulate their labor markets and household arrangements. Women's increased participation in the labor force, combined with longer life expectancies, steadily dropping birth rates, and the emergence of diverse forms of family life, has undermined long-standing gender arrangements.

Just as the industrial revolution created a new way of life by separating earning an income from domestic caretaking, the rise of a new economy is again reshaping the ways people organize work and care. This new economic revolution, however, is undoing the clear division that once assigned women and men to different physical, social, and economic spheres (Gerson, 2017). At the height of this period, in the mid-20th century, three out of five U.S. households consisted of a breadwinning husband and homemaking wife. While this option was never available to—or desired by—everyone, structured career ladders and secure unionized jobs made it possible for the majority of middle- and working-class men to become their household's primary provider, while stable marital bonds meant that most women could depend on men's earnings. Even among the large proportions of working-class and minority families who were unable to attain this cultural ideal, the norm itself held great sway.

Since that period, however, widespread and deeply anchored economic and social shifts have eroded the institutional underpinnings of this 20th-century gender-divided arrangement.[1] The rise of what is often termed a "new economy" (characterized by the dominance of technology-, information-, and service-based economic activity) has included a decline in stable jobs and a concomitant rise in insecure work, creating unpredictable occupational prospects for all but the most privileged employees.[2] In a parallel shift, the decline of stable marriages and the rise of more fluid intimate partnerships have created similarly uncertain interpersonal prospects. The growth of these interpersonal uncertainties has implications for women and men of all class backgrounds, with the better educated more likely to postpone marriage and the less educated more likely to see marriage as a "luxury" they may not be able to afford.[3] However diverse the consequences, the rise in financial and interpersonal uncertainty has undermined the institutions and blurred the boundaries that once demarcated a clear division between work and caretaking as well as the existence of distinct pathways for American women and men to follow.

Although a system of separate gender spheres neither meets the needs nor reflects the aspirations of most 21st-century adults, the contours of a new system—and its implications for gender arrangements—remain unsettled and contested.[4] Some argue that the gender revolution has stalled (England, 2010) and may have reached its end (Cotter, Hermsen, and Vanneman, 2011). There is certainly considerable evidence to support this view, including the emergence of a plateau in women's labor force participation, a continuing gender gap in earnings and occupational attainment, an intensification of cultural pressures to practice "intensive mothering" (Hays, 1996), and the decision among some professional women to "opt out" (Belkin, 2003; Stone, 2007).

Others, however, posit a countervailing trend. Pointing to evidence that women are outpacing men in educational attainment and men are falling behind in earnings and ambition (Rosin, 2012; DiPrete and Buchmann, 2013), these analysts see women's aspirations on the upswing and men becoming increasingly adrift as opportunities to secure stable blue- and white-collar jobs contract. For some, these shifts in the fortunes and outlooks of American women and men represent not just a declining gender gap but a growing gender reversal. Still, others see related developments—such as the rise of cohabitation, postponed marriage, single motherhood, and single adults living alone—as a troubling trend away from enduring marital commitments and toward unmoored individualism (Wilcox, 2010).

There are elements of truth in each perspective, but they are partial truths. Like the proverbial blind men who touch different parts of the elephant, those looking at only parts of the current transformation are likely to reach different—and misleading—conclusions. Uncertain, uneven change may prompt even the most careful analysts to view social change through disparate lenses, but this unevenness should also make us wary of unilinear views about the direction such change is taking. Whether the stress is on a return to tradition or a new world of disconnected adults, neither scenario represents the only way forward. It is more accurate—and, we argue, more useful—to consider the full range of patterns emerging in response to the fundamental economic and social shifts that are dissolving the boundaries between home and work and creating new insecurities at jobs and in relationships.

This chapter thus has two primary goals. The first is to present some findings of how current economic and social changes have affected the ways people organize work, care, and gender relationships, with special attention paid to the U.S. case. While the U.S. offers a strategic example of the transnational economic and demographic shifts that are transforming work and care worldwide, it lags behind many other post-industrial nations in its efforts to create new institutional forms able to adequately address new breadwinning and caregiving needs. The second goal is to gain a clearer understanding of the U.S. case by examining the main findings of a research project, conducted by Gerson, that consists of 120 in-depth interviews with American adults living and working in the heart of the new economy—specifically the Silicon Valley area of Northern California and the New York metropolitan area. These women and men are in the life stage, when the conflicts between earning a living and building a family are likely to be most acute.

As the nation that has arguably embraced the logics of the "new economy" most extensively, the U.S. case provides an appropriate and potentially paradigmatic context for understanding the core issues that characterize the current work and family debate. In a similar way, by adopting a mixed-methods approach that uses both quantitative and qualitative data to highlight critical issues in our understanding of the connections between gender, work, and care in the new economy, this chapter offers some tools for analyzing the transformation of the work–family relationship in a variety of national and local settings.

2.   METHODOLOGICAL NOTES

A main characteristic of work and family studies is the linked nature of their topics and the complexity this produces in their research foci. According to Poelmans (2005), scholars around the world who study the work–family interface do so with theoretical and methodological approaches that are as diverse as the nations they inhabit and the cultural backgrounds they represent. The study of work and family life also encompasses a broad range of disciplines and disciplinary perspectives. When considering the relationship between these two broad areas of social life, we must consider them not only as distinct dimensions, but also as dimensions that consistently overlap and interact in both people's daily lives and their unfolding life trajectories. To add to this complexity, as two of the most important dimensions of individual lives, the work–family interface must ultimately address both policy issues and personal experiences, behaviors, and attitudes. Indeed, modern welfare systems were built on the premise that ensuring social and individual well-being depends on addressing the economic and social consequences of workplace and family policies. In sum, addressing the work–family interface inevitably involves sharing paradigms and perspectives as well as focusing on micro and macro dimensions and the connections between the two.

To understand the complexity of the work and family dimensions, we draw on both qualitative and demographic data. The quantitative analysis provides an overview of the larger context within which the dynamics between institutional structures and individual actions unfold, and the qualitative interview data uncovers the behaviors and practices that men and women develop as they confront and respond to these structures in their work and family lives. This mixed-methods strategy "is the type of research in which a researcher or team of researchers combines elements of qualitative and quantitative approaches (e.g., use of qualitative and quantitative viewpoints, data collection, analysis, inference techniques) for the purpose of breadth and depth of understanding and corroboration" (Johnson, Onwuegbuzie, and Turner 2007).

Like any methodological approach, the mixed-methods approach has strengths and limitations. Venkatesh, Brown, and Bala (2013) identify three main strengths. First, it can address both confirmatory and exploratory research questions within the same study or analysis. Second, it allows for more robust inferences than a single method. Third, the integration of qualitative and quantitative data offers a fuller understanding of the research foci and theoretical concepts.

There are, nevertheless, some limitations worth noting. Combining a mix of methodological approaches can take more time and requires use of a fuller array of analytic techniques to successfully combine different methodological points of view. Mixed-methods research can spark disagreement if researchers believe that a research design should never combine quantitative and qualitative data in a single study (Cronholm and Hjalmarsson, 2011). If used appropriately, however, a mixed-methods approach offers the opportunity to analyze social dynamics more broadly and deeply than any one method alone would allow.

As numerous researchers have shown, using mixed methods can enhance the quest for sociological explanation (Howe, 2012; Ivankova, Creswell and Stick, 2006), even if clear examples of this added value may be lacking in some sociological fields (Stolz, Lindemann and Antonietti, 2019).

We highlight how a mixed-methods approach can help us understand the diversity and the complexity of work and family connections and dynamics. Our mixed-methods approach affords a perspective that illuminates how macro-structural arrangements and trends shape individual lives and how, in turn, people respond to these arrangements in diverse ways. According to Pearce, while sociology has long been a discipline where empirical research benefits from the integration of a varied set of methods, including both qualitative and quantitative approaches, this mixed-methods approach has rapidly gained adherents and codification across all the social science disciplines (Pearce, 2012). When social scientists refer to "mixed methods," they mean a research method that advances the systematic integration of quantitative and qualitative information within a single investigation or program of inquiry. The basic assumption is that such integration permits a more complete and synergistic utilization of data and understanding of the topic than separate quantitative and qualitative inquiries can achieve. We use the mixed-methods approach to integrate macro and micro dimensions and provide evidence to better understand how the convergence of work and family conditions shapes both social trends and individual lives.

In this chapter, we analyze the work and family interface through a sociological lens and by employing both quantitative and qualitative data. Using demographic and related data sources, we analyze the trends and major axes and dynamics that characterize how work and family changes in the U.S. compare with such changes in Europe and the Organisation for Economic Co-operation and Development (OECD) countries. We analyze data from the main national and international sources, including the U.S. Census and the U.S. Bureau of Labor Statistics as well as the OECD. We then analyze qualitative interviews to understand how U.S. women and men organize and manage the work and family constraints created in a context with little support for integrating earning an income with caring for others. For the qualitative material, Kathleen Gerson conducted face-to-face in-depth interviews with 120 women and men between the ages of 33 and 47, when Americans face their peak years for both work and family-building. To capture the dynamics of work and family life in the heart of the "new economy," the interview participants were randomly selected from residents in Silicon Valley (stretching from San Jose to the East Bay) and the New York metropolitan area. This approach yielded a group with diverse racial, class, and educational backgrounds who were currently living in a variety of family arrangements, including singles, cohabiters, and married couples with and without children.

3.   ANALYTIC FRAMEWORK

To provide an overview of the core transformations in work and family arrangements, we need to know the main contours of change—and lack of change—especially concerning gender differences and the relative changes in women's and men's lives. To do this, we focus on the trends in four general areas: the labor market, the family, the state of gender equity, and the policy context.

3.1   The Labor Market

Paid work is a key driver of material well-being, economic security, equality of opportunity, and human well-being in modern societies. Yet being employed does not always guarantee a living wage or income. Indeed, a growing proportion of the world's working-age population, even among the currently employed, is at risk of falling into poverty. According to prevailing socioeconomic analyses, countries around the world show different trends in employment outcomes. While many developed countries have experienced a decline in the unemployment rate, even among these many report high rates of labor underutilization, with large shares of discouraged, underemployed, and low-wage workers and the growing incidence of involuntary part-time employment (ILO 2018, 2019). In the U.S., moreover, the labor force participation rate has declined alongside a decrease in the unemployment rate.

Table 12.1   *Labor force main indicators. U.S., EU28, OECD countries, 1990–2018*

Country	Series	1990	1994	1998	2002	2006	2010	2014	2018
U.S.	Employment/population (pop.) ratio	72.2	72.0	73.8	71.9	72.0	66.7	68.1	70.7
	Labor force participation (part.) rate	76.5	76.7	77.4	76.4	75.5	73.9	72.7	73.6
	Unemployment rate	5.7	6.2	4.5	5.9	4.7	9.8	6.3	3.9
OECD countries	Employment/pop. ratio	65.6	64.0	65.0	64.9	66.1	64.5	65.7	68.5
	Labor force part. rate	70.0	69.5	69.9	69.8	70.5	70.6	71.1	72.4
	Unemployment rate	6.3	7.9	7.0	7.1	6.3	8.6	7.6	5.5
EU28	Employment/pop. ratio	61.5	59.9	61.4	62.4	64.5	64.3	65.0	68.8
	Labor force part. rate	67.1	67.5	68.2	68.7	70.3	71.2	72.5	73.9
	Unemployment rate	8.3	11.3	9.9	9.2	8.3	9.7	10.4	6.9

Source: OECD data

The U.S. labor force participation rate has been falling for two decades (by almost 1.7 percentage points from 1990), and this represents a significant decline. But this decline is not as large as the European average or the OECD average, which is lower by more than double. This decline also reflects the fact that more people are simply unable or unwilling to work at the current wage level. Men of prime working age in particular show sharp declines in labor force participation, and this fall has been particularly severe among Black men.[5] The effects of men's nonparticipation are notable for myriad reasons, including the slowing of economic growth and the rising dependency ratio for households of all kinds (Dotsey, Fujita, and Rudanko, 2017).

In the U.S., the declining of the participation rate also suggests changes in women's employment fortunes. While U.S. women's participation rate has historically been higher than most of the other developed countries, this is no longer the case. In the last 30 years, that rate has increased more slowly than in most other countries and has leveled off since reaching its peak in the 1990s. If U.S. women's participation rate was significantly higher in 1990 than European and OECD averages, the situation is different if we focus on those in their prime working ages. The OECD data show that women's labor force participation in 2018 is notably higher in Europe (80 percent) than in the U.S. (75.3 percent), compared with 74.3 percent in the U.S. and 64 percent in Europe in 1990.[6] Despite this plateauing of paid employment among U.S. women, the concomitant decline in U.S. men's work participation means the U.S. labor force participation rate has reached near gender parity, with 53 percent of men and 47 percent of women now in the labor force (PRC, 2019).

Yet parity is not equality. The unequal dynamics and characteristics of women's work participation, notably in comparison to men's, represent a fundamental key to understanding how work–family connections are changing. Indeed, the American case illustrates how these shifts have changed the nature of gender inequality but not eradicated it. Instead, the inequalities of class, race, and ethnicity combined with the absence of a strong welfare system that guarantees a safety net for everyone (such as those found in most European systems) change the nature and meaning of U.S. women's participation at the labor market and have created differences along the dimensions of educational access, occupational opportunity, and family composition. Despite the historical rise in women's employment, the U.S. workforce remains largely segregated by gender, class, and race. As a result, employed women work predominantly in female-dominated jobs that are devalued in both their pay and social status. Despite the fact that these jobs are essential and require physical and emotional skills and often a postsecondary education, they typically offer low wages and scant benefits (IWPR, 2016). Analysis of data from the U.S. Bureau of Labor Statistics shows that women workers tend to be concentrated in several occupational sectors (notably service sectors), including jobs that are growing in the new economy. In 2018, women's presence was concentrated in financial activities (53 percent), education and health services (74 percent), leisure and hospitality (52 percent), and other services (54 percent). At the same time, women's presence was underrepresented (relative to their share of total employment) in other sectors, such as agriculture (26 percent), construction (10 percent), manufacturing (29 percent), and transportation and utilities (24 percent), that are more closely linked to the "old economy" (BLS, 2019).

While many women now work in the service and information sectors that most exemplify the new economy, they are significantly underrepresented in the highest-paid jobs in tech, computing, and digital media. The share of American women employed in the three largest tech occupations (computer scientists and systems analysts, software developers, and computer support specialists) actually fell over the last 20 years. Gender and racial status is strongly linked to the likelihood of working in computing jobs, with white men far more likely to hold such jobs and move up in these companies (IWPR, 2019).

Additional changes in the nature of the labor force—specifically changes in U.S. working time and educational attainment—also shape the contours of work–family connections. In terms of the time Americans devote to paid work, the BLS reports that in 2018, 24 percent of employed women usually worked part-time (less than 35 hours per week), a percentage that has not changed significantly in 50 years, while only 12 percent of employed men (or half of women's share) usually worked part-time. On the other hand, in 2017, 63 percent of women worked full-time, compared with 41 percent in 1970. The proportion of men who worked full-time and year-round also rose over this period, but not to the same extent, rising from 66 percent in 1970 to 75 percent in 2017. Similarly, American men—especially in the professional sector—are more likely to put in excessively long workweeks that extend well beyond 40 hours a week, while American women are more likely to have shorter workweeks (Jacobs and Gerson, 2004). Notably, amid the persistence of gender inequality in the labor market, American women's educational attainment has risen substantially over the past five decades and now exceeds the average for men. In 2018, 44 percent of women between the ages of 25 to 64 held a bachelor's degree or higher, compared with only 11 percent in 1970. Similarly, in 2018, only 6 percent of women in the labor force had less than a high school diploma (that is, did not graduate from high school), down from 34 percent in 1970 (BLS, 2019).

3.2 The Family

In addition to the vast changes in the labor market, changes in marriage and childbearing have reshaped the family over the past half-century in virtually all developed nations. Across Europe and the U.S., adults are more likely to marry later, to live together without being married, to separate and divorce, and to never marry. In the U.S., the rise in unmarried people has contributed to an increasing rate of births taking place outside of marriage and to children living with a single parent, overwhelmingly a mother. Yet the appeal of an enduring marriage remains strong in some sectors of American society. According to a Pew Research Center survey, a majority—albeit a narrow one—says society is better off if couples in long-term relationships eventually get married (PRC, 2019).

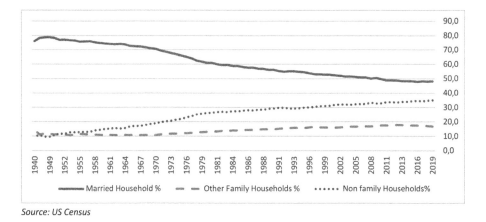

Source: US Census

Source: U.S. Census

Figure 12.1   Percentage of households by type (1940-2019). % value

The increasing proportion of women—especially mothers—as household breadwinners represents another major aspect of changes in American marital and workforce patterns. Mothers are not only contributing a higher proportion of a household's income than ever before; they are also much more likely to be an essential and even primary or sole source of that income. The Center for American Progress thus reports that 66 percent of American mothers are primary or co-breadwinners, with 41 percent providing more than half of a household's total income and 23 percent providing a quarter to a half (Glynn, 2019). Breadwinning mothers include both married women who earn as much or more than their husbands and unmarried employed women with children, while co-breadwinning mothers are either married or cohabiting with a partner. While most breadwinning mothers are white, racial and ethnic differences still persist and nonwhites are disproportionately likely to depend on a mother's income. When it comes to fathers' domestic participation, the picture is mixed. While fathers' domestic participation remains on average substantially lower than mothers', a growing group of men are increasingly involved in family caregiving and another group expresses a desire to be more involved if working time allowed (Gerson, 2011; Pedulla and Thebaud, 2015; Harrington, Van Deusen, and Sabatini Fraone, 2016).

3.3   Gender Equity and Equality

In the last several decades, American women have made significant strides toward reducing the gaps that have kept them from achieving equality with men, but the move toward greater gender equality in American society nevertheless remains uneven and stalled (England, Levine, and Mishel, 2020). As we have noted, despite the rise in women's employment, women remain largely segregated in "women's work" and continue to earn less than men on average, despite the fact that women are now outpacing men in gaining college and graduate degrees. According to the Institute for Women's Policy Research, women who worked full-time, year-round in 2018 made only 82 cents for every dollar earned by men, a gender wage gap of 18 percent. An IWPR analysis of women's and men's earnings over 15 years found that women made just half (49 percent) of what men earned, and earned less than men on average in nearly every single occupation. In middle-skill occupations, workers in jobs mainly done by women earn less than 70 percent of workers in jobs mainly done by men[7] (IWPR, 2019). In occupations where men predominate, moreover, a pervasive "glass ceiling" continues to limit the proportion of women who are able to rise to the higher echelons in public and private organizations, as the low number of women on the corporate boards and in upper-level managerial positions demonstrates.

Table 12.2   Gender wage gap. % value

	2001	2005	2009	2013	2017	2018
U.S.	23.6	19.0	19.8	17.9	18.2	18.9
OECD – Average	17.4	15.8	14.8	14.3	13.2	13.2

Source: OECD data, 2017

Table 12.3   Share of female managers. % value

	2011	2012	2013	2014	2015	2016	2017	2018
U.S.	38.3	38.3	37.9	38.0	38.5	38.8	39.5	39.8
OECD – Average	31.1	31.1	30.9	31.3	31.4	32.0	32.1	32.4

Source: OECD data

Table 12.4   Female share of seats on boards of the largest publicly listed companies. % value

	2016	2017	2018	2019
U.S.	20.3	21.7	23.4	26.1
OECD – Average	21.2	22.3	23.7	25.5

Source: OECD data

Despite the persistence of obstacles to gender equality in the workplace, there are signs that millennial and younger generations of women may make progress toward reducing the gender gap in occupational attainment. Millennials in the U.S. are not only the most highly educated generation to date, but a larger share of that increase has come from the educational attainment of women. Since younger cohorts of women are attending college and attaining degrees in unprecedented numbers, there is reason to conclude that their future work prospects will exceed those of earlier generations.

Wage inequalities and blocked opportunities are aspects of a wider range of concerns about the nature and persistence of gender inequalities. An overview presented by the Pew Research Center identifies a number of these dimensions, including: sexual harassment, where one in five employed women report being sexually harassed at the workplace; discrimination, where four in ten employed women report experiencing some form of gender discrimination at work; online harassment, which seven in ten women see as a major problem – and one in five of those under 30 say they have been sexually harassed online; and, finally, a general concern about equal rights, where a large proportion of women believe the country has not gone far enough to ensure them (PRC, 2017).

On many of these issues, a gender divide emerges. Among women, 44 percent say gender discrimination is a major problem, while only 29 percent of men agree. While most Americans say women face a lot of pressure to be an involved parent and be physically attractive, half of American men also say they face a lot or some pressure to join in when other men talk about women sexually. And although three-quarters of American adults see gender discrimination in the tech industry as a problem (at least a minor one), majorities of both women and men also say that neither women nor men have it easier. In general, women in the U.S. have made significant strides toward closing the gaps that have kept them from achieving equality, but the country is divided over how much work remains to be done. These divisions are rooted in the cultural and demographic divisions that pervade American society. Yet gender inequality is not simply a matter of individual beliefs and behaviors. It is also rooted in American institutions and social policies that shape the options that individual Americans confront in their public and private lives.

3.4   The Policy Context

As the U.S. economy has shifted toward a system that depends on lengthening workweeks and nonstandard work schedules, the expansion of work demands has spilt over into the time once reserved for private pursuits and has thus created ever-deepening conflicts between the demands of paid work and the needs of family life. And as salaried work and self-employment in the gig economy have become America's predominant forms of earning income, national policies that once required overtime pay only for wage labor are no longer able to enforce a norm that says a typical workweek should be limited to 40 hours and a predictable schedule. Now that such "overtime" policies have become inadequate, nonstandard work schedules have become pervasive in both professional and low-wage work, creating challenges for families in their efforts to care for children, the elderly, and other dependents who need care.

Adding to these difficulties, U.S. family policy continues to presume that caring for others is a private responsibility and that families can count on a devoted and unpaid caregiver—especially a mother—to do this work. Yet American motherhood has changed dramatically in recent decades. American women are more likely to become mothers later in life, with the median age at which women become mothers at 26, up from 23 in 1994. Mothers are spending more time in the labor force, but they are also spending more time on childcare, creating severe strains and a "sandwich condition." And nearly one-quarter (24 percent) are solo moms raising children on their own, which intensifies the conflicts that all employed parents face. With research demonstrating that American parents experience the largest "happiness gap" (that is, the gap between the level of happiness expressed by parents with children living in their household and the higher level of happiness expressed by adults without children in the household) among most developed nations, it is not a surprise that foreign-born moms account for a rising share of U.S. births, and annual births have decreased among American-born women (Glass, Simon, and Andersson, 2016; PRC, 2019).

Taken together, these interlocked changes mean that most American children now live in households where all parents work, whether they are married couples or single parents. Indeed, more than six of every ten households with children live in a home where all the resident parents are employed, up from four out of ten in 1965. They include dual-earner couples and single working parents, both of whom have been increasing over the last 40 years, even among families in which the youngest child is under 1. Under these conditions, the quality of family life and children's well-being are at risk. Yet they are not the only group. This growing care crisis endangers economic prosperity and social cohesion as well. Parents, and especially mothers, are facing new pressures in particular. Most women with a young child are employed, more children depend on their mothers' earnings, and the proportion of mothers who desire or are able to stay home remains low. Yet American women and men alike have few government or employer supports to draw on as they face new challenges in resolving the conflicts between earning and caregiving. As a result, publicly provided, high-quality, and affordable childcare is difficult to find and out of reach for lower-income parents as well as those who must work nonstandard hours or on unpredictable schedules (Zaslow, Crosby, and Smith, 2013; Stanczyk, Henly, and Lambert, 2017).

These changes place America's lack of a thoughtful, well-financed set of family and workplace policies in bold relief. With the exception of scattered efforts in a handful of states and localities, the state sector has also largely left individual families to fend for themselves. The U.S. is only one of several countries globally that does not guarantee a right to paid parental leave in the event of a birth or family health emergency. Universally available childcare remains a dream that seems politically out of reach, and high-quality childcare is largely unaffordable to all but the most affluent parents. In lieu of such needed parental supports, parents of all classes and genders are facing ever-growing pressures to follow a norm of "intensive parenting," whose demands are undefinable and can thus seem limitless (Ishizuka, 2019).

Despite the new insecurities and caregiving demands that families face, a new and adequate safety net for American workers and their families has yet to appear. Yet the case for building new polities and strengthening old ones to create work and childcare supports has rarely been stronger.

4. WORK–FAMILY INSTITUTIONAL REGIMES: INDIVIDUALIST, FAMILISTIC, OR EGALITARIAN?

What are the policy options available to societies to support workers and families amid such sweeping global changes? Government policies that focus on families, fertility, and work–

family reconciliation highlight the complex interactions among these issues and the way they combine to create "care regimes" (Daly and Lewis, 2000; Leitner, 2003; Gornick and Meyers, 2009; Saraceno and Keck, 2010; Naldini and Saraceno, 2011). Defining policy systems as a bundle of policies that constitute a regime helps us understand why countries differ not only in terms of their policies but also in terms of the outcomes they produce. To take a key issue in modern family policies, countries that provide supports for employed mothers tend to have a positive correlation between the fertility rate and women's labor force participation, while countries that do not support employed mothers are more likely to engender low birth rates even if the goal is to support women who stay home. The type of work–family policy regime found in each country provides the key to unraveling this puzzle: whether or not a policy offers services, leaves, or cash benefits, does a country's policy regime support an integration of work and family life or, instead, promote a forced choice—especially for women—between pursuing economic security and work achievement on the one hand, and caregiving commitments on the other?

Looking cross-nationally, work–family institutional regimes take three general forms, which can be termed "individualistic," "familistic," and "egalitarian." Each represents a different approach to structuring the links among the workplace, family life, and gender. To understand where the U.S. fits in this schema, it helps to begin by considering how it compares with other, specifically European, approaches. As we will show, Southern European countries provide a good example of a familistic regime, and Northern European countries (especially among the Nordic countries) a good example of an egalitarian regime. Though quite different, both of these cases stand in vivid contrast with current U.S. work–family policies, which are better characterized as individualistic.

4.1   European Contrasts

The relationship between social policies and demographic dynamics has attracted attention for over three decades, especially in Europe, where an aging population has placed pressure on existing systems and where the Nordic model appears to offer a winning example of a system that is able to support women's presence in the labor force while also maintaining stable birth rates, thus promoting gender parity by providing public support for integrating employment with childbearing and childrearing. The relationship between social policies and fertility rates nevertheless remains complex, and the support provided to families with children varies substantially among European countries (Gornick and Meyers, 2009; Lappegård, 2014).

Although its meaning in any given system may vary, a "familistic" model refers to the principle that a system should focus on protecting the welfare of families and especially children and other dependents rather than aiming to reduce inequality within families. While the goal of these systems is to help families provide for their dependents, they differ in the mix of policies used to accomplish this outcome, including policies that provide explicit fiscal support and policies that encourage women to perform unpaid carework. Southern European countries, such as Italy and Spain, are thus inclined to stress policies that rely on families rather than collective alternatives to provide care and, by implication, discourage mothers from engaging in full-time employment. Saraceno and Negri (1994) call such a system, which offers little in the way of childcare, long-term care services, or other measures that help people reconcile obligations to jobs and family life, "unsupported familism." Yet in an ironic twist, instead of prompting women to have more children, these maternalistic policies tend to depress fertility rates even as they constrain women's work opportunities (León and Migliavacca, 2013).

The family policies of these Mediterranean countries co-exist with low scores on indicators of gender equality in both the public (for example, employment) and private (for example, the division of childcare and housework) spheres. Whether as cause or consequence, they are associated with the prevalence of a traditional male breadwinner model that expects women to retreat from paid jobs to rear children and perform unpaid domestic work. This intergenerational solidarity helps to legitimate these familistic practices and dampen prospects for creating a more egalitarian approach to family and gender support. As a result, these countries have a limited capacity to make a smooth transition to a "dual-earner model" in which all adult members of a household participate in paid work (León and Migliavacca, 2013; Migliavacca and Naldini, 2018).

While the comparative literature has accepted the continuity of the familistic "male breadwinner model" in Southern Europe, several questions remain. First, is support for the male breadwinner/female carer model equally strong in all four Southern European countries (or significantly different from non-southern European countries, especially those with a Bismarckian tradition)? Second, do recent welfare reforms in these countries (such as innovations in childcare, work/family balance, and the guiding principles of social assistance and family policy) point to future departures from a familistic paradigm? And even if familism is a feature that Southern European countries share, is this a useful way to conceptualize welfare state clusters (Guillén and León, 2011; León and Migliavacca, 2013)?

When the concept of "familism" is used comparatively to classify care regimes, Southern Europe clearly emerges as distinct from other approaches. Such a comparison is descriptive and does not imply judgment about the benefits or shortcomings of any country's welfare development (León and Migliavacca, 2013). It is thus not only possible but useful, according to Anttonen and Sipilä's (1996) models of care, to classify countries according to whether care is mostly provided formally by the state or the market or informally by the family. Pfau-Effinger's (2005) and Bettio and Plantenga's (2004) also both situate Southern European countries as more familistic in the sense that they delegate the bulk of care to the private domain. When we view work–family regimes on a continuum, the Southern European countries represent one end—specifically one in which the privatized family is the main provider of (unpaid) care.

The policies stressed in Nordic countries represent the other end of the spectrum—ones in which public provision of care, efforts to create equal employment opportunities, and work–family integration predominate. Sweden represents a paradigmatic example of this egalitarian model. Historically, Sweden has been viewed as the reference point for depicting a universalistic welfare state that many other European countries may wish to attain (Esping-Andersen, 1990). Today, after years of concern about a growing crisis in European welfare states, Sweden remains an exemplar of egalitarian work and family policies. Sweden's approach to regulating working hours provides a good example of the consequences of this approach. A recent HSBC survey (HSBC, 2019) thus ranked it best in the world for work–life balance. A recent OECD analysis of their "How's Life" survey (OECD, 2020) came to a similar conclusion, reporting that only about 1.1 percent of Swedish employees work very long hours, the second-lowest share among OECD countries. Swedish policies also provide support for parents of children of all ages. Generous paid parental leave reduces working hours for parents with young children, while high-quality childcare and extensive out-of-school-hours care are available at a low price to families with school-age children.

The comprehensive supports Sweden provides for reconciling work and family commitments contributes to some notable outcomes, including comparatively high levels of women's employment, greater involvement in caretaking among Swedish fathers, high marks on measures of children's well-being (including low levels of child policy, and stable birth rates; OECD, 2005, 2020). Yet Sweden's approach contains its own challenges. Providing public supports for reconciling work and family life is expensive, and the government faces pressures to contain costs while also maintaining the high quality of services that Swedish citizens expect. To sustain such a comprehensive system financially in the long term requires avoiding significant increases in spending while simultaneously providing good-quality childcare, generous parental leaves, and ample work opportunities for women and men alike.

4.2   The U.S. Case in Comparative and Historical Perspective

In contrast to the European models, the U.S. has taken a different path. While a principle of familism (or what Orloff, 2011, calls "maternalism") formed the basis for the earliest policy approaches, it has given way to a more "individualistic" package of work and family policy approaches. In the beginning years of the American welfare state, policies were predicated on the assumption that most households would be anchored by a breadwinning husband and father. Accordingly, social rights were allocated to households, and social programs aimed to fill this void by providing supports to those—such as single mothers and unemployed men—who were not able to achieve this status. This paradigm stressed family cohesion rather than gender equality and built social policy around the primacy of the married, heterosexual couple. This familistic approach informed much of American social welfare policy throughout the middle decades of the 20th century, but it began to fray as women joined the labor force in unprecedented numbers and family structures rapidly diversified with the growth of divorced, single, and cohabiting households.

Amid these work and family changes, which peaked in the closing decades of the 20th century, an "individualistic" social policy regime began to supplant the earlier principle of supporting single mothers and their children. This approach, which predominates today, stresses equal opportunities—but not equal outcomes—for individuals rather than social rights for households. Drawing on the American tradition of individualism, an "individualistic" policy logic focuses on the rights of all citizens, regardless of gender, race, class, or sexual status, to compete (presumably though rarely actually) on an equal basis for social resources such as jobs and education. Since the emphasis is on opportunities rather than outcomes, anti-discrimination policies that aim to secure equal rights at the workplace take center stage, while policies providing a financial safety net as well as support for unpaid caregiving are downplayed or non-existent, leaving caregiving as a largely private responsibility.

Yet the American tradition of individualism and family self-sufficiency, though never able to provide equality or security to everyone, is especially inadequate to address the challenges of the new economy. Neither a familistic nor an individualistic approach can address the revolutionary shifts that have upended the gender system. By depending on women as unpaid caretakers, a familistic policy paradigm swims against the tide of history. Rather than persuading women to relinquish economic autonomy in favor of motherhood, it is more likely to create a birth dearth as women avoid marriage and childbearing in favor of paid work (as falling birthrates in countries such as Japan and Italy attest).

An individualistic policy regime, in contrast, may protect the individual rights of some in the marketplace, but it ignores the rights of those who give and receive care in the private sphere as well as those who face discrimination in the economic sphere. Each of these institutional logics presumes the market takes precedence over nonmarket activities and that the state is not responsible for protecting or supporting families or individuals who "fall through the cracks" of a market economy. Both thus fall far short of a workable and humane framework that provides both equal rights and caregiving support.

5.   INSIDE THE U.S. CASE

To understand how the rise of new forms of economic and interpersonal insecurity are transforming the work–care strategies of new generations of American workers and their families, Gerson's face-to-face, in-depth interviews reveal how changes in the nature of jobs and intimate relationships have influenced patterns of work and caregiving in the new economy. Home to the high-tech economy and its ancillary occupations, these locations offer a high concentration of cutting-edge jobs that form the core of the new economy, while also containing a mix of both old and new occupational niches as well as what Kalleberg (2011) terms "good" and "bad" jobs, providing fertile ground for examining how new jobs and occupational trajectories compare with more traditional ones and how the growth of new workplace and career structures is shaping the social and economic options for everyone. This approach yielded a group with diverse racial, class, and educational backgrounds who were currently living in a variety of family arrangements, including singles, co-habiters, and married couples.

5.1   The New American Landscape of Work and Care

How are these women and men experiencing and responding to the new challenges of earning a living and caring for others? And what are the implications for gender—and class— inequality? The interviews revealed four major patterns of response to the challenges of earning a living and caring for others. At one end of the spectrum, one-fifth of the participants adopted a "hyper-traditional" pattern that emphasized overwork for fathers and intensive parenting for mothers. Concerns about job security prompted husbands to put in very long workweeks (ranging from 60 to as much as 100 hours) to assure employers of their work commitment. In a parallel way, concerns about living up to a standard of "intensive parenting" left wives facing equally strong pressures to devote their utmost attention to childrearing. Although these mothers and fathers felt overworked in their separate spheres and deprived of both personal time and time together as a couple, they did not believe they could risk doing anything else.

At the other end of the spectrum, 24 percent opted to remain "unencumbered." These adults remained single and childless or became estranged from offspring in the wake of a breakup. An equal number of women and men followed this path, but they did so for different reasons. The men were typically unable (or unwilling) to find steady work and concluded they could not afford to take on the financial or emotional responsibilities of marriage and parenthood.

The women found they valued work too much to dilute their career commitment by taking on commitments to care for husbands as well as children.

In important ways, the "hyper-traditionals" are recreating traditional gender-divided patterns in an especially extreme form, while the unencumbered are opting to preserve their independence by avoiding all such traditional family commitments. Yet together these two extremes account for only 44 percent of the respondents. Two additional groups comprise the remaining 56 percent.

About a quarter (26 percent) of the participants are in relationships that reflect the simultaneous decline of the (male) breadwinner wage and the persistence of the (female) caregiver norm. These families rely on a woman's earnings as much as they do on a man's (and in some instances more) but they also depend on her for the bulk of caregiving. In these cases, women do not "have it all" so much as they "do it all." It is hardly surprising that carrying the load as both a primary or co-breadwinner and the main caretaker leaves most of these women feeling tired, disheartened, and unappreciated, but they are not alone in their frustration. Most of the men in these relationships also express frustration, saying they wish they could do more caregiving, but fear that taking the necessary time would endanger their job security and future prospects. What is more, these are not unrealistic fears. Research has demonstrated that unlike the Nordic countries where fathers as well as mothers are granted paid parental leave, a "flexibility stigma" penalizes American workers—especially professional men—who choose to pull back even slightly to engage in carework (Williams, Blair-Loy, and Berdahl, 2013).

The remaining 30 percent of the respondents can be described as egalitarians—couples who are experimenting with building an equal partnership despite the obstacles. With no clear path to follow, they do so in varying ways and with varying degrees of success. A third of this group (or about 12 percent of the entire sample) decided to avoid the difficulties of equal caretaking by forgoing parenthood altogether, with many looking to relatives, friends, and pets to forge other forms of caregiving ties. The rest were willing to limit their working time, risk their financial prospects, and forgo sleep and personal time to divide work and caregiving equally. Yet the dearth of institutional supports has left most of these work–care egalitarians wondering how long and at what cost they can sustain their efforts.

It is clear that contemporary Americans are fashioning a variety of strategies in response to the growing challenges of earning a living and caring for others. This diversity includes couples who are recreating separate gender spheres and singles who are living without the support of or obligations to a committed partner, but it also includes those who continue to rely on women to do it all and those who are trying, often against the odds, to divide work and caregiving equally. The question remains: Why did some choose traditionalism while others opted for singlehood, and still others for work–care equality?

5.2   Explaining Divergent Strategies: Shared Dilemmas, Different Compromises

First, individual preferences and desires do *not* explain the differences among traditionalists, the unencumbered, couples relying on a woman to do it all, and egalitarians. On the contrary, most women and men aspired to a better balance and integration of work and care than they were able to achieve. Each of the four strategies inevitably produces some degree of dissatisfaction, although those seeking to sustain a balanced egalitarian strategy report being the least dissatisfied. Figure 12.2 shows that 55 percent of hyper-traditional women and 38 percent of hyper-traditional men would prefer a different arrangement, while 84 percent of the women who "do it all" and 75 percent of men who rely on a woman to do it all would also prefer a different arrangement. Among the unencumbered, 58 percent of women and 76 percent of men report that a different situation would be preferable. In contrast, those expressing the least dissatisfaction are the egalitarians, where only 7 percent of women and 29 percent of men would prefer a different arrangement.

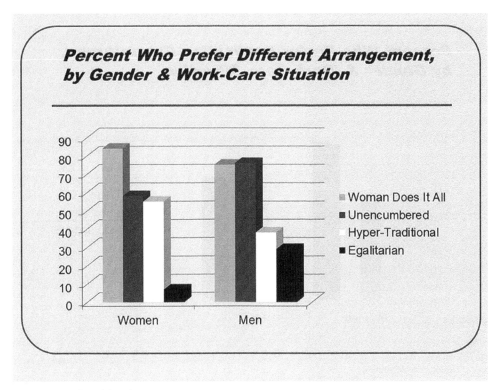

Percent Who Prefer Different Arrangement, by Gender & Work-Care Situation

- Woman Does It All
- Unencumbered
- Hyper-Traditional
- Egalitarian

Source: Gerson data elaboration

Figure 12.2   Percentage who prefer a different situation, by work–care arrangement and gender

What arrangement do people prefer instead? Figure 12.3 shows that most of those who are not sharing breadwinning and caregiving in an egalitarian way would prefer to do so if that were a more realistic option. Women are understandably more likely to prefer sharing, with 74 percent of those currently "doing it all," 58 percent of the unencumbered, and 55 percent of those in hyper-traditional relationships preferring more equal sharing. Although men express less enthusiasm for sharing, a significant proportion—including 38 percent of hyper-traditional men, 50 percent of men who rely on a woman to do it all, 53 percent of unencumbered men, and 71 percent of those in egalitarian relationships—express a preference for an egalitarian partnership. Among the egalitarians, a full 93 percent of women prefer their situation to remain that way.

Neither gender identity nor individual personal preferences can account for the shape of a person's work–care strategy. And despite the obstacles and difficulties facing egalitarian couples, they come closest to enacting their preferences. Instead of focusing on individual preferences, however, each group's work–care strategy is best explained by focusing on how a set of factors at work and in the domestic sphere converge in different ways to prompt different reactions to shared work–care conflicts.

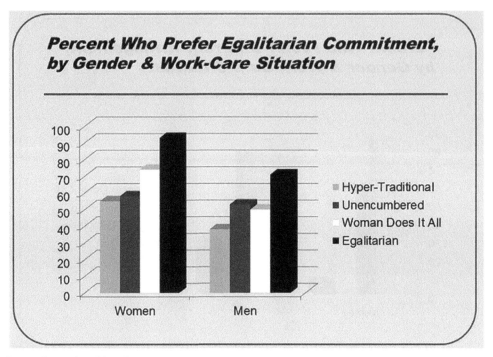

Source: Gerson data elaboration

Figure 12.3   *Percentage who prefer egalitarian commitment, by current situation and gender*

In the case of hyper-traditional couples, the partner with the higher paid but also more time-demanding job became the main breadwinner, leaving the partner with less promising work options to take on the lion's share of caretaking. In these instances, fathers enjoyed the best prospects at work but also faced the highest work demands and pressures, while mothers took on the job of intensive parenting almost single-handedly.

In contrast, the unencumbered were unable or unwilling to commit to marriage, although the causes and consequences varied by gender. Many unencumbered men were either unable to find secure work or chose a nontraditional form of work that could not offer a large or steady enough paycheck to support a family. Accepting the traditional view that a married man should be able to provide for his family, they concluded they were "unmarriageable" and disinclined to take on obligations to wives or children. Unencumbered women faced a different set of trade-offs. With promising work trajectories, they concluded that marriage and parenthood threatened to undo their hard-won accomplishments. The dilemmas facing these women and men formed mirror images, but they led both groups to opt for personal autonomy rather than commitments to partners or children.

A number of situational factors prompted women to add primary responsibility for caregiving onto equally demanding jobs. Some were left to rear children without the help or support of an intimate partner, leaving these single mothers to shoulder the work of earning an income and caring for offspring on their own. Most, however, were in married-couple relationships that nevertheless left the woman to "do it all." Often the women in these partnerships held an "old economy" job (in administration, teaching, retail, and the like) that offered a steady if not especially high income, while her partner sought less flexible but more appealing opportunities in new economy sectors such as high technology. These women not only brought equal or higher earnings to the partnership, but also put in more time and effort caring for others at home. Whether married or single, women in these situations not only shouldered breadwinning responsibilities but also could not look to a partner to share the unpaid work of caregiving.

Finally, egalitarians confronted a different set of options than their traditional, unencumbered, or "the woman does it all" peers. They were able to find satisfying jobs and to create long-term relationships with partners equally committed to paid work. Some concluded that these equal work ties left insufficient room to adding parenthood to the mix, at least without risking the well-being of their relationship, would-be children, careers, and mental health. Most, however, decided to take these risks, bear children, and share the work of earning and caretaking despite the obstacles. To do so, they chose jobs that offered some degree of flexibility as well as a partner who was willing to do the same, even if that meant sacrificing some degree of financial security and a great deal of sleep and personal time. Yet these egalitarian parents found the challenges daunting. With few supports at work or in their communities, their makeshift equal arrangements seemed fragile and difficult to sustain. Pulling back from work, even temporarily, threatened their long-term financial security, while working long hours threatened their relationship and personal well-being. Like single parents, egalitarian parents found that doing it all did not mean having it all. Whether they opted to remain childless or to share caregiving, all egalitarian partnerships faced a distinct set of pressures and trade-offs.

Despite their obvious differences, all these strategies are responses to a similar set of institutional conflicts and pressures. Rising job insecurity has upped the ante for workers, forcing them to put in long hours or risk losing their employment and endangering their future security. On the home front, concerns about rising inequality and declining social mobility have upped the ante on childrearing, creating a sense that only intensive parental attention can prepare children to navigate an uncertain future. These dual pressures have created work–care conflicts for everyone, and each strategy inevitably produces frustration, dissatisfaction, and even fear. What is more, because they emerge from situational constraints rather than inherent internal predispositions, each response represents a fluid state not a rigid position. It can—and indeed is likely to—change if and when the circumstantial opportunities and constraints are altered.

Each pattern illustrates one aspect of the diversity in how Americans are coping with the intractable conflicts and trade-offs between work and care. While the distinctions among them can become blurred as some people move from one category to another in response to changes in their economic and interpersonal fortunes, taken together they provide a framework for charting the options Americans face today and the strategies they use to build life paths amid the contradictions and conflicts of an increasingly uncertain economic and interpersonal landscape.

Stepping back to survey this landscape, it becomes clear that while the growth in economic insecurity and interpersonal uncertainty makes change inevitable and unavoidable, the shape of that change depends on how people navigate this new context. These two domains— access (or lack of access) to secure work and the ability (or inability) to establish a stable partnership—can and do converge in different ways, generating a patchwork of work–care strategies that reflect the changing nature of opportunities at work and in our private lives.

5.3   Beyond "Having It All"

Despite their differences, these strategies all represent Americans' efforts to fashion a coherent life path amid mounting work–family conflict. In an earlier era, gender offered a resolution to these institutional conflicts. For better or worse, men specialized in market work and women in nonmarket domestic activities. Yet even as the rise of unpredictable work paths and optional intimate relationships has undermined this gendered order, the norms and structures forged in that earlier era have persisted and even intensified, with American workers expected to spend an ever-expanding amount of time on the job (Jacobs and Gerson, 2004) and American parents expected to devote ever-expanding attention to each child (Hays, 1996). The traditional bargain between breadwinning husbands and caretaking wives may be increasingly unappealing and out of reach, but the cultural and structural supports for a more balanced, egalitarian gender bargain remain elusive.

The new economy may have irreversibly eroded a system of strict gender differences, with secure work available to most men and secure marriages available to most women, but it has not replaced this once-entrenched order with new and more satisfying ways to resolve the conflicts between paid work and private care.

In this context, "having it all" is a misleading and dangerous metaphor. Most often used to imply that earning and caregiving are incompatible and that women who try to combine them are unrealistic and selfish, this frame obscures the institutional roots of everyone's difficulties. Yet there is no necessary conflict between work and care. It is rooted instead in American institutional arrangements that devalue both paid and unpaid care work, fail to regulate the conditions of market work, and leave households to fend for themselves. Amid the new uncertainties facing women and men alike, the wish to combine work and caretaking is anything but selfish. On the contrary, gender-equal options for participating in paid work and integrating it with unpaid caregiving are key ingredients to securing the welfare not only of children and families but of all segments of American society.

6.   CONCLUSION: U.S. PROSPECTS AND POLICY POSSIBILITIES

As with the rise of the industrial system more than a century ago, the rise of the new precarious economy is an irreversible transformation that calls for structural and cultural realignments as vast as the shifts they need to address. Given the realities of an economic and social system that relies on women as workers but no longer offers job security to men or women, the costs of doing nothing are far greater than the costs of helping everyone—women and men alike—forge a more balanced, equal, and secure division of work and caregiving. What policies would ease the hardships change has produced? And what are the political possibilities in the U.S. context? Rather than relying on the tired lens of "having it all," the U.S. needs to embrace an egalitarian policy regime based on the principles of gender justice and work–care integration. The most effective and just response to the work–care conflicts wrought by the new economy would stress three general principles: gender equality in work and caregiving, integration between the public sphere of the market and the private sphere of family life, and support for all workers who wish to integrate earning an income with caring for others.

This analysis has shown the power of combining qualitative and quantitative approaches to understand work and family dynamics. The quantitative analysis provides an overview of the economic and the labor market frames that shape work and family options cross-nationally. The qualitative analysis within the U.S. context reveals the diverse behavioral and perceptional reactions women and men develop to the conflicts they face in an "individualist" work–family regime. This mixed-methods approach has made it possible to discover and explain the role that social policy plays in shaping the work–family conflicts citizens face and the strategies they develop in response.

Achieving these goals requires policies that make it possible for women to attain equality at work, for men to become equal partners at home, and for families to weather unpredictable changes in their economic fortunes and household composition. Such policies would seek to combine economic security with gender equality by constraining inequality within and between families and granting social rights to all citizens, regardless of the composition of their households. Concretely, this means regulating time norms at the workplace so no worker must choose between excessive workweeks and job insecurity. In communities, it means creating caretaking supports that extend beyond the privatized household for children of all ages. In American political institutions, it means ensuring equal economic opportunities and caregiving rights for everyone and creating a strengthened safety net that provides the basics, such as a livable income, decent healthcare, and supports to weather the unpredictable changes in people's economic fortunes and household composition.

Though no society has fully attained these outcomes, the Nordic model comes closest by providing all citizens with a minimum economic floor, universal childcare (along with healthcare and education), and "use it or lose it" paid parental leave policies that encourage men's caregiving and lessen the penalties for taking time out from work. As a package, such policies provide greater economic security, lessen work–care conflicts, and constrain inequality within and between families. They also begin to redress the imbalance that places a higher social and economic value on market work than on caregiving in its many forms.

The possibilities for creating an egalitarian policy regime—and the steps needed to achieve it—depend on the constraints and opportunities offered by diverse political contexts. The American context poses especially daunting obstacles. Americans possess a well-known skepticism toward strong state-based policies, which many see as "government intervention" in the private realm. The rise of family diversity has also created a deeply polarized political stalemate, often called a "culture war," between those who wish to restore an earlier gender and family order and those who favor a more egalitarian one. Additionally, the rise of work–care conflicts leaves ordinary citizens facing severe time crunches that shrink the time available for political activism that presses for new policy initiatives (Putnam, 2000).

Despite these roadblocks, American support for gender equality and work–family integration is on the rise, especially among younger generations (Pedulla and Thebaud, 2015). The growing support for paid family leave and nationally subsidized health insurance, and a higher minimum wage, suggests that most Americans wish to overcome past political stalemates and entertain transformative policies. If the moment has arrived, the first step is to distinguish between the social changes that are unavoidable and the options available to shape social arrangements through collective choices. Economic uncertainty and relationship fragility, along with diversity and fluidity in family forms, are integral aspects of inexorable economic and demographic shifts that are likely to continue, whether or not some pockets of American society wish it were not so.

As the new economy continues to transform the lives of successive generations, the conflicts between work and care will only become more apparent. Change is inescapable, and going back to an outdated gender system is not an option. It is neither humane nor just to continue to measure a man's worth by his ability to be a breadwinner or a woman's worth by her willing-ness to be a selfless caregiver. Going forward, the choice is between new forms of inequality and insecurity or the creation of new supports for equalizing and integrating responsibility for work and care. The good news is that the revolutionary shifts taking place in work and family life have created an unprecedented opportunity to achieve greater gender and family equality and to create a new social contract based on these principles. In a society as diverse as the U.S., the political challenge is to find common ground for realigning state and market institutions to address the needs of America's 21st-century families, whatever form they may take so that Americans need not have to choose between viable work and a rich personal life.

NOTES

1. We use the term "institutional" to refer both to structural arrangements, such as the family wage that made it possible for an employed father to support a household on his income, and to cultural norms, such as the ideal of the "good provider" father and the "homemaking" mother.
2. In today's environment, women are almost as likely as men to hold a paid job and consequently face job insecurity. Job insecurity is on the rise at all class levels, but is especially high among employees in the service sector, where women are especially likely to find employment.
3. Rates of divorce and single parenthood are higher among the less affluent, but these rates have risen among all classes and economic levels. Cherlin (2014) provides an in-depth analysis of changes in the economic prospects of working-class families that make stable marriage difficult to obtain or sustain.
4. Recent research has confirmed Gerson's findings that aspirations for more egalitarian relationships and a more equal personal balance between work and family life are rising, especially among younger generations of Americans (Gerson, 2011; Pedulla and Thebaud, 2015).
5. For all the U.S. indicators, the rates varied across race and ethnicity groups. Some studies stated that by 2045, the U.S. is projected to become a "majority-minority" nation in which non-Hispanic whites of all ages will constitute less than 50 percent of the total population (Vespa, Armstrong, and Medina, 2018).
6. Concerning the U.S. case, the main cause of the falling labor force participation rate is the retire-ment of the baby boomers. The analysis proposed said that the decline of the participation rate will continue for the next decade, and achieve a rate not seen since the years between 1950 and 1960, before women began to enter the labor force in increasing numbers (Dotsey, Fujita, and Rudanko, 2017).
7. As for all the U.S. topics, race and ethnic differences are relevant.

REFERENCES

Anttonen, A., and Sipilä, J. (1996), "European social care services: Is it possible to identify models?" *Journal of European Social Policy* **6** (2), 87–100.

Belkin, L. (2003), "The opt-out revolution," *New York Times Magazine*, October 26.

Bettio, F., and Plantenga, J. (2004), "Comparing care regimes in Europe," *Feminist Economics* **10** (1), 85–113.

BLS (U.S. Bureau of Labor Statistics) (2019), BLS reports, www.bls.gov/opub/reports/womens-databook/2019/home.htm.

Cherlin, A.J. (2014), *Labor's Love Lost: The Rise and Fall of the Working-Class Family in America*, New York, NY: Russell Sage Foundation.

Choen, P.N. (2019), "The coming divorce decline," *Socius: Sociological Research for a Dynamic World* **5**, 1–6.

Cotter, D., Hermsen, J., and Vanneman, R. (2011), "End of the gender revolution? Gender role attitudes from 1977 to 2008," *American Journal of Sociology* **117**, 259–89.

Cronholm, S., and Hjalmarsson, A. (2011), "Mixed Methods in Use: Experiences from Combining Qualitative and Quantitative Approaches," in M. Ashwin (ed.), *Proceedings of the 10th European Conference on Research Methodology for Business and Management Studies, Caen, France, June 20–21, 2011*.

Daly, M., and Lewis, J. (2000), "The concept of social care and the analysis of contemporary welfare states," *British Journal of Sociology* **51** (2), 281–98.

DiPrete, T., and Buchmann, C. (2013), *The Rise of Women: The Growing Gender Gap in Education and What It Means for American Schools*, New York, NY: Russell Sage Foundation.

Dotsey, M., Fujita, S., and Rudanko, L. (2017), "Where is everybody? The shrinking labor force participation rate," *Economic Insights* **2** (4), 17–24.

England, P. (2010), "The gender revolution: Uneven and stalled," *Gender & Society* **24**, 149–66.

England, P., Levine, A., and Mishel, E. (2020), "Progress toward gender equality in the United States has slowed or stalled," *Proceedings of the National Academy of Sciences* **117** (13), 6990–97. https://doi.org/10.1073/pnas.1918891117.

Esping-Andersen, G. (1990), *The Three Worlds of Welfare Capitalism*, Cambridge: Polity Press.

Gerson, K. (2011), *The Unfinished Revolution: Coming of Age in a New Era of Gender, Work and Family*, New York, NY: Oxford University Press.

Gerson, K. (2017), "Different Ways of Not Having It All: Work, Care, and Shifting Gender Arrangements in the New Economy," in A. Pugh (ed.), *Beyond the Cubicle: Job Insecurity, Intimacy, and the Flexible Self*, New York, NY: Oxford University Press.

Glass, J., Simon, R., and Andersson, M. (2016), "Parenthood and happiness: Effects of work-family reconciliation policies in 22 OECD Countries," *American Journal of Sociology* **122**, 886–929.

Glynn, S.J. (2019), "Breadwinning mothers continue to be the U.S. norm," Center for American Progress, 10 May, www.americanprogress.org/issues/women/reports/2019/05/10/469739/breadwinning-mothers-continue-u-s-norm/.

Gornick, J.C., and Meyers, M.K. (2009), *Gender Equality: Transforming Family Divisions of Labor*, New York, NY: Verso.

Guillén, A.M., and León, M. (eds) (2011), *The Spanish Welfare State in European Context*, Farnham: Ashgate.

Harrington, B., Van Deusen, F., and Sabatini Fraone, J. (2016), *The New Dad*, Boston, MA: Boston College Center for Work & Family.

Hays, S. (1996), *The Cultural Contradictions of Motherhood*, New Haven, CT: Yale University Press.

Howe, K.R. (2012), "Mixed methods, triangulation, and causal explanation," *Journal of Mixed Methods Research* **6** (2), 89–96, https://doi.org/10.1177/1558689812437187.

HSBC (2019), The expat explorer survey, www.expatexplorer.hsbc.com/survey/.

Ishizuka, P. (2019), "Social class, gender, and contemporary parenting standards in the United States: Evidence from a national survey experiment," *Social Forces* **98** (1), 31–58, https://doi.org/10.1093/sf/soy107.

ILO (International Labour Organization) (2018), *World Employment and Social Outlook: Trends 2018*, Geneva: ILO.

ILO (International Labour Organization) (2019), *World Employment and Social Outlook: Trends 2019*, Geneva: ILO.

Ivankova, N.V., Creswell, J.W., and Stick, S.L (2006), "Using mixed-methods sequential explanatory design: From theory to practice," *Field Methods* **18** (1), 3–20, https://doi.org/10.1177/1525822X05282260.

IWPR (Institute for Women's Policy Research) (2016), Fact sheet: The gender wage gap 2016 – Earnings differences by race and ethnicity, https://iwpr.org/wp-content/uploads/2017/03/C454.pdf.

IWPR (Institute for Women's Policy Research) (2019), Pay equity and discrimination, https://iwpr.org/issue/employment-education-economic-change/pay-equity-discrimination/.

Jacobs, J., and Gerson, K. (2004), *The Time Divide: Work, Family, and Gender Inequality*, Cambridge, MA: Harvard University Press.

Johnson, R.B., Onwuegbuzie, A.J., Turner, L.A (2007), "Toward a definition of mixed methods research," *Journal of Mixed Methods Research* **1** (2),112–133.

Kalleberg, A. (2011), *Good Jobs, Bad Jobs: The Rise of Polarized and Precarious Employment Systems in the United States, 1970s to 2000s*, New York, NY: Russell Sage Foundation.

Lappegård, T. (2014), "Changing European Families," in J. Treas, J. Scott and M. Richards (eds), *The Wiley Blackwell Companion to the Sociology of Families*, Hoboken, NJ: Wiley Blackwell, 20–43.

Leitner, S. (2003), "Varieties of familialism: The caring function of the family in comparative perspective," *European Societies* **5** (4), 353–75.

León, M., and Migliavacca, M. (2013), "Italy and Spain: Still the case of familistic welfare models?" *Population Review* **52** (1), 25–42.

Migliavacca, M., and Naldini, M. (2018), "Tra famiglia e lavoro, quattro sistemi a confronto. I casi di Australia, Stati Uniti, Italia e Giappone," *Rivista delle politiche Sociali* **1**, 23–47.

Naldini, M., and Saraceno, C. (2011), *Conciliare famiglia e lavoro Vecchi e nuovi patti tra sessi e generazioni*, Bologna: Il Mulino.

OECD (Organisation for Economic Co-operation and Development) (2005), *Babies and Bosses: Reconciling Work and Family Life, Volume 4 – Canada, Finland, Sweden and the United Kingdom*, Paris: OECD Publishing. https://doi.org/10.1787/9789264009295-en.

OECD (Organisation for Economic Co-operation and Development) (2020), *How's Life? 2020: Measuring Well-Being*, Paris: OECD Publishing. https://doi.org/10.1787/9870c393-en.

Orloff, A.S. (2011), "Policy, politics, gender: Bringing gender to the analysis of welfare states," *Sociologica* **1**, 1–19.

Pearce, L.D. (2012), "Mixed methods inquiry in sociology," *American Behavioral Scientist* **56** (6), 829–48, https://doi.org/10.1177/0002764211433798.

Pedulla, D., and Thebaud, S. (2015), "Can we finish the revolution? Gender, work-family ideals, and institutional constraint," *American Sociological Review* **80** (1), 16–139.

Pfau-Effinger, B. (2005), "Welfare state policies and the development of care arrangements," *European Societies* **7** (2), 321–47.

Poelmans, S.A.Y. (2005), *Work and Family: An International Research Perspective*, Mahwah, NJ: Lawrence Erlbaum Associates.

PRC (Pew Research Center) (2017), 10 things we learned about gender issues in the U.S. in 2017, www.pewresearch.org/fact-tank/2017/12/28/10-things-we-learned-about-gender-issues-in-the-u-s-in-2017/.

PRC (Pew Research Center) (2019), 6 facts about U.S. moms, www.pewresearch.org/fact-tank/2019/05/08/facts-about-u-s-mothers/.

Putnam, R. (2000), *Bowling Alone: The Collapse and Revival of American Community*, New York, NY: Simon & Schuster.

Rosin, H. (2012), *The End of Men and the Rise of Women*, New York, NY: Riverbed.

Saraceno, C., and Keck, W. (2010), "Towards an integrated approach for the analysis of gender equity in policies supporting paid work and care responsibilities," *Demographic Research* **25**, 371–406.

Saraceno, C., and Negri, N. (1994), "The changing Italian welfare state," *Journal of European Social Policy* **4** (1), 19–34, https://doi.org/10.1177/095892879400400102.

Sassler, S., and Miller, A. (2017), *Cohabitation Nation: Gender, Class, and the Remaking of Relationships*, Los Angeles, CA: University of California Press.

Stanczyk, A.B., Henly, J.R., and Lambert, S.J. (2017), "Enough time for housework? Low-wage work and desired housework time adjustments," *Journal of Marriage and Family* **79** (1), 243–60.

Stolz, J., Lindemann, A., and Antonietti, J.-P. (2019), "Sociological explanation and mixed methods: The example of the *Titanic*," *Quality & Quantity: International Journal of Methodology* **53** (3), 1623–43.

Stone, P. (2007), *Opting Out? Why Women Really Quit Careers and Head Home*, Berkeley, CA: University of California Press.

Venkatesh, V., Brown, S., and Bala, H. (2013), "Bridging the qualitative–quantitative divide: Guidelines for conducting mixed methods research in information systems," *MIS Quarterly* **37** (1), 21–54.

Vespa, J., Armstrong, D.M., and Medina, L. (2018), *Demographic Turning Points for the United States: Population Projections for 2020 to 2060 – Current Population Reports*. U.S. Census Bureau, March 2018.

Wilcox, W.B. (2010), *When Marriage Disappears: The Retreat from Marriage in Middle America*, Charlottesville, VA: National Marriage Project.

Williams, J., Blair-Loy, M., and Berdahl, J. (2013), "Cultural schemas, social class, and the flexibility stigma," *Journal of Social Issues* **69**, 209–34.

Zaslow, M., Crosby, D.A., and Smith, N. (2013), "Issues of Quality and Access Emerging from the Changing Early Childhood Policy Context: Toward the Next Generation of Research," in E.T. Gershoff, R.S. Mistry and D.A. Crosby (eds), *Societal Contexts of Child Development: Pathways of Influence and Implications for Practice and Policy*, Oxford: Oxford Scholarship Online. https://doi.org/10.1093/acprof:oso/9780199943913.001.0001.

13. The effect of childcare facilities on labour market participation among young adults in Estonia: a mixed-methods study

Kadri Täht, Marge Unt and Epp Reiska

INTRODUCTION

The availability of care arrangements for young children plays an important role in parents' (especially women's) labour market participation (Stier et al. 2001, Uunk et al. 2005). Evidence from previous studies suggests that lower childcare costs and available formal care arrangements decrease the cost of employment, and in turn increase the likelihood that parents are employed and lengthen their working hours (see, for example, Del Boca et al. 2009, Han and Waldfogel 2001, Tekin 2007). Attending non-parental early care and education facilities (day-care centres, preschools, and so on) has become a common experience in the lives of young children in our (Western) societies. In 2017, on average 34 per cent of children under the age of 3 attended centre-based early childhood education and care (ECEC) in European Union (EU) countries, ranging from less than 1 per cent in Slovakia to almost 72 per cent in Denmark. The same year, of children between the age of 4 and compulsory primary education age, on average 95 per cent participated in ECEC in the EU (EC/EAECEA/Eurydice 2019).

Next to the increasing prevalence and use of formal care, informal care has remained important for parental labour market participation as well. Studies show that informal care remains a significant factor for parental labour market participation in many countries, including those where formal care is already quite prevalent (Larsen 2004). Or, as suggested by several studies, informal care and formal care strategies are possibly intertwined and complementary (Raeymaeckers et al. 2008, Sümer et al. 2008). However, the effect of (informal) care varies across countries (Aassve et al. 2012, Di Gessa et al. 2016).

The aim of this chapter is to analyse the effect of having young children on labour market participation and the (mediating) role of care arrangements in Estonia. The central research question is "What is the effect of formal and informal care on the labour market participation of parents of young children?" Estonia provides an interesting country case, with a high labour market participation rate by women, including women with (young) children. Moreover, the norm is to work full-time. Public childcare is available, accessible and highly used – families have the legal entitlement to public ECEC as of the age of 1 year and 6 months, there is no top-level regulation restricting the ECEC hours and even when the ECEC is not free, the fees are low. However, similar to many other European countries, there exists a considerable childcare gap, with the result that, for example, in 2017 only 27 per cent of children under the age of 3 participated in ECEC (EC/EAECEA/Eurydice 2019). Although care leave is available for both parents, it is mostly taken by women – in 2013, of all recipients of parental leave benefit, 6.5 per cent were men, and this number has remained quite unchanged over recent years (Eurofound 2015). Thus, despite the high labour market attachment of men and women, the careers of women are marked by rather long care breaks (1.5 to three years per child). Respectively, the main burden and challenge of returning to labour market after a (long) care break falls disproportionally on women. Therefore, the second central research question focuses on whether and how the childcare-availability effect on labour market participation differs for men and women.

We limit and focus our analysis on young adults (18–34 years old) who are in the beginning of both their labour market career and parenthood. This narrows our target population to a more homogeneous group in terms of the labour market and work–family situation – the labour market participation challenges and struggles are in general different for those just at the beginning of their career and those who have their careers already established (or have had time to establish them). Next to the challenge of entering the world of employment, young adults are also often in the life stage of starting their own family, which makes the employment challenge even bigger and respectively their situation more vulnerable (Inanc 2015, Liefbroer and Corijn 1999). Moreover, due to the overlapping and intersectionality of two relevant life stages – labour market entry and family formation – there is a higher risk of accumulation of disadvantages. For example, young adults with a low education already have higher risks of labour market exclusion, while at the same time they are more likely to enter into early parenthood (Kreyenfeld 2010), which increases their labour market exclusion risk or makes labour market participation even more challenging and more dependent on external (care) support. Therefore, we offer an insight into the challenges of and coping strategies for combining childcare and labour market participation for vulnerable labour market participants among young adults.

The current study will apply a mixed-methods approach, where both quantitative and qualitative data will be used. The main source for quantitative analysis will be the Estonian Time-Use Survey 2009 (Statistics Estonia 2011), which enables the study of the detailed time-use of household members, including participation in paid work and time spent on care. It provides data on the use of both external (public childcare, grandparents) and internal (grandparents living in the household) care. The quantitative time-use data will be complemented with interviews from a qualitative study conducted within the EXCEPT project (Bertolini et al. 2018). For this, we have selected two cases from an Estonian country study to illustrate how the use of formal and informal childcare may affect young parents' labour market participation. We outline the life story of two young mothers with low education to illuminate their coping strategies and challenges in combining working and being a parent. The interviews reveal how the labour market participation is linked to the interplay between formal and informal childcare opportunities, and even widely available and affordable childcare may not always foster labour market participation of those in vulnerable positions in the labour market.

THE EFFECT OF FORMAL CARE SERVICES ON LABOUR MARKET PARTICIPATION

Previous studies have shown that childcare reduces the labour market participation of parents, especially for women (Angrist and Evans 1998, Uunk et al. 2005). One of the common strategies for combining work and care for children is part-time employment. However, the availability and use of part-time work varies across countries and is strongly dependent on the country's institutional, labour market and wealth contexts (Mínguez 2005).

Alternatively, childcare needs are met by the use of external care facilities such as public day-care. There exists a vast amount of literature on female labour supply, emphasizing the importance of the availability of public childcare on it (Del Boca and Vuri 2007, Stier et al. 2001, Uunk et al. 2005). Institutional support towards the use of formal childcare services has been related to encouraging young adults' and parents' participation in the labour market, and increasing female labour force participation and fertility (Blau and Robins 1988). While the general finding tends to be that childcare costs and availability affect parental labour force participation, the effect and association tends to vary across countries and welfare regimes. A meta-analysis of 37 peer-reviewed articles on care access (costs) and female labour market participation by Akgunduz and Plantenga (2011) summarizes that the general participation response can be characterized by a positive inverse U-shaped relationship with aggregate labour market participation, and decreases with high rates of part-time work and social spending. In other words, in high-participation or high-part-time countries such as Sweden, Norway or the Netherlands, the mere focus on childcare prices appears to be unproductive and alternative aspects such as quality of care may be more relevant. On the other hand, in developing countries or countries with low rates for female participation, the reason and solution for non-participation rates may not be care subsidies, but may lie somewhere else, owing presumably to more structural and cultural reasons (Van der Lippe and Siegers 1994). A literature review by Morrissey (2017) on the effect of childcare costs and availability on parental employment comes to similar conclusions – while research literature suggests that a reduction in childcare costs and an increase in childcare availability increases parents' (especially mothers') labour force participation, the effect sizes vary widely. The heterogeneity of findings likely results from variations in policy, cultural or historical contexts, but also in the methodological approaches and data used.

THE EFFECT OF INFORMAL CARE ON LABOUR MARKET PARTICIPATION

Next to formal care arrangements, informal arrangements keep being important. According to a comparative study by Larsen (2004) in all the countries representing different welfare regimes, formal care arrangements tended to be insufficient to cover all the families' child-care needs. "Informal childcare" used by parents is overwhelmingly grandparent care, as it is usually viewed as the closest to the care that mothers themselves provide (Kuhlthau and Mason 1996, Wheelock and Jones 2002). Previous research has shown that across EU countries, grandparents are the most common providers of informal childcare (Jappens and Van Bavel 2012, Rutter and Evans 2011). Hank and Buber (2009) found in their study a high prevalence of childcare by grandparents in all European countries – about 32 per cent of European grandmothers are engaged in regular childcare (that is, almost weekly or more often). Tan et al. (2010) reported in their study about the UK that 94 per cent of maternal grandmothers met their grandchildren at least twice a year, while 57 per cent met them on a weekly or daily basis. Given the demographic trends – increased life expectancy and an increasing proportion of elderly adults in the population – the number of grandparents is rising. Moreover, grandparents and grandchildren have nowadays more shared years than ever before, and due to lower fertility rates grandparents have fewer children to take care of and will be able to be more present in each grandchild's life. Thus, family multigenerational relations, namely the roles of grandparents, are expected to grow in importance (Bengtson 2001, Giarrusso and Silverstein 1996) even in more advanced societies.

The use of grandparents as carers results from two main factors: (1) the unavailability of formal childcare and (2) normative values and attitudes towards childcare. There have been several recent studies showing the role of grandparents in increasing parents' (mostly mothers') labour force participation (Aassve et al. 2012, Compton and Pollak 2014, Dimova and Wolff 2008). For parents, particularly mothers, in many European countries with low investment in formal childcare services, the only possible way to enter the labour market is to have grandparents' help with childcare (Herlofson and Hagestad 2012). Next to pointing out the often substantial role played by grandparents in parental labour force participation, the studies highlight the considerable differences in the size of effects between countries (Di Gessa et al. 2016). For example, in their study, Aassve et al. (2012) found considerable variation across countries with regard to whether grandparents' childcare raised mothers' labour force participation: in France, Germany, Bulgaria and Hungary grandparents' childcare had a positive significant impact on mothers' participation, while in Russia, Georgia and the Netherlands it did not.

The cross-country differences both in grandparents' childcare and grandparents' effect on parental labour market participation illustrate how the welfare state context and features of the labour market influence the expression of intergenerational relationships (Szydlik 2012). However, these trends do not follow always the widely used welfare state typologies (see, for example, Esping-Andersen 1990). For example, Estonia has been characterized as a liberal welfare regime regarding labour market protection and labour market flexibility, but it ranks high in public childcare provision (EC/EACEA/Eurydice 2019). The UK, another so-called liberal welfare regime, fell into the medium category among EU member states with regard to (public) provision of childcare (Saraceno and Keck 2010), whereas in the US, which is also often classified as a liberal regime, grandparents were the main source of childcare for up to 23 per cent of pre-schoolers (Laughlin 2013).

Grandparents' participation in taking care of grandchildren is also related to their proximity; that is, how close or far away they live. Jappens and Van Bavel (2012) examined the proportion of grandparents (respondents aged 55 or older) living together with at least one of their children and found a clear difference between Northern and Western European countries, and Mediterranean and Central and Eastern European countries. Pilkauskas and Martinson (2014) find in their comparative study that nearly one-quarter of US children live in a three-generation household during early childhood, compared to 8 per cent of children in the UK and 11 per cent in Australia. In most Northern and Western European countries, co-residence with children was reported by less than 15 per cent of respondents. In contrast, co-residence between elderly parents and children in Southern, Central and Eastern European regions and Ireland was reported by 48 per cent or more of respondents.

Although there are large differences in the frequency of co-residence cross-nationally, similar demographic groups live in three-generation households across contexts – younger, less educated, lower-income and minority mothers are more likely to live in three-generation households. Along the same lines, lone parents, parents working long or nonstandard hours and parents from financially disadvantaged families are most likely to use grandparent care. The age of children also influences the pattern of grandparents' care, with grandparents most likely to provide care for pre-school children, except very young children and toddlers (Igel and Szydlik 2011, Jappens and Van Bavel 2012). An association with socioeconomic status has been pointed out by other studies, showing that the grandparent effect is stronger in the case of economically deprived households, and in households of single mothers (Attar-Schwartz et al. 2009, Ruiz and Silverstein 2007).

THE CASE OF ESTONIA: HYPOTHESES

In Estonia, the labour market participation rate for both men and women is high – in 2017, 79 per cent of men and 71 per cent of women aged 15–69 were mostly full-time active participants in the workforce. Having children makes workers, mostly women, withdraw from the labour market, but usually only temporarily. Parents are entitled to a care leave of up to three years, the first one and a half years being covered by social insurance (100 per cent of his or her last work year's earnings, calculated based on social tax contributions). Although care leave could be taken by either parent, it is mostly taken by women – less than 10 per cent of men take some parental leave. Although parents in Estonia, mostly mothers, stay home for a considerable period of time – 27 per cent for one and a half to two years, 35 per cent for more than two years – after their childcare leave they usually return to the labour market. The norm for both men and women is to work full-time – in 82–85 per cent of households with children aged under 18, both parents work full-time (Statistics Estonia 2020).

Public childcare is available, accessible, of high quality and highly used. Ninety-one per cent of pre-school institutions are municipal kindergartens and private care is rather rare, and even when the ECEC is not free, the fees are affordable. Families have the legal entitlement to public ECEC for their child as of the age of 1 year and 6 months; however, in reality there is still higher demand for places for children under 3 years old than there is supply. In 2017, 27 per cent of children under the age of 3 participated in ECEC in Estonia, whereas the participation rate for those between 3 and 7 (the age to start compulsory education) was 92 per cent, in both cases remaining slightly under the EU average (EC/EAECEA/Eurydice 2019). In Estonia, the actual time spent in formal care for children both under and over 3 years old is above the EU average, reaching an average of 34.7 hours a week for those under 3 years old and 38.5 hours a week for those over 3 (ibid.: 69).

Given the trends and associations pointed out in previous research, it is expected that formal childcare raises the labour market participation of parents of young children (Hypothesis 1), whereas the impact is stronger on women's labour market behaviour (Hypothesis 1.1).

Next to extensive use of formal care, informal care also remains relevant in Estonia. According to the study by Jappens and Van Bavel (2012), the highest level of intergenerational support and care can be found in the Central and Eastern European countries, although with substantive differences within and between individual countries. According to the study by Mills et al. (2013), Estonia placed somewhere in the middle of Central and Eastern European countries in terms of the percentage of children in informal care (in 2010). Moreover, the use of grandparent care for children under or over 3 years old is above the EU average, whereas the general European level was considered very high. At the same time, it should be kept in mind that labour market participation among older people (that is, the potential grandparents) is high in Estonia – the labour force participation rate for men and women aged 50–64 is between 60 and 89 per cent.

Given these trends and associations, it is expected that informal care raises the labour market participation (even when formal care is accounted for) of parents of young children (Hypothesis 2), whereas the effect is stronger for women's labour market behaviour (Hypothesis 2.1).

DATA AND VARIABLES

Quantitative Data and Analysis

The main data used for the current analysis comes from the Estonian Time-Use Survey 2009 (Statistics Estonia 2011). This is a household survey that collects data on time-use of individual household members, including a time diary filled in by each household member older than 10. The data has been collected by Statistics Estonia and so far the survey has been carried out twice in Estonia, in 1999 and 2009. In the current analysis, the data from 2009 is used. The sample of the time-use study includes approximately 3,100 households with approximately 7,000 individuals/members interviewed. The effective sample of the current study involves young adults aged 18–34 who are currently working, unemployed or inactive. Young adults in full-time education were left out of the analysis. This leaves us with a sub-sample of 1,744 cases.

The central dependent variable of the analysis is the labour market status – being employed, unemployed or inactive. The central independent variables include several types of childcare arrangements:

- Use of formal childcare – childcare that takes place in a formal childcare institution (ECEC). In the current analysis it is operationalized as the total number of hours the young child(ren) of the household spent in ECEC last week;
- Use of informal childcare – free (non-paid) childcare received from a grandparent (or some other relative).

As most commonly young children in European countries live in a household with their parent(s) (and siblings), childcare by a grandparent is usually "external" help as grandparents do not live together with their grandchildren. However, there are still countries, especially in Eastern Europe, where a three-generational household is not as rare and a considerable amount of children live with their grandparents. In 2008, 11 per cent of children in Estonia lived in a three-generational household, which is almost twice the EU average (6.6 per cent) (Iacovou and Skew 2011). As shown in earlier research, those more likely to live in a three-generation household as well as being more likely dependent on grandparent care are younger, less educated, lower-income and minority mothers (Pilkauskas and Martinson 2014). Thus, another relevant source of grandparent care may be "internal"; that is, taking place inside the household. Therefore, in the current analysis we take into account and differentiate between both types of informal childcare – the one received from family members (mostly grandparents) living outside the household and the one from the grandparent(s) living in the same household – which will be operationalized as follows:

1. The child(ren) under the age of 10 was/were taken care of last week by somebody who is not living in the household and who provided it for free (usually a grandparent or some other relative).

2. The total minutes a grandparent (to an under-10-year-old child in the household) living in the same household spent on childcare (both care and play) during working days last week. The data is received from the time-use diary filled in by the respective grandparent.

Other control variables included in the analysis are: age, ethnicity (being Estonian or non-Estonian), level of education, place of residence, partnership status and number of young children (under 10 years old) in the household.

For the quantitative analysis we use descriptive analysis and Ordinary Least Squares (OLS) regression analysis for assessing the probability to be in unemployment or in inactivity compared to being in employment. Note that although the dependent variable is a binary measure, we use here a linear regression model, because the coefficients can be interpreted on the probability scale. Especially for the interpretation of interaction effects, linear models imply, in contrast to non-linear regressions, a straightforward interpretation.

Qualitative Data and Analysis

To complement and illustrate the results of quantitative analysis, we draw on a qualitative study conducted as part of the EXCEPT project. It involved qualitative interviews with young people in nine countries to explore how they perceive their situation and their coping strategies in different institutional, economic and cultural contexts. Young adults in the age range of 18–30, mostly at the margins of the labour market and with a low educational level were sampled for this study (for methodological details, see Bertolini et al. 2018). For the current analysis the life stories of two young mothers in Estonia, both with low education and poor labour market perspectives, were selected to illuminate the challenges and respective copying strategies in combining paid work and parenthood for young adults in a vulnerable labour market situation. The focus of the analysis is on the relationship between the employment situation and opportunities and the role of informal and formal childcare in it. In order to narrow the focus on similar institutional settings, both examples are drawn from a similar context – from the capital city with a more vibrant labour market and a wider range of job opportunities.

The first case, Aveli, is a 26-year-old woman with three children (aged 9, 7 and 2). She dropped out of lower secondary education in the 9th grade (the last year of compulsory education) as she became pregnant with her first child and "didn't have the courage to go to school with a big belly". She eventually managed to finish her lower secondary education two years later, just before her second child was born, but did not continue in upper secondary or vocational education. She currently thinks that she will continue her education career sometime in the future, but has no concrete plans related to it as her main goal for the moment is to raise her children and make ends meet.

The second case, Mai, is a 28-year-old woman with two children (one aged 8 years and the other 8 months) whom she is currently raising alone. She has acquired lower secondary (compulsory) education and tried higher secondary twice and vocational training once, but has failed to graduate for different reasons. An important turning point for her was a conflict with her mother when she was in the beginning of her higher secondary education, and because of it she was put out of her parental home. She has been unemployed for most of her labour career. However during these unemployment periods, with the support of the Public Employment Office, she has attended several training courses, such as for babysitting, customer support and secretarial work.

Thus, both women are facing the challenge of combining work and family, while both have limited negation power in the labour market due to having little work experience and low educational resources. Both have managed to gain access to jobs with a minimum salary, which does not allow them to use any paid childcare services, and they rely on public care facilities or on informal care provided by a close network.

FINDINGS

The Use of Formal and Informal Care

Mothers' (but not fathers') labour market participation is clearly related to the age of their child and the availability and use of (formal) care in Estonia. As can be seen in Figure 13.1, when the youngest child is under 1 year of age, only a very small share of women are actively participating in the labour market. Fathers' labour market participation rates, in turn, remain relatively unchanged for that age period – the mean participation level for fathers goes down by only a few percentage points during the first few years of their youngest child's life. Mothers start returning to the labour market after 1.5 to two years of care leave, and parallel to this increase the use of formal care (here measured as the mean number of hours a week a child spends in ECEC). According to our data, with the youngest child being 3–4 years old, 70–80 per cent of their mothers are in paid labour, and the children of that age spent on average 30–34 hours a week in ECEC.

Next to the "external" care, both formal and informal, "internal" grandparent care – childcare carried out by a grandparent living in the household – is used in Estonia. Table 13.1 presents the average minutes a grandparent living in a three-generation household with at least one child under 10 years old spent during the week on childcare activities (this includes both care and interaction time). The first thing to be emphasized here is the share of three-generation households – households with a pre-school aged child where there are two parents (a couple) present: 14–15 per cent are a three-generation household where at least one grandparent lives. The share is even bigger when we include single parents (mostly households of single mothers) in the analysis – about every fifth home has a grandparent living in the same household.

Secondly, a co-residential grandparent reports on average 1–2 hours a week (on working days) with childcare as their main activity (both care and so-called quality time: playing, reading, and so on). Also, here the contribution is related to the age of the youngest child – when children are very young, grandparent care is less used because parents (mostly mothers) are doing the care work. However, once children enter formal care and mothers return to the labour market, grandparents' contribution becomes more prominent. The care is more intense for grandparents living in a mono-parental household (mostly single mothers'). In any case, these findings suggest that childcare by grandparents forms an important part of care arrangements in Estonia, where the use of formal care is already very widespread.

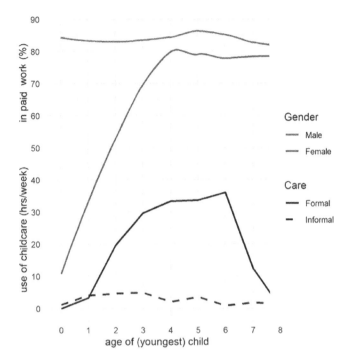

Notes: Formal care – hours (mean) spent in ECEC during a week; Informal care – free childcare provided by an external family member or friend, number of hours a week
Source: Estonian Time-Use Survey 2009 (Statistics Estonia 2011), authors' calculations

Figure 13.1   *Labour market participation (%) and use of care arrangements (hrs/week) by age of the youngest child in the household*

THE EFFECT OF CHILDCARE ARRANGEMENTS AND AVAILABILITY ON LABOUR MARKET PARTICIPATION

The findings from the regression analysis (Table 13.2) show that for young adults in Estonia, being out of employment – being unemployed or being inactive – has to do with (among other things) having children and the availability and use of childcare. The association is, however, clearer for inactivity (Models 4, 5 and 6 in Table 13.2), which could be expected as "children's issues" still tend to be very much "women's issues" when it comes to an effect on labour market behaviour.

Regarding unemployment risk, according to our data there is no clear association between having young children and experiencing labour market exclusion. The risks are – in line with previous studies – rather associated with a lower education level, living in the countryside, and so on. In the same way, we cannot observe any significant association between childcare arrangements and labour market exclusion risk. There can be observed a negative association between informal care (when provided both by somebody who is not a member of the household or by a grandparent living in the household), which means that more weekly hours of childcare help tend to lower the unemployment risk, but statistically the association is not significant. Part of that could be due to a lack of statistical power in the data (small N).

The association between childcare arrangements and labour market participation for young adults is clearer and statistically significant when it comes to the status of inactivity. The "reason" for inactivity is often related to caring for children and affects more women than men (as can be observed in our data; see Models 4–6 in Table 13.2). Here, a significant association can be observed for both formal and informal care arrangements. Firstly, the negative association between formal care and probability to be in inactivity rather than in employment indicates that more hours in ECEC relates to a higher probability to be working than in inactivity. On top of that (when controlling for time in formal care), informal care also still tends to matter – the more childcare help received from somebody out of the household, the lower the probability to be in inactivity (meaning to be employed). A negative association can be observed also between parents' labour market inactivity and the hours spent on childcare by a grandparent living in the household. The association is, however, statistically not significant. These findings partly confirm our hypotheses that formal childcare arrangements relate to higher labour market participation (H1), and that the role of informal care is relevant for labour market participation even when formal care is (also) used (H2).

Table 13.1   Grandparent care provided inside a household, by household type

	Age of youngest child	Care activities + playing with children (minutes)[1]		Grandparent living in the hh, %
		On working days	On weekends	
Couples only	0–2 years	47	5	14
	3–6 years	72	22	15
	7–10 years	109	9	11
Couples + single parents	0–2 years	59	26	21
	3–6 years	111	35	20
	7–10 years	100	5	14

Notes: Sub-sample of families where there is at least one child under 10 years old (N=1,081); [1] only the main activity is shown
Source: Estonian Time-Use Survey 2009 (Statistics Estonia 2011), authors' calculations

Regarding the hypotheses H1.1 and H2.1 that claimed there were gender differences in the effect of childcare use on labour market participation, the interaction effects presented in Figure 13.2 (see also Table 13.A1 in the Appendix) suggest that for men and women care availability indeed tends to play a different role. The total number of hours of formal care received has either no or a modest positive effect on men's unemployment risk (Figure 13.2), whereas for women the association is the reverse – more hours of formal care are associated with lower probability of being in unemployment, which is in line with our hypothesis that externalizing childcare matters more for women's labour market participation than for men. For inactivity (Figure 13.2), we see that in particular the effect of informal care differs for men's and women's labour market participation rates (relative to being in inactivity). Having a relative or friend out of the household who can provide free childcare reduces women's inactivity in particular, and even more so when looking at the hours of childcare provided by a (grand)parent living in the household. The latter interaction is also statistically significant, which once more confirms our gender-difference hypothesis.

Table 13.2   The effect of childcare facilities on unemployment and inactivity risk

	Unemployment			Inactivity		
	Model 1	Model 2	Model 3	Model 4	Model 5	Model 6
Gender (Ref = male)						
Female	-0.06*	-0.06*	-0.06*	0.17***	0.17***	0.17***
Age	-0.06***	-0.06***	-0.06***	-0.16***	-0.16***	-0.16***
Ethnicity (Ref = Estonian)						
Non-Estonian	0.14***	0.14***	0.14***	0.05	0.06	0.06
Education (Ref = primary level)						
Secondary level	-0.15***	-0.15***	-0.15***	-0.14***	-0.14***	-0.14***
Tertiary level	-0.24***	-0.24***	-0.24***	-0.23***	-0.22***	-0.23***
Place of residence (Ref = rural area)						
Small town	-0.01	-0.01	-0.01	-0.06*	-0.05*	-0.05
Big town	0.00	0.00	0.00	0.00	-0.00	0.00
Capital	-0.08*	-0.09*	-0.09*	-0.10**	-0.10**	-0.10**
Partnership status (Ref = single)						
Partner	-0.13***	-0.13***	-0.13***	-0.18***	-0.18***	-0.18***
Separated/divorced	0.11	0.12	0.12	-0.17	-0.14	-0.15
Number of children under 10 years old in household	0.00	0.01	0.01	0.12***	0.13***	0.13***
Formal childcare (kindergarten), hrs/week	0.00	0.00	0.00	-0.08***	-0.07***	-0.07***
Informal childcare by somebody outside the hh		-0.02	-0.02		-0.03**	-0.03**
Informal childcare by grandparent living in the hh			-0.01			-0.02
N	1107	1107	1107	1479	1479	1479
R2	0.15	0.15	0.15	0.30	0.30	0.30

Notes: *** $p < 0.001$; ** $p < 0.01$; * $p < 0.05$. Formal childcare – total number of hours per week the child(ren) spend(s) in ECEC; Informal childcare by somebody outside the hh – total number of hours per week free childcare is received by household that has been provided by somebody outside of the household; Informal childcare by grandparent living in the hh – total number of hours a grandparent living in the household has reported to be active in taking care of the child(ren), playing with them, reading with them, and so on.
Source: Estonian Time-Use Survey 2009 (Statistics Estonia 2011), authors' calculations

QUALITATIVE FINDINGS: LIFE STORIES

Aveli (cohabiting) first started working when the Estonian economy was recovering from the Great Recession and her second child (aged 3) could attend formal childcare. She had several short-term jobs until her third child was born. The same pattern repeated after she returned to employment following parental leave with her third child. All her contracts have been with an undefined end, but she has left them on her own initiative, so until the time of her interview her longest working experience in one place was five months. She has never been unemployed longer than a few weeks. Her ease at finding jobs is related to her low expectations (she accepts any type of job) and to structural factors (a shortage of labour in low-skilled jobs, especially in the capital area where she was living).

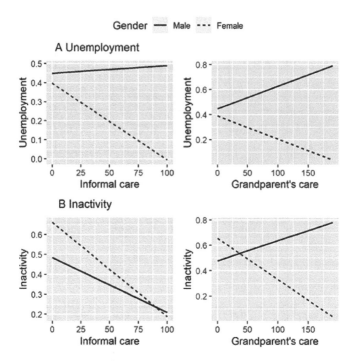

Note: Figures based on analysis presented in Table 13.A1
Source: Estonian Time-Use Survey 2009 (Statistics Estonia 2011), authors' calculations

Figure 13.2   *Predicted values of unemployment (13.2a) and inactivity (13.2b) for men and*
            women

During the time of the interview, she was working as an attendant at a gas station, doing night shifts. Her choice of jobs is clearly related to the need to combine work and family life.

> I started working nights because of my children, to spend the days with them. I have three little boys … My youngest is in kindergarten, but when he is ill, he has to stay home. That's why I ... started working in [the] night shift, so when needed I can be at home during the day.

Thus, available and affordable childcare is a precondition for her to be able to work. But even like this, she still needs additional flexibility and backup, as despite having a full-day care place available for her youngest son, the child often gets ill and cannot go to care. Although she has a right to stay home with a sick child (which includes a pay reduction for these days), she is trying not to use this option, but prefers to rely on the support of her family. Thus, in reality she can accept flexible work and night shifts due to the fact that her partner and grandparents are ready to support her with childcare. She lives with her partner, who is the father of her third child, and her children on the second floor of her grandparents' house. They live in separate households – Aveli's household pay for their electricity bills, but they do not pay rent. The current living arrangement seems to be suitable for both the grandparents and her family as she has affordable housing and help with the children, and the grandparents get help they need with harder household chores.

Mai (single) has very little official work experience and has been unemployed for most of her adult life. Before the birth of her first child she worked officially for a short time at a counter selling strawberries. When she became pregnant this job was not suitable for her anymore as it included the task of lifting heavy boxes. Since then she has worked occasionally and unofficially as a babysitter. Due to her acquired babysitting training, she could have also worked officially as a babysitter, but the potential clients were not interested in arranging it this way, in order to avoid paying taxes.

Currently she is on parental leave with her youngest son, but according to her, if she could find employment which would allow her to work from home she would like to be working. Her opportunities are limited, because she cannot accept "typical low skilled (service) jobs" which often include so-called "bad hours", which is work during nonstandard days or hours, as she has nobody to leave her children with.

> Back then I had only one child, now I have two, so it becomes even harder for me, because kindergartens are open to a certain time. And ... since I am raising my children alone, I have no-one I can rely on. My mom would help but she is also working long hours every day.

In other words, informal childcare support is missing, and this limits her choices at the labour market, in addition to her limitations related to low education and work experience. Also, Mai herself feels uncertain when she thinks about her future, since she experienced that it was hard to find a job when having one child, and now she has two.

Both Aveli and Mai demonstrate the will and readiness to work, but due to their limited education level and labour market experience, they are both faced with poor labour market perspectives and precariousness. Their participation in the labour market is made even more complicated by their family situation, where they both have young children and experience high care demands. Availability of low-cost public childcare alleviates the work–family reconciliation challenge considerably. However it seems to be insufficient to assure it – early education and care centres usually operate on weekdays and during standard working hours, which often do not coincide with the "bad hours" of low qualified and so-called bad jobs. Thus, both women experience additional need and demand for informal care arrangements and support in order to be able to participate in the labour market. In one case, the support is there, allowing the young mother to work, although her labour market position remains precarious in this situation. For the other case, the situation is much more complicated as she has no family or other close network support to carry out the care responsibilities. Both examples clearly outline how both formal and informal childcare are crucial for providing the opportunity window to be engaged in employment and help against the accumulation of disadvantage, especially for young adults in already vulnerable labour market situations.

SUMMARY

The current study explored the effect of childcare, both formal and informal, on the labour market participation chances for young adults. The results showed that having access to early care facilities reduces the chances of women in particular being in unemployment or in inactivity rather than being employed. The effect is clearer and stronger for inactivity, which suggests that part of long care leaves is related to limited childcare facilities, even in a country like Estonia where access to affordable and good-quality public care is considered rather high.

The chances of being out of employment reduce even more when received informal care (free care provided by some other family member, relative, friend, and so on, who does not form part of the same household) is considered. Thus, despite the availability of public care, informal care remains important. One explanation for this is the "care gap"; that is, the period where many women are already willing to return to the labour market but still do not have access to formal care (for a child somewhere between the age of 1.5 and 3), or the child is still getting used to the care facility. The informal care need is plausibly bigger for those working nonstandard schedules of hours, which often form part of low-qualification (service) jobs, which in turn increases the risk for accumulation of disadvantage for labour market participants who are already in more vulnerable and precarious situations. Although the data did not allow testing for the moderator effect of socioeconomic status, the qualitative interviews used for illustrating the care needs and possible coping mechanisms of young adults in disadvantaged labour market situations demonstrated the importance of care support, both formal and even more so informal, for being able to participate in the labour market.

The analysis has some limitations that should be considered. Firstly, the limitations in the data. Time-use data is cross-sectional data, which limits our possibilities for testing causality in the association, and we should just talk about associations. Also, the small N of the effective sample – that is, the young adults with young children – sets limits to the analysis and to the statistical power of the model. Secondly, it could be argued that the target group of the analysis, which is young adults in their early career track and having children, is somewhat selective, meaning in particular that young adults with poorer labour market perspectives and from lower-socioeconomic-status groups could be over-represented. Still, in Estonia no clear bias could be pointed out here, as most Estonians have children and having at least one child is not related to education level, social class, and so on. Thirdly, we have only limited information about grandparents, which means we are not able to control in the models for grandparents' age, gender, and so on, which may be relevant regarding the amount of care provided. Thus, it is assumed that the grandparent in the household is more of a "contributor" than a "receiver" of care.

ACKNOWLEDGEMENT

This analysis has received funding from the Estonian Research Council grant "My time, your time, our time. Household time allocation: choice or inevitability?" (PUT1182).

REFERENCES

Aassve, A., B. Arpino and A. Goisis (2012), "Grandparenting and mothers' labour force participation: a comparative analysis using the generations and gender survey", *Demographic Research*, 27, 53–84.

Akgunduz, Y.E., and J. Plantenga (2011), *Child Care Prices and Female Labour Market Participation: A Meta-Analysis*, Utrecht School of Economics, T.J. Koopmans Research Institute Discussion Papers Series, 11-08.

Angrist, J., and W. Evans (1998), "Children and their parents' labor supply: evidence from exogenous variation in family size", *American Economic Review*, 88(3), 450–477.

Attar-Schwartz, S., J.-P. Tan, A. Buchanan, E. Flouri and J. Griggs (2009), "Grand-parenting and adolescent adjustment in two-parent biological, lone-parent, and step-families", *Journal of Family Psychology*, 23, 67–75.

Bengtson, V. (2001), "Beyond the nuclear family: the increasing importance of multigenerational bonds", *Journal of Marriage and Family*, 63, 1–16.

Bertolini, S., M. Bolzoni, V. Moiso and R. Musumeci (2018), "The comparative qualitative research methodology of the EXCEPT project", EXCEPT Working Papers, WP No. 56, Tallinn University, Tallinn.

Blau, D.M., and P.K. Robins (1988), "Child care costs and family labor supply", *Review of Economics and Statistics*, 70(3), 374–381.

Compton, J., and R.A. Pollak (2014), "Family proximity, childcare, and women's labor force attachment", *Journal of Urban Economics*, 79, 72–90.

Del Boca, D., S. Pasqua and C. Pronzato (2009), "Motherhood and market work decisions in institutional context: a European perspective", *Oxford Economic Papers*, 61(Supplement 1), 147–171.

Del Boca, D., and D. Vuri (2007). "The mismatch between employment and child care in Italy: the impact of rationing", *Journal of Population Economics*, 20(4), 805–832.

Di Gessa, G., K. Glaser, D. Price, E. Ribe and A. Tinker (2016), "What drives national differences in intensive grandparental childcare in Europe?", *Journals of Gerontology Series B: Psychological Sciences and Social Sciences*, 71(1), 141–153.

Dimova, R., and F.-C. Wolff (2008), "Grandchild care transfers by ageing immigrants in France: intra-household allocation and labour market implications", *European Journal of Population*, 24(3), 315–340.

Esping-Andersen, G. (1990), *Three Worlds of Welfare Capitalism*. Princeton, NJ: Princeton University Press.

Eurofound (2015), *Promoting Uptake of Parental and Paternity Leave among Fathers in the European Union*. Luxembourg: Publications Office of the European Union.

European Commission/EAECEA/Eurydice (2019), *Key Data on Early Childhood Education and Care in Europe – 2019 Edition*, Eurydice Report. Luxembourg: Publications Office of the European Union.

Giarrusso, R., and M. Silverstein (1996), "Family complexity and grandparent role", *Generations*, 20(1), 17–23.

Han, W.-J., and J. Waldfogel (2001), "Child care costs and women's employment: a comparison of single and married mothers with pre-school-aged children", *Social Science Quarterly*, 82(3), 552–568.

Hank, K., and I. Buber (2009), "Grandparents caring for their grandchildren: findings from the 2004 Survey of Health, Ageing, and Retirement in Europe", *Journal of Family Issues*, 30(1), 53–73.

Herlofson, K., and G. Hagestad (2012). "Transformations in the role of grandparents across welfare states". In: Arber, S., and Timonen, T. (eds), *Contemporary Grandparenting: Changing Family Relationships in Global Contexts*. Bristol: Policy Press, pp. 27–49.

Iacovou, M., and A.J. Skew (2011). "Household composition across the new Europe: where do the new member states fit in?", *Demographic Research*, 25, 465–490.

Igel, C., and M. Szydlik (2011), "Grandchild care and welfare state arrangements in Europe", *Journal of European Social Policy*, 21(3), 210–224.

Inanc, I. (2015), "Unemployment and the timing of parenthood: implications of partnership status and partner's employment", *Demographic Research*, 32, 219–250.

Jappens, M., and J. Van Bavel (2012), "Regional family cultures and child care by grandparents in Europe", *Demographic Research*, 27(4), 85–120.

Kreyenfeld, M. (2010), "Uncertainties in female employment careers and the postponement of parenthood in Germany", *European Sociological Review*, 26(3), 351–366.

Kuhlthau, K., and K. Mason (1996), "Market child care versus care by relatives: choices made by employed and nonemployed mothers", *Journal of Family Issues*, 17(4), 561–578.

Larsen, T. (2004), "Work and care strategies of European families: similarities or national differences?", *Social Policy & Administration*, 38(6), 654–677.

Laughlin, L. (2013), *Who's Minding the Kids? Child Care Arrangements*. Washington, DC: U.S. Census Bureau.

Liefbroer, A.C., and M. Corijn (1999), "Who, what, where, and when? Specifying the impact of educational attainment and labour force participation on family formation", *European Journal of Population*, 15(1), 45–75.

Mills, M., P. Präg, F. Tsang, K. Begall, J. Derbyshire, L. Kohle and S. Hoorens (2013), "Use of childcare serevices in the EU member states and progress towards the Barcelona targets", Short Statistical Report No. 1, prepared for the European Commission Directorate-General for Justice.

Mínguez, A. (2005), "A comparative view of working women and the family in the welfare systems of southern Europe: the continuance of the male breadwinner", *Revista Española de Investigaciones Sociológicas*, 112, 131–164.

Morrissey, T.W. (2017), "Child care and parent labour force participation: a review of the research literature", *Review of Economics of the Household*, 15, 1–24.

Pilkauskas, N., and M. Martinson (2014). "Three-generation family households in early childhood: comparisons between the United States, the United Kingdom, and Australia", *Demographic Research*, 30(60), 1639–1652.

Raeymaeckers, P., C. Dewilde, L. Snoeckx, and D. Mortelmans (2008) "Childcare strategies of divorced mothers in Europe: a comparative analysis", *European Sociological Review*, 24(1), 115–131.

Ruiz, S.A., and M. Silverstein (2007), "Relationships with grandparents and the emotional well-being of late adolescent and young adult grandchildren", *Journal of Social Issues*, 63(4), 793–808.

Rutter, J., and B. Evans (2011), *Listening to Grandparents*. London: Daycare Trust.

Saraceno, C., and W. Keck (2010), "Can we identify intergenerational policy regimes in Europe?", *European Societies*, 12(5), 675–696.

Statistics Estonia (2011), *2009–2010 Time Use Survey: Methodology Report*. Tallinn: Statistics Estonia.

Statistics Estonia (2020), data accessed March 23 2020 at http://pub.stat.ee/px-web.2001/Database/Sotsiaalelu/15TOOTURG/15TOOTURG.asp.

Stier, H., N. Lewin-Epstein and M. Braun (2001), "Welfare regimes, family supportive policies, and women's employment along the life-course", *American Journal of Sociology*, 106(6), 1731–1760.

Sümer, S., J. Smithson, M. Guerreiro and L. Granlund (2008), "Becoming working mothers: reconciling work and family at three particular workplaces in Norway, the UK, and Portugal", *Community, Work & Family*, 11(4), 365–384.

Szydlik, M. (2012), "Generations: connections across the life course", *Advances in Life Course Research*, 17(3), 100–111.

Tan, J.-P., A. Buchanan, E. Flouri, S. Attar-Schwartz and J. Giggs (2010), "Filling the parenting gap? Grandparent involvement with UK adolescents", *Journal of Family Issues*, 2010(31), 992–1015.

Tekin, E. (2007), "Childcare subsidies, wages, and employment of single mothers", *Journal of Human Resources*, 42, 453–487.

Uunk, W., M. Kalmijn and R. Muffels (2005), "The impact of young children on women's labor supply: a reassessment of institutional effects in Europe", *Acta Sociologica*, 48(1), 41–62.

Van der Lippe, T., and J.J. Siegers (1994), "Division of household and paid labour between partners: effects of relative wage rates and social norms", *Kyklos*, 47(1), 109–136.

Wheelock, J., and K. Jones (2002), "'Grandparents are the next best thing': informal childcare for working parents in urban Britain", *Journal of Social Policy*, 31(3), 441–463.

APPENDIX

Table 13.A1   The effect of childcare arrangements and availability on labour market participation, interactions with gender

	Unemployment			Inactivity		
	Model 1	Model 2	Model 3	Model 4	Model 5	Model 6
Gender (Ref = male)						
Female	-0.06*	-0.06*	-0.06*	0.17***	0.17***	0.17***
Age	-0.06***	-0.06***	-0.06***	-0.16***	-0.16***	-0.16***
Ethnicity (Ref = Estonian)						
Non-Estonian	0.14***	0.14***	0.14***	0.05	0.06	0.06
Education (Ref = primary level)						
Secondary level	-0.15***	-0.14***	-0.14***	-0.14***	-0.14***	-0.14***
Tertiary level	-0.24***	-0.24***	-0.24***	-0.23***	-0.22***	-0.23***
Place of residence (Ref = rural area)						
Small town	-0.01	-0.01	-0.01	-0.06*	-0.05*	-0.05
Big town	0.01	-0.00	0.00	0.00	-0.00	-0.00
Capital	-0.08*	-0.08*	-0.08*	-0.10**	-0.10**	-0.10**
Partnership status (Ref = single)						
Partner	-0.13***	-0.13***	-0.13***	-0.18***	-0.18***	-0.18***
Separated/divorced	0.11	0.13	0.12	-0.17	-0.14	-0.15
Number of children under 10 years old in household	0.00	0.00	0.01	0.12***	0.13***	0.13***
Formal childcare (kindergarten), hrs/ week	-0.02	0.00	0.00	-0.09***	-0.07***	-0.07***
* Female	0.04			0.03		
Informal childcare by somebody outside the hh		0.00	-0.02		-0.02	-0.03*
* Female		-0.04			-0.01	
Informal childcare by grandparent living in the hh			0.02			0.02
* Female			-0.04			-0.05*
N	1107	1107	1107	1479	1479	1479
R2	0.15	0.16	0.16	0.30	0.30	0.31

Data: Estonian Time-Use Survey 2009 (Statistics Estonia 2011), authors' calculations

Notes: *** $p < 0.001$; ** $p < 0.01$; * $p < 0.05$. Formal childcare – total number of hours per week the child(ren) spend(s) in ECEC; Informal child care by somebody outside the hh – total number of hours per week free childcare received by household that has been provided by somebody outside of the household; Informal child care by grandparent living in the hh – total number of hours a grandparent living in the household has reported to be active in taking care of the child(ren), playing with them, reading with them, and so on.

14. Flexible work arrangements and diversity through a comparative and multilevel lens

Eleni Stavrou and Myrto Anastassiadou

INTRODUCTION

Relevant research on flexible work arrangements (FWAs) and diversity has been conducted in a multitude of ways. Namely, such research has been approached from a qualitative as well as a quantitative perspective at different levels of analysis. However, it has predominantly been approached from a micro, individual-employee perspective (Fischer et al., 2005; Hitt et al., 2007; Parasuraman and Greenhaus, 2002). Nevertheless, more recently research on the topic has expanded to the meso and even macro level of analysis (Ilies et al., 2007; Kopelman et al., 2006; McCarthy et al., 2013; O'Neill et al., 2009). Furthermore, studies have combined levels of analysis (micro, meso and macro) across different organizational and employee outcomes (distal and proximal outcomes), involving, for instance, employee turnover, absenteeism and organizational performance (see Ierodiakonou and Stavrou, 2015; 2017; Stavrou, 2005; Stavrou et al., 2010; Stavrou and Ierodiakonou, 2013b, 2016, 2018; Stavrou and Kilaniotis, 2010; Stavrou and Solea, 2018).

In addition to the above, diversity is of particular significance in regard to the study of FWAs due to the suitability of specific FWAs to different diverse groups and their preferences. There is strong evidence of particularities in relation to diversity and the implications of FWAs. Specifically, certain demographic groups seem to have different experiences of FWAs, and the latter have unique implications for those groups (Stavrou and Ierodiakonou, 2013b), possibly, among other reasons, due to societal norms that support or restrict the utilization of FWAs (Michielsens et al., 2014). For instance, FWAs do not specifically help working mothers who wish to advance their careers (Brown, 2010). Further, the barriers to balancing work and life are more salient for women who belong to religious ethnic minority groups that have strong ties to their communities (Kamenou, 2008). Also, specific FWAs – such as part-time work and in general arrangements with reduced hours – are largely taken up by working mothers while men tend to refrain from taking up such arrangements (Gregory and Milner, 2009). Finally, certain minorities, such as LGBT employees, seem to experience flexibility differently from their heterosexual counterparts (Languilaire and Carey, 2017; Sawyer et al., 2015; Stavrou and Ierodiakonou, 2018).

In turn, we propose a multilevel comparative framework (see Figure 14.1) that should guide the study of FWAs. The framework concentrates on three levels: the individual, the meso/organizational in the centre, and the macro/supra-organizational. When examining FWAs at the organizational level, researchers should focus on whether these are employee- or employer-friendly arrangements and, methodologically, whether they should be examined one by one or grouped together. At the individual level, we suggest that demographic diversity, such as gender, sexual orientation and caring responsibilities, should be considered and incorporated in the study of FWAs. As discussed above, individual characteristics such as demographic ones affect the adoption as well as the outcomes of FWAs. Further, at the macro level, this framework highlights the importance of incorporating supra-organizational predictors such as industry, national and regional policies along with cultural dimensions. Along with individual-level characteristics, supra-organizational predictors influence the adoption of FWAs. Lastly, as mentioned above, FWAs have effects on individuals and also on organizations (that is, proximal and distal outcomes), involving, for instance, employee turnover, productivity, organizational financial performance, absenteeism, the proportion of women in the organization, organizational effectiveness and job satisfaction. Thus, proximal and distal outcomes should be incorporated in the examination of FWAs. By utilizing this framework, FWAs will be approached in a holistic way through the consideration of multiple levels in a comparative way.

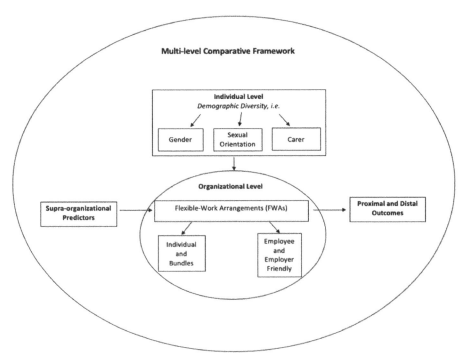

Figure 14.1   *Proposed multilevel framework for the study of flexible work arrangements*

In the following sections, we discuss empirical examples from one of the authors' work on FWAs. Specifically, we explore the study of FWAs in clusters versus individual measures, the distal and proximal outcomes of FWAs, the importance of including diversity and specifically women and LGBT people in the study of work–life balance (WLB), and lastly, the significance of examining supra-organizational factors in this line of research. By presenting these empirical approaches, we also propose that FWAs and these factors should be explored through quantitative as well as qualitative methodologies and multilevel analyses, highlighting their usefulness along with some of their limitations. Finally, we make two suggestions for future research. First, we propose that invisible minorities should be considered as a beneficial and value-adding tool in the study of FWAs. In this respect, we suggest that such research should become more inclusive by focusing on employees who are caregivers. Second, we recommend the use of non-parametric methods as tools, which can provide further understandings on WLB issues.

STUDYING FLEXIBLE WORK ARRANGEMENTS

In this section, we present how Stavrou and her colleagues empirically approached FWAs and the methodological implications that emerged from these empirical investigations. Firstly, we discuss the clustering of FWAs while describing when and how FWAs have been explored in bundles and/or one by one and how they have been categorized as employee- and employer-friendly in Stavrou's research. Secondly, we propose incorporating distal and proximal outcomes in the study of FWAs by demonstrating Stavrou et al.'s empirical examples that dealt with these. Thirdly, we examine the reasoning and particular implications of incorporating supra-organizational predictors in the examination of FWAs and organizational-level effects and the need to adopt multilevel methodological approaches when studying the aforementioned aspects. Lastly, we discuss the significance of taking into consideration various demographic groups, namely women and LGBT people, when examining FWAs, and suggest a specific methodological approach when doing so, namely combining qualitative and quantitative methodologies.

Bundles versus Individual FWAs

It has been stated that FWAs are neither homogeneous nor universal. From Stavrou's work, it has emerged that FWAs should not be studied as one unified set of practices but either grouped in bundles (Kassinis and Stavrou, 2013; Stavrou, 2005; Stavrou and Ierodiakonou, 2011; Stavrou and Kilaniotis, 2010) or individually (Ierodiakonou and Stavrou, 2015; Stavrou et al., 2010; Stavrou et al., 2015a). Primarily, the most common FWAs are weekend work, shift work, annual hour contracts, overtime, part-time work, job sharing, flexitime, temporary employment, fixed-term contracts, home-based work, teleworking and subcontracting (Stavrou, 2005).

In one of the first attempts to group FWAs into bundles, a typology of employee- and employer-driven ones was proposed (Stavrou, 2005). By using principal components analysis, four bundles of specific FWA practices were suggested. These are: employee-friendly bundles such as Non-Standard Work Patterns (Bundle 1) that include annual hour contracts, part-time work, job sharing, flexitime and fixed-term contracts, and Work Away from the Office (B2) that include home-based work and teleworking; and employer-friendly bundles, namely Non-Standard Work Hours (B3) that include weekend work, shift work and overtime, and Work Outsourced (B4) that include temporary employment and subcontracting.

Following the above typology in an analysis of the motives of unemployed Cypriot women in finding work through FWAs, it was found that women are positively related mainly with intentions to adopt employee-driven FWAs. Further, women who consider childcare support and employer requirements limiting were more interested in telework, while the latter were also more interested in temporary employment (Stavrou and Ierodiakonou, 2011). Furthermore, a discrepancy was found between the FWAs women prefer compared to what managers consider as the most suitable for their organization, implying that there is indeed a distinction between employer- and employee-friendly FWAs (Stavrou and Ierodiakonou, 2013a).

Apart from the aforementioned typology, FWAs have also been grouped into bundles of non-standard work arrangements (NSWAs), namely: (a) flexibility patterns and (b) part-time options. The relationship between these bundles and public expenditure on national family-leave policies, employment legislation and culture differs based on the context and the type of the NSWA, highlighting the premise that NSWAs should not be studied all-together (Kassinis and Stavrou, 2013).

Further to these, the study of FWAs in bundles has proved beneficial when examining specific organizational outcomes, such as the association between HR practices (that is, FWAs) and competitiveness. A number of authors have argued that when innovative HR practices are combined in different forms, the effects on organizational performance are much greater than when they are applied individually (see Ichniowski et al., 1997; Perry-Smith and Blum, 2000). The empirical work of Stavrou and her colleagues has shown that different bundles of FWAs are related to particular organizational and employee outcomes, such as changes to organizational performance, employee turnover and absenteeism. To illustrate, following the aforementioned typology, only the bundle of Non-Standard Work Patterns (B1) was found to be inversely related to employee turnover among private sector organizations, while the bundle of Work Outsourced (B4) was positively associated with employee turnover, although only in the public sector (Stavrou, 2005). In a similar fashion, significant differences were found in an exploration of the association between employee turnover and three bundles of FWAs, namely unsocial hours (overtime, shift work and weekend work), part-time arrangements (part-time and job sharing) and schedule flexibility (telework, working from home and flexitime) in two societal clusters (Anglo and Nordic). Specifically, schedule flexibility was found to be significantly negatively associated with employee turnover. Differently, a significant positive association was observed between part-time arrangements and employee turnover. Furthermore, differences have been found between the two societal clusters, where the increase of schedule flexibility was significantly associated with a decrease in employee turnover among the Nordic cultures while the increase of part-time arrangements and unsocial hours was significantly related to an increase in employee turnover in the Anglo cluster (Stavrou and Kilaniotis, 2010).

While bundling FWAs is often recommended, Stavrou's empirical work shows that certain practices should be considered as distinct. One such practice is part-time work, which may be treated as a hybrid one. It has both employer- and employee-driven characteristics and regular hours as well as FWAs (Ierodiakonou and Stavrou, 2015); thus it should be studied individually. In this respect, part-time work has been studied as an isolated practice in an effort to observe any possible associations between part-time work and organizational, institutional and national contexts and factors, such as productivity, employment legislation, gender empowerment and women's employment patterns (Ierodiakonou and Stavrou, 2015; Stavrou et al., 2015a). Lastly, apart from part-time work, other FWAs such as shift work and job sharing have been examined individually with organizational predictors and within various national contexts (Stavrou et al., 2010).

The aforementioned review of studies shows that the exploration of FWAs either in bundles or individually is not straightforward. While the employer- and employee-friendly demarcation seems consistent, the significant relationships seem to vary depending on a number of factors, such as outcomes or context. That is why it becomes important that in this chapter we explore some of these more salient factors as well.

Distal/Proximal Outcomes of FWAs

In turn, next we will discuss FWAs in relation to their various effects on the organization as well as on employees. Such can be considered as distal and proximal outcomes and involve, for example, employee turnover, productivity, organizational financial performance, competitiveness, absenteeism, the proportion of women in the organization, organizational effectiveness and job satisfaction.

The use of FWAs is characterized by contextuality, as organizational as well as employee outcomes depend on, among other factors, the sector of the organization and country-specific characteristics (Stavrou et al., 2010). For instance, non-standard work practices were found to be associated with reduced turnover only in the private sector. To illustrate the significance of country-specific dimensions, non-standard work hours were associated with increased performance but only among Swedish organizations. Moreover, reduced absenteeism and improved performance were associated with working away from the office; and non-standard work hours along with work being outsourced had a positive association with turnover, although only in the public sector (Stavrou, 2005). Further to the country-specific predictors, national work–family balance policies partially affect the relationship between FWAs and firm performance across different countries (Stavrou and Ierodiakonou, 2013b). Apart from country-level distinctions, countries have also been grouped and studied as societal clusters. To illustrate this, as mentioned above in the examination of the relationship between FWAs and turnover in two different societal clusters, namely the Anglo and the Nordic, it was shown that based on the specific bundle of FWAs and the societal cluster, the effect of FWAs on turnover differed. Specifically, in the Anglo cluster turnover increased when unsocial hours and part-time arrangements increased. Differently, turnover decreased in the Nordic cluster when schedule flexibility increased (Stavrou and Kilaniotis, 2010).

Apart from the aforementioned dimensions, the broader institutional environment should also be considered as an important contingency that affects organizational decisions and outcomes in relation to FWAs. To illustrate, the industrial relations system, social expenditure and working-time legislation at national level were found to be important contingencies in the association between use of flexitime and turnover (Ierodiakonou and Stavrou, 2017). Lastly, productivity was found to be associated with part-time work while it was moderated by employment legislation in a study of the complexity of the relationships among part-time work, institutional context and productivity used as a distal organizational outcome (Ierodiakonou and Stavrou, 2015).

Given the above discussion of existing studies on distal and proximal outcomes of FWAs, it becomes clear that extant literature on this relationship is in its infancy and needs further enrichment. While including a variety of contextual factors, researchers should engage in a deeper exploration of the possible positive and negative proximal and distal effects of FWAs, either individually or in bundles. For example, Kotey and Sharma (2019), acknowledging the mixed results in existing research, enumerate the positive effects of FWAs that range from improved job satisfaction, work commitment, absenteeism and productivity to better organizational performance and reduced employee turnover. At the same time, they explain that FWAs may also lead to instability, increased stress, and a lack of cohesion and trust in the workplace, with adverse performance consequences for the organization (Kotey and Sharma, 2019).

Finally, as Stavrou and Ierodiakonou (2018) have proposed, WLB in general and FWAs in particular should take context into account and be approached both quantitatively and qualitatively and at different levels of analysis. Context could be placed at multiple levels of analysis: individual level, such as diversity of employees in terms of gender and sexual orientation, as discussed in this chapter; organizational level, such as type of organization or industry; or supra-organizational level, such as national or supra-national context. We discuss each level below, proposing the combination of these various levels of analysis in order to explore FWAs and diversity from a comparative and multilevel lens. Originally conceptualized as cross-national but later expanded into different forms of comparisons, such a lens offers many relevant insights into organization processes and systems in context (Lazarova et al., 2008). It challenges the universalistic approach that supports only one best way of functioning (Brewster, 2007).

Context and FWAs

WLB in general and FWAs in particular should be studied from the lens of demographic diversity that characterizes workplaces. Various demographic groups, based on their varying personal needs and preferences, might require different types of support mechanisms in relation to WLB (Stavrou and Ierodiakonou, 2013b). In the following section we give special consideration to gender and sexual orientation as an illustration. Further, we argue for the use of methodological pluralism in studying the connection between WLB and diversity.

Gender

Fundamentally, gender employment patterns are not universal. Thus, they should be studied comparatively as these patterns belong to distinct organizational, cultural and labour market environments (Stavrou et al., 2015b). Further, gender-based work and family role expectations differ among countries due to variations based on, among other factors, employment systems and cultural values and norms, including constructions of femininity and masculinity and gender roles within societies. These are important parameters to take into consideration when studying women's employment patterns. For instance, gender egalitarianism should be studied comparatively based on the country-level index of gender empowerment measure (GEM). Gender empowerment is considered an important institutional factor that serves as an antecedent to the organizational decision of supporting part-time work and employing more women (Ierodiakonou and Stavrou, 2015; Stavrou et al., 2015a). Although widely used given a lack of consensus in terms of the best measure of gender empowerment in general, most of the criticism lies on the fact that GEM does not consider gender equality from various angles, it utilizes absolute levels of income and it entails a complex process of measuring gender gaps (Stavrou et al., 2015a). Thus, GEM should be used cautiously, while other similar measures may be utilized instead.

When WLB practices are being studied based on a gender dimension, it is also important to take into account the preferences of women employees along with managers because a discrepancy might exist between them that affects the suitability of certain FWAs. For instance, as mentioned above, in Cyprus a discrepancy was observed between the practices that unemployed women prefer to those that managers consider as a good fit for their organizations, highlighting also the contextuality of FWA suitability (Stavrou and Ierodiakonou, 2013a).

Methodologically, integrating qualitative and quantitative methodologies in studying gender employment patterns and WLB is beneficial, as unemployed women are an under-researched population (Stavrou and Ierodiakonou, 2011, 2013a). In general, as Parasuraman and Greenhaus (2002) said, most research on gender variations on work–family experiences is narrowly framed, and the aforementioned methodological choices can enrich the results of an empirical work for a population that is usually understudied. Thus, despite the fact that epistemological as well as ontological perspectives of qualitative and quantitative methodologies have been debated extensively in relation to mixed-methods research, mainly because the complexity of integrating qualitative and quantitative results coherently is considered one of the biggest challenges that scholars in the mixed-methods literature have noted so far, we argue that addressing the complications of such an approach would benefit the study of WLB and women (Bryman, 2007; Greene et al., 1989; Johnson and Onwuegbuzie, 2004; Johnson et al., 2007; Kelle, 2006; Lieber and Weisner, 2010; Molina-Azorín, 2011; Sale et al., 2002; Tashakkori and Teddlie, 2010). Although the aforementioned challenge has been identified as a complication of mixed methods, it has been remarked that mixed methods is not necessarily a practice of testing qualitative results against quantitative ones. Rather, results should be integrated at the analytical stage instead of just being reported as separate qualitative and quantitative ones. In this respect, several barriers that researchers face in combining mixed-methods results have been identified. These limitations include the existence of different audiences and their expectations for each methodology; the methodological preferences of the researchers; the structure of the project, as one methodology might mark its character; the issue of timeliness, as one kind of result might be produced faster than the other; a lack of skills or specialization of the researcher in both methodologies; the nature of the data; and the bringing together of ontological perspectives (that is, objectivism and constructivism, publication problems) (Bryman, 2007).

Apart from the challenge of integrating results, scholars have also indicated the problematic nature of the sequencing of research questions and methodology in the research process. The method chosen should be informed by the research question and the research puzzle, and not by the methodological choices and preferences of the researchers as the latter is considered to be a bad research practice (Greene et al., 1989; Johnson and Onwuegbuzie, 2004; Kelle, 2006). In a similar manner, Johnson et al. (2007) have also marked the importance of considering beforehand what philosophical position to choose when employing mixed methods, although they suggest the 'pragmatism of the middle' (p.125) as the most suitable stance when employing mixed methods. Furthermore, quality assessment, conceptualization, design and the language of mixed methods have been identified as potential challenges for researchers conducting mixed-methods research (Tashakkori and Teddlie, 2010). In addition to the aforementioned challenges, Johnson et al. (2007) highlight the significance of the credibility, trustworthiness and validity of mixed methodology and they suggest that researchers should seek for 'multiple validities legitimation' (p.128).

Additionally, a mixed-methods approach could benefit researchers in helping them identify, for example, the multiple reasons of unemployed women in attempting to get employed through FWAs (Stavrou and Ierodiakonou, 2011). Indeed, according to a number of authors, epistemological as well as methodological pluralism can provide a more inclusive, comprehensive and credible view of more complicated, inter-disciplinary and multidimensional issues (Johnson and Onwuegbuzie, 2004; Kelle, 2006; Molina-Azorín, 2011; Tashakkori and Teddlie, 2010). In doing so, researchers should follow a methodological eclecticism, which is the freedom that researchers hold in combining the finest methodological tools while attempting to better answer research questions (Tashakkori and Teddlie, 2010) and thus can advance the strengths of both qualitative and quantitative methods while compensating for each other's weaknesses as methods should be viewed as part of a continuum rather than distinct and dichotomous (Johnson and Onwuegbuzie, 2004; Kelle, 2006; Molina-Azorín, 2011; Lieber and Weisner, 2010). For instance, through mixed methods, theory could be synchronously developed and verified, as meaning and quantity are fused in the same project (Molina-Azorín, 2011; Morse, 2010). More specifically, problems that characterize qualitative methods – such as case selection, transferability and purposive sampling – and limitations of quantitative methods, like theory building and measurement, could be eliminated by combining both methods and promoting their strengths. In this respect, quantitative research could lead the selection of cases in qualitative projects with small sample sizes and then corroborate results and transfer them. Further, qualitative methods could advance quantitative results by broadening the understanding of unobserved heterogeneity in unexplained variables and also providing a more exhaustive explanation of statistical findings. Apart from that, qualitative research could enhance the validity of quantitative measurement, operations and instruments (Kelle, 2006).

Sexual orientation

Another important dimension to be considered in terms of needs and preferences regarding WLB is the sexual orientation of employees (Özbilgin et al., 2011; Stavrou and Solea, 2018). However, the LGBT group is often characterized as an 'invisible minority' as it has characteristics that are not visible to others but yet are substantial and should be considered (Ragins, 2008). This is the reason why LGBT employees have been largely excluded from literature and research on diversity (Stavrou and Ierodiakonou, 2018; Stavrou and Solea, 2018). It is a population globally understudied; thus its research should initially focus on being descriptive (Stavrou and Solea, 2018). Due to the lack of relevant empirical work in this field, we suggest that both quantitative and qualitative methodologies be employed. In fact, the validity of results could be strengthened through triangulation as data and findings could be mutually validated (Kelle, 2006), although triangulating might not be the only goal of mixed methods, as it could also serve the purpose of complementarity, development, initiation and expansion (Molina-Azorín, 2011; see also Greene et al., 1989).

When examining WLB practices among LGBT employees, a comparative approach should be adopted as well. For example, perceptions of LGBT employees have been compared along with those of their heterosexual counterparts in regard to perceived supervisory support on life beyond work (LBW), job satisfaction and life-to-work-conflict (LWC). What emerges is the presence of identity-based conflict among LGBT employees in terms of the life-to-work sphere that does not exist among heterosexual ones (Stavrou and Solea, 2018).

Also, when WLB is examined among LGBT people, specific constructs (scales or measures) should be created that measure the unique work–life experiences of LGBT employees rather than use conventional ones that apply to all employees (Stavrou and Solea, 2018). Moreover, when WLB is studied while acknowledging the sexual orientation dimension, LGBT people should be approached as significant organizational stakeholders who can directly or indirectly advance organizational performance (Stavrou and Ierodiakonou, 2018). Because of the lack of extensive research on the aforementioned field along with the complexity of studying an 'invisible minority', we suggest that methodological pluralism can enrich the understanding of this population in regard to WLB.

Along similar lines to gender employment, we argue that the complexity of WLB in regard to LGBT people could be better understood through triangulation methodological approaches which better explain multilevel phenomena compared to monomethod attempts (Hitt et al., 2007). Additionally, as exemplified in the research examples noted in this chapter (see Stavrou and Ierodiakonou, 2011, 2013a), Tashakkori and Teddlie (2010) suggest that mixed methods highlight the humanistic conceptualization of the research process further, compared to each method independently. Taking into consideration the challenges and limitations mentioned above, methodological pluralism should be adopted with caution. Despite the proposed incommensurability of qualitative and quantitative results (Sale at al., 2002) and the lack of paradigms to guide mixed-methods research (Bryman, 2007; Greene et al., 1989), efforts have been made more recently to propose guidance on how to conduct such research. For instance, the comprehensive handbook by Tashakkori and Teddlie (2010) notes specific strategies and proposes an extensive framework for the advancement of integrating data for analysis and interpretation and for assessing the quality of a mixed-methods project (Lieber and Weisner, 2010; O'Cathain, 2010). Further, a typology of sampling techniques in mixed methods has been introduced to guide researchers (Teddlie and Yu, 2007).

Thus, we suggest, in accordance with Tashakkori and Teddlie (2010), that despite the limitations and challenges of mixed-methods research, as long as it is conducted with rigour and parsimony and researchers act as methodological connoisseurs, mixed-methods research can provide great insights and new opportunities for investigating the social world. Scholars have marked the benefits of such methodology from various perspectives. To illustrate, mixed methods give researchers the opportunity to utilize the benefits of each methodology and address more complex and multidimensional research puzzles. Further, the weaknesses of each methodology, such as transferability of results for qualitative methods, could be eliminated because of the use of quantitative methods as well.

Organizational and Supra-Organizational Predictors of FWAs

Studies on WLB in general and FWAs in particular should include organizational and supra-organizational predictors as they can affect the organizational-level relationships either directly or indirectly. The study of WLB is characterized by 'polycontexuality' that should be given special attention by including various organizational, supra-organizational, national and even supra-national predictors (Ierodiakonou and Stavrou, 2017). Such factors may include industry, national or regional (that is, European Union) policies and cultural dimensions. It is also possible to identify country-level predictors, suggesting that homogeneity and universality do not exist geographically, thus stressing the importance of adopting a multilevel framework (Ierodiakonou and Stavrou, 2017). This could be done through multilevel modelling (MLM) through various methods, the most common of which are hierarchical linear modelling (HLM) and structural equation models, allowing researchers to examine complex associations at various levels of analysis.

Firm systems along with societal configurations are important antecedents to the use of NSWAs. In a study of two different cultural clusters, namely the Anglo and Nordic from the Global Leadership and Organizational Behavior Effectiveness (GLOBE) research programme, a horizontal fit was supported, which involves the organizational internal fit system and market fit system in relation to FWAs, and a vertical fit, which involves the societal configurational systems (that is, Nordic and Anglo), the institutional environment and cultural values relevant to FWAs (Stavrou et al., 2015b). In line with the above study, the significance of both organizational- and national-level contingencies in women's employment patterns was highlighted as such patterns are situated within unique cultural and labour market contexts. When trying to understand organizational choices, such as supporting part-time work and its correlation with women's employment, the cultural and institutional context should be taken into account (Stavrou et al., 2015a).

Therefore, we provide further empirical examples from the work of Stavrou and colleagues to demonstrate that national policy, legal context and cultural aspects should all be studied along with organizational context in exploring the use of NSWAs in organizations. To illustrate, in a comparative study of 1893 companies operating in 15 countries, it emerged that family-leave policies, employment legislation and culture all have an effect on the use of NSWAs in organizations while the specific association varies based on context and the specific NSWA at hand (Kassinis and Stavrou, 2013). Further to the above, Stavrou et al. (2010) have studied a number of FWAs in terms of employee turnover and absenteeism while taking into consideration different national contexts and organizational predictors through a cross-country lens. Their results have highlighted the contextuality in the use of FWAs, which based on their analysis depends on both sector- and country-specific characteristics.

In an attempt to construct a work–family balance framework through a multilevel examination of organizational- and national-level factors in 21 countries in the use of firm mechanisms to support work–family balance, it was suggested that both organizational- and national-level predictors should be taken into consideration. In fact, the models formed in this study revealed that predictions were enhanced once organizational- and national-level factors were examined together (Stavrou and Ierodiakonou, 2013b).

Along similar lines, the universal applicability of FWAs among organizations has been challenged, as significant differences emerged between two societal clusters, the Anglo and the Nordic, in terms of the relationship between FWAs and turnover. In turn, the contextuality of FWAs and the importance of studying supra-organizational predictors was emphasized (Stavrou and Kilaniotis, 2010). In regard to national-level contingencies on part-time work and organizational effectiveness, it was shown that employment legislation acts as a moderator in the relationship between part-time work and organizational performance (Ierodiakonou and Stavrou, 2015).

Methodologically, one limitation that has been remarked in Stavrou et al.'s work was the use of the highest-ranking HR officers in each organization as key informants, highlighting the importance of incorporating different groups and levels of employees in examining the use of FWAs among organizations (Stavrou and Kilaniotis, 2010). In this respect, despite the fact that countries have been studied extensively in clusters, quite often it is country-level variations that matter. Country has been considered as a significant moderator and country-specific characteristics have been revealed in extant empirical work (Stavrou, 2005; Stavrou et al., 2010; Stavrou and Ierodiakonou, 2011; 2013a; Stavrou and Solea, 2018). For instance, Stavrou's (2005) empirical investigation on the use of FWAs and organizational competitiveness has revealed that the bundle of non-standard work hours was associated with increased performance only amidst Swedish organizations, pointing out that FWAs cannot be studied as a group of homogeneous practices. Although there is strong evidence supporting the existence and usefulness of cultural clusters (Gupta et al., 2002), their use should be adopted with caution, because meaningful within-culture and within-country variations may exist as well. For example, specific countries tend to be more similar in terms of cultural values, such as the ones that belong to the Anglo cluster, compared to, for example, African clusters, in which the countries within do not have as many similarities (Minkov and Hofstede, 2012).

Additionally, when a multilevel perspective is adopted, there is a possibility of spurious associations at the organizational as well as the national level. Hence, depending on the study, a number of confounders, as cited in extant studies (Ierodiakonou and Stavrou, 2015; 2017; Kassinis and Stavrou, 2013; Stavrou, 2005; Stavrou et al., 2010; Stavrou et al., 2015b; Stavrou and Ierodiakonou, 2013a; 2013b) should be considered when studying FWAs at various levels. At the organizational level, these may include proportion of specific employee groups (that is, women or LGBT people) in the firm, staff category level (that is, the percentage of the workforce that are managers, professional or technical staff), strategic role of human resource management (HRM), organizational size, industry, public versus private sector, workforce age composition, use of trade unions and local vs multi-national organization. At the supra-organizational level these may include gender empowerment/egalitarianism, labour force composition (that is, female participation in the labour force), structure of the economy, cultural variables (that is, performance orientation), and relevant national or supra-national policies (that is, leaves).

A multilevel methodological approach such as mixed-model analysis (HLM) is useful because organizations within a country may function similarly compared to those in other countries, allowing for differences in industry types as well (Kassinis and Stavrou, 2013; Stavrou and Ierodiakonou, 2016). Further, a multilevel statistical methodology provides researchers with the ability to observe associations that even occur over and above national-level factors, such as institutional and cultural context (Stavrou and Ierodiakonou, 2016, 2018). In multilevel analyses, as in HLM, organizational-level variables, for instance, are nested within national regulatory contexts (Ierodiakonou and Stavrou, 2015, 2017), and thus such analysis allows the study of independent variables that occur at multiple levels. Multilevel models are constructed in a way that enable the analysis of variables from different levels concurrently and thus allow researchers to synchronously test hypotheses at various layers of analysis. Also, they control for spurious associations at one level while testing hypotheses at the other. Additionally, context and lower-level effects could be modelled. Another benefit of MLM is that unbalanced data with different numbers of observations per group could be used (Hox et al., 2017; Peterson et al., 2012). In this respect, according to Peterson et al. (2012), MLM has proved beneficial in international business research when studying nation-states and within-nation regions.

Nevertheless, the adoption of a multilevel framework in relation to FWAs usually requires large samples and diverse data commonly associated with the use of secondary data. Although archival data can provide researchers with the ability to make cross-country and across-level comparisons, they also impose certain limitations. In fact, when using archival data, researchers have no control over measures and very limited flexibility at the design stage. For instance, the lack of control of secondary data has resulted in the omission of certain constructs that are generally considered as significant in examining job satisfaction of LGBT employees, such as openness and perceived discrimination based on sexual orientation. Additionally, the use of generic measures of LBW and LWC that are not specific to LGBT people due to the lack of specific variables in the data could be problematic as such constructs do not take into account the uniqueness of the experiences of LGBT employees (Stavrou and Solea, 2018).

Despite the usefulness of multilevel models, they should be utilized by researchers with caution. The greatest criticism of MLM lies in the specifications for sample size and observations per group that are required in the model (Hitt et al., 2007; Maas and Hox, 2005; Peterson et al., 2012; Snijders, 2005). In fact, the statistical power and accurate estimation of the findings depends on the total sample size of each level of analysis. In general, due to the fact that the maximum likelihood method is asymptotic but still common in MLM, large sample sizes are required. Yet the sample size of the highest level is considered to be the most significant one but still the most problematic because it is usually smaller than the lowest-level sample size. Specifically, the sample-size criteria that are considered to be the most deterministic are the number of predictors on each level, number of level-one units, intraclass correlation and whether fixed- or random-effects models are being explored (Maas and Hox, 2005; Peterson et al., 2012; Snijders, 2005). Hox et al. (2017) mark the dependence of observations at the lowest level as a significant challenge of hierarchical data, and they instead suggest the adjustment to clustered data in order to avoid inaccurate significance tests.

Another challenge of using MLM has been noted by Rousseau (1985), namely the 'fallacy of the wrong level' (p.5), which highlights the lack of establishment of specific-level construct validity. Also, Osborne (2000) has highlighted that when dealing with cross-level data, the unit of analysis should be chosen carefully. Further, the level of theory, measurement and analysis should be approached cautiously in MLM (Hitt et al., 2007; Peterson et al., 2012). Specifically, the level of analysis should be aligned with the level of theory and measurement of the constructs. Furthermore, researchers need to explicitly explain the process of how the collected data at one level of analysis are associated with higher-level constructs. The latter could be done through two aggregation principles, namely composition and compilation (Hitt et al., 2007).

Apart from the above, data quality and accessibility problems have been signified as limitations of MLM research. Due to the nature of MLM and its requirement for large samples, the choice of using available large datasets by the researchers is almost unavoidable. Nevertheless, such a decision entails measurement issues. As such, single-item scales are very common in these datasets, which hinder the assessment of translation equivalence and response bias. Also, simple words and dichotomous variables are frequent in them, which also limits the measurement of constructs. In relation to measurement when conducting mixed-methods research, researchers should examine if the variables that are described by group means are comparable to their individual-level measurement schemes (Peterson et al., 2012).

Yet we argue that organizational life could be better understood by multilevel studies, as national and institutional contexts could explain variations that research on only micro or meso levels cannot address. Further, most research on diversity so far has focused on the micro level in order to capture biases, discriminations, perceptions and roles in everyday interactions, yet the larger cultural context and social composition of organizations and work groups are important aspects in need of inclusion as well. Still, research that focuses only on the micro level neglects social dynamics that could only be explored at higher levels of analysis. In turn, the general idea of a multilevel approach is that the outcomes that ought to be explored are the results of effects at various levels of analysis (Hitt et al., 2007).

RECOMMENDATIONS FOR FUTURE RESEARCH

We have proposed that FWAs and diversity should be approached through methodological pluralism and a multilevel lens. Apart from the two aforementioned approaches, we also propose that future researchers should shift their focus from the more conventional/mostly discussed themes in relation to WLB, such as the exploration of WLB based on mothers of young children (Emslie and Hunt, 2009), to focus also on groups that are understudied yet significant. Specifically, as showcased earlier in relation to LGBT people, we propose that minorities whose characteristics are not noticeable (that is, invisible minorities) should be included in the study of WLB and diversity. Along similar lines, we argue that the definition of carers should be revised so as to include employees whose caring responsibilities are not that visible. Lastly, we recommend the use of non-parametric methods in WLB research.

Invisible Minorities: LGBT People and Informal Carers

In relation to diversity and minorities, WLB studies have primarily focused on employees with visible characteristics such as women and racial or ethnic minorities (Clair et al., 2005). Yet other minorities, often called 'invisible' (Ragins, 2008), whose characteristics are not visible, have been under-researched. These invisible minorities are, among others, LGBT people and employees with mental health problems and chronic illnesses. Because of the aforementioned invisibility, such minorities are often ignored, even though their needs and preferences seem to be unique in reference to WLB (Özbilgin et al., 2011; Stavrou and Solea, 2018). Further, although not stigmatized yet possibly invisible as the most conventional definitions and analyses of caregiving consistently exclude them, middle-aged caregivers should be examined as well in relation to WLB, as evidence suggests that their caregiving roles have been in conflict with their work ones.

As defined by Rocco et al. (2009, p.8), a minority belongs in 'a group that does not have dominant status, lacks social status, and is subordinated to the dominant group' (see also Blumenfeld, 1992; Leonard, 2004). Most empirical work on invisible minorities relies on Goffman's (1963) theory of stigma (Clair et al., 2005; McLaughlin et al., 2004; Ragins et al., 2007; Rocco et al., 2009). Identities comprise visible and invisible features that are deterministic in the categorization of individuals (Rocco et al., 2009). To illustrate, examples of visible stigmatized identities include racial, age, ethnic and sex minorities as well as people with physical disfigurements. Differently, other minorities who have invisible stigmas are LGBT people and people with invisible conditions such as epilepsy, mental illnesses and HIV (Clair et al., 2005; Ragins et al., 2007). Apart from stigma theory, minorities have been situated within the power and privilege discourse that affects organizational and stakeholder decisions (Rocco et al., 2009).

In general, invisible stigmatized minorities have unique interaction experiences in the workplace compared to those with visible characteristics; thus, special research attention should be paid to them. To illustrate, sexual minorities might face difficulties in maintaining balance between clashing relationship obligations (Clair et al., 2005). Also, because of heterosexist social norms, sexual minorities may have diminished opportunities in the workplace such as the denial of benefits to their partners and also inequitable policies and leave, medical and retirement benefits towards them. Apart from these, they may also be reluctant to bring their same-sex partners or friends to organizational social events (Githens and Aragon, 2009;

Hornsby and Munn, 2009; Rocco et al., 2009). Further, the fears that LGBT employees face in disclosing their sexual identity have been found to be associated with lower job satisfaction and organizational and career commitment as well as greater employee turnover (Ragins et al., 2007). In addition to sexual minorities, people with disabilities are also a stigmatized workforce population. In an exploration of employees' acceptance of co-workers with disabilities, it was suggested that stigma was significantly associated with employees' attitudes towards having a co-worker with disability, perceived fairness of accommodation of employees with disabilities and discriminatory employment judgements (McLaughlin et al., 2004).

Empirical work in reference to invisible minorities and WLB has been limited. Hornsby and Munn (2009) have examined the work–life benefits and policies of ten Midwestern public universities in relation to same-sex couples. Their conclusions suggested that institutions that belonged to the Council of Independent Colleges have made progress regarding the expansion of benefits to domestic partners and children of LG employees while complexities and inequalities still exist regarding benefits of LG couples compared to their heterosexual married counterparts. In another study of LGB employees and WLB, Stavrou and Solea (2018) have examined the perceptions of LGB and heterosexual employees of supervisory support of LBW, job satisfaction and LWC. Their results have suggested that LGB employees face an identity-based conflict related to their work–life realm compared to heterosexual employees. The lack of extensive empirical work on the experiences of WLB of LGBT employees calls for further extensive exploration of the topic.

In addition to the study of WLB and invisible stigmatized minorities, we propose that the examination of carers and WLB should become more inclusive and incorporate proportions of the workforce (that is, those responsible for elder care) that have not been extensively studied so far and yet whose caregiving work is significant (Parasuraman and Greenhaus, 2002). Specifically, we suggest that while possibly invisible even though not-stigmatized, middle-aged informal caregivers should be examined further as evidence suggests that their caregiving roles have been in conflict with their work ones. Carers are more likely to be employed in part-time than full-time work and are also more likely to face financial difficulties, poorer physical and psychological health, higher levels of stress and higher use of health care services compared to non-carers (Lee and Porteous, 2002). In another study, Casado-Marín et al. (2010) have concluded that significant costs are associated with the employment of intensive carers who provide support for more than 28 hours per week and/or reside with the dependent person(s). Further, Emslie and Hunt (2009) have examined the experiences of WLB of middle-aged men and women. Their results have pointed out that middle-aged employees indeed have caring duties, namely of their grandchildren and elderly parents. Also, the aforementioned study has highlighted the importance of considering gender and socioeconomic position, apart from age, when examining the WLB of middle-aged employees.

Further to that, as noted by various scholars (Casado-Marín et al., 2010; Dahlberg et al., 2007; Lee and Porteous, 2002; Sánchez-Ayéndez, 1998), a significant asymmetry is reported in regard to caregivers' gender. Specifically, the greatest proportion of middle-aged caregivers are women. Thus, we suggest that the intersectionality of the caregivers' identities should be taken into consideration when examined. Specifically, we propose that both age and gender dimensions should be studied in relation to WLB and caregiving.

Non-Parametric Methods

Lastly, we propose that non-parametric methods be used more extensively in HR research in general and WLB in particular as so far in WLB research, and specifically in studies that examined FWAs and diversity, parametric tools instead have been utilized extensively. According to Siegel (1956, p.31), 'a nonparametric statistical test is a test whose model does not specify conditions about the parameters from which the sample was drawn'. Although non-parametric statistics are rarely used among researchers in this field, they can prove useful. One of their advantages is that only few assumptions need to be made regarding the population from which the sample is drawn. Specifically, non-parametric methods do not endorse the assumption that the population under study is normally distributed, and compared to parametric methods, the shape of the population is not determining the accuracy of the probability statement. Further, they are in part not sensitive to outliers and sample size, and compared to parametric methods, they require only the rank of observations rather than their magnitude. Also, they are often more easily applied and understood compared to other statistical procedures.

By using non-parametric statistical procedures, researchers could also benefit from the fact that they allow the analysis of data from samples of different populations (Hollander et al., 2013; Leech and Onwuegbuzie, 2002; Siegel, 1956). Further, according to Hollander et al. (2013, p.1), non-parametric methods allow researchers to 'obtain exact p-values for tests, exact coverage probabilities for confidence intervals, exact experiment-wise error rates for multiple comparison procedures, and exact coverage probabilities for confidence bands without relying on assumptions that the underlying populations are normal'.

When the population distribution is not normal, non-parametric procedures are more efficient tools than parametric ones. Yet when the population is normal, they are slightly less efficient (Hollander et al., 2013). Four criteria need to be considered in order to choose the appropriate statistics: power of the test, the applicability of the statistical model, power-efficiency and the level of measurement. To illustrate, based on the level of measurement, data at the nominal or ordinal level should be analysed through non-parametric statistics. In turn, interval and ratio data may be analysed by both parametric and non-parametric statistical tests. Specifically, certain non-parametric tests can treat nominal data effectively, which are very common in social and behavioural research, while parametric methods fall short in doing so (Siegel, 1956).

Although scarce in HRM research, below we note some studies that have used non-parametric methods. In a study by Stavrou et al. (2010), a non-parametric tool, namely Kohonen's Self-Organizing Maps (SOMs), has been utilized, which allowed the reduction of the amount of data while finding potential clusters of FWAs as SOMs are a powerful tool for exploratory analysis. In another study, Nikandrou et al. (2005) have employed a non-parametric procedure, cluster analysis, in an attempt to explore the changes and trends in different European countries about specific HRM issues; cluster analysis has allowed them to classify countries into homogeneous groups.

Further, in an examination of subsidiaries of US companies in Europe and their calculative HRM practices in relation to national institutional contexts, Mokken's (1971) non-parametric latent trait model for unidimensional scaling was used in order to develop a scale for calculative HRM practices (Gooderham et al., 1998). Moreover, in another study, the Mann–Whitney U test was utilized to explore the differences among a disclosure and nondisclosure group of Japanese companies in relation to productivity. Specifically, this tool allowed the observation of a statistically significant variation in the distribution of productivity between these two types of companies (Sotome and Takahashi, 2014). As discussed above, various non-parametric tools are available with different useful applications that can benefit HRM research. Yet their use is rare, and more empirical work should utilize them.

CONCLUSION

Although the study of WLB in general and FWAs in particular has been approached through various epistemological and methodological perspectives, much of the empirical work in this field has focused on the individual-employee level (Hitt et al., 2007). As noted by Parasuraman and Greenhaus (2002) in a review of the extant research, most studies adopted a micro-lens perspective. Although some more recent studies (see Ilies et al., 2007; Kopelman et al., 2006; McCarthy et al., 2013; O'Neill et al., 2009) have shifted their focus to the meso and even macro perspective, future empirical investigations should examine all levels in a comparative manner in order to gain a more holistic, non-universalistic and in-depth understanding of the issue.

In turn, in this chapter we highlight that social systems are characterized by multilevel dynamics and that most data are indeed nested, clustered or hierarchical by default. For example, individuals almost always belong somewhere, such as in teams or organizations, and organizations belong in countries and country clusters, forming a logical hierarchy characterizing such nesting (Fischer et al., 2005; Osborne, 2000). Thus, we suggest the adoption of a multilevel framework as it can bridge the micro and macro separation characterizing empirical research so far, by linking individuals, teams, organizations, industries and even countries and better addressing their nested complexity (Klein et al., 1999; Klein and Kozlowski, 2000). A multilevel lens offers many relevant insights into organization processes and systems in context (Lazarova et al., 2008). It challenges the universalistic approach that supports only one best way of functioning (Brewster, 2007).

Therefore, we have proposed a holistic framework that can be used to examine FWAs at multiple levels. Specifically, through those comparative lenses we have highlighted the contextuality of FWAs and we have demonstrated how the extant empirical work had approached their complexities aiming at contributing to the debate on how they should be studied. Further, we have discussed what should be considered when FWAs are being studied. Namely, following a comparative and multilevel approach, we have argued for the study of the associations between WLB practices and distal and proximal outcomes at organizational level along with the study of supra-organizational macro-level predictors and individual micro-level ones. The aforementioned approach calls for the utilization of multilevel methodological frameworks by researchers, although with caution for their limitations. Lastly, the importance of paying attention to understudied demographic groups, and specifically women and LGBT people, and their unique needs and experiences was highlighted along with future research directions and particularly the usefulness of methodological pluralism. Taking it a step further, we have urged future empirical work in WLB and FWAs to pay special attention to other minorities whose characteristics are invisible (as 'invisible minorities'), thus including in the exploration diverse groups of carers whose caregiving roles are demanding and also clashing with their work ones.

REFERENCES

Blumenfeld, W. J. (ed.) (1992), *Homophobia: How We All Pay the Price*. Boston: Beacon Press.

Brewster, C. (2007), 'Comparative HRM: European views and perspectives', *International Journal of Human Resource Management*, **18** (5), 769–787.

Brown, L. M. (2010), 'The relationship between motherhood and professional advancement', *Employee Relations*, **32** (5), 470–494.

Bryman, A. (2007), 'Barriers to integrating quantitative and qualitative research', *Journal of Mixed Methods Research*, **1** (1), 8–22.

Casado-Marín, D., P. García-Gómez and Á. López-Nicolás (2010), 'Informal care and labour force participation among middle-aged women in Spain', *SERIEs*, **2** (1), 1-29.

Clair, J. A., J. E. Beatty and T. L. Maclean (2005), 'Out of sight but not out of mind: managing invisible social identities in the workplace', *Academy of Management Review*, **30** (1), 78–95.

Dahlberg, L., S. Demack and C. Bambra (2007), 'Age and gender of informal carers: a population-based study in the UK', *Health and Social Care in the Community*, **15** (5), 439–445.

Emslie, C., and K. Hunt (2009), '"Live to Work" or "Work to Live"? A qualitative study of gender and work-life balance among men and women in mid-life', *Gender, Work & Organization*, **16** (1), 151–172.

Fischer, R., M. C. Ferreira, E. M. L. Assmar, P. Redford and C. Harb (2005), 'Organizational behaviour across cultures: theoretical and methodological issues for developing multi-level frameworks involving culture', *International Journal of Cross Cultural Management*, **5** (1), 27–48.

Githens, R. P., and S. R. Aragon (2009), 'LGBT employee groups: goals and organizational structures', *Advances in Developing Human Resources*, **11** (1), 121–135.

Goffman, E. (1963), *Stigma: Notes on the Management of a Spoiled Identity*. New York: Simon & Schuster.

Gooderham, P., O. Nordhaug and K. Ringdal (1998), 'When in Rome, do they do as the Romans? HRM practices of US subsidiaries in Europe', *Management and International Review*, **11** (3), 47–64.

Greene, J. C., V. J. Caracelli and W. F. Graham (1989), 'Toward a conceptual framework for mixed-method evaluation designs', *Educational Evaluation and Policy Analysis*, **11** (3), 255–274.

Gregory, A., and S. Milner (2009), 'Work–life balance: a matter of choice?', *Gender, Work & Organization*, **16** (1), 1–13.

Gupta, V., P. J. Hanges and P. Dorfman (2002), 'Cultural clusters: methodology and findings', *Journal of World Business*, **37** (1), 11–15.

Hitt, M. A., P. W. Beamish, S. E. Jackson and J. E. Mathieu (2007), 'Building theoretical and empirical bridges across levels: multilevel research in management', *Academy of Management Journal*, **50** (6), 1385–1399.

Hollander, M., D. A. Wolfe and E. Chicken (2013), *Nonparametric Statistical Methods*. Hoboken: John Wiley and Sons.

Hornsby, E. E., and S. L. Munn (2009), 'University work–life benefits and same-sex couples', *Advances in Developing Human Resources*, **11** (1), 67–81.

Hox, J. J., M. Moerbeek and R. V. Schoot (2017), *Multilevel Analysis: Techniques and Applications*. New York: Routledge.

Ichniowski, C., K. Shaw and G. Prennushi (1997), 'The effects of human resource practices on manufacturing performance: a study of steel finishing lines', *American Economic Review*, **87** (3), 291–313.

Ierodiakonou, C., and E. Stavrou (2015), 'Part time work, productivity and institutional policies', *Journal of Organizational Effectiveness: People and Performance*, **2** (2), 176–200.

Ierodiakonou, C., and E. Stavrou (2017), 'Flexitime and employee turnover: the polycontextuality of regulation as cross-national institutional contingency', *International Journal of Human Resource Management*, **28** (21), 3003–3026.

Ilies, R., K. M. Schwind and D. Heller (2007), 'Employee well-being: a multilevel model linking work and nonwork domains', *European Journal of Work and Organizational Psychology*, **16** (3), 326–341.

Johnson, R. B., and A. J. Onwuegbuzie (2004), 'Mixed methods research: a research paradigm whose time has come', *Educational Researcher*, **33** (7), 14–26.

Johnson, R. B., A. J. Onwuegbuzie and L. A. Turner (2007), 'Toward a definition of mixed methods research', *Journal of Mixed Methods Research*, **1** (2), 112–133.

Kamenou, N. (2008), 'Reconsidering work–life balance debates: challenging limited understandings of the "life" component in the context of ethnic minority women's experiences', *British Journal of Management*, **19** (s1), S99–S109.

Kassinis, G. I., and E. T. Stavrou (2013), 'Non-standard work arrangements and national context', *European Management Journal*, **31** (5), 464–477.

Kelle, U. (2006), 'Combining qualitative and quantitative methods in research practice: purposes and advantages', *Qualitative Research in Psychology*, **3** (4), 293–311.

Klein, K. J., and S. W. Kozlowski (2000), 'From micro to meso: critical steps in conceptualizing and conducting multilevel research', *Organizational Research Methods*, **3** (3), 211–236.

Klein, K. J., H. Tosi and A. A. Cannella Jr. (1999), 'Multilevel theory building: benefits, barriers, and new developments', *Academy of Management Review*, **24** (2), 248–253.

Kopelman, R., D. Prottas, C. Thompson and E. Jahn (2006), 'A multilevel examination of work-life practices: is more always better?', *Journal of Managerial Issues*, **18** (2), 232–253.

Kotey, B. A., and B. Sharma (2019), 'Pathways from flexible work arrangements to financial performance', *Personnel Review*, **48** (3), 731–774.

Languilaire, J. C. E., and N. Carey (2017), 'LGBT voices in work-life: a call for research and a research community', *Community, Work & Family*, **20** (1), 99–111.

Lazarova, M., M. Morley and S. Tyson (2008), 'International comparative studies in HRM and performance – the Cranet data', *International Journal of Human Resource Management*, **19** (11), 1995–2003.

Lee, C., and J. Porteous (2002), 'Experiences of family caregiving among middle-aged Australian women', *Feminism & Psychology*, **12** (1), 79–96.

Leech, N. L., and A. J. Onwuegbuzie (2002), 'A call for greater use of nonparametric statistics', *Research in the Schools*, **26** (2), xiii–xxvi.

Leonard, A. S. (2004), 'Sexual minority rights in the workplace', *Brandeis LJ*, **43**, 145–164.

Lieber, E., and T. S. Weisner (2010), 'Meeting the practical challenges of mixed methods research', in A. Tashakkori and C. Teddlie (eds), *SAGE Handbook of Mixed Methods in Social & Behavioral Research*. Thousand Oaks: SAGE, pp.559–580.

Maas, C. J., and J. J. Hox (2005), 'Sufficient sample sizes for multilevel modeling', *Methodology*, **1** (3), 86–92.

McCarthy, A., J. N. Cleveland, S. Hunter, C. Darcy and G. Grady (2013), 'Employee work–life balance outcomes in Ireland: a multilevel investigation of supervisory support and perceived organizational support', *International Journal of Human Resource Management*, **24** (6), 1257–1276.

McLaughlin, M. E., M. P. Bell and D. Y. Stringer (2004), 'Stigma and acceptance of persons with disabilities', *Group & Organization Management*, **29** (3), 302–333.

Michielsens, E., C. Bingham and L. Clarke (2014), 'Managing diversity through flexible work arrangements: management perspectives', *Employee Relations*, **36** (1), 49–69.

Minkov, M., and G. Hofstede (2012), 'Is national culture a meaningful concept?', *Cross-Cultural Research*, **46** (2), 133–159.

Mokken, R. J. (1971), *A Theory and Procedure of Scale Analysis*. The Hague: Mouton.

Molina-Azorín, J. F. (2011), 'The use and added value of mixed methods in management research', *Journal of Mixed Methods Research*, **5** (1), 7–24.

Morse, J. M. (2010), 'Procedures and practice of mixed method design: maintaining control, rigor, and complexity', in A. Tashakkori and C. Teddlie (eds), *SAGE Handbook of Mixed Methods in Social & Behavioral Research*. Thousand Oaks: SAGE, pp.339–352.

Nikandrou, I., E. Apospori and N. Papalexandris (2005), 'Changes in HRM in Europe', *Journal of European Industrial Training*, **29** (7), 541–560.

O'Cathain, A. (2010), 'Assessing the quality of mixed methods research: toward a comprehensive framework', in A. Tashakkori and C. Teddlie (eds), *SAGE Handbook of Mixed Methods in Social & Behavioral Research*. Thousand Oaks: SAGE, pp.531–555.

O'Neill, J. W., M. M. Harrison, J. Cleveland, D. Almeida, R. Stawski and A. C. Crouter (2009), 'Work–family climate, organizational commitment, and turnover: multilevel contagion effects of leaders', *Journal of Vocational Behavior*, **74** (1), 18–29.

Osborne, J. W. (2000), 'Advantages of hierarchical linear modeling', *Practical Assessment, Research & Evaluation*, **7** (1). https://doi.org/10.7275/pmgn-zx89.

Özbilgin, M. F., T. A. Beauregard, A. Tatli and M. P. Bell (2011), 'Work-life, diversity and intersectionality: a critical review and research agenda', *International Journal of Management Reviews*, **13** (2), 177–198.

Parasuraman, S., and J. H. Greenhaus (2002), 'Toward reducing some critical gaps in work–family research', *Human Resource Management Review*, **12** (3), 299–312.

Perry-Smith, J. E., and T. C. Blum (2000), 'Work-family human resource bundles and perceived organizational performance', *Academy of Management Journal*, **43** (6), 1107–1117.

Peterson, M. F., J. Arregle and X. Martin (2012), 'Multilevel models in international business research', *Journal of International Business Studies*, **43** (5), 451–457.

Ragins, B. R. (2008), 'Disclosure disconnects: antecedents and consequences of disclosing invisible stigmas across life domains', *Academy of Management Review*, **33** (1), 194–215.

Ragins, B. R., R. Singh and J. M. Cornwell (2007), 'Making the invisible visible: fear and disclosure of sexual orientation at work', *Journal of Applied Psychology*, **92** (4), 1103–1118.

Rocco, T. S., H. Landorf and A. Delgado (2009), 'Framing the issue/framing the question: a proposed framework for organizational perspectives on sexual minorities', *Advances in Developing Human Resources*, **11** (1), 7–23.

Rousseau, D. M. (1985), 'Issues of level in organizational research: multi-level and cross-level perspectives', *Research in Organizational Behavior*, **7** (1), 1–37.

Sale, J. E., L. H. Lohfeld and K. Brazil (2002), 'Revisiting the quantitative-qualitative debate: implications for mixed-methods research', *Quality and Quantity*, **36** (1), 43–53.

Sánchez-Ayéndez, M. (1998), 'Middle-aged Puerto Rican women as primary caregivers to the elderly', *Journal of Gerontological Social Work*, **30** (1–2), 75–97.

Sawyer, K. B., C. N. Thoroughgood and J. N. Cleveland (2015), 'Challenging heteronormative and gendered assumptions in work–family research: an examination of LGB identity-based work–family conflict', in M. J. Mills (ed.), *Gender and the Work-Family Experience: An Intersection of Two Domains*. Cham: Springer, pp.77–98.

Siegel, S. (1956), *Nonparametric Statistics for the Behavioral Sciences*. New York: McGraw-Hill.

Snijders, T. A. (2005), 'Power and sample size in multilevel linear models', in B. Everitt and D. Howell (eds), *Encyclopedia of Statistics in Behavioral Science*. Chichester: Wiley, pp.1570–1573.

Sotome, R., and M. Takahashi (2014), 'Does the Japanese employment system harm productivity performance?', *Asia-Pacific Journal of Business Administration*, **6** (3), 225–246.

Stavrou, E., and C. Ierodiakonou (2011), 'Flexible work arrangements and intentions of unemployed women in Cyprus: a planned behavior model', *British Journal of Management*, **22** (1), 150–172.

Stavrou, E., and C. Ierodiakonou (2013a), 'Flexibility for women returners in Cyprus: a competency-based approach', *Gender in Management: An International Journal*, **28** (1), 6–27.

Stavrou, E., and C. Ierodiakonou (2013b), '"Rationalizing" organizational support for work-family balance', *Academy of Management Proceedings*, **2013** (1), 13625.

Stavrou, E., and C. Ierodiakonou (2016), 'Entitlement to work-life balance support: employee/manager perceptual discrepancies and their effect on outcomes', *Human Resource Management*, **55** (5), 845–869.

Stavrou, E., and C. Ierodiakonou (2018), 'Expanding the work-life balance discourse to LGBT employees: proposed research framework and organizational responses', *Human Resource Management*, **57** (6), 1355–1370.

Stavrou, E., and C. Kilaniotis (2010), 'Flexible work and turnover: an empirical investigation across cultures', *British Journal of Management*, **21** (2), 541–554.

Stavrou, E., and E. Solea (2018), 'In the eye of the beholder: employee sexual orientation, work-life interface and job satisfaction', *Academy of Management Proceedings*, **2018** (1), 12652.

Stavrou, E. T. (2005) 'Flexible work bundles and organizational competitiveness: a cross-national study of the European work context', *Journal of Organizational Behavior*, **26** (8), 923–947.

Stavrou, E. T., W. J. Casper and C. Ierodiakonou (2015a), 'Support for part-time work as a channel to female employment: the moderating effects of national gender empowerment and labour market conditions', *International Journal of Human Resource Management*, **26** (6), 688–706.

Stavrou, E. T., E. Parry and D. Anderson (2015b), 'Nonstandard work arrangements and configurations of firm and societal systems', *International Journal of Human Resource Management*, **26** (19), 2412–2433.

Stavrou, E. T., S. Spiliotis and C. Charalambous (2010), 'Flexible working arrangements in context: an empirical investigation through self-organizing maps', *European Journal of Operational Research*, **202** (3), 893–902.

Tashakkori, A., and C. Teddlie (2010), 'Putting the human back in "human research methodology": the researcher in mixed methods research', *Journal of Mixed Methods Research*, **4** (4), 271–277.

Teddlie, C., and F. Yu (2007), 'Mixed methods sampling: a typology with examples', *Journal of Mixed Methods Research*, **1** (1), 77–100.

PART VI

DIGITAL AND VISUAL METHODS

15. The gendered labour of work–life balance: using a new method to understand an enduring dilemma

Julia Cook and Dan Woodman

INTRODUCTION

Research on 'work–life balance' is ubiquitous in social sciences, related to anxiety among the public, policy makers and researchers about the impacts of changing work patterns on the social fabric (Pocock et al. 2012). This scholarship has shifted from focusing on balance to addressing 'interference' and 'integration' in the context of a blurring boundary between work and non-work in the context of new digital technology, demands to work from home and changing employment conditions, including growing insecurity (Fein et al. 2017). These changes have, however, also been accompanied by a move away from standardised work patterns. Work–life interference research has given this less consideration. These recent developments have a distinctly gendered dimension as, in Australia along with many other Western economies, the rise of non-standard work patterns has coincided with women overtaking men in educational attainment and greatly increasing their labour force participation. Notably, while Hochschild and Machung (2003), along with several other feminist scholars, have observed the disproportionate burden that women face while balancing workforce participation with domestic and caring work – producing insights about the ways in which women are often disproportionately responsible for coordinating the plans and schedules of their household – there is a need to further consider how such dynamics may manifest in the context of non-standard work patterns becoming more common (Woodman and Cook 2019).

In this chapter we discuss a recent study addressing how the rise of dual-income households, coupled with the rise of non-standard hours in paid employment, has resulted in an increasing need to schedule and manage lives, as well as an accompanying sense of temporal precarity. This study focuses specifically on heterosexual couples in their late 20s. This age cohort forms the focus of this study primarily because they sit just beyond or on the edge of the so-called 'rush hour of life' – generally located between ages 30–50 – in which the pressures of employment commitments and childcare demands collide (Craig and Powell 2011, Hewitt et al. 2012). Despite sitting outside the 'rush hour of life', Australian young adults aged 20–29 report almost as high levels of work–life 'interference' as adults aged 30–44, and higher levels than employees older than this (Pocock et al. 2012), suggesting factors at work in creating these pressures in addition to the demands of dual-income families juggling care and workforce participation. In previous work we have addressed how relationships change work and the challenges that individuals face when seeking to synchronise their own schedules with those of their significant others (Woodman and Cook 2019), and we have considered the use of digital methods to study participants' lived experiences of non-standard work (Cook and Woodman 2020). In this chapter we draw on and extend this previous research, focusing particularly on its implications for work–life interference.

This chapter uses a study conducted in an effort to address this empirical context as a means of discussing how to gain insight into the factors creating this sense of interference using an innovative method for accessing everyday life experiences, using a combination of digital and interview-based methods of data collection. We highlight the insights this method gives for understanding work–life pressures and persistent gender inequalities in the context of contemporary conditions. The chapter thus begins with a discussion of the empirical context in which the study is situated. The study, and the methods that it employs, are then discussed and findings are presented in order to demonstrate the nature of the data that it elicits. We then move on to evaluate the specific method that we have employed, focusing on its utility for research addressing the significance of gender in the context of work–life interference. Finally, we consider future directions for both the method we have employed and the empirical area that we have addressed.

THE NEW WORLD OF WORK FOR AUSTRALIAN YOUNG ADULTS

As we have already mentioned, the world of work is shifting for Australian young adults in ways that have strong implications for their experiences of work–life balance. With over half of casual employees in Australia young adults (ABS 2011), this group are clearly among those most likely to have 'non-standard' employment conditions. Additionally, the already disproportionate representation of young people among those with non-standard conditions and variable working patterns has increased over the past 15 years (Venn et al. 2016). Both casualisation and the rise of non-standard employment relations are important shifts in the way that people are working. However, a relatively overlooked aspect of changing employment patterns that may impact on people's challenges in integrating paid-work and non-work aspects of their lives is the rise of non-standard hours of work – including weekend, evening and variable hours. Differing levels of control over temporal schedules in an increasingly 24/7 economy is argued by some to be emerging as a primary dimension of inequality (Presser 2005, Goodin et al. 2008, Woodman 2012, Clawson and Gerstel 2014).

Although young adults are transitioning towards permanent contracts at a slower pace than in the past, most workforce participants are on a permanent or renewable contract by their late 20s (ABS 2011). The shift towards standard hours of work is, however, even slower. Australian research shows that working non-standard hours is very common for people in their 20s, with likely impacts on work–life interference (Woodman 2013). Yet work–life interference research has overlooked this age group. The problem of underemployment for the young would suggest too much 'leisure' time is the primary issue, depending on the demands of any active labour market programs or job search activities. The 20s are seen as a time when leisure with a friendship group or significant others is developmentally essential for 'emerging adults', but is also assumed to be easily available (Arnett 2014). Time-use data from Australia, however, suggests that young people have less free time than other age brackets, excluding those in the 'rush hour' of life (ABS 2006).

Long hours of work are only a partial driver of work–life intrusions (Presser 2005, Pocock et al. 2012, Wajcman 2014). The growth of a relatively '24/7' economy over recent decades, characterised by patterns of engagement that are outside weekday daytime hours becoming more common alongside more variability in hours of work across weeks, is arguably one of the most significant changes marking the lives of today's young people as different from those of previous generations (Woodman 2013). While non-standard hours have a long history, they have returned as the regulations of work that shaped the post-war period of the mid 20th century have been wound back (Venn 2004). In Australia, some aspects of 'non-standard' work stopped growing during the 2000s, at least for prime-aged workers, but so-called 'flexible' patterns of work hours have continued to increase (Venn et al. 2016), as has the blurring of work and non-work time (Gregg 2011). As Woodman (2012) has shown previously for young people aged 18–20, relatively individualised work patterns create new challenges for synchronising rhythms and schedules so that time can be regularly spent with significant others, another factor behind feelings of a lack of control and insecurity that tend to be understood as caused by other changes, like casual employment contracts expanding. The significance of this new context for young adults has been largely overlooked in research addressing work–life balance. The surprising levels of work–life interference claimed by those in their 20s suggests a puzzle through which some of the ways insecure work might be affecting lives beyond work can be unravelled, if we have the right methodological tools to address the puzzle. We begin to address this here, focusing specifically on the work–life experiences of people in their late 20s in intimate relationships (all heterosexual), most without children and largely middle-class, using an innovative digital method to gain insights into participants' everyday lives. Specifically, we draw on the claim that synchronising lives with others demands new efforts in an increasingly 24/7 economy to consider how this work is managed collectively in couples.

METHOD

The study that we address in this chapter was conducted in 2017 with a cohort of young adults drawn from the Life Patterns research program, a larger mixed-methods longitudinal panel study of young adulthood in Australia. The participants in this part of the study were from the Year 12 school-leaving cohort of 2006 and were recruited into the study in 2005 or 2006. They were aged 28–29 in 2017, when the data for this study were collected. The study involved the collection of digital data from a mobile phone app followed by in-depth interviews. While selecting participants to recruit from the broader Life Patterns sample, we focused on those who had experience of non-standard hours. We also asked these participants to invite a significant other who they tried to spend time with in a given week to take part in the study, with the aim of understanding not only their own lives, but how they intersected with the lives of those around them. A total of 53 people took part in the study. This included 37 existing Life Patterns participants and 16 significant others, meaning that just under half of the participants recruited someone into the study. The significant others included 11 partners of Life Patterns participants (all in heterosexual couples), three housemates, one friend/workmate and one sibling.

We focus on 11 heterosexual couples in this chapter, as they provide the clearest illustration of the gendered nature of work–life balance. While the 11 existing Life Patterns participants were all tertiary-educated and working in professional positions, their partners (four married and seven de facto) exhibited a greater degree of diversity. Seven were tertiary-educated, three had undertaken apprenticeships or vocational education, and one had not undertaken any post-secondary education. Seven worked in professional positions, while two worked in managerial roles and two in trades. All but one of the male participants worked at least full-time, with two also working a second job. Four of the couples were parents and seven of the female participants worked full-time, while the other four (all parents) worked part-time, with one on maternity leave at the time of the interview. Nine of the couples lived in a state capital city (Melbourne, Sydney or Canberra), while one lived in a large regional city, and one in a small regional town. However, the couples' location did not appear to have an overt impact on their management and experience of time.

The form that the digital mode of data collection could take was heavily determined by the Life Patterns participants' use of digital technologies. In the 2013 survey, the participants were asked to comment on what they used social media for, and how important it was in their life, via an open-response question. Although a range of responses were received, we found that a significant proportion of the participants used social media as a tool for keeping in touch with those who were important to them, and preferred to use private messaging over more visible functions (echoing the findings of previous studies; see boyd 2008). Data from the same survey also showed that most of the participants engaged with social media frequently, with 40 per cent checking it many times a day, 27 per cent a few times a day, and 18 per cent once or twice a day, leaving only 15 per cent using some form of social media less than once daily.

Although these data were collected four years prior to the design of the present study, they nevertheless provided an indication of the nature of the participants' engagement with social media, which has likely increased since 2013 as smartphones have become increasingly ubiquitous and a central tool for managing everyday life. The data suggested that while observation of participants' existing social media profiles was unlikely to provide a sufficiently detailed sense of their everyday lives, most of them were engaging with digital platforms regularly, meaning that doing so was probably part of their everyday routines. Based on these insights we determined that it was likely that a large proportion of the participants would be willing and able to engage with a digital space multiple times each day, but that it would be necessary to elicit a form of digital engagement from them rather than observing their existing modes of engagement.

Significantly, while we were originally inspired by the successes of digital ethnographic methods, these insights prompted us to diverge from what are often considered to be some of the key conventions of ethnography. Ethnography, along with its digital variant, remains deeply contested, evading definition despite myriad attempts (see Pink et al. 2015). Yet in much of the literature it appears that ethnographic methods generally diverge from other qualitative methods (such as interviewing) due to their focus on observation (Gobo and Marciniak 2016). While both the necessity and the feasibility of spending extended periods of time with a specific, often unfamiliar group of people as suggested by early ethnographers has been challenged on several fronts (see, for instance, Madison 2011), the ethnographic method nevertheless maintains an enduring relationship with the observation of already-occurring social phenomena. By inviting our participants to a specific digital space that they (for the most part) did not already inhabit, and by relying on data that they curated, but which was elicited from them, we stepped towards the margins of ethnography, even as we were able to gain access to their everyday experiences in a new way. Although, as we discuss in the course of this chapter, this meant that we could capitalise on some of the benefits that have resulted from ethnographic studies in youth research, it also provoked several challenges.

While searching for an appropriate digital platform we contended with concerns about privacy and data security. Although we initially considered using a social media website such as Facebook, well-publicised concerns about privacy policies and (mis)use of data (Baruh and Popescu 2017) ultimately deterred us from pursuing this option. We turned our attention to other platforms available as smartphone applications. The study of the implications and usage of smartphones signifies a rapidly expanding area of research interest (Lasén 2015). Apps form a central part of this. Curiously, while sociologists have studied apps by participating in their design (Neves et al. 2017), producing critiques and commentaries on them (Thomas and Lupton 2016) and studying individuals' use of them via both self-reported content (Hobbs et al. 2017) and log data (Kaufmann 2018), we are aware of little research that has made use of apps to solicit data from participants. Indeed, the only studies doing so stem from market research (see Erickson 2017). For this reason, there was little guidance that we could find as to an appropriate app for our study. Ultimately, we selected an app based on our requirements for data security as well as functionality. Specifically, we chose an app named Slack because it provided us with a password-protected digital space that was visible only to the participant and ourselves, and because the administrators could provide stronger guarantees about the security of the data that was uploaded to the app. Additionally, it was free to download and use (aside from costs associated with internet connectivity and uploading and downloading data) and allowed the participants to easily post text, images and videos in real time. Despite the ubiquity of smartphones in Australia, we considered that some of the potential participants may not own or use smartphones, and determined that if this were the case we would request that they use the app online via a computer. However, this situation did not arise during recruitment.

The week-long digital data collection was followed by a one-on-one interview which averaged 60–90 minutes. The interview schedule, much like the prompts used for the digital mode of data collection, included a broad range of questions which sought to gain understanding of the intersecting commitments that formed the participants' lives. The first part of the interview was based on posts, selecting 3–4 of the participant's posts and either asking participants questions about them or asking them to elaborate upon them.

The data were initially analysed using a priori coding based on the interview questions, which allowed us to identify commonalities and differences between the participants' responses. A closer round of thematic open coding then allowed us to identify patterns that were reflected across various parts of their lives (for instance, work, leisure, family life). At this stage we focused on the formation, use and experience of time, routines and scheduling. This step was important for gaining insight into how the participants organised and coordinated their time. It also allowed us to incorporate the app posts into the analysis. In doing so we were able to compare the participants' reflections on their scheduling and organisation of time with some of the in-the-moment realities that they had posted about and, in some cases, uncover points of difference between their perceptions and experiences. While we initially focused on schedules and time use due to an interest in work–life interference and leisure time, it quickly became apparent that gendered dynamics were at play not only in the use of the participants' time, but in the organisation of it. Moreover, the gendered dynamics that we observed in the organisation of time directly informed the use of time. Simply, the participant who managed scheduling and coordination (women in this study) generally took primary responsibility for ensuring that necessary tasks (such as organising childcare) were completed. Inequalities in labour and leisure stemmed from, and were even naturalised by, the gendered nature of scheduling and its intensification, and this informed our focus on this area as a key aspect of wider gender inequalities in intimate relationships.

KEY FINDINGS

As outlined in our discussion of data analysis, this study produced findings relevant to the participants' schedules and organisation of time. While the question of what the participants did with their time was relevant, this topic has been pursued at great length in previous research on work–life balance and gender. Of more interest for us, and less previous scholarly consideration, was the issue of how schedules were planned and coordinated. We found that when the participants were asked who, within the couple, was responsible for finding or planning time together they generally stated that this was either distributed evenly or slanted slightly towards one partner. However, closer examination of the participants' specific schedules, and the ways in which they were managed (facilitated in large part by the qualitative time-use data from the app) demonstrated that the practices through which an 'egalitarian split' in organising and managing shared time was achieved were commonly implemented, managed and maintained by the female partner. We now turn to three case studies of heterosexual couples within our study to outline some of the key findings emerging from the study.

Samantha and Jacob

Samantha, an accountant, and her de facto partner Jacob, a web developer, both worked full-time, undertook voluntary work and belonged to multiple clubs and professional associations. On top of this Jacob ran his own side business, meaning that their hours of work typically exceeded a conventional full-time schedule, and that their work often took place outside of 9 to 5 hours. Their schedules were therefore full and complex – something that they each attributed to their desire for professional development and advancement. This desire appeared to be shaped by the insecure nature of their work – Samantha in particular was employed on a 12-month fixed-term contract to cover another staff member's maternity leave and did not have a position lined up to correspond with the end of this contract. Samantha and Jacob appeared to have a relatively egalitarian split with regard to managing their schedules and finding time together. For instance, Samantha reported that:

> We both contribute ideas about what we wanna do, and then we plan out the time to do some, most of them. Now, every Sunday night we have a meeting and we will discuss all what our weeks look like, and then what we are going to do on Friday night … We both share ideas.

However, when asked how long they had this routine, Samantha told us it had only been in place for approximately a month at her instigation in response to her frustrations with not having enough time together. Prior to this arrangement the couple had used a shared calendar-based mobile phone app which allowed them to see each other's schedules. However, Samantha found that Jacob did not always keep his calendar updated, and that for this reason she often did not know what he was doing or where he was:

> Sometimes like in the past I was like "Where are you?" And I would never get a reply, I would get so upset. We share the calendars together, and I could see what he is on tonight, but if we don't update

our calendars on time we would just lose track of each other. So that's why sometimes I got … I got a bit cranky and was like "Why don't you update your calendar?"

Jacob echoed Samantha's narrative, reporting that she was frustrated with his failure to update his calendar and that their coordination of time together had recently improved. Indeed, while addressing his work–life balance he stated:

Overall, I'm relatively content with the distribution of where I'm putting my time and energy. I feel like I've got enough time for investing in a relationship, and work, and doing a little bit of stuff for fun.

However, he did not attribute this to their Sunday night planning and increased diligence with recording his plans. Rather, he attributed it to weekly meetings with a life coach:

So, I meet with [coach] on a Monday night and plan out what my priorities are over the next week. Put that into my calendar, and then I'll have a bit of an accountability check of how I went the previous week. As part of the goals, I'll put in not just work stuff but business, relationship, finance, career progression, all the things that I think are important.

When asked why he sought coaching, Jacob stated:

I went to her and said, "Look, I want help with balancing everything", because I knew that, in theory, that I did want to have a more balanced life.

While Samantha and Jacob each appeared to contribute to facilitating and managing their time together and reported that the work involved in doing this was relatively evenly distributed, when these practices were interrogated further a complex gender division and inequality emerged. Specifically, Samantha originally instigated calendar-sharing and then, when that was not successful, the Sunday night planning. Jacob complied with these plans, but essentially outsourced his scheduling when Samantha expressed dissatisfaction with his original efforts.

Nathan and Carla

Rather than outsourcing to a life coach, many of the men in heterosexual relationships across the sample instead appeared to essentially 'outsource' to their partner. For instance, when Carla, a self-employed hairdresser who worked from home and routinely worked evenings, was asked who organised social events for herself and her husband Nathan, a property valuer with whom she shared two children, she initially stated that Nathan was more proactive about planning social events:

Nathan is a lot more, "Let's go do this", where I'm more a, "Can't we just stay at home and spend time together?" And Nathan is more like … he'll say, "Let's invite some people over for tea", and I'm like, "I've literally just finished work. The last thing I want to do is deal with more people."

However, it appeared that although Nathan was more likely to suggest social events, the labour of actualising these events – inviting family and friends, cooking – generally fell to Carla. Additionally, Carla found herself disproportionately responsible for managing their children's social and extra-curricular commitments. Specifically, her 7-year-old daughter undertook three weekly extra-curricular classes, while her 2-year-old son attended a weekly swimming lesson, and both children had regular social plans with friends that Carla organised and coordinated.

Seemingly due to her lack of time and lack of flexibility in her schedule, when Carla was asked if she spent much social time with friends she replied:

> I'm very close with my clients. A lot of my friends obviously come to me, which is a really crappy excuse. So I do catch up with my friends while doing their hair.

Aside from catching up with friends in the course of her paid work as a hairdresser, Carla also played netball. However, she identified getting to her weekly netball game as a challenge, as she performed complex scheduling work to facilitate it:

> While I was playing netball, it was hard because I would literally go from swimming, drop [daughter] home to [Nathan], and then go straight to netball. But then sometimes netball would be quite late, so it would be an 8:30 game. So you don't get home til 10:00.

Notably, Carla's netball games and socialising during work signified a markedly different time commitment when compared to Nathan's leisure activities – most commonly hunting trips, which typically involved long periods of time (several hours, and in some cases an overnight stay) away from the family and outside of mobile phone coverage.

Abigail and Simon

In some cases, identifying how scheduling work was divided within couples proved challenging. A strong example of this was provided by Abigail, an occupational therapist, and her husband Simon, a public servant, who had three children. Abigail and Simon had busy and complex schedules. Simon worked full-time, while Abigail mixed tertiary study with full-time work while taking primary responsibility for the care of their children, one with additional needs, necessitating a large volume of specialist appointments. While Simon and Abigail both officially worked 9 to 5 hours, they each typically used evenings to catch up on work and, in Abigail's case, study. Additionally, while they lived with Abigail's father who undertook a caring role for the children, this caring was negotiated by Abigail. When asked who took responsibility for organising the family's time, Simon responded:

> I'm probably more of the organiser but that's partly because of the role I have at work now, it comes a bit more naturally, and because [Abigail] is always busy with, you know, doing her work or uni or the kids or … so yeah, I think I've taken on more of that role.

However, Simon appeared to view being the 'organiser' as determining events to be attended. This contrasted with Abigail's views. While acknowledging that Simon chose activities, she nevertheless felt responsible for the scheduling involved in making them possible:

> I do all the scheduling as you might have picked up on. [Simon] doesn't do much of that. Um, but yeah. So I take care of that, I suppose. And that helps us to run things smoothly.

Simon's reference to his workplace role as a manager, and the way in which management – including the delegation of tasks – came naturally to him in his personal life as well, was exemplified in his reflections on the impact on work–life balance of recently losing his driver's licence. He saw it as having a positive impact while also making planning easier for Abigail:

> Since losing my licence and doing the public transport it's going a lot better, which I mentioned earlier. I'd say from August last year to maybe July this year it was heavily leaning towards, you know, towards work instead of [the] life side. Since getting the train and stuff to work has definitely evened up a lot more. I know when I nearly get home that makes it easier for [Abigail] to plan what dinner is and all that kind of stuff and if she's working I'm home at a certain time to watch the kids, so that's definitely helped in that aspect.

However, Abigail's digital posts illustrate that dropping off and picking up Simon from the train station daily added a new task into an already complex schedule, one that needed to be coordinated with her own work, the schedules of their three children, domestic tasks such as preparing dinner and coordinating with her father when necessary. Evidently, while this development rendered Simon's schedule more predictable and facilitated additional time with the children, it added to Abigail's coordination work, which Simon did not discuss in his posts or subsequent interview.

Notably, while Abigail recognised that she completed the bulk of the scheduling labour for the household, and expressed frustration with this arrangement, she nevertheless attributed this to her own personality or personal aptitude. For instance, while discussing the organisation of schedules and distribution of domestic labour, Abigail stated:

> The general day-to-day running of our family. That's sort of like what I handle. You know, [Simon] helps out where he can. And I just pretty much tell everybody where they need to be … So, that's just my personality. I think that was never something that we decided. It was just how it kind of fell into place.

The participants reported a relatively equal sharing of the work of managing the complex schedules of their lives. Yet in the detail of the posts and interviews it was clear that for these participants, the organisation of time has continued to unfold through a seeming delineation between men's and women's time, even as both partners are heavily invested in paid employment (Davies 1990, Bryson 2007). This was not completely naturalised, with the women presenting some exasperation at their partner's lack of organisation and some of the men apologetic about the inequality. Yet the participants rarely presented the differences within their relationships to us directly in gendered terms, framing them instead in terms of choice and preference, and in so doing brushing over the structured gendering of the work of managing the synchronisation of at least two complex schedules.

EVALUATION

Now that we have established the design of the research as well as some of its key findings, we turn to an evaluation of the utility of this approach for addressing gendered issues in the context of work–life balance. We begin by discussing some of the interpretive and practical challenges that were associated with our digital mode of data collection, before moving on to considering how this method was able to access data that could speak to the complexities that characterise implicit gender inequalities.

Interpretive Challenges

Beginning with a discussion of the data elicited from the app, we found that the type of data that this stage of the research produced was highly specific in some ways. For instance, we found that many of the photos that the participants uploaded onto the app were of food, often with a stylised presentation, that they were either preparing or about to consume. Food and meals were not mentioned directly in the document given to the participants outlining the aspects of life that they may like to post about (although they were implicit in activities such as domestic labour and socialising). The ubiquity of food posts may highlight the importance of food practices to conviviality and sociality (Neely et al. 2014). However, the images tended to be of food alone, and appear prompted by the popularity of the practice of sharing stylised images of food via social media platforms (Holmberg et al. 2016). While the broad social implications of this practice have been addressed (Bouvier 2018), little research has considered its place within and utility for understanding individuals' everyday lives.

The volume of food-based images was unexpected. However, we again sought to consider how it may be of relevance to the aims of our study. While the aesthetics of the participants' images and the specifics of the food that they photographed was not of great utility to the aims of our study, more likely evidence of a contemporary social media aesthetic than an emergent finding about sociality, we nevertheless found that the images that they provided allowed us to elicit insight into their lives. For instance, in many cases we were able to use these images to prompt discussion of whether they ate alone or with others, whether they took breaks from activities such as work to eat, whether they left their desk or workplace to eat, and whether they cooked or found themselves too tired to do so, instead ordering takeaway (as we observed in many cases). Preparation and planning of meals was also often gendered, and provided insight into an everyday way in which gendered forms of labour played out for our participants.

Technological Challenges

While some unanticipated implications of this digital mode of data collection produced unexpected insights about our participants' routines, the use of technology to facilitate data collection nevertheless introduced additional challenges that needed to be managed. For instance, at one point the servers at the app's central headquarters went down for approximately six hours. We worked around this issue by contacting participants and asking them to temporarily record posts elsewhere and upload them when Slack returned online. However, while this minimised the impact of the disruption, it did not negate its effects completely. For instance, we found that participants recorded fewer posts during this time, and these were generally briefer and did not include images. Ultimately, this disruption highlights a peril of using cloud-based digital technology when attempting to collect data in real time.

We also found that participants' familiarity with mobile phone apps was both an opportunity and a challenge. As already mentioned, all participants asked to take part in the study owned a smartphone and were familiar with its use, including those initially interested but who did not ultimately take part. Hence, we did not need to ask participants to post to an alternative forum. However, while familiarity with smartphones meant participants found and downloaded the app with relative ease, many did not closely follow the provided instructions about the specific way we wanted them to post data to the app, possibly viewing them as unnecessary. Hence, initially several participants did not post in the specific 'channel' (forum or online space within the app) that we requested, meaning that we had difficulty identifying where they were posting, and in some cases were not able to view their posts. While this necessitated asking the participants again to post to the right channel, and in some cases a phone conversation to direct them to the correct channel, we eventually found that our instructions were more likely to be followed when included in a condensed form in an email or text, rather than in the fact sheet that we had originally provided. This experience demonstrated to us some of the considerations that must be attended to while asking participants to interact with a familiar platform (mobile phone applications).

Added Depth and Specificity

While the use of the app tool directly produced several fruitful insights in isolation – highlighting the complexities of young lives as shown above – the posts were also utilised for a second purpose, as an elicitation tool during an interview that took place in the weeks that followed. We used the posts at the beginning of the interviews, selecting 3–4 posts and either asking them questions about them or asking them to elaborate upon them. These posts were selected because they presented some degree of ambiguity, or they touched directly upon an area of interest to the project, such as the participant's experience of balancing work with other aspects of their life.

This generally provided a very successful entry point into the interview. We were able to discuss aspects of their everyday lives, as well as their plans and ambitions. For instance, some of them posted about a house they wanted to buy, or a job that they were applying for, and familiarity of this type helped to build rapport. Beginning the interview by discussing specific experiences or anecdotes also appeared to lead the participants to continue to provide answers, suggesting a degree of comfort in expanding on everyday life with the interviewer, aided by participants' awareness that the interviewer already had a general understanding of their circumstances, as well as by reference back to posts from the app where relevant throughout the interviews. This resulted in interview data based more on stories and discussions of specific experiences than it was on more general explanations. The example below provides a snapshot of how an interview conducted using the app data as an elicitation tool compares to an interview conducted with the same participant in a previous round. While the issue of quality or validity in qualitative interviewing has received a number of oft-cited treatments (Seale 2004, Flick 2007, Kvale 2007) and is dependent on the epistemological and methodological underpinnings of the research in question (Roulston 2010), recommendations have generally converged on the claim that rich, detailed and specific data offer a greater resource than generalised discussion based, for instance, on justifications rather than explanations and experiences.

2008 interview with Laura
(After establishing that the participant lived in a residential college associated with her tertiary institution)

Interviewer: OK. Have you ever lived in Melbourne in a, in a shared accommodation or outside the residential house?
Participant: Umm no, I have only ever lived in this student village at Deakin.
Interviewer: Oh.
Participant: I have never lived anywhere else in Melbourne.
Interviewer: And why is that? Why did you decide to live in the residential village?
Participant: Umm well, when I first got into my course at Deakin, umm, my sister already lived there so she could vouch for me that it was a good place to live. Umm and it is a very secure environment because there is a whole management team there who make sure everything is running smoothly and everyone is safe and comfortable, umm, in that living environment. Umm so I had that recommendation and once I got there I just really liked it and didn't want to leave so there I stayed.

2017 interview with Laura

Interviewer: The way in which your hours are concentrated a bit later in the days – it seems to have moved your whole day up a bit.
Participant: Moved forward, yeah.
Interviewer: You also touched on the fact that it can be difficult to get together with friends who have a standard work week. Is there any other kind of impact on your life?
Participant: Umm, when I get home from work, I, yeah, it kind of changes a bit of my home routine, because you know, I'll wanna put on washing or, you know, kind of cook dinner at ten o'clock or whatever. And then I'll think, "Oh, maybe I won't do that because I don't want to make too much noise in the house." Of … everyone else who doesn't do that. Um, but sometimes I think, "No. I'm sorry guys. I've got to do it, I've got to do it tonight." *(Laughs)*
Interviewer: I'm interested, because you work slightly different hours to the rest of the people in the house, do you think that that helps you to get some time when everyone's not sitting around, some time alone in the house?
Participant: That's true. Yeah. That's a good point. Yeah, that's kind of my time to access, you know? The kitchen, the laundry.

Ultimately the digital mode of data collection, by prompting our participants to focus on their everyday experiences, provided a tool for focusing the beginning of the interviews on this level of experience and maintaining it throughout. This resulted in more detailed data than we had collected in previous years, solely using interviews. Although the utility of this method is dependent on the aims of the research in which it is being deployed, it was particularly successful at illuminating the everyday experiences through which the gendered dimension of work–life balance can be drawn out.

Enhanced Scope for Reflexivity

In addition to encouraging more detailed responses within interviews, the digital mode of data collection also appeared to enhance participants' reflexivity. Several authors have addressed participant reflexivity in the context of various research methods, such as interview (see, for instance, Riach 2009) as part of a broader project of taking seriously the reflexivity that people use in their everyday lives (Giddens 1991). The digital mode of data collection appeared to encourage the participants to reflect upon their own posts. For instance, several of the participants read over their posts at the conclusion of the week-long period of posting and made a final post reflecting on how documenting their time in this way had prompted them to think about their time use and interactions in a different way. An example of this was provided by Catherine, a primary school teacher who lived with her husband in metropolitan Melbourne. In her final post Catherine wrote:

> Well, time to tuck in for the night, ready for another week. This has been an interesting process. I've enjoyed being forced to reflect on my days and week as I've gone. It's given me a more methodical take on my life. It's been clear to me for some time now, that the intensity of my work is not sustainable for me in the long term and that I have a growing sense of "missing out" when I observe my life going by. By that I mean, I feel like I miss the small, seemingly insignificant, moments of my life because I'm so busy trying to get by and "fit it all in". At the end of a weekend I feel let down that there isn't more time to take it all in and I have to prepare myself for the onslaught of the working week. I'm constantly shocked at how much time has passed and I haven't even seemed to notice, or really enjoyed all the moments for what they are. [Husband] and I got married in April and it feels like we just had this most magical moment in time and then had to move on straight away, like pressing "play" again on the life remote. I wish we had more moments like that to feel like we've pressed the pause button and really appreciated our lives and the things in them. It shouldn't take something as big as a wedding to allow us to do that.

Alongside this message, Catherine posted a photograph from her wedding, an image of a joyous moment that contrasted with the pressure and speed of her current everyday life. Taking part in the digital portion of the study seemingly allowed some of the participants to reflect in a way that they were not otherwise prompted to do so, and to articulate these reflections in a way that can be difficult for researchers to access otherwise. This was particularly useful in the context of our study, in which we were seeking insights into the ways in which gendered experiences were shaped and manifest in participants' everyday lives.

FUTURE DIRECTIONS

The future directions for research combining digital and 'traditional' methods to study enduring areas of concern for social researchers, such as the topic of gender and work–life balance, are myriad. They are also, necessarily, tied to the development of emerging digital tools for research and data collection, an area that encompasses many particularly exciting and promising developments. It has been one of our aims in this chapter to demonstrate how a digital research method can work not only in conjunction with, but in a way that enriches, a traditional method, such as the research interview. Indeed, we have shown that the use of a digital method, both as a standalone data source and as a primer for interviews, enhanced our ability to meet our research aims, ultimately uncovering new insights about how work–life balance is managed for Australian young adults in heterosexual partnerships – many of whom are facing a labour market crowded with increasing uncertainty, and an increasing volume of jobs requiring non-standard hours.

Rather than focusing on any one potential development in digital research – a topic that has been discussed at great length elsewhere (see Marres 2017) – we instead end this chapter by arguing that the future of research such as our own lies in part in its alignment with traditional, quantitative time-use studies. 'Traditional' time-use studies (such as the Australian Bureau of Statistics' *How Australians Use Their Time* survey) ask respondents to fill out a diary for a set period of time (two days in the case of the ABS's survey). In such surveys the time-use diary is broken down into five-minute increments, and respondents are asked to record their main activity, who they did it for, what else they were doing at the same time, where they were and who they were with. While such research produces eminently useful data – especially for those studying issues of gender and work–life balance – it nevertheless provides a quantitative measure of time use. By asking our participants not just what they were doing but also how they were feeling, and then speaking to them about it more directly in an interview, we were able to identify valuable information that does not emerge from purely quantitative time-use studies. Specifically, we found that even in cases in which men were performing unpaid domestic and caring work, it was often at the behest of their female partner. Put simply, while male partners were contributing to the household in these ways – thus presenting a veneer of egalitarianism – women overwhelmingly remained responsible for managing, coordinating and overseeing the broader architecture of the family's schedule, including the expanding work of creating a schedule in the context of individualised working patterns. Our data therefore revealed that women's role as the 'time and motion' experts within families was still firmly in place for our participants, and even enhanced in some respects (Hochschild and Machung 2003).

We therefore see the use of qualitative measures of time use, as well as experience of time, alongside 'traditional' time-use studies as the most significant future direction for research like ours. Without a measure of this type there is a risk that, in better documenting and comparing women's and men's use of time, we inadvertently miss, and even encourage, a new space for invisible, and gendered, labour.

REFERENCES

ABS (2006), *4153.0 – How Australians Use Their Time, 2006*. Canberra: Australian Bureau of Statistics.
ABS (2011), *6310.0 – Employee Earnings, Benefits and Trade Union Membership*. Canberra: Australian Bureau of Statistics.
Arnett, J. (2014), *Emerging Adulthood: The Winding Road from the Late Teens through the Twenties*. New York, NY: Oxford University Press.
Baruh, L., and Popescu, M. (2017), 'Big data analytics and the limits of privacy self-management', *New Media & Society*, **19** (4): 579–596.
Bouvier, E. (2018), 'Breaking bread online: social media, photography, and the virtual experience of food', in N. Namaste and M. Nadales (eds), *Who Decides? Competing Narratives in Constructing Tastes, Consumption and Choice*. Leiden: Brill, 157–172.
boyd, d. (2008), 'Why youth (heart) social network sites: the role of networked publics in teenaged social life', in D. Buckingham (ed.), *Youth, Identity, and Digital Media*. Cambridge, MA: MIT Press, 119–142.
Bryson, V. (2007), *Gender and the Politics of Time: Feminist Theory and Contemporary Debates*. Bristol: Policy Press.

Clawson, D., and Gerstel, N. (2014), *Unequal Time: Gender, Class, and Family in Employment Schedules*. New York, NY: Russell Sage Foundation.

Cook, J., and Woodman, D. (2020), 'Digital modes of data collection in mixed-methods longitudinal youth research', in P. Billett, D. Martin and M. Hart (eds), *Complexities of Researching with Young People*. London: Routledge.

Craig, L., and Powell, A. (2011), 'Non-standard work schedules, work-family balance and the gendered division of childcare', *Work, Employment and Society*, **25** (2): 274–291.

Davies, K. (1990), *Women, Time, and the Weaving of the Strands of Everyday Life*. Aldershot: Gower.

Erickson, G.S. (2017), *New Methods of Market Research and Analysis*. Cheltenham, UK and Northampton, MA, USA: Edward Elgar Publishing.

Fein, E.C., Skinner, N., and Machin, M.A. (2017), 'Work intensification, work–life interference, stress, and well-being in Australian workers', *International Studies of Management & Organization*, **47** (4): 360–371.

Flick, U. (2007), *Managing Quality in Qualitative Research*. London: SAGE.

Giddens, A. (1991), *Modernity and Self-Identity: Self and Society in the Late Modern Age*. Cambridge: Polity.

Gobo, G., and Marciniak, L. (2016), 'What is ethnography?', in D. Silverman (ed.), *Qualitative Research*, 4th edition. London: SAGE, 103–118.

Goodin, R.E., Rice, J.M., Parpo, A., and Eriksson, L. (2008), *Discretionary Time: A New Measure of Freedom*. Cambridge: Cambridge University Press.

Gregg, M. (2011), *Work's Intimacy*. Cambridge: Polity.

Hewitt, B., Craig, L., and Baxter, J. (2012), 'Family, work and wellbeing over the life course', *Journal of Population Research*, **29**: 289–292.

Hobbs, M., Owen, S., and Gerber, L. (2017), 'Liquid love? Dating apps, sex, relationships and the digital transformation of intimacy', *Journal of Sociology*, **53** (2), 271–284.

Hochschild, A., and Machung, A. (2003), *The Second Shift*. London: Penguin.

Holmberg, C., Chaplin, J.E., Hillman, T., and Berg, C. (2016), 'Adolescents' presentation of food in social media: an exploratory study', *Appetite*, **99** (1): 121–129.

Kaufmann, K. (2018), 'The smartphone as a snapshot of its use: mobile media elicitation in qualitative interviews', *Mobile Media & Communication*, **6** (2), 233–246.

Kvale, S. (2007), *Doing Interviews*. London: SAGE.

Lasén, A. (2015), 'Rhythms and flow: timing and spacing the digitally mediated everyday', in J. Wyn and H. Cahill (eds), *Handbook of Children and Youth Studies*. Singapore: Springer, 749–760.

Madison, S. (2011), *Critical Ethnography: Method, Ethics and Performance*. Thousand Oaks, CA: SAGE.

Marres, N. (2017), *Digital Sociology: The Reinvention of Social Research*. Oxford: Polity Press.

Neely, E., Walton, M., and Stephens, C. (2014), 'Young people's food practices and social relationships: a thematic synthesis', *Appetite*, **82** (1), 50–60.

Neves, B.B., Franz, R.L., Munteanu, C., and Baecker, R. (2017), 'Adoption and feasibility of a communication app to enhance social connectedness amongst frail institutionalized oldest old: an embedded case study', *Information, Communication & Society*, https://doi.org/10.1080/1369118X.2017.1348534.

Pink, S., Horst, H., Postill, J., Hjorth, L., Lewis, T., and Tacchi, J. (2015), *Digital Ethnography: Principles and Practice*. London: SAGE.

Pocock, B., Skinner, N., and Williams, P. (2012), *Time Bomb: Work, Rest and Play in Australia Today*. Sydney: UNSW Press.

Presser, H.B. (2005), *Working in a 24/7 Economy: Challenges for American Families*. New York, NY: Russell Sage Foundation.

Riach, K. (2009), 'Exploring participant-centred reflexivity in the research interview', *Sociology*, **43** (2): 356–370.

Roulston, K. (2010), 'Considering quality in qualitative interviewing', *Qualitative Research*, **10** (2): 199–228.

Seale, C. (2004), 'Quality in qualitative research', in C. Seale, G. Gobo, J.F. Gubrium and D. Silverman (eds), *Qualitative Research Practice*. London: SAGE, 407–419.

Thomas, G.M., and Lupton, D. (2016), 'Threats and thrills: pregnancy apps, risk and consumption', *Health, Risk & Society*, **17** (7–8), 495–509.

Venn, D. (2004), *Work Timing Arrangements in Australia in the 1990s: Evidence from the Australian Time Use Survey*. Melbourne: University of Melbourne (Doctoral dissertation).

Venn, D., Carey, G., Strazdins, L., and Burgess, J. (2016), 'What explains trends in Australian working time arrangements in the 2000s?', *Labour & Industry*, **26**: 138–155.

Wajcman, J. (2014), *Pressed for Time: The Acceleration of Life in Digital Capitalism*. Chicago, IL: University of Chicago Press.

Woodman, D. (2012), 'Life out of synch: how new patterns of further education and the rise of precarious employment are reshaping young people's relationships', *Sociology*, **46** (6): 1074–1090.

Woodman, D. (2013), 'Young people's friendships in the context of non-standard work patterns', *Economic and Labour Relations Review*, **24** (3): 416–432.

Woodman, D., and Cook, J. (2019), 'The new gendered labour of synchronisation: temporal labour in the new world of work', *Journal of Sociology*, **55** (4): 762–777.

16. 'My work is full of gossipers so I tried to keep my pregnancy secret': 'distant' netnography as a qualitative method for exploring work–life balance among pregnant and breastfeeding employees

Caroline Gatrell

INTRODUCTION

In this chapter I discuss the use of 'netnography' (or internet research) as a qualitative methodology for exploring work–life balance (here, among pregnant women and new mothers). My approach is a personal one – I have been researching work and family among employed parents (both mothers and fathers) since I started my PhD in 1998. I began using netnography as a means of understanding work, life and health among employed, pregnant and newly maternal women in 2006. The purpose of the present narrative is to share my experiences, rather than presenting a framework for 'how to' be a netnographer.

I tell the story of how I used a netnographic approach with two studies about motherhood, work–life balance and employment. One of these studies was focused on pregnancy, the other on breastfeeding and employment. I show how netnographic methods offered opportunities to access groups of women and their stories, which might otherwise have been hard to elicit, as well as extending the scope of my data. Throughout this research, I utilized netnography always in a non-participative form: what I term 'distant' netnography; that is to say, observing interactions within internet space through open-access sites, but not personally joining these communities. Acknowledging how internet communications (what Kozinets, 2015, describes as 'online sociality') have changed dramatically since I began researching in this area, with opportunities for researcher participation increasing rapidly, my own approach has remained relatively stable. I have continued to gather data from websites and discussion groups which are publicly available, and within which users usually choose an internet 'identifier' which renders them anonymous. I consider that this 'distant' form of netnography has preserved women's anonymity in a manner which other media methods (for example, following Facebook threads as part of a friendship group) might not have done. It has also reduced the likelihood of blurring the boundaries regarding what I may, or ought not to, use as part of my research. It seemed less likely, using the 'distant' netnographic method, that I might accidentally discover information about acquaintances who were not part of my study, yet whom I know personally, than if I had used 'friendship' technologies such as Facebook. Using distant netnography, there was always a possibility that I might have recognized someone via posted photographs, but this has never occurred. Below, I tell the story of using distant netnography to inform my qualitative research studies, and I discuss the benefits and the disadvantages of using such a method.

1.   USING NETNOGRAPHY AS A QUALITATIVE TECHNIQUE

Netnography (or internet research) was first defined by Robert Kozinets (1998) in relation to marketing and consumption – on his personal website he describes the technique as adapting 'the anthropological approach of ethnography to work with the many types of social experience and interaction that emerge through networked digital communications' (Kozinets, 2019). Specifically, as a 'distant' netnographer, I have used netnographic techniques to draw upon data which may be found on the internet, usually through accessing open conversations which occur as part of digital communications networks (chat rooms, question-and-answer sessions or advice fora which enable correspondence among and between interested parties). Such data may originate from commercial sources. In my case, for example, where pregnancy and new motherhood was the focus, I looked to organizations such as What to Expect, a company established in the 1980s which publishes best-selling advice books on pregnancy, birth and infancy. Sites established by corporate hosts such as this offer health and social advice to pregnant women and new mothers, as well as setting up and facilitating chat rooms and discussion fora for mothers to exchange experience and views. Interestingly, the style of provision of such facilities, hosted by commercial entities for the use of interested parties, has changed very little since I began first using netnography as a research method. Government health agencies might also offer public health information and case studies and/or mediate question-and-answer sessions, perhaps also offering 'expert' advice. Consumer-led sites, which might begin with small numbers of subscribers, might build up a following sufficient to pull in advertising revenue, launching themselves as entities in their own right (that is, not on the back of a commercial brand).

At the time of writing this chapter, for example, the What to Expect (2019) site is headlining an ovulation diary to identify the best days for conception, a 'due date' calculator and a 'week by week' calendar of maternal (and baby's) body developments as the baby grows inside the uterus and the mother's body changes shape. What to Expect is also hosting a discussion forum in which women are invited to join and share 'stuff people say to you when you get pregnant'. This last thread includes maternal reporting of comments such as: 'You're too small, there's no bump, that's not normal', 'Is there a dad', 'I don't like that name', 'Child birth is agony', 'How long did it take', 'How will the dog cope' … Mothers within these conversations share comments and views about the tendency for co-workers, acquaintances and sometimes complete strangers to ask intrusive questions, make personal comments or offer unsolicited advice. Women argue that such public interest in the pregnant body is intrusive, and many report feeling uncomfortable and being under scrutiny not only by their family and health professionals (which can sometimes feel overwhelming) but also by others with no familial or clinical interest in the pregnancy, including co-workers. Pregnant women often feel that they are managing their work–life balance while being unfairly monitored, or 'policed', by others (Gatrell, 2011; Longhurst, 2001).

Netnographers use conversations (such as the above discussions on the What to Expect site) as data for exploring and interpreting experience and opinion. While the idea of netnography was first developed in the context of marketing, many other disciplines now, inevitably, draw upon this method to explore social phenomena, including geography, anthropology and information science (see Kozinets, 2015). In my case, as an organization theorist working from a qualitative and socio-cultural perspective, I used netnographic methods to examine pregnancy, motherhood and breastfeeding practices within the context of work–life balance and employment. I sought to better understand women's perceptions and experience of balancing pregnancy and new motherhood with employment; I was not measuring or monitoring their views, and I was not seeking to generalize the research across wider populations. I did not seek to join any of the discussion groups, but confined myself to observing what occurred within them.

My own view about adopting a 'distant' or non-participatory approach to gathering netnographic data is that this is distinct from the examination of people's lives through invitation-only websites, or social media communications systems such as Facebook. The form of netnography which I describe below does not require access to particular friendship or interest groups; rather, data are drawn from sites which are in the public domain – that is, sites which are open to anyone with capacity to access and search the internet. This approach has, of course, its own ethical challenges, and I reflect on these within the chapter.

I first considered the idea of netnography in around 2006, when I sought new ways of gathering data about employment, pregnancy and new motherhood. At this time, my research on work–life balance and motherhood was ongoing, and my approach centred on face-to-face interviews among professionally employed women – doctors, lawyers, academics, teachers, engineers and other senior roles requiring education to degree level or equivalent. Such roles might be imagined to offer good access to maternity leave and maternity protection policies (Stumbitz et al., 2018). The face-to-face interviewing was quite intensive, which, given I was working as a lecturer with a full teaching load, restricted the number of interviews I was able to conduct over time. I considered then (and still believe) that interviews concerning sensitive subjects such as health in pregnancy and post-birth, and breastfeeding experience, are best conducted in person, especially if participants are not previously known to the interviewer. Allowing time for interviewees to settle into the interview, enabling breaks if necessary, being acutely sensitive to body language and offering space for the interviewee to talk as long as they wished (see Gatrell, 2013) felt (and still feels) very important to me. Although I have since used what I term 'one-step-removed' methods such as Skype and audio conferencing, I am not convinced that these are an equivalent substitute for personal contact when discussing deeply personal and sensitive issues such as maternal health.

2. THE CHALLENGES OF FACE-TO-FACE INTERVIEWING, AND THE DRAW TOWARDS NETNOGRAPHY

Between 1998 and 2006, having gained small grants and allowances from various sources to assist with travel and subscription costs, I had conducted face-to-face interviews with around 70 women. These interviews had been complicated to arrange. I was employed as a university lecturer and had two small children. All my interviewees were employed and either pregnant, or mothers, or both. Thus, scheduling interviews was often a complex task. The interview process itself usually involved travel and overnight stays. Usually, women preferred to be interviewed away from their workplace contexts unless they could be sure of privacy in their own office space. This meant sometimes visiting respondents in their own homes, often with babies and animals requiring attention while interviews took place. Often interviewees were keen to maximize their space to talk, and arranged for grandparents to stay over, or fathers to take time away from work, so as to look after infants while the interview proceeded. However, even these arrangements involved interruptions and the need for flexibility regarding time taken to complete the discussions.

Some notes from a seminar which I gave in 2006, regarding qualitative research and the interview process, revealed the following:

> All interviews were carefully recorded. Although in some cases, I was fortunate enough to conduct the interviews in quiet conditions without interruptions, this was not always the case. In some instances, (usually at people's homes) there were babies, children and animals present. In one case a cat kept sitting on the tape recorder, in another there were five children under seven present. If interviews took place in women's workplaces, the women were sometimes called out urgently – perhaps to deal with a distressed client or a sick patient. This meant that some interviews took a great deal longer than the three hours which I had originally allocated for the process, as participants managed their interviews alongside domestic and employment related interruptions.

As I undertook an increasing number of interviews with mothers (and also, in some instances, with fathers) a number of questions, often sensitive and health-related, were raised regarding women's work–life balance. These questions involved issues such as mothers' health, and how women coped with maternity-related symptoms while continuing with their paid employment. It was clear from participant responses that such issues were complex, personal and potentially serious.

One woman drove 250 miles from her home at the other end of the country to be interviewed at my home, so she could tell me her story without interruptions or fear of being overheard. This mother explained how she felt pressured into continuing with her paid work (she was the main earner for her family) during pregnancy while she was ill. Her illness involved spending weekends in hospital, yet somehow hiding this from line managers so she could continue working. As a result, she became gravely ill, risking her own well-being and that of her child, who she believes still to be affected. Other participants talked about the difficulties of trying to continue what one person termed the 'nightmare' of breastfeeding at work following their return from maternity leave (see Gatrell, 2005, 2007, 2011; Haynes, 2008a, 2008b). For example, one mother who worked as a lawyer described how:

> I was at the whim of the magistrates … so they decided we were going to work until nine at night but I had left the house at eight in the morning which meant that my breasts became engorged and leaky, which was acutely embarrassing. I somehow got through with breast pads and so on, but I was so upset leaving my baby for [14 hours], it was the emotional aspect as well as the physical.

As I listened over the years to mothers' narratives it became increasingly clear to me that experiences such as these were shared by many women. I recall one interviewee's account of how she sat silently crying, with breasts leaking, as she sat a professional exam (she passed). And another woman's story of how she struggled to work on crutches while pregnant, due to pelvic pain and instability. A further interviewee returned to work after maternity leave, feeling vulnerable and exhausted only to find that her belongings had been packed up in her absence and her desk shunted out onto a corridor, where she was expected to work for two years until she gained employment elsewhere.

Many expectant women, frightened of the repercussions should they announce their pregnant state, hid pregnancies from line managers and co-workers, sometimes for up to five months. One mother (an academic) admitted not having even been to see a doctor until she was 18 weeks pregnant because she was employed on a temporary contract and frightened of losing her job should her pregnancy by discovered by line managers (she kept the job, but only after a fight). Several women had experienced a miscarriage yet reported continuing at work without taking sick leave or telling colleagues.

It seemed to me that my interviews must be the tip of a large iceberg, a feeling which was affirmed by qualitative research on similar topics by feminist philosophers and sociologists such as Höpfl and Hornby Atkinson (2000), Tyler (2000), Longhurst (2001) and Haynes (2006). Yet on the occasions when I presented my work at conferences and policy events, audiences were often cynical and sceptical. A common response when I shared mothers' stories was: 'Oh, but this must be an extreme case.' Yet the more interviews I undertook, the more convinced I became that the challenges of what I have termed 'maternal body work' (or the combining of pregnancy/new motherhood with employment, while trying to satisfy the demands of both; see Gatrell, 2013) were likely to be shared across a wider population of women beyond those women I had interviewed, including those in less prestigious jobs.

Two significant events prompted me to look for additional ways of gathering data on motherhood and employment. The first of these was a particularly difficult occasion at a management studies conference, where delegates questioned the qualitative nature of my findings, suggesting that my sample must be comprised of 'outliers', and was thus likely to be unrepresentative of the wider population of professional mothers in the workplace. The logic of this argument was then applied to policy. Specifically, the argument was put forward that no policy changes were required on the basis of one scholar's qualitative sample. This suggestion seemed to me highly questionable regarding the sample of professional women with high social capital, and even more problematic in the case of women in low-paid work, who would be even more vulnerable to discrimination (Stumbitz et al., 2018) and whose situation I sought to learn more about. The second incident that prompted me to widen my qualitative sample beyond my ongoing interviews was one occasion when a respondent became tearful in her interview. Although I suggested she might wish to stop the discussion, this participant expressed her determination to continue. She stated:

> I find it difficult to talk about this stuff but it needs to be talked about. I want you to publish it; push it as far as you can.

While my research would remain qualitative – I sought to examine the cultural experience of balancing motherhood and work, rather than seeking to produce a repeatable representative study – I nevertheless felt motivated to do more to augment my interviews with further data. I anticipated that widening my sample and method would help substantiate my arguments, which might then assist in the 'push' for greater understanding, and more inclusive policy initiatives among employers and organizations.

Looking at the options at the time, the ideal solution seemed to be gaining a major grant which could enable me to extend the research and the sample. I soon learned that applying for large grants is time-consuming, with limited chance of success. Interestingly, to date, I still have not received major grant funding to explore the situation of work–life balance among employed mothers, although I have gained two significant awards to investigate the experiences of employed fathers. Are research projects with male subjects more likely to receive funding than those foregrounding women's interests, I wonder?

3.   MOTHERS AND THE INTERNET

It became evident that major grant funding was unlikely to supply me with the required resources, especially in a short timeframe. I thus began to look elsewhere for ideas, and an important (for me) article by Lagan et al. (2006) led me in the direction of netnography. Lagan and team were writing about women's experiences of anxiety during pregnancy and exploring maternal desire to seek counsel and comfort from other women, anonymously, over the internet. They observed how netnography was a method used with increasing frequency for investigative social research into women's health (Lagan et al., 2006). Most especially, they noted how netnography was popular among researchers seeking to explore experiences among research groups who were regarded by research teams as hard to reach, especially in relation to respondents with low status and/or temporary employment. They advocated distant netnography not as a quantitative tool (they were not counting or measuring numbers and types of discussions) but as a qualitative means of exploring the cultural and social experience of women who shared health queries and concerns within internet discussion fora. These observations by Lagan et al. (2006) made netnography particularly relevant to my own research, which had to date foregrounded women in professional roles, but which I sought to broaden in order to embrace a range of different occupations (see Kozinets, 1998; also Gatrell, 2011).

I thus began to explore the possibility of using netnography as a research method (see Kozinets, 2017). A review of developing literatures on this research method suggested significant benefits of a netnographic approach. Netnography promised to allow access to anonymized, yet relevant and plentiful, data within virtual communities, offering the chance of cutting across social and organizational hierarchies as well as geographical settings (Hine, 2001; Gatrell, 2011). It was apparent from within existing research (and this was affirmed by my own subsequent studies) how internet users welcomed the space to consider health and personal matters in open-access settings, with people whom they did not know, while keeping their own identity secret (Whitty and Carr, 2003; Gustavsson, 2005). Netnography appeared to offer an alternative way of accessing a larger and more diverse sample, given that at the time I had access only to a modest budget and was operating as a 'lone scholar' with no research team to draw upon.

In order to elucidate how employed mothers organize and experience pregnancy, new motherhood and breastfeeding at work, I thus began to gather (in addition to and alongside the gathering of further interview data) data from the internet. Specifically, I sought to undertake a 'netnographic' analysis of online public and commercial health advice, as well as communication within open-access discussion groups, on pregnancy, new motherhood and breastfeeding. Netnography promised to provide an optimum research method for embracing wider numbers of mothers in my research, as well as opportunities to access women working in occupations less prestigious than those I had already interviewed.

The first hurdle I faced in beginning my netnographic study was to gain ethical approval from my employer (at that time, Lancaster University in the UK). I prepared an application explaining that the netnographic element of my research was part of a wider project entitled 'Embodying Maternal Management', the purpose of which was to examine women's health and personal experiences of combining motherhood and paid work.

The ethics application assisted me in thinking through the research design for a method which I had not previously used, and which at the time was not commonly used by my colleagues.

I explained that I would use netnography to consider interactions among and between individual pregnant and newly maternal/breastfeeding women within open-access virtual chat rooms, as well as the online advice offered to this group by 'experts'. I pledged not to join or accept invitations to participate in such groups. As in research by Warren and Brewis (2004), which investigated the views of employed pregnant women towards their own expectant bodies (through face-to-face interviews), I explained that my research was not intended to be representative of the experiences of all employed pregnant women. Rather, I sought to understand better the specific experiences of women included in the internet sample. I expressed my intention to extend, within the context of feminist debates on motherhood and the female body, considerations of how employed pregnant and newly maternal women were treated by co-workers and line managers within their workplace environments, and how they managed their work–life balance. In so doing, I sought to define and articulate strategies upon which women drew in order to combine pregnancy and new maternity with workplace requirements (see also Ladge, Clair and Greenberg, 2012).

Perhaps unsurprisingly, due to its relative newness as a method, my then department questioned the wisdom and the appropriateness of using internet data to contribute to my research. This view was significant in terms of progressing the study, as departmental sign-off was required for my proposal to be classified as low-risk (which meant I could proceed with the research) or high-risk (in which case the proposal would go to the university's central ethics committee and thus require a longer time frame before I could start). In the end, the proposal was signed off by my department and within a short time I was ready to begin the project.

Questions regarding the ethics of using, for scholarly purposes, internet data which are open-access to researchers remain pertinent, however. While such data might be readily available to researchers (and anyone else who wishes to view it) and is therefore public, it is important to recognize that the individuals who have posted views and joined online discussions have not given permission for their words to be used for other purposes. It was the usage of internet data without the knowledge of participants which most concerned my department. In order to try to ameliorate, as far as possible, concerns about using data without the permission of the originator, Eriksson and Kovalainen (2008, p. 106) counsel netnographers to 'strip all identifying information' from netnographic materials so as to preserve anonymity among those studied. It may not be feasible to find the originator of a discussion thread or seek permission to use their words as data (uncovering the identity of a respondent would in itself pose complex ethical questions), but it is possible, and important, to protect the identity of chat room users. For these reasons I never discuss or publish photographs or other images in my published work.

Such guidance about anonymity I now follow as a matter of course when dealing with netnographic data. Thus, for example, where internet discussions might offer information about mothers' employment situation and where this is pertinent (perhaps if they are undertaking shift work or have duties involving lifting during pregnancy) I would indicate this in subsequent publications. However, I would carefully exclude any personal details that could lead to women's identification. In any published materials, I always cite the posts of pregnant women and new mothers using pseudonyms rather than women's chosen internet identifiers; for example, changing an identifier such as 'Spanish mum, three sons' to 'busy mum'. I never link quotes to specific websites.

In addition to concerns regarding netnography and ethics, there continue to be debates about how netnographic research compares with more conventional qualitative research techniques;

in particular, face-to-face interviewing. A question of validity, truth and how far internet research may be considered trustworthy is raised, with queries about whether netnographic data may be considered to be more or less truthful than face-to-face interviews. Gustavsson (2005, p. 404) observes how 'the internet is often seen as an arena separate from the "real world" ... the social actions of real life [being] firmly anchored in bodies'. Parr (2002) and Gustavsson (2005) both comment on feelings of closeness yet separation between online life and everyday personal lives, which they regard as a methodological dilemma. As Parr has observed, debates about how the personal, face-to-face social world relates to 'virtual' social worlds are complex. In contemporary societies, twentieth-century-style boundaries of human relationships, notions of embodiment and social understandings are changing constantly and notions of what is 'true' might vary depending on situations, structures and perspectives (Parr, 2002).

Bearing this in mind, as I began my formal investigations of pregnancy and breastfeeding through exploring internet discussions, I acknowledged (and indeed hoped) that internet data might produce nuanced results that might differ from those gathered using more traditional qualitative methods (in my case, face-to-face interviews), not least because netnography would facilitate the exploring of hard-to-reach groups such as breastfeeding mothers. For example, drawing upon Lagan et al.'s (2006) research on internet use among women who are pregnant, I was aware that this group turn to the internet for support and interaction with other pregnant women due to feelings of anxiety, isolation and confusion regarding the preponderance of health and nutrition advice imposed on them. Lagan et al. (2006, p. 20) argued that, for many women, the internet offers a safe haven, a continual source of discussion and reassurance, and with the capacity to link individuals who may be geographically distant but who share, celebrate and worry about common issues. This view aligns with claims made by the commercial advice site BabyCenter, which facilitates social interaction and in-depth correspondence between mothers, who meet virtually seeking advice and support from site 'experts' and from one another. (In 2011, BabyCentre UK reported hosting 715,000 conversations, 4.3 million posts and 123,000 photo uploads; Gatrell, 2014.)

In the case of my pregnant and newly maternal respondents, I considered that narratives shared within the intimate yet otherworldly space within maternity chat rooms and discussion fora might offer wider and alternative perspectives than could have been obtained through engaging only in qualitative interviews. In all my netnographic research I have thus adopted the strategy advocated by Gustavsson (2005), understanding the virtual as inextricably linked with (rather than separate or different from) the embodied world, always treating the accounts of chat room participants as equal in validity to the accounts of research interviewees. (Such an approach accords with the findings of Whitty and Carr, 2003, who, in their study of cyber flirting, reported that netnographic research enhanced understandings of interconnections between bodies and socialization.) Like Lagan et al. (2006), Whitty and Carr regarded the internet as a safe space (so long as users remain anonymous), in which users can share anonymously their feelings yet may 'disconnect at any time' should they feel uncomfortable with certain conversations (2003, p. 880).

4.   COLLECTING AND ANALYSING NETOGRAPHIC DATA

In the next section I outline what was involved in collecting and analysing netnographic research data for the project 'Embodying Maternal Management'. Although it has changed shape and form, my interest in motherhood and work–life balance is still ongoing, and over the years I have continued to collect and work with data encompassing the experiences of pregnant women and new mothers as they negotiate the complex challenges of combining employment and motherhood. My purpose in using internet data has always been to explore cultural and social experience among pregnant women and new mothers, analysing these findings in the context of extant feminist and socio-cultural observations about motherhood, gender and work–life challenges. Below, I describe in detail two specific studies, which led to the publication of two papers, regarding first pregnancy (Gatrell, 2011) and second breastfeeding and new motherhood (Gatrell, 2019).

4.1   Pregnancy

As Eriksson and Kovalainen (2008) and Gatrell and Elliott (2008) have observed, one of the key difficulties as regards sourcing, classifying and analysing data collected from the internet is in relation to managing the extraordinary volume of information available. For my study, to try to alleviate the problem of volume I separated out, from the beginning, information about pregnancy from the data on new motherhood. To give some context, an initial search in 2006–07 on 'pregnancy and work' using Google brought up 27,300,000 references. It was apparent that I would need to be selective. I thus narrowed my exploratory searches on the experiences of employed pregnant women, focusing on sites that would enable me to reflect on the 'lives and culture of participants' (Eriksson and Kovalainen, 2008, p. 105) as well as accessing guidance offered by those individuals who were presented on these sites as 'experts' (in some instances justifiably so, in others rather more questionably so). Commercial sites designed to facilitate communication among 'interested audiences' (Eriksson and Kovalainen, 2008, p. 102) were helpful access points to chat rooms, at the same time as offering official guidance.

Box 16.1 gives an idea of which websites were studied, as well as numbering the quantity of chat room 'threads' which I accessed and classified. My chosen method of storage and analysis was paper, as I printed out chat room threads, a strategy which seemed reasonable at the time. I would be unlikely to adopt such an approach now, given the volume of material produced, the need to conserve resources, and the laboriousness of manually analysing each page. However, this method seemed appropriate at the time and it did give me the advantage of carefully reading and effectively submerging myself in the data, a feeling which in some ways replicated the sensitivity with which I prefer to deal with transcripts from face-to-face interviews. Between August 2006 and May 2007 I thus printed off information from these sites in batches. To the best of my knowledge, most sites originated within either the USA or the UK, and these two locations provided the focus of the study.

BOX 16.1: PRINCIPAL PREGNANCY WEBSITES DRAWN UPON AND DATA COLLECTION TIME FRAMES

- babycenter.com; 3 September 2006 to 4 June 2007; 359 threads analysed
- babyworld.co.uk; 23 August 2006 to 5 May 2007; 371 threads analysed
- Berkeley Parents Network; 29 August 2006 to 30 May 2007; 93 threads analysed
- familyeducation.com; 3 September 2006 to 28 May 2007; 51 threads analysed
- madmums.com; 5 September 2006 to 20 May 2007; 232 threads analysed
- mumsnet.com; 15 September 2006 to 22 May 2007; 131 threads analysed
- verybestbaby.com; 7 September 2006 to 24 May 2007; 343 threads analysed
- whattoexpect.com; 27 August 2006 to 23 May 2007; 139 threads analysed
- Yahoo! Answers; 2 September 2006 to 22 May 2007; 426 threads analysed

The sample embraced employed pregnant women (some of whom already had children) working in varying capacities and at differing grades within their organizations. My interest was in the questions posed and situations experienced in relation to work–life balance and equality among and between pregnant women in their workplaces, rather than their pay grade or level or responsibility within their roles.

To analyse the data I used a thematic analysis, observing key patterns and shared themes that appeared and were referred to in almost all chat room discussions and expert advice pieces (Cassell et al., 2005). These key patterns concerned notions of secrecy and silence: women's anxiety regarding the announcement of pregnancy or subsequent discussion about it at work, related attempts on the part of some women to conceal pregnancy, and the idea of supra-performance – the perception among employed pregnant women that they were under pressure to perform their roles at higher levels than prior to pregnancy. These key themes and patterns transcended job titles and descriptions, although women in higher-status roles sometimes had greater access to workplace flexibility and private space such as their car, or even personal office space if they needed respite from the workplace environment. Having identified these themes, I classified the data accordingly. Following the advice of Crang (1997), I then further analysed the data manually with highlighters and different coloured page markers and by cutting and pasting excerpts (literally, from hard copies, using scissors). These methods of analysis did facilitate me in achieving closeness to the data in the most material sense, handling and organizing virtual discussions into different piles and boxes as I drew out 'connections, patterns and explanations' (Crang, 1997, p. 187). Establishing order among the data in this manual way felt direct and personal – different from the experience of doing this electronically using a software analysis package, which from my perspective gives a greater sense of liminality, data being mediated via the software as opposed to being dealt with first-hand by the researcher. However, the resulting quantity of paper, sticky markers and colour codes cannot be underemphasized – our (quite large) spare room and study was rendered almost unusable, literally for years, as the growing piles of data were stored and analysed. In addition, while analysing data through the materiality of printed materials, which could be moved and marked up to represent a given classification, was an effective strategy on the basis of single-researcher usage, this would be impossible for a team to manage. Today, all my data (whatever their source) are stored, classified and analysed electronically.

Having classified the netnographic data, I then considered the emergent themes in the context of socio-cultural and feminist literatures concerning pregnant bodies, as well as policy literatures regarding maternity protection.

As noted earlier, the internet sites researched derived mainly from the UK and the USA, and it is thus British and American pregnancy policies which framed the basis for the publications which derived from the research (Gatrell, 2011, 2014). However, although the websites may have originated from the UK or the USA, writers did not necessarily offer information regarding their geographical region. Of the many pregnant employees sharing experience, some gave details about their working lives: their jobs and the kinds of organization they worked for. Others offered less information. Given that a key concern of the research was to gain a picture of women's workplace roles (that is, whether they were working at a managerial or less skilled level) I looked for signposts indicating what type of work they were doing. As noted earlier, I followed Eriksson and Kovalainen's guidance (2008, p. 106) to 'strip all identifying information' from netnographic materials. Thus, where I did have clues and details about women's working conditions and individual circumstances, I disguised or excluded any details which could have in any way identified them.

Although the process of collecting and analysing the data was slow and laborious, and the material effect of keeping it at home inconvenient, the results were rich and assisted in answering the questions to which I had sought answers following earlier qualitative interviews. In order to offer a picture of the rich data produced by this netnographic research, I summarize below my findings, which were published in the journal *Gender, Work and Organization* in 2011.

4.2 The Pregnant Body as Taboo

Netnographic conversations between pregnant workers gave a strong indication that pregnant bodies were regarded as often 'taboo' within workplace settings. Maternity protection policies offered limited assistance, and pregnancy discrimination seemed very common. Occupational status did not appear to make much difference to unfair treatment, and work–life balance among pregnant women appeared generally to be poor (although some women, usually those with greater social capital, had better access to resources which might enable gaining short respite from workplace pressures, perhaps by sitting in a car or private office space).

Some women were in higher-status roles such as law, medicine, accountancy, academia or general management. Others were in lower-paid jobs such as shop work or waitressing. Regardless of job type, the themes were the same. Correspondence among and between women showed how pregnant bodies at work may be treated as inappropriate, out of place and alien in the sense described by Tyler (2000) and Longhurst (2001). Feminist philosopher Margaret Shildrick (1997) has described how women's reproductive bodies (especially in the context of 'public' environments such as the workplace) may be regarded as socially inappropriate due to their potential to 'leak', perhaps literally (the need to visit the lavatory more frequently, the production of breast milk, and so on) and metaphorically (hormones might be imagined by co-workers in theory to threaten emotional outbursts, even if such things do not occur in practice). Hostility towards the 'leaky' pregnant body suggests hidden social assumptions that pregnant women should remain at home, rather than being welcome at work, while they are expecting. Shildrick's theory aligned with what the netnographic data revealed. The expanding, unpredictable and potentially 'leaky' pregnant body (Gatrell, 2013) was treated often by line managers and co-workers as a source of disruption and inconvenience. Pregnancy underlined women's sexual difference from male norms and posed a 'threat to social control and order' (Longhurst, 2001, p. 41).

Thus, many pregnant women interacting in chat rooms felt under pressure to erase pregnancy from workplace space. They did this using two strategies. The first was secrecy and silence, in which their pregnancy was concealed for as long as possible and not discussed at work. In keeping with research by Tyler (2000), Longhurst (2001), Gatrell (2005) and Haynes (2006), the physical manifestations of the maternal body – nausea, an expanding waistline and the threat of breaking waters and leaking breasts – were concealed. That women chose these strategies was unsurprising given that expert advice on pregnancy websites exhorted women to remain silent about their pregnancy for as long as possible and offered 'handy tips' on how they might keep hidden their expectant status. The site Babyworld indicated to readers that pregnancy, and the literal forms of 'leakage' associated with this, might be regarded by co-workers not only as symptomatic of illness and shame, but also with notions of unreliability and reduced work commitment. Women were advised to conceal as far as possible from colleagues symptoms such as nausea and vomiting, keeping their pregnancy and associated health challenges hidden where possible. The website Verybestbaby.com (2007, p. 1) suggested concealing pregnancy into the second trimester (between three and six months) before announcing this at work. The What to Expect website (whattoexpect.com, 2007, pp. 1–2) also recommended that pregnant employees might be advised to wait till the 20-week mark, assuming that they could hide pregnancy until then, in case line managers might not be family-friendly (Gatrell, 2011). If women felt tired and nauseous during pregnancy, they were advised to hide this and work through it, rather than taking a break or seeking support from co-workers by sharing this experience. 'Expert' guidance from Kilby (2007, as quoted in Gatrell, 2011, p. 169) counsels: 'What you will really need from workmates throughout your pregnancy is their continued support and understanding which might be hard if you spend half the day in the toilet [throwing up] and the other half telling people about [this].'

Women's accounts of their experience suggested that combining pregnancy with employment was, in practice, just as problematic as the expert advice had predicted. Time and again, women's posts showed how pregnant women were treated differently (and unfairly) at work once line managers and co-workers became aware of their pregnant status, with women variously being eased out of their roles, accused of low work commitment (even if there was no justification for such censure) and asked if they might prefer to remain at home once babies were born. Incidences of women being offered support and flexibility in order to manage their work–life balance were almost non-existent. In the USA and the UK, discriminatory treatment of pregnant employees is illegal and contravenes law and policy (Tahmincioglu, 2007). Nevertheless, it was apparent that women were (as they are still; EHRC, 2018) likely to experience discrimination when expecting, this leading them to hide their pregnant status for as long as they were able. Women reported being told variously that they were 's**t' at their jobs; that they 'ought' to leave and that their expanding pregnant body was distasteful (Gatrell, 2011).

The second strategy adopted by women seeking to maintain their position at work was supra-performance, in which women appeared to feel under pressure to demonstrate workplace commitment through working harder than normal and to an exemplary standard. Expert advice, anticipating the probability of discrimination, recommended that women eschew the notion of seeking work–life balance, exhorting them instead to protect their jobs by undertaking significant extra work in spite of their pregnant status. The Family Education website

(2007, p. 1) put forward the idea that employed pregnant woman should present themselves at work as always healthy and resilient, making sure to 'stay[ing] on top of [their] workload during pregnancy'. Many women were shown to remain at work regardless of ill health (sometimes relating to pregnancy, sometimes due to other causes). They continued at work while experiencing severe morning sickness, urinary tract infections and general exhaustion. Sometimes, workers who were unable to continue at work found themselves out of a job. For example, Sophie, who was hospitalized following a serious vaginal bleed at her workplace but continued working, found herself marginalized on her return to work from hospital, to the point where she felt obliged to leave, at which her line manager expressed his delight (Gatrell, 2011).

Drawing upon the volume of data available within netnographic space and my own findings in the context of socio-cultural and feminist analyses of women's work (for example, Höpfl and Hornby Atkinson, 2000), I was able to reflect upon the conceptual notion that expectant women might be treated at work as unwelcome because the pregnant body is seen by co-workers to violate cultural norms within workplace space. The use of netnography therefore facilitated me in developing the idea that cases of pregnancy discrimination were neither extreme nor rare. Pregnant women commonly experienced highly compromised work–life balance. They continued in their employment while they were unwell in order to keep their jobs and position, and many dealt with unfair treatment from line managers and co-workers by working harder or leaving. Few appeared to fight their corner, or to complain.

Lagan et al. (2006) observed how pregnant women might access websites while anxious or in need of support, and I have acknowledged within my various netnographic studies that such netnographies might produce a preponderance of anxious subjects, perhaps more so than in the general population. However, I view netnography as a qualitative method, the purpose of which is to reveal social and cultural experience, not to provide findings which apply to wider populations.

4.3 Breastfeeding and Employment

The second study, which formed the second part of the 'Embodying Maternal Management' project, concerns the experiences of new mothers, and the challenges of combining breastfeeding and work (Gatrell, 2017). The purpose of the netnographic data was to explore how employed, breastfeeding mothers balanced their commitments to breastfeeding and paid work (a concern defined as a priority for organizational research; van Amsterdam, 2015). Like pregnant women, breastfeeding employed mothers are regarded as a hard-to-access group, especially if in low-status and/or temporary employment (Turner and Norwood, 2013a, 2013b). The experiences of employed breastfeeding women are known to be under-researched because this group seek to deflect attention, often preferring to conceal their breastfeeding status so as to avoid workplace discrimination (Haynes, 2006; Gatrell, 2013; Turner and Norwood, 2013a, 2013b). As in the pregnancy research, netnography offered a possibility of capturing experiences of breastfeeding respondents who would otherwise have been difficult to reach.

The breastfeeding study was not intended to be representative, and it required an epistemology which could recognize maternal bodies as material and inhabited (Evans and Lee, 2002) given that women sought to balance and integrate the physical experience of breastfeeding with their commitment to paid work. As such, the project adopted a socio-cultural approach (Gatrell, 2017) acknowledging how breastfeeding and breast milk may be viewed differently depending upon context. That is, breastfeeding may be regarded as fundamental to maternal roles within public health narratives, but treated by co-workers as inconvenient and distasteful within workplace settings (Haynes, 2006).

As in the pregnancy study, the breastfeeding project drew upon publicly available netnographic discussion fora, in which expert advice was provided and new mothers shared with one another experiences and ideas about breastfeeding, employment and work–life balance. As previously, the data were not intended to be representative, but to reveal shared patterns and themes which would be analysed in the context of feminist and socio-cultural research on motherhood.

To source relevant conversations, I used search terms such as 'breastfeeding and policy', 'breastfeeding and work' and 'breastfeeding and employment'. Over 1,000 discussions on breastfeeding and employment, posted between 2009 and 2013, were selected, most of which were drawn from commercial or government websites designed to engage users in virtual conversations (Eriksson and Kovalainen, 2008). These include breastfeeding advice fora such as Public Health Wales, NHS England and Web MD, as well as commercial websites such as Babyworld, BabyCentre, Mumsnet and What to Expect. In keeping with the ethical commitments of the research project, I sought to ensure anonymity of participants through removing or changing details which could hint at respondent identity, also changing internet 'identifiers' in case these might be recognizable by others.

5.   ANALYSIS OF BREASTFEEDING DATA

By the time I came to analyse the data for the breastfeeding study, many new and additional papers on maternity and work, written from a socio-cultural and feminist perspective, had been published. In particular, I found helpful Marianna Fotaki's (2013) paper about women in academia. Fotaki's study recommended analysing data through what she described as 'retroductive reasoning'; that is, a form of analysis which acknowledged the complex and iterative movements between data and theory, especially regarding topics which are well known to the researcher. Retroductive reasoning offered a compromise, representing a balance between claiming either a grounded or a more deductive approach. As such, the utilization of retroductive reasoning enabled me to ascribe equal status to extant theoretical debates on breastfeeding and employment, and to newly sourced netnographic data on maternal experience. It allowed me to conduct inductively data analysis, not making presumptions about how employed mothers might experience breastfeeding, even though I was very familiar with literature in the field.

I began to analyse my data using template analysis (Cassell et al., 2005), interpreting thematically the data on breastfeeding which I had drawn from community discussion fora. As previously, I manually classified the data, and this involved the printing out of internet conversations and identification of common themes and patterns using highlighters and coloured stickers (see also Fotaki, 2013, and Kenny, 2016, each of whom adopted a similar manual approach in examining their data). Although this method was laborious, it did, as with the pregnancy study, facilitate 'closeness' with the data, enabling the identification of 'patterns' and 'connections' (Crang, 1997, p. 187).

Although the research approach was qualitative and socio-cultural (I was not trying to produce repeatable findings, nor to generalize these across wider populations), the volume of data was extensive and required careful classification. At this stage of the research project, I considered that the original thematic approach needed to be supported by a further, systematic process which would enable me to manage my qualitative data in a thorough and meticulous manner, thus ensuring that all important themes were noted and included (Corley and Gioia, 2004). Adopting the Corley and Gioia (2004) method of narrowing down categories of findings to produce a series of meta-narratives, I used my coloured stickers and markers to identify themes on hard-copy print-outs. This approach facilitated initially the articulation of eight 'first order' categories of themes which embraced, variously, the challenges of breast-feeding in accordance with health standards, mothers' experiences of combining breastfeeding and employment, and the effort required as mothers tried to comport themselves in accordance with what they perceived as appropriate embodied behaviour at work (Tyler, 2000).

The eight themes were then narrowed down into clusters (or 'second order' themes), forming three 'overarching' narratives which enabled a clear picture of the data to be provided (Corley and Gioia, 2004). These second-order themes, or overarching narratives, included specifically the labour of breastfeeding at work (as women sought to balance commitments to both employers and infant feeding), the treatment of breastfeeding workers as abject subjects (treating the 'maternal body' as 'out of place', an object of disgust within the workplace), and the maternal body work undertaken by employed breastfeeding workers trying to 'blend in' (women seeking to conceal and minimize breastfeeding requirements so as to fit in with cultural norms at work).

The three second-order themes provided the basis of iterative movements between the original source data and extant literatures on maternal bodies. Such recursive analysis enabled me to conceptualize the theoretical contribution of the research (see Gatrell, 2019).

Specifically, I developed the notion of 'abjection as practice' whereby (while policy might appear to support breastfeeding at work) breastfeeding may be seen by co-workers and line managers as a threat to workplace routines (see Kenny, 2016). The conscious preference among some co-workers to exclude the nursing body (and any 'whiff' of maternity; Cockburn, 2002, p. 185) from everyday workplace space may result in overt rejection of the lactating body (or abjection as practice) with breastfeeding treated as a 'distasteful' process more suited (for example) to the car, or to the lavatory. Under such circumstances, the work–life balance experienced by breastfeeding women can only be described as seriously deficient. The (2019) breastfeeding paper concluded by putting forward the concept of breastfeeding employees as liminal: 'boundary creatures' of uncertain position, caught between the health ideals of what constitutes 'proper' motherhood and organizational visions of the ideal worker (Phillips and Rippin, 2010), these competing narratives rendering it almost impossible for women to easily balance the requirements of breastfeeding with organizational demands.

6.   ADVANTAGES AND DISADVANTAGES OF 'DISTANT' NETNOGRAPHY

The above examples provide a description of how netnographic research informed the 'Embodying Maternal Management' study, enabling the gathering of rich data to explore work–life balance among pregnant and breastfeeding women. It was the 'right' method for me at a time when I sought to extend the range of data beyond face-to-face interviewing (my usual chosen method) and to embrace groups which might otherwise have been hard to reach. For me the approach was feasible, and at a time when I had a limited research budget it was relatively inexpensive. Advantages of using the 'distant' netnographic approach have been the opportunity to extend the reach of my research, and to understand the experiences of hard-to-contact groups such as pregnant and breastfeeding women who are trying to keep their maternal status secret, perhaps especially if working in low-status jobs. As a lone, early-career researcher, netnography offered me the chance to access a rich vein of data, in addition to my usual method of conducting face-to-face qualitative interviews, without needing a large budget or a research team. Gathering the data in this way has enabled me to publish my findings (Gatrell, 2011, 2014, 2019) and to make recommendations for policy. In conference presentations, the volume of data (although I analysed this always from a qualitative perspective) assists me in challenging the notion that the cases I quote are 'extreme', given that my netnographic research suggests discriminatory treatment and seriously deficient work–life balance to be commonly shared experiences among pregnant women and breastfeeding mothers; meaning the need for changes in both policy and attitudes is acute. As far as I know, the identity of the individuals upon whose views I have drawn has never been compromised. In these respects, the 'distant', non-participatory netnographic approach has worked well. For me, it added a new and beneficial strand to the qualitative interviews which had been previously the mainstay of my research.

CONCLUSIONS

There are, however, challenges in using 'distant' netnographic research as a qualitative method. Some of these challenges are ethical. It remains a source of some concern for me that I do not know the identity of, and have not gained permission from, those whose words I quote. While I have drawn only on open-access sites where information is available to any general reader, I cannot know whether the pregnant women and new mothers whose stories I have written about would wish to be, or would prefer not to be, involved in my research. Further, from a methodological perspective, the 'unknown' aspect of participants' situation and location is also a limitation, given that women's geographical, ethnic and cultural backgrounds are not known, and cannot therefore form any part of the analysis.

Furthermore, in relation to 'hard to reach' groups, it should be noted that even in supposedly 'developed' countries in the global north, millions of people with low incomes and limited literacy skills do not have access to the internet. Thus, individuals in insecure and poorly paid forms of employment, perhaps working in 'grey' sectors within the economy or with no access at all to paid work, may be excluded from netnographic studies such as mine, because they are prevented from using the internet (Royal Geographical Society, 2016). This omission suggests the need for future, in-depth and funded research using other methods to try and access these very-hard-to-reach groups, whose experiences are, at least in netnographic terms, hidden from view.

As observed by Gatrell and Elliott (2008), the volume of data available from the internet is itself a challenge. The choices I made as regards analysis of the netnographic data offered both an opportunity and a trial (in the sense of an ordeal!). I made the decision in 2006 to analyse my internet findings from hard copy. This process was elaborate and time-consuming, increasingly so as the volume of material I collected expanded. As noted earlier, I probably would not make such a choice again. Should I decide to undertake further netnographic studies I would probably store and analyse the data electronically. This would be essential if the project was funded and if it involved a research team, who would all require viewing and accessing the data within shared folders. It would also be more environmentally friendly than printing out vast swathes of data.

While I might not repeat the time-consuming challenge of managing hard-copy storage and analysis, there were advantages of using this method. As Kozinets (2015) observes, it is not always feasible or advisable to apply extant 'offline' research techniques to online data. At the same time, however, Kozinets notes how the intelligent adaptation of past approaches might be an appropriate decision if this enables the continuation of core research principles. In my case, as a qualitative researcher who sought closeness to my data (and with a habit of reading and re-reading, or listening to interview transcripts many times), the usage of printed copies did allow me to experience the same sense of being close to the data and the stories contained within them, even though I had never met the participants in person. Despite the volume of data, I managed to feel familiar with the narratives and themes contained within this, and as a lone researcher it was a feasible approach which produced results appropriate for scholarly publication and policy recommendations. The laboriousness of the paper approach meant that the timelines from research proposal to publication were lengthy. However, I am not sure that these timelines were any longer than might have been involved for other methods of qualitative research, which tend always to take longer than I anticipate!

The publication of the breastfeeding paper in particular required persistence and long-term determination on my part, though the end result was worth the wait as it was finally published in the journal *Organization Studies*, which is highly regarded within my discipline and which has an interest in both theory and policy. While it took some time to gain acceptance for this paper, I suspect this had more to do with the sensitivity of breastfeeding as a topic, rather than the netnographic methodology.

In all, 'distant' netnography proved a helpful approach for me, as I was able to gather rich data to help answer my research questions and raise awareness of the situation of pregnant and newly maternal women as regards work–life balance and employment. I do consider this approach could inform a wide range of research topics (relating, for example, to health, or to marketing and consumption). However, netnographic research strategies require careful thought from start to finish, as there are many directions which may be taken, and researchers need to choose the path which is right for them and their research.

REFERENCES

Cassell, C., Buehring, A., Symon, G., Johnson, P., and Bishop, V. (2005). *Qualitative Management Research: A Thematic analysis of Interviews with Stakeholders in the Field*. ESRC Report, ESRC Grant No. H33250006.
Cockburn, C. (2002). Resisting equal opportunities: the issue of maternity. In Jackson, S., and Scott, S. (eds) *Gender: A Sociological Reader*, pp. 180–191. London: Routledge.
Corley, K. G., and Gioia, D. A. (2004). Identity, ambiguity and change in the wake of a corporate spin-off. *Administrative Science Quarterly*, 49, 173–208.
Crang, M. (1997). Analysing qualitative materials. In Flowerdew, R. and Martin, D. (eds) *Methods in Human Geography*, pp. 183–196. London: Addison Wesley Longman.
EHRC (2018). Pregnancy and maternity discrimination research findings. www.equalityhumanrights.com/en/managing-pregnancy-and-maternity-workplace/pregnancy-and-maternity-discrimination-research-findings. Accessed 9 September 2019.

Eriksson, P., and Kovalainen, A. (2008). *Qualitative Methods in Business Research*. London: Sage.

Evans, M., and Lee, E. J. (2002). *Real Bodies: A Sociological Introduction*. London: Palgrave.

Family Education (2007). Working parents and pregnancy. http://life.familyeducation.com/workingparents/pregnancy/40389. Accessed 5 June 2008. No longer available online.

Fotaki, M. (2013). No woman is like a man (in academia): the masculine symbolic order and the unwanted female body. *Organization Studies*, *34*, 1251–1275.

Gatrell, A., and Elliott, S. (2008). *Geographies of Health*, 2nd edn. Oxford: Wiley-Blackwell.

Gatrell, C. (2005). *Hard Labour: The Sociology of Parenthood*. Maidenhead: Open University Press.

Gatrell C. (2011). Policy and the pregnant body at work: strategies of secrecy, silence and supra-performance, *Gender, Work and Organization*, *18*, 158–181.

Gatrell, C. (2013). Maternal body work: how women managers and professionals negotiate pregnancy and new motherhood at work. *Human Relations*, *66*, 621–644.

Gatrell, C. (2019). Boundary creatures? Employed, breastfeeding mothers and 'abjection as practice'. *Organization Studies*, *40*(3), 421–442.

Gatrell, C., Cooper, C. L., and Kossek, E. E. (2017). Maternal bodies as taboo at work: new perspectives on the marginalizing of senior-level women in organizations. *Academy of Management Perspectives*, *31*(3), 239–252.

Gatrell, C. J. (2007). Secrets and lies: breastfeeding and professional paid work. *Social Science & Medicine*, *65*, 393–404.

Gatrell, C. J. (2014). Monstrous motherhood versus magical maternity? An exploration of conflicting attitudes to maternity within health discourses and organizational settings. *Equality, Diversity and Inclusion: An International Journal*, *33*(7), 633–647.

Gustavsson, E. (2005). Virtual servants: stereotyping female front-office employees on the internet. *Gender, Work & Organization*, *12*, 400–419.

Haynes, K. (2006). Linking narrative and identity construction: using autobiography in accounting research. *Critical Perspectives on Accounting*, *17*, 399–418.

Haynes, K. (2008a). (Re)figuring accounting and maternal bodies: the gendered embodiment of accounting professionals. *Accounting, Organizations and Society*, *33*, 328–348.

Haynes, K. (2008b). Transforming identities: accounting professionals and the transition to motherhood. *Critical Perspectives on Accounting*, *19*, 620–642.

Hine, C. (2001). Web pages, authors and audiences: the meaning of a mouse click. *Information, Communication and Society*, *4*, 182–198.

Höpfl, H., and Hornby Atkinson, P. (2000). The future of women's careers. In Collin, A., and Young, R. (eds) *The Future of Career*, pp. 130–143. Cambridge: Cambridge University Press.

Kenny, K. (2016). Organizations and violence: The child as abject-boundary in Ireland's Industrial Schools. *Organization Studies*, *37*, 939-961.

Kilby, S. (2007). I'm pregnant, not mad, bad and dangerous. www.babyworld.co.uk/information/pregnancy/pregnancyandwork.asp. Accessed 5 June 2008.

Kozinets, R. V. (1998). On netnography: initial reflections on consumer research investigations of cyberculture. In Alba, J. W., and Hutchinson, J. W. (eds) *ACR North American Advances*, Volume 25, pp. 366–371. Provo: Association for Consumer Research.

Kozinets, R. V. (2015). *Netnography Redefined*. Thousand Oaks: SAGE.

Kozinets, R. V. (2017). Management netnography: axiological and methodological developments in online cultural business research. In Cassell, C., Cunliffe, A. L., and Grandy, G. (eds) *SAGE Handbook of Qualitative Business and Management Research Methods*. Thousand Oaks, SAGE.

Kozinets, R. V. (2019). Personal web page. https://annenberg.usc.edu/faculty/journalism/robert-kozinets. Accessed 31 August 2019.

Ladge, J., Clair, J., and Greenberg, D. (2012). Cross-domain identity transition during liminal periods: constructing multiple selves as 'professional and mother' during pregnancy. *Academy of Management Journal*, *55*, 1449–1471.

Lagan, B., Sinclair, M., and Kernohan, W. G. (2006). Pregnant women's use of the internet: a review of published and unpublished evidence. *Evidence Based Midwifery*, *4*, 17–23.

Longhurst, R. (2001). *Bodies: Exploring Fluid Boundaries*. London: Routledge.

Parr, H. (2002). New body-geographies: the embodied spaces of health and medical information on the internet. *Environment and Planning D: Society and Space*, *20*, 73–95.

Phillips, M., and Rippin, A. (2010). Howard and the mermaid: abjection and the Starbucks' foundation memoir. *Organization*, *17*, 481–499.

Royal Geographical Society (2016). Digital divide in the UK. http://21stcenturychallenges.org/what-is -the-digital-divide/. Accessed 20 March 2016.

Shildrick, M. (1997). *Leaky Bodies and Boundaries: Feminism, Postmodernism and (Bio) Ethics*. London: Routledge.

Stumbitz, B., Lewis, S., and Rouse, J. (2018). Maternity management in SMEs: a transdisciplinary review and research agenda. *International Journal of Management Reviews*, *20*(2), 500–522.

Tahmincioglu, E. (2007). Pregnancy discrimination is on the rise, EEOC seeing more complaints. MSNBC. www.msnbc.msn.com/id/18742634/. Accessed 29 May 2008.

Turner, P., and Norwood, K. (2013a). Unbounded motherhood: embodying a good working mother identity. *Management Communication Quarterly*, *27*, 396–424.

Turner, P., and Norwood, K. (2013b). I had the luxury …': organizational breastfeeding support as privatized privilege. *Human Relations*, *67*, 849–874.

Tyler, I. (2000). Reframing pregnant embodiment. In Ahmed, S., Kilby, J., Lury, S., McNeil, M., and Skeggs, B. (eds) *Transformations: Thinking Through Feminism*, pp. 288–301. London: Routledge.

Van Amsterdam, N. (2015). Othering the 'leaky body': an autoethnographic story about expressing breast milk in the workplace. *Culture and Organization*, *21*, 269–287.

Verybestbaby.com (2007). www.verybestbaby.com/MyPregnancy/SecondTrimester.aspx?ArticleId= 39922. Accessed 29 May 2008. No longer available online.

Warren, S., and Brewis, J. (2004). Matters over mind? Examining the experience of pregnancy. *Sociology*, *38*, 219–36.

WhattoExpect.com (2007). The What to Expect Foundation. www.whattoexpect.com/pregnancy/work -issues/politics-and-policies/when-totell-your-boss.aspx. Accessed 5 June 2008.

What to Expect (2019). Stuff people say to you when you are pregnant. https://community.whattoexpect .com/forums/october-2019-babies/topic/the-stuff-people-say-to-you-when-your-pregnant-78944673 .html. Accessed 27 August 2019.

Whitty, M. T., and Carr, A. N. (2003). Cyberspace as potential space: considering the web as a play-ground to cyberflirt. *Human Relations*, *56*, 869–891.

17. The performance of oneself through visuals in interviews: queering the work–life binary

Marjan De Coster and Patrizia Zanoni

INTRODUCTION

The scholarship on work–life balance, or 'the satisfaction of and good functioning at work and home, with a minimum role conflict' (Clark, 2000, p. 751; see also Beauregard and Henry, 2009), has traditionally assumed two ontologically distinct and separated spheres of life that can be brought to an equilibrium by a subject who pre-occupies them. Tying into earlier work that questions the binary nature of work and private life (for example, Glucksmann, 2005), and the phantasy of balance (for example, Bloom, 2016), this chapter scrutinizes the role of commonly used quantitative and qualitative research methods in the discursive reproduction of the work-versus-life binary (Bochantin and Cowan, 2016). Drawing on Judith Butler's work, we plead for a performative ontology in which the subject is considered as an outcome of its narrative performance rather than preceding it. In line with such ontology, we introduce visual methods as offering an anti-narrative space where a more 'entangled subjectivity' can be performed in interview settings. In other words, we argue that the use of visuals creates affordances for participants to 'queer the frame of legibility' – to question, deconstruct and transform the normative discourses and, in so doing, create new subject positions (see Butler, 1990; Sedgewick, 1993) – allowing them to emerge beyond their narrative inscription in the binary.

In what follows, we start with an overview of the current onto-epistemological and methodological approaches to work–life balance and interrogate the categorical subjectivities they reproduce. We then introduce Butler's performative ontology in order to denaturalize the frame that scripts the work–life binary and present visual methods as a suitable methodology to empirically investigate the coming into being of subjectivities that queer the hegemonic binary normative script. Finally, we offer two illustrations of how specific visual methods – elicitation based on objects brought by participants and elicitation based on online content – provide subjects with the opportunity to perform oneself in interview settings through anti-narratives, enabling the deconstruction of the binary framework.

1. ONTO-EPISTEMOLOGICAL APPROACHES TO WORK–LIFE BALANCE

The work–life balance literature relies on the ontological assumption of work and life as two separated domains, a strict rupture that was introduced in the industrial revolution, which divided waged work from reproductive work and private life both in time and space (Gambles et al., 2016). Studies of work–life balance often narratively start by stating that, until recently, the boundary between work and private life was maintained through a gendered division of labour, with a male breadwinner in paid work and a female care-taker carrying out unpaid work in the household. The rising participation of women in paid work since the 1970s and, to some extent, the higher participation of men in care tasks has however increasingly blurred these gendered roles. Furthermore, the increase of dual-earner and single-parent families (Minnotte, 2012; Pedersen and Minnotte, 2012), combined with the diffusion of flexible forms of work supported by new communication technologies, has rendered the boundary between these two spheres more permeable, resulting in an increased conflict between role demands stemming from work and private life (Greenhaus and Beutell, 1985).

Building on this premise, a vast body of work in work–life balance literature has sought to understand the individual consequences of persons' participation in both domains. While some scholars have examined the potential advantages of the combination of different roles, through concepts such as 'work–family enrichment' or 'role enhancement' (for example, Greenhaus and Powell, 2006; Ruderman et al., 2002), the majority have focused on the negative consequences. The relation between work and private life can be harmful in both directions: work can intrude into and disrupt private life and private life can intrude into and disrupt work (Byron, 2005). Most often, the management of conflicting time demands, the negative effect of tensions spilling over from one domain into the other, and contradictory behaviour expected in the two domains are identified as important sources of conflict (Greenhaus and Beutell, 1985). In order to understand the specific antecedents and consequences of conflict, scholars have deployed data collection methods, such as surveys, that allow them to empirically test hypotheses derived from extant theory (Bochantin and Cowan, 2016; Byron, 2005; Eby et al., 2005).

Grounded in a positivist ontology, this tradition of work–life balance literature understands subjects as gender-neutral, rational decision makers, able to manage the conflict between these interfering roles and to literally 'balance' their work and life domains. Most often, these studies investigate how subjects attempt to reduce conflict; for instance, through coping strategies (see Behson, 2002) and boundary management (for example, Ashfort et al., 2000), or by making use of one of the flexible work arrangements implemented by their employers (for example, Allen, 2001). Studies taking this perspective and conceptualizing the subject in this way are of use to management, as they provide insights into how organizations can adapt their policies to optimize the wellbeing of their employees (Beauregard and Henry, 2009).

A second substantial body of research in the domain of work–life balance has rather focused on the meaning-making process through which individuals make sense of and justify their work–life choices. Here, studies largely rely on gender and feminist theories to analyse how internalized heteronormative understandings of work, private life and the 'balanced self' operate as powerful norms in the construction of meaning, leading to individualized and gendered 'choices' with regard to work and private life (for example, Blair-Loy, 2001; Smithson and Stokoe, 2005; Toffoletti and Starr, 2016). Importantly, this body of work argues that the internalization of gendered norms and the discourse of individual choice entail that penalties in the work domain (for instance, being denied career opportunities) or in the private life (for instance, spending little time with children and family) are understood by individuals as consequences of their own decisions, obscuring the power of underlying structural mechanisms (Dick and Hyde, 2006). In this way, gendered norms about work–life are reproduced. Grounded in a non-positivistic, constructivist ontology, this research calls for methods that can capture narratives in the field to inductively understand how social reality is constructed through language. Whereas positivistic, quantitative studies shed light on *why* or *when* conflict may or may not emerge for gender-neutral individuals, interpretivist, qualitative ones show *how* gendered individuals give gendered meanings to such conflict (Bochantin and Cowan, 2016).

The interpretivist body of work in work–life balance literature contests the notion of subjects as rational decision makers and instead conceptualizes it as one that (unconsciously) acts upon gendered norms that give meaning to the self and the situation, resulting in different professional and life choices by men and women. Here, the subject is recognized as gendered because of the heteronormativity of the discourses guiding her/his choices. The recognition of the power of social norms underlying subjects' decisions is important to understand how 'imbalance' is not a personal failure of a rational decision maker who has made the 'wrong' choices, but rather, the consequence of irreconcilable discourses the subject engages with (De Coster and Zanoni, 2018).

While the positivist and the interpretivist approaches have each yielded rich insight, both traditions tend to represent social reality as a trade-off between work and private life. Positivist accounts stress the characteristics of work versus private life as antecedents to work–life conflict, whereas interpretivist accounts put emphasis on competing discourses, identities and ethics of professionalism and parenthood. Some scholars have, however, questioned the categorical separation between work and 'non-work' and emphasized that they are more 'entangled, embedded and differentiated with regard to the various socio-economic relations and spaces in which an activity takes place' (Strauss and Fleischman, 2019, p. 2; see also Glucksmann, 2005). This entanglement is fostered by technological developments, such as IT and the internet, as well as by the surge of 'flexible' work carried out outside traditional employment relations by project workers, portfolio workers, freelancers and the like (Cappelli and Keller, 2013; Kalleberg, 2000). In the 'social factory' (Tronti, 1966) – where work no longer occurs within the walls of the factory and according to the factory clock – the question arises about whether work and life are still strictly separated and whether they can be balanced at all (for example, Bloom, 2016). Relatedly, the definition of 'work' itself has become the object of an intense debate, one that emphasizes the structural interdependencies between wage work and reproductive work on the one hand (Bhattacharya, 2017; Federici, 2012) and that points to the renewed blurring of work and non-work (Peticca-Harris et al., 2018; Vidaillet and Bousalham, 2018) beyond processes of mere spatio-temporal flexibilization of waged work (Pettinger et al., 2006).

Although the current literature on work–life balance has, to some extent, considered the evolution in the way we work/live, we argue that our methodological approaches have not followed. Neither surveys nor interviews adequately grasp deeply entangled contemporary subjectivities. Because both are grounded in a social reality that is binarily conceived along work–life, they force subjects to inscribe themselves within it. Surveys largely rely on closed questions, while interviews collect narratives allowing the subject to provide more nuance. Nevertheless, as both data-generation methods rely on language, they force participants to 'tell' and 'perform' themselves within the shared binary script. Doing so, subjects inevitably reproduce the binary from which they depart, in an interminable vicious circle. This additionally feeds the illusion of an individually achievable balance; a desire produced, under capitalism, to regulate its imbalanced subjects (Bloom, 2016).

2.   TOWARDS A PERFORMATIVE ONTOLOGY OF WORK–LIFE

2.1   Performing the Subject through the Normative Framework of Intelligibility

In this contribution, we advance an approach to the 'work–life' subject that draws on the work of Judith Butler. Adopting a radically non-essentialist stance, Butler argues that the subject does not precede social norms, which it subsequently internalizes and enacts, but rather comes into being through the performance of such norms (Butler, 1990, 1997). The subject is inherently social, as it emerges by 'giving an account' of itself in the relation with others, who hold it accountable for its actions (Butler, 2005). Responding to the other in the scene of address, the subject will try to constitute itself as ethical and responsible through performance along a 'regime of truth' (Foucault, 1982). It is by narrating itself coherently along a predefined normative script imposed in the relation that the subject becomes readable to its audience and hence 'becomes'.

Butler's emphasis on 'subjective existence as the outcome, rather than the basis, of a process of social recognition' (Riach et al., 2016, p. 2072) is at the core of her performative ontology. The subject does not precede language – like envisioned in the interpretivist paradigm – as it does not author the script it needs to narrate, but instead constitutes itself through the narration of a script that was already written. It is only by performing the self within the framework of intelligibility, by chronologically narrating the words that were already written down, that she can give an account and thus become subject (Butler, 1990). This performative ontology allows us to recognize not only our own binary assumptions – for instance, man or woman – about the subject, but also the limits within which the subjects can become. The language we speak constitutes the symbolic framework through which we can give an account and become intelligible to ourselves and others, imposing a first severe limit on whom or how we can become. The subject is inherently vulnerable, because of this unavoidable dependency on sociality and the field of power prescribing the script through which it can 'become', and because its performance always occurs in the scene of address in the relation of accountability with an 'Other', a social audience who might misrecognize the subject (Butler, 1990, 1997, 2005; see also Roberts, 2005, 2009). Like an audience watching a play, others will only be able to read our performance, to recognize it as a 'worthy performance', when the right words are spoken, when the script is followed in the interaction with others (Butler, 1997). Driven by the desire to be recognized, we repetitively perform ourselves in coherence with the scripts at hand. Any subject is thus essentially 'opaque' towards itself, as it can never fully grasp the script it needs to perform to make itself readable in the relation, yet it needs to speak the language it prescribes in order to become. This means that the subject produces itself in coherence with the framework and always 'at the cost of its own complexity' (Butler, 1993, p. 115). A deviant performance entails taboo, the possibility of being mocked or, worse, violated, and can even result in the misrecognition of one's very humanity.

Butler's theorization of the performativity of the subject is best known for her understanding of gender as prescribed by the heterosexual matrix and normatively performed in social interaction, constituting the gendered subject. The drag queen is exemplary of a performance that deviates from the normative scripts and of the misrecognition of one's humanity (Butler, 1990, 1993). Indeed, the performance of the drag is often thought of as a parody, not to be taken as a serious performance. To avoid such misrecognition, the subject keeps performing itself along the heterosexual matrix, thereby constituting itself as gendered and reproducing the binary. Emphasizing the key role of language and more specifically opposed binaries in the production of subjectivities, Butler's performative ontology provides a theoretical lens that helps unveil the discursive limits of the onto-epistemological and methodological approaches of current work–life balance research.

2.2   Queering the Framework Through Which We Become Subject

The social is, however, according to Butler, not a stable reality, as 'any hegemonic position is always exposed to the risk of being subverted' (Butler et al., 1997, p. 3). The field of power can only be subverted if the framework at the basis of our becoming is denaturalized (see also Mumby et al., 2017). To do so, we have to recognize our vulnerability, our dispossession from ourselves and dependency, in the relation with others, to constitute ourselves through a language we have not written ourselves (see also Butler and Athanasiou, 2013; Butler et al., 2016). In other words, we need to become aware of the struggle to narrate ourselves in coherence with a script that we have not authored ourselves and hence to perform ourselves at the cost of our own complexity (Butler, 1993; see also Riach et al., 2016). Only if we do so can the taken-for-grantedness of our performances and the frames of intelligibility prescribing it be scrutinized, allowing for the constitution of new, legible subject positions.

In her early work on queer theory, Butler (1990, 2004) explains how by narrating our gender differently we can take a transformative position on the heterosexual matrix that predefines masculinity and femininity, and perform our gender differently. By 'queering' the gender binary, we can unveil its constructed nature, denaturalize it and create new meanings of gender resulting in the constitution of more subject positions. Queering thus entails the opportunity of resistance, the broadening of the conditions through which we can become and constitute ourselves differently. Organization scholars have drawn on this theory to understand gender performativity and its subversion in organizations (for example, Pullen et al., 2016; Tyler and Cohen, 2008), but also, more broadly, to understand how we can 'queer' other normative frameworks (for example, Gibson-Graham, 1996; Parker, 2002; Rumens et al., 2018).

Scholars taking a performative ontological stance have maintained in a similar vein that, in our research approach, we need to think self-reflectively about the subject positions at hand and the limits they impose on participants to perform themselves (differently) in research settings (Riach et al., 2016; Wray-Bliss, 2003). This is particularly relevant in interview settings, where the interviewer and the interviewee are mutually vulnerable in their relation. They both rely on language as a tool to narrate themselves in a readable way towards each other. Yet this language is already scripted beforehand and entails a 'particular version of reality' that 'achieves authority as a consequence of the power relationship that characterizes the interaction' (Dick, 2013, p. 647), trapping us into it. In other words, as the interviewer and interviewee depend on each other's recognition to become, they are both caught in the frame of legibility to make sense of themselves and the other, and are thus performing the script at hand to be recognized as viable human beings.

Building on these insights, we argue that the methodologies of data-creation commonly used in the positivist and interpretative traditions of research on work–life balance inevitably *perform* binarily inscribed subjects they claim to investigate, as they rely on the language – in survey items and interview questionnaires – that constitutes it along the work–life binary in sociality. Narratives are not 'just telling stories' about ourselves, but an active 'giving of an account', a performance through which the subject constitutes an ethical self by means of the language that is already out there, that precedes its existence in order to be recognized as a responsible and viable human being (Butler, 2005). Taking a performative onto-epistemological stance, we therefore advocate the use of visual methods as a way to constitute an 'anti-narrative space' where the 'cracks' between our own complexity and our narrative inscription in the frames of intelligibility emerge. This way, in the anti-narrative space, performances of the subject are afforded that queer the binary work–life framework.

2.3   Queering the Work–Life Binary Through Visual Methods

While scholars in anthropology and sociology have long drawn on visual research methods – a range of research methods drawing on visual materials to make an interpretative account of respondents' complex realities (Rose, 2001) – their use in organization studies remains to date scant. It is only in the last decade that interest in visual materials to approach the field has risen (Davison et al., 2012). This is surprising, considered the ubiquity of visuals in contemporary society and the specificity of the symbols and the codes that characterize them (Rose, 2001; Spencer, 2011). In this era of ocularcentrism, social reality should no longer be conceived only in terms of structures – as in a positivist research – or of meaningful language – as in an interpretivist research. Rather, we should acknowledge the key role visuals play in shaping our understandings of the world. Embracing the 'visual turn', we should address the role of visuals in the way we constitute ourselves and the reality surrounding us, and adopt new research methods to capture this role (Bell and Davison, 2013). We need to move towards an epistemology and methodologies which recognize that visuals are not transparent or neutral but, similar to language, constitutive of our social reality (Rose, 2001). Visuals can help us to grasp better how subjects give meaning to themselves and the environment they are embedded in (Bell and Davison, 2013).

Broadly speaking, visuals can be used for data generation in two distinct ways. One option is to use visuals to stimulate a conversation in the interview setting (Bell and Davison, 2013), as a form of 'visual elicitation'. The visuals – for instance, objects, photos, network drawings, and so on – can be introduced by the researcher in order to elicit particular interests or feelings, but most often participants are asked to bring or create something (Bell and Davison, 2013). Another option is to use visuals as a data source themselves, on which a content analysis is conducted; for instance, an online analysis of image branding or organizations' use of social media.

Particularly when introduced as elicitation, we argue that the use of visuals allows participants to think otherwise, reflectively and more holistically about the topic of interest and bring their own meanings and associations in a more expressive way (Bagnoli, 2009). Asking them to bring objects, make drawings, take photos and similar not only broadens the codes through which participants can perform themselves beyond the narratives they know (Gauntlett, 2007), it also suspends their narrative inscription in the frames of legibility. In this 'delay' an anti-narrative space is opened up, where the subject can critically reflect on its appearance and emerge in all its complexity, whereas an interview guide or questionnaire instantly forces the subject to produce a simplified narrative coherent to the frames offered through it (Riach et al., 2016). It is only when participants are asked about the meaning of the visuals introduced that they are required to give an account, to inscribe themselves in the frames of legibility they know. In order to prevent conversations from relapsing in linear narratives in this phase of inscription, participants should be encouraged to jump back and forth between the complexity in the anti-narrative visual and their narrative inscription. More precisely, this means asking them to 'articulate disruptions, tensions and negotiations within their narratives, considering the work involved in maintaining apparent coherence and in conforming to the norms' (Riach et al., 2016, p. 2079). Doing so, the cracks and connections between both will emerge, allowing for a reflection on the different layers that are constitutive of themselves and the denaturalization of the frames they know, thereby giving rise to a more complex understanding of their coming into being.

Visuals have hardly been used to study work–life balance. A study by Cassell et al. (2016) used photograph-eliciting to investigate the 'balance' between work and private life. However, their use of visuals was still largely premised on a division between work and private life, instructing respondents, for instance, as follows: 'over the next two weeks please take some photographs that illustrate your daily experiences of work–life conflict or work–life balance' (p. 162) and 'the interview continued with further questions probing for in-depth and detailed information about their work–life balance and conflict experiences' (p. 151). The instructions are formulated in such a way that the visuals generated are from the beginning inscribed in the linguistic categories of work and life, rather than to interrogate them. This use thus renounces the potential of creative research to allow for a new form of performativity beyond the code of language that 'avoid[s] clichés and "readymade" answers which could easily be replied' (Bagnoli, 2009, p. 566).

In what follows we reflect on the use of visuals in our own research practice to study 'work–life'. Based on two empirical cases, we show how they have helped us queer the work–life binary in interview settings, allowing subjects to perform themselves in novel, more 'entangled' ways.

2.4   Illustration 1: The Emergence of Complex Subjectivities Through Objects

In one of our studies on precarious workers, we used visual elicitation in interviews with project workers. The study investigated the case of a cooperative that sought to reduce project workers' precarious conditions of work and life. Members of the cooperative were invited to participate in the study, which aimed at better understanding how they manage their work (relations) and how the cooperative helps them to do so. Work–life balance was not explicitly mentioned in this initial communication, but was part of the study as the extant literature on project workers emphasizes the challenges they encounter in balancing work and life.

Fifteen project workers – seven men and eight women – agreed to be interviewed. About half of the respondents lived together with their partner and children, while the other half were relatively young (in their mid-twenties and early thirties), lived alone or with their partner and did not have children. A few days before the interview, which was conducted by the first author, participants received an email with the following instructions: 'Can you please bring a few objects (maximum three) that represent or describe you? This can be something that you have created yourself (for instance a drawing, collage, photo …) or an object that is very important to you.' By sending this email a few days in advance, we provided research participants with time to thoroughly think about which artefacts they could bring, stimulating them to reflect on themselves. Additionally, as the instructions were formulated in a very general sense, with no reference to the topic of interest, research participants were able to bring something that they themselves found important to share. Upon arrival, the interviewer made respondents feel comfortable by introducing herself and engaging in some small talk to break the ice. Once participants seemed to feel at ease, they were asked to introduce the objects they brought with them.

As an example of our use of visual elicitation, we reflect on the interview with Kate (pseudonym), a 32-year-old art director and scenographer who, at the time of the interview, lived together with her partner and dog in a rented apartment.

When I ask Kate about the objects she brought, she first refers to the clothes she is wearing and then brings me[1] to the truck she recently bought.

Figure 17.1   Kate's truck

Before inscribing herself narratively in the framework of intelligibility – before she is even asked to produce meaning about work and life through the language available to us – Kate performs herself only through her clothes and her truck, the objects she has chosen to represent her and by which she hopes to make herself 'visually readable' to the interviewer.

Kate is dressed in an almost 'masculine' way, wearing some sort of overall and working boots. Through her outfit, I 'read' her as some kind of handy(wo)man, whose comfortable work outfit suits the idea that work might occur at any moment throughout the day. Furthermore, I 'read' her visual performance through the truck as the constitution of herself in three words: *tough* ('driving a truck like that is so kick-ass!'), *nomadic* ('she must be always on the road') and *handy* ('she probably knows a lot of mechanic maintenance'). Additionally, looking at the outdated, almost 'vintage' character of the truck, I 'read' her as someone who does not have sufficient money to buy a more recent model and probably also prefers an older model because a 'retro' look – certainly taking note of the old mint-green paint – fits her more.

Through these objects, she initially visually performs herself without inscribing herself in the work–life binary framework. She appears more as a whole subject, someone for whom different aspects in life are highly entangled and meaningful to the constitution of herself as a whole rather than giving distinct meaning to her. In this sense, Kate queers the work–life binary as the objects she brought deconstruct the strict division between them, allowing her to perform herself differently. Only when asked about the meaning of the visuals were participants required to perform themselves along the work–life binary in order to make themselves readable in the relation with the interviewer. For instance, when Kate was asked about the meaning of her truck, she responded:

> That's because … it is very difficult to find affordable work space and, also, a bit this idea of … working while travelling.

Here, Kate uses the binary language she knows to make herself readable, a language that pushes her to name the distinction between work and private life. Yet, as the question is formulated in a general sense, Kate does not perform herself in complete coherence with the normative binary of work–life balance. Rather, she constitutes a unitary self for whom work and life are congruent and spatio-temporally overlapping.

Kate was in the remainder of the conversation repeatedly encouraged to move back and forth between object, narrative and the frameworks she has to comply with, a technique that helps illuminate the cracks between the different layers in the constitution of herself (Riach et al., 2016). Throughout this process, the truck functioned as a thread to emphasize the tensions and struggles when trying to comply with the normative frameworks at hand in different relations of accountability. Indeed, rather than making a sharp distinction between work and private life or trying to balance them, Kate narrated different relations in the field, 'a complex space of accountability', holding her accountable against different norms. For instance, respectively narrating the meaning of her outfit and the truck, she argued:

> just because you never know what the day will bring or when it will end. And most often … yes, you are always working.
> We [art directors and scenographers] are often on the road for a long period of time, I mean from very early in the morning until late at night. It seems nice that when you're recording somewhere a few days in a row, that you can stay there.

In these accounts, Kate does not perform a self that seeks to balance her work and private life. Rather, when reflecting on the meaning of her visual performance, she emerges as an entangled subjectivity for whom there is no separation – 'you are always working' – let alone balance, but instead is flexible in overlapping relations of accountability. Her clothes as well as the truck here refer to her relation with her clients towards whom she performs herself in a very flexible way, in order to be recognized as a credible and responsible professional art director in this relation. Further stressing the requirement of performing a flexible self in order to obtain future projects, she adds:

> You don't really have a choice, you really need something like this [truck] (…) Actually, you get the most bookings when you invest a lot. The more autonomous you can work, the better.

By making Kate jump back and forth between the visual performance of her objects and her narrative, she queers the work–life binary constituting a subjectivity that transgresses it.

Her awareness of this transgression was expressed in the uneasiness she felt with the gendered and age-related expectations along this binary. She explained:

I've reached an age … [Kate is 32 at the time of the interview] and that's also very ironic, that I *have* to make certain decisions, and that's also about buying houses and hmm (…) It's also a lifestyle. It's also like … I think that's also the reason why I'm doing what I do. I can … this idea of settling down … I've been panicking about it and now it seems … now it seems OK to me, I seem to find my peace with this idea but still … still it seems an absurd idea … But it's also a bit about building in some certainties in life, to invest your money instead of muddling on.

Throughout this account, the struggle of constituting herself along the normative framework describing the gendered division of work and life surfaces in the constant contradictions, on the one hand paying a narrative tribute to the normative 'necessity' to settle down, while on the other hand dismissing it as absurd, unthinkable. She queers the gendered norm imposing her to invest in a 'proper' private sphere – a house – through the highly significant purchase of a truck, symbolizing a nomadic (male) life. Kate thus constitutes herself as ethical in the space of accountability by queering the gendered work–life balance norms imposed upon her in the space of accountability. Her outfit and truck help her inscribe herself at once in the (feminine) domestic life and the (male) flexible life and, so doing, where she performs an 'entangled subjectivity' with regard to the gendered division of work and private life.

2.5   Illustration 2: The Online Performance of Complex Subjectivities

Visuals were also key in two studies, co-supervised by the authors, conducted by two master's students as part of their theses on the work–life balance of social media influencers. The students contacted influencers for whom influencing was the core professional activity. Most of them had, however, side jobs to make ends meet. In total, nine women aged between 23 and 30 and one man aged 46 agreed to participate in the research. Half of them were married and three of them had children.

Visuals are an undeniably important part of the work and in the self-constitution of influencers. It is by continuously and massively sharing visual content about themselves online that they perform themselves properly as influencers. As organizations pay them for 'the right picture' (Abidin, 2016), in this work the self that is performed online is not 'just an image', but a thoroughly considered visual performance to advertise particular products. The visually performed self thus becomes a commodity. Taking note of the central position of this online performance in influencers' lives, an in-depth content analysis of participants' online visual material was carried out in a first stage of the research process, before meeting the influencers. This material was further used to elicit conversations with them during the interviews.

Consider below the online visual constitution of Sarah (pseudonym), a 22-year-old professional influencer in the field of beauty, fashion and lifestyle, through her Instagram pictures.

To her online audience, Sarah performs herself visually through these, and many other similar, images. By this online visual performance beyond the narrative, before giving meaning to it, Sarah constitutes herself in a particular way.

When taking a look at Sarah's Instagram profile she becomes 'readable' to me as someone who is very social ('a lot of friends run through her pictures, she must be hanging out with them all the time'), outgoing ('seems as if she has a lot of leisure time to do fun stuff') and overall 'life enjoying' ('having drinks and food with friends and family, taking time to relax, petting the dog'). To me, she presents herself through these images as almost having the perfect life in which she is surrounded by warmth, laughter and fun.

Figure 17.2   Sarah's Instagram profile

Through her visual performance, Sarah makes herself readable to me as a care-taking subject, as someone who has a lot of time to take care of friends, family and pets, thereby re-affirming an ideal image of femininity in the private sphere.

Although all Sarah's online performances take place in a non-work sphere – adding to an understanding of her as having a lot of free time – these are in fact staged to sell them as a gendered ideal to those companies that hope to advertise 'beauty, fashion and lifestyle' products. Her visual performance thus operates on two levels, reproducing the gendered division of work and private life in the relation with her audience, while simultaneously constituting a professional self by performing herself as a reliable influencer in the relation to her clients. In this sense, her visual performance does not reveal a strict separation between her professional versus her private self – even though she portrays it in such a way to her audience – but rather allows to constitute herself through an overlap between both. Doing so, from these images an entangled subjectivity emerges by which she queers the gendered division between work and private life.

During the interviews, the influencers were asked to narrate themselves and, doing so, were required to inscribe themselves into the normative frameworks at hand in order to make themselves readable and recognized in the relation with the interviewer. When asked about how they perform themselves through their visuals, influencers constituted themselves as entangled, whole selves, for whom work and private life are overlapping. For instance, Sarah explained:

> I work with projects that I like, that interest me. It's important. It's also what makes it fun to do. (…) What I often get is that, for instance, McDonald's or Quick ask me something. I mean … I don't have a problem with that, but then I'll respond "No, I won't do it." Just because I don't think this [brand] suits me, I don't want to present myself like that.

In her account, Sarah does not make a distinction between an 'online professional self' and an 'offline personal self'. Instead, she queers the work–life binary by constituting an entangled self in her online posts in which she performs an 'authentic', if commodified, self.

In the continuation of their conversation, the students repeatedly asked Sarah and other influencers about the visuals posted online in order to prevent the conversation from relapsing in a linear story in which influencers constituted themselves in coherence with the binary framework. The moving between their anti-narrative visual performance and the narrative inscription in the frames of intelligibility allowed them to reflect on the cracks and connections between their complex selves and the coherent story of themselves along the normative frames. Like in Kate's case, jumping back and forth reveals how Sarah does not constitute herself along a work–life binary but rather through different relations of accountability holding her accountable along different normative frameworks and expecting different behaviour from her. She said:

> Nowadays, people are expecting so much of me. Because … I have three sides, I have my followers who expect that I do certain things and don't do other things. I have my clients, those who pay me, like brands who also expect me to do certain things. And then I also have, for instance, my boyfriend … he does not really expect something from me … But I also want to spend time with him.

The struggle to constitute herself as a coherent legible subject in this space of accountability surfaces throughout her account, as the demands imposed upon her in different relations of accountability often conflict with one another. She expressed this conflict by adding: 'it drives me crazy'.

Additionally, Sarah's narration of the visual material reveals how she is often tossed and turned to perform herself along a binary. She recounted how the burden to 'do the right thing' along the binary of influencer (work) versus partner (private) can become too high, resulting in a conflicted self. She explains:

> My current boyfriend handles it very well, he is very positive about it, so that's really nice. But my previous boyfriend found it difficult, which I understand. Because … When we were on holiday I wanted to take photos all the time. Yes of course, I wanted to enjoy the trip, but I also wanted to have a lot of photos and a lot of content, that is what I like so much about it (…) That's one of the reasons that we grew apart.

On her Instagram account, Sarah indeed includes visual performances of herself on holiday while advertising particular products, thereby revealing again her entangled coming into being rather than a coherent story along the work–life binary. However, the explanation of this type of photos at once emphasizes the cracks and difficulties in constituting an ethical self through the binary work–life frameworks at hand: while on holiday her boyfriend expects her to make time for their relationship; she simultaneously feels the demand to share good content with her followers and clients. The impossibility to reconcile the two cost her the relationship in the end. Trying to cope with the struggles emerging from the impossibility to constitute herself as ethical in this particular space of accountability, she queers the norms along which she feels required to be 'the perfect girlfriend', by starting a new relation with someone who – as she stressed – does not complain about her performing herself as an influencer. Doing so, she is able to simultaneously give an account in the relation towards her boyfriend, and in the relation towards clients and followers, thereby constituting an entangled subjectivity that is responsible in the space of accountability.

CONCLUSION

Drawing on the work of Judith Butler, this chapter tied into earlier work that has scrutinized the ontological presumption of work and private life as two strictly separated spheres of life in need to be balanced (for example, Glucksmann, 2005). We argued that the dominance of surveys and interviews in organization studies reproduces this binary, as they rely on participants' inscription in the predefined frames of legibility, a normative script they do not author themselves yet need to be performed in order to make themselves readable (see also Butler, 1988).

As an alternative, our chapter advocates the use of visual research methods to provide participants with an anti-narrative space in which the subject can emerge in its complexity, beyond the binary between work and life. Resting on a performative ontology – which posits that the subject does not pre-exist language but is rather performed (Butler, 1997, 2004; for example, see Butler, 2005; see also Riach et al., 2016) – we show how, through visuals, participants queer the work–life binary by performing an 'entangled subjectivity'. Jumping back and forth between visuals and narrative exposes the cracks between the complexity of the self and the imposed binary framework, inviting them to denaturalize it.

A further analysis of the jumping between visual and narrative performances additionally reveals how the conflict experienced by participants is not a conflict *between* different predefined (gendered) roles in work and private life (Blair-Loy, 2001; Smithson and Stokoe, 2005; Toffoletti and Starr, 2016). Instead, it reflects an ontological struggle in constituting an ethical self through multiple relations of accountability *across* work and private life. In this struggle, they do not simply abide by the (hetero)normative norms imposed on them, but rather attempt to re-negotiate them (see also De Coster and Zanoni, 2018).

Finally, the chapter talks back to scholars that use visual materials in their qualitative studies. They have advocated for the use of visuals to complement participants' stories, as it allows participants to think differently about a particular topic and/or bring their own associations and meanings to the story (Bagnoli, 2009; Gauntlett, 2007). We rather suggest that visuals are most useful when they are deployed to reveal tensions, contradictions and struggles in participants' stories. Our illustrations suggest that it is precisely in the cracks between anti-narrative and narrative that the visuals add to the analysis. Unmasking inconsistencies helps to account for the ontological struggles of the subject seeking to constitute itself at the 'cost of its own complexity' in the relation to others. It is in these cracks that the normative nature of the frames of legibility we ourselves impose on participants through common qualitative and quantitative methods become visible.

NOTE

1.   Marjan De Coster.

REFERENCES

Abidin, C. (2016), '"Aren't these just young, rich women doing vain things online?": influencer selfies as subversive frivolity', *Social Media + Society*, **2**(2), https://doi.org/10.1177/2056305116641342.
Allen, T. (2001), 'Family-supportive work environments: the role of organizational perceptions', *Journal of Vocational Behavior*, **58**, 414–35.
Ashfort, B., Kreiner, G., and Fugate, M. (2000), 'All in a day's work: boundaries and micro role transitions', *Academy of Management Review*, **25**(3), 472–91.
Bagnoli, A. (2009), 'Beyond the standard interview: the use of graphic elicitation and arts-based methods', *Qualitative Research*, **9**(5), 547–70.
Beauregard, T., and Henry, L. (2009), 'Making the link between work-life balance practices and organizational performance', *Human Resource Management Review*, **19**, 9–22.
Behson, S. (2002), 'Coping with family-to-work conflict: the role of informal accommodations to family', *Journal of Occupational Health Psychology*, **7**(4), 324–41.
Bell, E., and Davison, J. (2013), 'Visual management studies: empirical and theoretical approaches', *International Journal of Management Reviews*, **15**, 167–84, https://doi.org/10.1111/j.1468-2370.2012.00342.x.
Bhattacharya, T. (2017), *Social Reproduction Theory: Remapping Class, Recentering Oppression*. London, Pluto Press.
Blair-Loy, M. (2001), 'Cultural constructions of family schemas: the case of women finance executives', *Gender and Society*, **15**(5), 687–709.
Bloom, P. (2016), 'Work as the contemporary limit of life: capitalism, the death drive and the lethal fantasy of "work-life balance"', *Organization*, **23**(4), 588–606, https://doi.org/10.1177/1350508415596604.
Bochantin, J., and Cowan, R. (2016), 'Focusing on emotion and work-family conflict research: an exploration through the paradigms', *Journal of Management Inquiry*, **25**(4), 367–81, https://doi.org/10.1177/1056492616642330.
Butler, J. (1988). 'Performative acts and gender constitution: an essay in phenomenology and feminist theory', *Theatre Journal*, **40**(4), 591–31.
Butler, J. (1990), *Gender Trouble*. London, Routledge.
Butler, J. (1993), *Bodies that Matter: On the Discursive Limits of 'Sex'*. London, Routledge.
Butler, J. (1997), *The Psychic Life of Power: Theories in Subjection*. Stanford, CA, Stanford University Press.
Butler, J. (2004), *Undoing Gender*. London, Routledge.
Butler, J. (2005), *Giving an Account of Oneself*. New York, NY, Fordham University Press.
Butler, J., and Athanasiou, A. (2013), *Dispossession: The Performative in the Political*. Cambridge, MA, Polity Press.
Butler, J., Gambetti, Z., and Sabsay, L. (eds) (2016), *Vulnerability in Resistance*. Durham, Duke University Press.
Butler, J., Laclau, E., and Laddaga, R. (1997), 'The uses of equality', *Diacritics*, **27**(1), 2–12.
Byron, K. (2005), 'A meta-analytic review of work–family conflict and its antecedents', *Journal of Vocational Behavior*, **67**(2), 169–98, https://doi.org/10.1016/j.jvb.2004.08.009.

Cappelli, P., and Keller, J. R. (2013), 'Classifying work in the new economy', *Academy of Management Review*, **38**(4), 575–96.

Cassell, C., Malik, F., and Radcliffe, L. (2016), 'Using photo-elicitation to understand experiences of work-life balance'. In K. Townsend, R. Loudoun and D. Lewin (eds), *Handbook of Qualitative Research Methods on Human Resource Management: Innovative Techniques*. Cheltenham, UK and Northampton, MA, USA, Edward Elgar Publishing, pp. 146–61.

Clark, S. C. (2000), 'Work-family border theory: a new theory of work-family balance', *Human Relations*, **53**(6), 747–70.

Davison, J., Maclean, C., and Warren, S. (2012), 'Exploring the visual in organizations and management', *Qualitative Research in Organizations and Management: An International Journal*, **7**(1), 5–15.

De Coster, M., and Zanoni, P. (2018), 'Governing through accountability: gendered moral selves and the (im)possibilities of resistance in the neoliberal university', *Gender, Work and Organization*, 1–19, https://doi.org/10.1111/gwao.12304.

Dick, P. (2013), 'The politics of experience: a discursive psychology approach to understanding different accounts of sexism in the workplace', *Human Relations*, **66**(5), 645–69, https://doi.org/10.1177/0018726712469541.

Dick, P., and R. Hyde (2006), 'Line manager involvement in work-life balance and career development: can't manage, won't manage?', *British Journal of Guidance & Counselling*, **34**(3), 345–64, https://doi.org/10.1080/03069880600769480.

Eby, L., Casper, W., Lockwoord, A., Bordeaux, C., and A. Brinley (2005), 'Work and family research in IO/OB: content analysis and review of the literature (1980–2002)', *Journal of Vocational Behavior*, **66**, 124–97.

Federici, S. (2012), *Revolution at Point Zero: Housework, Reproduction and Feminist Struggle*. Oakland, CA, PM Press.

Foucault, M. (1982), 'Afterword: the subject and power'. In H. Dreyfus and P. Rabinow (eds), *Michel Foucault: Beyond Structuralism and Hermeneutics*. Chicago, IL, University of Chicago Press, pp. 208–26.

Gambles, R., Lewis, S., and Rapoport, R. (2016), *The Myth of Work-Life Balance: The Challenges of Our Time for Men, Women and Societies*. Chichester, John Wiley & Sons.

Gauntlett, D. (2007), *Creative Explorations: New Approaches to Identities and Audiences*. New York, NY, Routledge.

Gibson-Graham, J. K. (1996), 'Queer(y)ing the capitalist organization', *Organization*, **3**(4), 541–45.

Glucksmann, M. (2005), 'Shifting boundaries and interconnections: extending the "total social organisation of labour"', *Sociological Review*, **53**(2suppl), 19–36.

Greenhaus, J., and Beutell, N. (1985), 'Sources of conflict between work and family roles', *Academy of Management*, **10**(1), 67–88.

Greenhaus, J., and Powell, G. (2006), 'When work and family are allies: a theory of work-family enrichment', *Academy of Management Review*, **32**, 71–92.

Kalleberg, A. J. (2000), 'Nonstandard relations: part-time, temporary and contract work', *Annual Review of Sociology*, **26**(1), 341–65.

Minnotte, K. L. (2012), 'Family structure, gender, and the work-family interface: work-to-family conflict among single and partnered parents', *Journal of Family and Economic Issues*, **33**, 95–107, https://doi.org/10.1007/s10834-011-9261-4.

Mumby, D. K., Thomas, R., Martí, I., and Seidl, D. (2017), 'Resistance redux', *Organization Studies*, **38**(9), 1157–83, https://doi.org/10.1177/0170840617717554.

Parker, M. (2002), 'Queering management and organization', *Gender, Work and Organization*, **9**(2), 146–66.

Pedersen, D. E., and Minnotte, K. L. (2012), 'Self- and spouse-reported work-family conflict and dual earners' job satisfaction', *Marriage & Family Review*, **48**(3), 272–92, https://doi.org/10.1080/01494929.2012.665015.

Peticca-Harris, A., deGama, N., and M. Ravishankar (2018), 'Postcapitalist precarious work and those in the 'drivers' seat: Exploring the motivations and lived experiences of Uber drivers in Canada', *Organization*, **27**(1), 36–59, https://doi.org/10.1177/1350508418757332.

Pettinger, L., Parry, J., Taylor, R., and Glucksmann, M. (2006), *A New Sociology of Work?* Malden, MA, Blackwell.

Pullen, A., Thanem, T., Tyler, M., and Wallenberg, L. (2016) 'Sexual politics, organizational practices: interrogating queer theory, work and organization', *Gender, Work and Organization*, **23**(1), 1–6, https://doi.org/10.1111/gwao.12123.

Riach, K., Rumens, N., and Tyler, M. (2016), 'Towards a Butlerian methodology: undoing organizational performativity through anti-narrative research', *Human Relations*, **69**(11), 2069–89, https://doi.org/doi:10.1177/0018726716632050.

Roberts, J. (2005), 'The power of the "imaginary" in disciplinary processes', *Organization*, **12**(5), 619–42.

Roberts, J. (2009), 'No one is perfect: the limits of transparency and an ethic for "intelligent" accountability', *Accounting, Organizations and Society*, **34**, 957–70.

Rose, G. (2001), *Visual Methodologies: An Introduction to the Interpretation of Visual Materials*, London, SAGE.

Ruderman, M., Ohlott, P., and Panzer, K. (2002), 'Benefits of multiple roles for managerial women', *Academy of Management Review*, **45**(3), 322–40.

Rumens, N., de Souza, E. M., and Brewis, J. (2018), 'Queering queer theory in management on organization studies: notes toward queering heterosexuality', *Organization Studies*, https://doi.org/10.1177/0170840617748904.

Sedgewick, E. K. (1993), *Epistemology of the Closet*, Berkeley, CA, University of California Press.

Smithson, J., and Stokoe, E. (2005), 'Discourses of work-life balance: negotiating "genderblind" terms in organizations', *Gender, Work and Organization*, **12**(2), 147–68.

Spencer, S. (2011), *Visual Research Methods in the Social Sciences*, London, Routledge.

Strauss, A., and Fleischman, A. (2019), 'Reconceptualising solidarity in the social factory: cultural work between economic need and political desires', *Work, Employment and Society*, **34**(1), 109–25, https://doi.org/10.1177/0950017019866649.

Toffoletti, K., and Starr, A. (2016), 'Women academics and work-life balance: gendered discourses of work and care', *Gender, Work and Organization*, **23**(5), 489–504, https://doi.org/10.1111/gwao.12133.

Tronti, M. (1966), *Operai e capitale*. Torino, Einaudi.

Tyler, M., and Cohen, L. (2008), 'Management in/as comic relief: queer theory and gender performativity in *The Office*', *Gender, Work and Organization*, **15**, 113–32.

Vidaillet, B., and Bousalham, Y. (2018), 'Coworking spaces as places where economic diversity can be articulated: towards a theory of syntopia', *Organization*, **27**(1), 60–87, https://doi.org/10.1177/1350508418794003.

Wray-Bliss, E. (2003), 'Research subjects, research subjections: exploring the ethics and politics of critical research', *Organization*, **10**(2), 307–25.

Index

Täht, K. 5, 32, 40
Talouselämä 164
Tan, J.-P. 219
Taris, T. W. 137
Tashakkori, A. 39, 242
"Task Participation Index" 77
Teddlie, C. 39, 242
Teigen, M. 179
tertiary education 100
Thebaud, S. 55
thematic-oriented analysis 178
theory-based sampling approach 147
Thomson, R. 146
Tichenor, V. 55
"time and place" paradigm 72
'time-based demands' 116
time-based family demands 117
Time-Use Survey 5, 40, 218, 222
"trading off" strategy 79
traditional division of labour 78, 107
traditional ethnographic studies 29
traditional family model 30
traditional gender arrangements 102, 103
traditional gender beliefs 56
traditional gendered organization of families 53
traditional gender roles 102, 165
traditional gender socialization 56
traditional gender values 39
traditional male-breadwinner model 3, 113, 205
"traditional" model of complementary roles 149
'traditional' time-use studies 268
traditional work–life balance concept 19
transPARENT project 147, 148, 155
traumatised masculinity 166
triangulation methodological approaches 242
Twenge, J. M. 94
Tyler, I. 275, 281, 282

"unconditional adult worker" model 142
unpaid work 3, 15, 34, 37, 43, 73, 77–8, 88, 92, 94, 95, 100, 101, 142, 144, 147, 211, 291
"unsupported familism" 149, 150, 204
Unt, M. 5
U.S.
    in comparative and historical perspective 206–7
    divergent strategies 208–12
    family 200–201
    gender equity and equality 201–2
    "having it all" 212
    households 194
    labor market 197–9
    new American landscape of work and care 207–8
    policy context 202–3

prospects and policy possibilities 212–14
U.S. Bureau of Labor Statistics 199
US National Longitudinal Survey of Youth (NLSY79) 74

Van Bavel, J. 220, 221
Venkatesh, V. 196
'visual elicitation' 6, 295–7
visual methods, work–life binary through 295–6
visual narrative analysis 178, 189

wage inequalities 202
Warren, S. 277
Warren, T. 32, 35, 38, 94
welfare policies 150
welfare state policies 153
welfare state typologies 220
West, C. 51
Wharton, A.S. 34
Whitty, M. T. 278
widowhood 78
Williams, C. 119, 121
Williams, J. 60
Willig, C. 161, 164
Women's Roles Survey 75
Woodman, D. 5, 257
work
    arrangements 121, 124, 128, 134, 135
    gender and care in new economy 194–214
    men and fathers in and 160–173
Work and Family in the United States: A Critical Review and Agenda for Research and Policy (Kanter) 8
work–care arrangement and gender 209
work–care conflicts 210, 211, 213
work–family arrangements 50, 53, 54–6
work–family balance 4, 27, 63, 72, 88, 90, 163, 165, 171
    framework 243
    policies 149
    qualitative longitudinal research for (*see* qualitative longitudinal research)
'work–family border' theory 38, 117
'work–family boundary' 11
work–family conflicts 3, 4, 10, 29, 33, 55, 56, 59, 60, 80, 91, 117, 119, 128, 129–30, 137
    self-employment and 124–35
    subjective (*see* subjective work–family conflicts)
work–family discussions 162, 172
'work–family enhancement' 10
'work–family enrichment' 10, 291
work–family gender differences 143
work–family institutional regimes 203
    European contrasts 204–6

Printed and bound by CPI Group (UK) Ltd, Croydon, CR0 4YY

16/04/2025

14658396-0002